CW01021194

The Age of Central Banks

Curzio Giannini

Formerly Deputy Director, International Relations Department, Bank of Italy

Edward Elgar
Cheltenham, UK • Northampton, MA, USA

© Vera Lukic Giannini 2011

First published in Italian as *L'età delle banche centrali: forme e governo della moneta fiduciaria in una prospettiva istituzionalista*, Bologna: Il Mulino.
© Vera Lukic Giannini 2004
Translated by Bank of Italy's translating staff.

All rights reserved. No part of this publication may be reproduced, stored in a retrieval system or transmitted in any form or by any means, electronic, mechanical or photocopying, recording, or otherwise without the prior permission of the publisher.

Published by
Edward Elgar Publishing Limited
The Lypiatts
15 Lansdown Road
Cheltenham
Glos GL50 2JA
UK

Edward Elgar Publishing, Inc.
William Pratt House
9 Dewey Court
Northampton
Massachusetts 01060
USA

A catalogue record for this book
is available from the British Library

Library of Congress Control Number: 2011925760

ISBN 978 0 85793 213 6

Typeset by Servis Filmsetting Ltd, Stockport, Cheshire
Printed and bound by MPG Books Group, UK

Contents

Figures

Tables

Foreword

Curzio Giannini, 1957–2003, was a brilliant economist. He was a passionately dedicated scholar of central banking, having worked most of his life, since 1983, at the Banca d'Italia. In the last months of his life he fought against his illness, supported by Vera, his wife, while working on this book in which he collected his published and unpublished works on the evolution and functioning of central banking. He was able to finish it only a few weeks before his death; entitled *L'età delle banche centrali*, 'The Age of Central Banks', it was first published in Italian by Il Mulino in 2004.

Besides this book, a selection of his published works include: 'Credibility without rules? Monetary frameworks in the post-Bretton Woods era' (IMF Occasional Paper, 1997); *Enemy of None but a Common Friend of All?* (Princeton Essays in International Finance, 1999); 'Moneta e Istituzioni Monetarie' (Hoepli, 2001); 'Pitfalls in international crisis lending' (in Charles Goodhart and Gerhard Illing (eds), *Financial Crises, Contagion and the Lender of Last Resort*, Oxford University Press, 2002); 'Lender of last resort', (ibid.); 'Promoting financial stability in emerging-market countries: the soft law approach and beyond', (*Comparative Economic Studies*, 2002); and 'Bedfellows, hostages or perfect strangers? Global capital markets and the catalytic effect of IMF crisis lending', (IMF Working Paper, WP/02/193, 2002, co-authored with Carlo Cottarelli).

Curzio was born in Chieti in 1957, and studied at LUISS Guido Carli in Italy, at the London School of Economics (LSE) and Oxford University in the UK, and at the University of California, Berkeley in the USA. In 1983 he joined the Research and International Relations Department of the Banca d'Italia and in 1999 was appointed Deputy Head of the Bank's newly created International Relations Office. He died of cancer in 2003.

Curzio had one of the most fertile and original minds ever to be deployed on questions relating, first, to the interactions between the central bank, private sector financial intermediaries and the government, and second to the working of the international monetary system in general, and to the role of the International Monetary Fund (IMF) specifically within that.

Until a couple of years ago, the concept had taken hold that the central bank could, and should, largely separate itself from the hurly-burly of the financial system, setting official interest rates in Olympian macroeconomic solitude, leaving market developments to the beneficent workings of efficient markets on one side, while maintaining complete independence from government on the other. As that concept has become discredited, so we need to return to the much more nuanced and subtle institutional analysis that Giannini presents here. As Giannini states: 'The mistake that neo-classical theories make is to consider money as a commodity. Instead, it is really an institution that is held up by trust: trust in its future purchasing power and trust in the continued convention that payment is complete when money changes hands.' What Giannini outlines here is the essential institutional role that central banks should play in each country in maintaining that trust, a role that gives the financial stability objective at least equal billing to their price stability purpose.

Whereas the role of central banks within each country had seemed, mistakenly, to be settled and clarified a few years ago, the international monetary system, if it can be properly so called, has remained defective. International imbalances remain and fester. The IMF has no capacity to exert much influence, if any, on the most important countries whose policies really drive global developments. Curzio was a clear-sighted observer of all this, even if he had no blueprint for overcoming such intractable problems.

His approach has been to apply a 'theory of history', which provides a beautifully written and illuminating book, much easier and nicer to read and more rounded than the limited mathematical models that have so monopolized academia in recent decades.

Overall it is a privilege to present and to recommend this book to, I hope, a host of new readers.

Charles A.E. Goodhart
Emeritus Professor, London School of Economics

Foreword to the Italian edition

What role do central banks play and how has it evolved over the two centuries since they came into existence? How and why, in the course of time and in different places, have central banks acquired distinct but complementary functions that continue to be a topic of debate: issuing bank, lender of last resort, monetary policy-maker, banking supervisor, payment system operator? What mutations, from Bretton Woods to the European System of Central Banks and perhaps beyond, have given central banking its international dimension? How do these questions tie in with the history of money and its progressive dematerialization from commodity money to fiat money and to the advancing forms of electronic money? None of the paradigms of economic analysis – classical, Marxian or neoclassical – can fully explain the *raison d'être*, the development or the effects of economic institutions; monetary institutions are no exception.

In this elegant work, Curzio Giannini offers a compelling, overarching interpretation of the manifold responsibilities that have gradually fallen to central banks, which he views as complex institutions and not only as makers of monetary policy. The nature of central banks has been examined from different perspectives over the years: they are a natural response to the crises that accompanied the growth of bank money during a period of incomplete contracts and information problems in the credit and financial markets; they are entities whose purpose is to use the currency as a hidden tool of taxation for the state; they are agents whose task is to ensure the achievement of the final objectives of monetary policy – objectives that the increasing abstraction of money and growing complexity of intervention have reduced to the core requirement of price stability, to be pursued autonomously. Analysis, guided by history, has explored each of these dimensions, producing important theoretical and practical contributions. Yet these contributions all share a perplexing feature: none offers a comprehensive interpretation that can account for the enormous differences in the structure and functioning of economic systems, in public intervention in the economy, and in international trade and cooperation.

It is just such a comprehensive interpretation that *The Age of Central Banks* seeks to offer. The basic thesis is that central banks are neither a historical accident, the fruit of changing political interests, nor the inevitable product of the instability and incompleteness of credit contracts, nor even a means of guaranteeing the price stability of money as a 'good' (not, in this instance, a standard good with a market of its own, but an institution that is necessary for the operation of all markets). The 'central bank' is the outcome of a gradual institutional evolution, the rationale of which resides in money's distinctive features compared with the other goods and services produced in the economic circuit. This evolution is not deterministic but path-dependent, correlated with the historical evolution of our political, social and economic systems. It depends largely on the fact that if money is to survive and perform its functions in economic transactions effectively in space and time it must instil and maintain a sufficient degree of confidence in its acceptability and future value. The role and the powers of central banks – indeed their very existence – derive from the ultimate purpose of sustaining that confidence.

This book provides an all-round view of the phenomenon of central banking, proposing an original and complex interpretation of the evolution of central banks at every level. Methodologically, it adopts a 'neo-institutionalist' approach. Social institutions such as firms, political parties, trade unions or, in this case, money are essential to allow individual decisions to be coordinated given high transaction costs, crucial information shortcomings and incomplete contracts. In the case of money, the analysis turns on the concept of 'payment technology' as the set of conventions, objects and procedures that make it possible to extinguish obligations arising from economic exchange. Here the fundamental problem is the incompleteness of the monetary contract, which must be remedied. The means of doing so are unavoidably flawed and determined by history, consisting in investment in the 'brand name' of a currency, upheld by rules and institutions designed to bolster confidence among those who use it.

In terms of instruments, Giannini's approach draws on the authoritative precedent of the 'theory of history' proposed by John Hicks, although without aiming for historiographical completeness. Through the examination of secondary sources, the analysis of the evolution of payment technologies in the pre-industrial age and the subsequent emergence of convertible currency, the study of banking crises and of the establishment of the first central bank, with the rise and fall of the various monetary regimes that preceded the fiat standard, the book marshals extensive and convincing evidence in support of the basic thesis. The debate on the independence of central banks, the credibility of their action and the recent proposals for a more or less flexible form of inflation targeting are also examined, with close attention for the occurrence and recurrence of general phenomena in different situations in time and space.

As to results, there is clear evidence that payment technologies have been designed, although not by intention or determinism, to increase the flexibility of money supply and its prompt adjustment to the needs of economic growth and to cyclical friction. Money supply thus becomes increasingly abstract, entailing a growing degree of risk, although it is also better able to respond to the 'deflationary drift' that is the true common denominator of the various payment technologies, all of which tend to be based on a rigid money supply, at least in the short to medium term. Clearly, this is a very different approach to that normally used to study the 'money market' and consequent formation of monetary policy. Nowadays, monetary issues are considered in the light of a token money that is easy to manipulate, not one that is relatively inflexible and impedes growth. From a 'theory of history' standpoint, however, although this view is useful for immediate operational purposes, it is not adequate for a fully satisfactory study of the institutions of money and central banks and their evolution over time, especially – and here lies the innovative force of Giannini's work – their future prospects.

These prospects encompass the evolution of the international monetary system itself. Globalization tends to alter the relationships between nation-states and central banks. The series of solutions proposed since the collapse of the Bretton Woods system show that the evolutionary process is in full swing, with new equilibria being sought in the institutional field as well. One strand of this search is the essentially supranational consortium model of central banking embodied by the European System of Central Banks as part of the monetary internationalism that has prevailed throughout history, regardless of the developments of the last century based on 'regional currencies'. Although profoundly different, the regimes of monetary union and of hegemony (the present dollarization of the economy) have a key feature in common: the renunciation of national monetary sovereignty. The result, however, is a highly unstable equilibrium; an 'imperfect bipolarism' that only a cooperative solution can overcome. Given the failure of the cooperative arrangements of Bretton Woods, the only possible solution is closer institutional integration. In the author's opinion one advisable direction would be that of cooperation within a soft-law system, a natural evolution of cooperation among central banks that is exemplified by the Basel capital accords and non-binding recommendations and best practices designed to promote financial stability. This is the method of cooperation adopted by the Financial Stability Forum, set up by governments, central banks and other market regulators in response to the financial crises of the late 1990s.

The book also examines the prospective relationships between central banks and the financial industry and between central banks and governments. The first of these relationships is becoming increasingly complex, partly as a result of financial innovation. This has led, on the one hand, to the coexistence of payment technologies based on legal tender with exchanges based on bank money, which is likely to become predominantly electronic in the future; and on the other hand to the emergence of huge cross-border intermediaries. Thus the payment system has acquired a pre-eminent role and become a focus of attention, emphasizing the need to take account of the cash and securities settlement services now offered by private sector non-bank intermediaries but that were once the preserve of central banks. The result, in the author's description, is a 'pyramid under attack', which could have serious implications for monetary policy as well. Since providers of private payment services are likely to face major conflicts of interest and will be unable, on their own, to preserve the necessary confidence in money – the *raison d'être* of central banks – the latter are unlikely to disappear with the switch to electronic money or the development of elaborate financial superstructures.

What is happening to the role of central banks in assuring continued supervision of credit systems (broadly defined as financial systems) and acting as lender of last resort? Changes are taking place in this field as well, although their direction is less clear. In some countries the solution for the time being has been to strengthen the central bank's role and expand its functions; in others, the central bank has been stripped of its supervisory powers. In the field of monetary policy, with price stability now the key objective and the central bank entrusted with an institutional role at the highest level while remaining independent from the executive in the performance of its functions, how is it possible not to take account of movements of assets and liabilities in the stock and property markets, be it only in the interests of price stability? No answer has yet been found to these questions and the book addresses them only briefly, although from a very interesting angle. Although the most important developments will probably occur in the fields of supervision and regulation, that intangible but essential factor, confidence, will still have to be safeguarded. If the central bank as an institution rests on this principle, it will certainly not need to seek new lines of business. On the contrary, according to the arguments and evidence put forward in this book, it will become necessary to turn to it (how, is not yet clear) when evolutionary crises inevitably strike the capitalist system.

In July 2003 Curzio Giannini died at the end of a brief but relentless illness. Although aware that the battle was lost, he fought on to the end with fierce determination. His place in the hearts of his family, his friends and his fellow economists can never be filled. Apart from the courage with which he faced the last months of his life, many will also remember his contribution in the professional field. Formal and casual exchanges alike benefited from his quick and lively intelligence, his erudition and his wide knowledge of culture beyond the bounds of economics. To his work he brought a rigorous analytical and methodological approach and broad historical and political perspective. Alongside these recollections and the many papers he wrote in 20 years of his career we now have the contribution of this 'unfinished' book, as he described it. Nonetheless, it remains an extremely valuable contribution and one that is certainly complete in its overall design, in the construction of its arguments, in the historical evidence it presents and in the conclusions drawn.

Curzio Giannini did not have time for the final discussions that an author normally seeks before turning a work such as this over to a wider readership, although the work does take account of many of the points raised in frequent discussions over the years. The book is a general theory of central banking based on money as an institution, although it is not unmindful of the fact that money itself is an evolutionary phenomenon. As far as the implications of his analysis go, it would be true to say that in the trade-off between a flexible and a rigorous conduct of monetary policy the second receives less attention than the first. It is a deliberate choice, and the author certainly does not consider the objective of price stability to be of secondary importance. It is partly a reaction to a sometimes overly deterministic view of economic relationships and the 'methods' of economic policy. I believe this book not only provides a firm and reliable guide to newcomers wishing to explore the difficult issues surrounding the role and evolution of central banking, but also raises new questions, generates useful doubts, offers some unexpected answers and opens up new vistas for those already familiar with this field. It remains for the reader to pass judgement on the finished product.

Ignazio Visco
Deputy Director General, Bank of Italy
April 2004

Preface

The idea for this book has been in my mind for most of my professional life. I began working on the history of the creation of the central bank in Italy while studying at Brasenose College in Oxford in 1984–85. However, I soon realized that the time was not ripe for the sort of research I had in mind. At that time, the Bank of Italy was considering setting up a Historical Research Office, primarily in order to give scholars access to documents pertaining to the history of money in Italy; there were enormous gaps in the existing data, but everything suggested they would soon be filled. The experience left me convinced that large tracts of the history of central banking were still very much unexplored, and prompted various observations and considerations that would prove useful in the years to come. During those months I also read Benjamin Klein's 1974 essay on the link between money and trust, which was to become a constant point of reference over the next years. Upon my return to the Bank of Italy I soon found myself involved in a project that helped greatly to forge my ideas about the evolution of central banks. That project was the drafting of the White Paper on the Payment System in Italy, published in April 1987. Nowadays, it may seem unimportant, another technical paper on one of the many aspects of central banking. At the time, though, its publication was a major event. The prevailing opinion in both academic and banking circles was that central banking began and ended with the conduct of monetary policy, and that this had always been more or less the case. According to this approach, the other functions, from management of the payment system to supervision, were merely coincidental, deposits left by history on the main body of the institution of the central bank. In reality it was an anachronistic view, or worse, an opinion without justification even when it was formed. The White Paper shed light on the many complex interactions linking payment system, structure of the banking system, conduct of supervision and monetary policy management. Taking part in drafting it was an exceptional and highly formative experience, with many exciting moments. Traces of analytical contributions remain in two articles already outlining many of the ideas I put forward in this book.[1]

I came back to those ideas while attending the University of California at Berkeley in 1992–93. During my stay I was able, through Oliver

Williamson's lessons, to broaden my knowledge of neo-institutionalist theory, which was gaining currency in academe thanks to the contributions of Williamson himself, along with Douglass North, Richard Langlois and other scholars. At the end of that year of study I published two articles in which I expanded the idea that central banks had developed and evolved around the function of ensuring trust in what were beginning to be known as 'payment technologies'.[2]

During the next years I worked on other topics, ranging from European monetary integration to the reform of monetary institutions in the 1980s and 1990s and to the role of the International Monetary Fund as international lender of last resort. Some of the studies I undertook, often in collaboration with other economists from the Bank of Italy and the International Monetary Fund, form the backbone of the third part of the book.[3]

Inevitably after such a long gestation, I have accumulated numerous, profound debts of gratitude during the writing of the book. My greatest debt, however, is not to a person but to an institution, the Bank of Italy. It may resemble old-fashioned anthropomorphism to attribute a conscious role to an institution, but anyone who experienced the intellectual atmosphere in the Bank of Italy in the 1980s and 1990s (I cannot speak for the years before) will have no difficulty agreeing with the anthropologist Mary Douglas that 'institutions think'. In my case certainly much of what I am and what I think in the field of economics, as elsewhere, is the fruit of 20 years in the Bank. When I re-read my work I often find it difficult to trace the real source of a particular idea, a particular empirical result or a particular idiosyncrasy.

I also owe much to the people who contributed in various ways to my intellectual development: Cesare Caranza, Guido Carli, Pierluigi Ciocca, Anthony Courakis, Tommaso Padoa-Schioppa, Franco Passacantando, Ezio Tarantelli and Ignazio Visco. Over the years I have also had discussions with numerous friends and colleagues on the issues that were researched in preparation for this volume. Regrettably, I cannot thank them all here, but I would like to mention in particular Carlo Cottarelli, with whom I co-authored a number of papers, Paolo Angelini, Lorenzo Bini Smaghi, Claudio Borio, Marco Committeri, Renato Filosa, Marc Flandreau, Andrea Gerali, Giorgio Gomel, Carlo Monticelli, Fabrizio Palmisani, Giovanni Battista Pittaluga, David Pyle and Fabrizio Saccomanni. Ignazio Visco read the whole manuscript and provided many useful comments. Special thanks also go to Maria Teresa Pandolfi for her unfailing kindness to this often wayward user of the Bank's library, which she manages with knowledgeable and loving care. I also have fond recollections of my dear colleague and friend Stefania Tortiello, without whose help and encouragement I would never have found the strength to resume a project that professional commitments and family responsibilities had forced me to give up. Maria Rosaria Lazzarini not only showed me constant affection, which never hurts, but also provided diligent editorial assistance over many years. I am also grateful to Chiara Mariani, Angela Di Maria and Giorgio Trebeschi for their help with tables and graphs.

Personal problems have prevented me from revising the text as I would have wished, or indeed as would have been appropriate with a view to publication. In this sense it is unfinished. I have decided to publish nonetheless, in the hope that others will find inspiration and encouragement to formulate a convincing institutionalist theory of central banking.

I dedicate the book to my companion Vera and our two children, Dara and Damjan, in gratitude for the love they have given me and in the hope that they will always remember that in a world without certainty only trust in oneself and one's neighbour can bring serenity.

C.G.
June 2003

Acknowledgements

The publishers wish to thank the following who have kindly given permission for the use of copyright material.

The Federal Reserve Bank of Richmond *Economic Review* for table from Michael D. Bordo, 'The Lender of Last Resort: Alternative Views and Historical Experience' (Jan.–Feb. 1990 issue).

Campus Verlag for table from Peter Flora et al., *State, Economy, and Society in Western Europe, 1815–1975: A Data Handbook in Two Volumes*, 1983, Vol. 1, Chapter 3.

The University of Chicago Press for table from Kenneth W. Dam, *The Rules of the Game: Reform and Evolution in the International Monetary System*, 1982.

Cengage Learning EMEA Ltd for tables from Charles P. Kindleberger, *A Financial History of Western Europe*, 1984.

The International Monetary Fund for table from Nicholas Crafts 'Globalization and growth in the twentieth century', March 2000.

The Brookings Institution for table from Dani Rodrik, 'Governance of economic globalization', in Joseph S. Nye and John D. Donahue (eds), *Governance in a Globalized World*, 2000.

The MIT Press for chart from Peter Temin, *Lessons from the Great Depression*, 1989.

Bollati Boringhieri editore for table from Pierluigi Ciocca, *La nuova finanza in Italia: una difficile metamorfosi (1980–2000)*, 2000.

Every effort has been made to trace all the copyright holders but if any have been inadvertently overlooked the publishers will be pleased to make the necessary arrangements at the first opportunity.

This book contains the text left by Curzio Giannini. Apart from checking and completing the references and general editing, at the author's request Chapter 7 on money and the payment system has been updated and the section on informal cooperation and soft law (the only one left unfinished) in Chapter 6 on international money has been completed from an article published in 2002. Special thanks are due to Paolo Angelini, Carlo Cottarelli, Andrea Gerali, Pino Marotta, Maria Teresa Pandolfi, Giovanni Battista Pittaluga and Francesco Spadafora for their assistance in these matters and to Gabriella Bernardi, Maria Rosaria Lazzarini and Stefania Tortiello for editing of the final text and for bibliographical research.

Special thanks are due to Alba Guidi and Rita Tosi for their dedicated work and precious assistance in bringing all the pieces of the English edition together.

Introduction

Non aes, sed fides[1]

If the success of an institution can be fairly judged by its diffusion, then the central bank is without doubt a very successful institution. When Will Rogers, the American humorist, said, 'There have been three great inventions since the beginning of time: fire, the wheel, and central banking', it may have been mere journalistic hyperbole, but like all hyperboles it contained an element of truth. In 1900 there were only 18 central banks. By 1950 that number had risen to 59 and by 1999, the last year for which accurate figures are available, it was 172. Today, over 90 per cent of the United Nations member states have a central bank.

More telling than these figures, which reflect the proliferation of nation-states following, first, the break-up of the great European empires and then the demise of colonialism, is the change that took place during that period in the perception of the role and the prerogatives of the central bank and its place in the organization and apparatus of the state. At the turn of the twentieth century, the central bank, still known by the less imposing name of 'issuing bank', was an institution with an uncertain future. Not all of the leading countries had one, notably the United States, which had a long-standing distrust of centralized power. In other countries, such as Italy and France, the central bank continued to lead a precarious existence between balance sheets constricted by large volumes of non-liquid financial assets, trifling legal constraints, and constant debates on the advantages of decentralizing issuance. Nowadays, the central bank has become an essential attribute of the state, if not a symbol of sovereignty.

Given the importance attributed, for better or for worse, to the central bank it may seem surprising that until quite recently it attracted very little theoretical interest. As Fausto Vicarelli remarked some 15 years ago on the question of the central bank's 'independence' from political power:

> When the economist begins to tackle such an important and topical subject as central bank autonomy, one question immediately arises: can the autonomy or independence of an economic institution be discussed without taking into consideration a theory which justifies its existence and explains the logic of its evolution? Assuming there are grounds for this question, if the answer to it is a negative one, the economist who begins to explore central bank autonomy will

encounter certain difficulties since, even today, central banking theory has yet to be developed or, more optimistically, is still in the development phase.[2]

There are many reasons why it has taken so long for a theory of the 'evolution' of central banking to emerge. The main reason is probably entirely analytical, that is, that the neo-classical theoretical paradigm's great heuristic potential in other fields does not reach to institutions – any institution, not just the central bank. In attempting to create a more rigorous discipline, neo-classical scholars have restricted both their method and their field of analysis to the point of reducing their theory of institutions virtually to an oxymoron. Firms, trade unions and even money are thus left out of the neo-classical paradigm.

Without a coherent theoretical framework, it was easy, given the close relationship that had linked central bank and state since the former began to evolve, for the adversaries of central banking to attribute the institution's existence to the prince's greed, to the constant attempts of the person in power to entangle the economy in a web of privileges and prohibitions designed to increase the power to raise taxes, whether openly or secretly. We can call this the 'fiscal' theory of central banking; Friedrich von Hayek and James Buchanan were its founders, Kevin Dowd, Lawrence White and David Glasner are its present leading exponents.[3]

The fiscal theory of central banking is backed by an incontrovertible historical fact, that in the early days of many central banks the state's action was specifically designed to reap advantages from the creation of a large bank endowed with special privileges enabling it to mobilize rapidly substantial amounts of funds with which to finance war. This passage in institutional history was an experience shared, for example, by the Bank of England, the Banque de France, the Bank of Prussia and the Banca Nazionale nel Regno d'Italia. Nonetheless, it is anachronistic, and often blatantly incorrect, to argue on this basis that such a mechanism is the *raison d'être* of central banks as we know them today. Other central banks, for instance, were not created for an immediate return in the form of financing public expenditure but for the advantages to the community of rationalizing the payment system, which was in complete chaos at the time, whether by historical accident or from poor legislation. This was the case of the Reichsbank, the Banca d'Italia, the Schweizerische Nationalbank and numerous other smaller institutions. Moreover, the nature of the financial advantage that would accrue to the state from setting up a privileged bank is unclear. For instance, on closer inspection, the creation of the Bank of England can be attributed to an attempt on the part of Britain's emerging middle class to exert fiscal control over the sovereign, not to facilitate secret taxation. The state certainly gained in creditworthiness.[4] All told, identifying the contingent factors that lead to the creation of this or that issuing bank is not the same as searching for the evolutionary mechanism that produced what we now term a central bank. For that, fiscal theory is of little help.

At the time that Vicarelli voiced his disappointment about the state of the theory of central banking, Charles Goodhart[5] exploited the intervening progress in the analysis of the informational problems of financial markets in a book that marked a major step forward in the thinking on this subject. Goodhart viewed the central bank as the fruit of an institutionalization of restrictive competitive practices required by the very nature of banking. He argued that because bank loans cannot be traded on secondary markets, depositors find it difficult to assess their true value. Hence, doubts about the soundness of a bank's capital can spread to the whole system, placing its stability at risk. It is therefore in the interests of the soundest banks to club together in order to safeguard their reputation, adopting any method of selection and rule of conduct for their members that will minimize opportunistic or fraudulent practices. However, and this is Goodhart's main thesis, such a governance structure is unlikely to emerge spontaneously or to be able to withstand the clash of interests that would ensue from increased competition in the credit markets. For the club president to have sufficient authority to issue rules, ensure their observance, and impose sanctions on recalcitrant members, he must remain outside the fray and not enter into competition with the subjects he governs. This would explain the state's intervention in the banking sector. By legislating to support a club structure hinged on a non-competitive central bank that is not constrained to maximize profit, the state exercises its coercive powers for the purpose of maintaining internal discipline. This is not an arbitrary action, therefore, but one designed to safeguard the stability of the banking system and so, in the final analysis, also the interests of depositors and of the economic system as a whole. All in all, such a development is a 'natural' one, as Goodhart stated in the subtitle to an early edition of his essay, published in 1985.

Goodhart's analysis has several merits, including the fact that it is presented as a logical extension of the doctrines of the 'fathers' of Anglo-Saxon-style central banking such as Henry Thornton and Walter Bagehot. It also has some evident limitations. To begin with, it is not a 'monetary' theory of central banking. If the problem of banking crises related only to the opaqueness of loans, it would be sufficient to separate credit circuit from money circuit in order to root out instability, following an old prescription dear to the monetarist school of thought. Why does a bank account that can be used for payments seem so inextricably linked to the granting of non-negotiable loans? What has led modern societies to accept such an evidently explosive mix and then 'invent' the central bank to defuse it? Moreover, in Goodhart's vision the central bank is born already fully developed, as it were. Against all evidence it undergoes no evolution, either in its functions or its instruments, and even less in its institutional role. On top of this, Goodhart's central bank has nothing to do with monetary policy or with the payment system, two areas that are instead in the forefront of discussions among central bankers and of reconstructions of the history of the individual central banks. Last of all, how can one explain the transformation of a decentralized banking system into a pyramid structure with the central bank at the top? Studies by Mancur Olson and his followers have familiarized us with the notion that it takes more than a shared interest for a group of individuals, however small, to decide to cooperate together. Remaining on the subject of banking, how is it possible that where a tight-knit group of bankers failed, politics, which depends on the consensus of much broader sections of the population, can succeed, not forgetting that the advent of central banks pre-dates universal suffrage? And how can one explain the repeated connection between banking reforms and crises of confidence? Or the fact that the evolution of central banking has been interspersed with 'waves' of reform affecting numerous countries whose legislators appear to have been inspired by the same model, adapted in each case to local conditions?

None of these questions are answered in Goodhart's analysis. Indeed, they are never even raised. The reasons for this silence are easily understood and come down to two. First, there is the aim of reflections at the time, which was essentially polemical. Goodhart's contribution was intended as a response to the reappearance in academic debate of what I have called the 'fiscal' theory of central banking. During the proliferation of new labels such as the 'theory of legal restrictions' or 'new monetary economics', all sharing a profound aversion for state intervention in monetary matters, it was a way of drawing the attention of academia and politics back to the 'lofty' motives for giving substance, a century earlier, to the embryonic institution of the central bank. Among such 'lofty' motives, the performance of the role of lender of last resort in financial emergencies was undoubtedly the most important. Second, Goodhart's analysis reflects the tools available to him at the time, which, despite the addition of the concept of imperfect information, barely acknowledged the concepts of transaction cost and uncertainty in the Keynesian sense. As Oliver Williamson demonstrates in his analysis of firms, Avner Greif, Barry Weingast and Paul Milgrom in their studies of mediaeval corporations, and Douglass North and Barry Weingast in relation to the English revolutions of the seventeenth century, it is virtually impossible to describe complex institutional changes without somehow linking the underlying assumptions of theoretical analysis to the reality being explained.[6] In the rarefied world in which substantial rationality, stable preferences and parametric uncertainty coexist, no role can be found for institutions.

Therefore, while Goodhart's important contribution must be the point of departure, it must be taken further by building around it a complex mosaic of many hues and shades. Lawrence Broz attempted this in 1997 in an essay on the creation of the Federal Reserve System.[7] He specifically followed the route carved by Goodhart but proposed his own solution to the problem of explaining the institutionalization of central banking, that is, the establishment of a body for the pursuit of a public good, financial stability, in a world of atomistic agents dedicated to maximizing their own personal utility function. That solution is based on the concept of joint production: in the case of the United States, the central banking model became acceptable when a small group of bankers at the head of the leading New York banks were finally convinced of the advantages central-ization would bring in terms of greater international use of the dollar. By promoting legislation in favour of central banking, and hence the public good of financial stability, at their own expense, those bankers in effect reaped benefits from the spread of their business across the Atlantic as the dollar became a currency of international reserves and trade.

The theory of public and private joint production may help to explain the sensational about-turn that took place in the United States, a country with a deep and long-standing aversion to central banking, with the passage of the Federal Reserve Act of 1913. However, it still does not explain why the about-turn occurred when it did and not earlier or later. Indeed, the radical nature of that institutional innovation begs the ques-tion how a group of bankers, however powerful, could successfully oppose the rest of the nation, and even suborn it to their own ends. However, it is when Broz attempts to apply his explanatory model to other countries that he becomes less convincing. In order to keep faith with the notion of joint production Broz is forced to find a private commodity with broad enough significance to elicit demand for reform even in countries with no ambition for an international role of their currency. That commodity, once again, is 'fiscal', although Broz takes account here of the lessons of North and Weingast on the origins of the Bank of England: the fiscal mechanism in this case is the benefit to the state from an improvement in creditworthi-ness following the creation of a central bank.

The explanation is not convincing for a number of reasons. While, as noted earlier, considerations of a fiscal nature do indeed lie behind the evolution of many central banks, equally it is anachronistic to try, at that early stage, to attribute the emerging bank with the role of guardian of financial stability, which only developed much later. The Bank of England of 1694, for instance, is a far cry from the Bank of England of 1913, and resembles even less the Federal Reserve set up in that year. Moreover, for some central banks such as the Banque de France and the Bank of Prussia the fiscal objective was not so much to improve the state's creditworthiness as to provide the Treasury with low-cost financing. The fact is that trying to reduce the long and varied evolution of central banks to a single mechanism – one adhering, moreover, to the assumptions of methodological individualism and substantial rationality – entirely out of regard for the theoretical clarity of an analytical apparatus, that of neo-classicism, evidently unable to offer tools of interpretation from an institutionalist viewpoint, is not a laudable enterprise, either on the theoretical level or, even less, on the historiographical one.

These are the premises behind the attempt that resulted in this book. The idea from which the analysis stems is that in order to understand the central bank, it is necessary first to understand money. The mistake that neo-classical theories make is to consider money a commodity. Instead, it is really an institution that is held up by trust: trust in its future purchasing power and trust in the continued convention that payment is complete when money changes hands (even if this is now something of a metaphor). The institutional nature of money is emphasized by building the analysis around the concept of 'payment technology', meaning the set of conventions, objects and procedures that allow obligations arising from trade to be extinguished. The fundamental problem of any payment technology is the incomplete monetary contract: it is impossible to define the future value of money beforehand without socializing the whole economy. Owing to this uncertainty, the spread of a given payment technology will depend on the existence of institutions and roles to safeguard users' trust in it. This is because as soon as a stock of money has been built up, the resulting utility flow becomes a quasi-rent, which can be expropriated by manipulating the supply of money. From this standpoint, the evolution of central banking is merely one aspect of the institutional adaptation set in motion by the development of payment technologies; as these became increasingly abstract and hence easier to manipulate, they made it more and more difficult to preserve the value of the outstanding stocks of money over a period of time.

In this approach the problem of transition from one payment technology to another inevitably becomes important. Once a particular payment technology has taken hold, why does the community feel the need to develop another, and how does the process of innovation occur? Who are the participants, what are the constraints, and what are the relative roles of the market and of politics? In order to shed light on the problem of transition we need to start from another, often neglected, characteristic of money: that it is present as counterparty in all exchanges taking place in the economic circuit. This characteristic, from which it follows that the price of money is none other than the inverse of the average of the prices of all other goods, means that any imbalance in the money market, given rigid supply, can only be eliminated by making adjustments in all the other markets. Nowadays, we imagine a typical money market shock as a sudden, unexpected increase in supply, because our way of looking at monetary matters is shaped by our familiarity with a form of money, token money, that can be manipulated at pleasure. However, for much of recorded history the main problem was the very opposite. From the late Middle Ages on, financial innovation was driven by the need to find more flexible forms of money in order to counter the long-standing tendency of the demand for money to increase as a result of economic development and the growing social division of labour. Thus, monetary innovation arises out of the need to counter the inherent deflationary drift of payment technologies based on rigid money supply, at least in the short to medium term.[8] The fact that the process did not immediately lead to the generalized adoption of a token money was due not so much to technical limits – paper credit money was well known to Renaissance merchant bankers and paper money was already widely used in China in the Middle Ages – as to a lack of institutions to uphold confidence in payment technologies built around a money that had no intrinsic value.

With the industrial revolution and virtually contemporaneous development of the representative state a structural split occurred. On the one side, as the economic circuit became increasingly complex it fuelled the social incentive to develop more flexible payment procedures. On the other side, under the new political and institutional framework monetary institutions could, for the first time, develop outside the control of the prince. Any attempt to move beyond commodity money, even in its most advanced form of coinage, must entail an intermingling of money circuit and credit circuit. This is the great innovation implicit in the notion of banking, in a process wonderfully described by John Hicks:

> This is the point at which deposits in banks, withdrawable deposits, are made transferable: either by cheque, which is an instruction to a bank to transfer an existing deposit, or by note – which is in effect a cheque payable to bearer, having the guarantee of the bank behind it, without reference to the depositor against whose deposit it was originally issued. This is vital; for it is at this point that the bank becomes able to create what is in effect money. When it makes a loan, it does not have to hand out the old 'hard' money; all it does is to exchange claims. Against the obligation of the borrower, to repay by some fixed date, it provides an obligation of its own, which is transferable upon demand, and for that reason has a money quality. The money which it lends is money that it itself creates.[9]

The intermingling of money and credit thus set in motion a long and somewhat tortuous process of institutional adaptation centred around the figure of the central bank. To date, the process has consisted in three separate phases. In the first phase, believed to have ended in 1844 with the adoption of the Bank Charter Act in England, which was imitated and adapted throughout the world in the following decades, it became an established principle that the issuance of convertible banknotes was a 'special' activity, subject to limits and performed under the control of the state. This period saw the emergence of the first great issuing institutes operating under a monopoly, although in several countries there were still forms of monetary competition, albeit subject to tight restrictions. In the second phase, the problem was how to govern bank money, which developed as banknote supply became increasingly rigid during the earlier round of reforms. This was when the private issuing institutes were transformed into true publicly owned or semi-publicly owned central banks. Operationally, it was also during this phase that the central banks became lenders of last resort and banking supervisory bodies, although how and when this happened varied from one country to another. Finally, the third phase was marked by the introduction of the inconvertible banknote as legal tender and of the concept of 'managed currency' – the revolutionary idea that monetary policy should actively aim to boost production and increase employment. Institutionally, this phase saw the definitive nationalization of the central banks and subsequent rise of the 'principle of autonomy' announced by David Ricardo in an essay published posthumously in 1824. According to Ricardo a condition for the successful control of the money supply by the state is that the technical body responsible for monetary policy should not be subject to the power of the executive but should answer to the legislature for its actions after the fact. At the same time as the notion of managed currency took hold, new methods of operation in the conduct of monetary policy were developed, notably open-market operations.

The three phases described above are defined on the basis of logic rather than of time. They occurred at different moments in different countries and not all of them in every country. Their contours are often hazy. For example, when it came to the point of regulating convertible banknotes, the spread of bank accounts had already begun. Similarly, the wave of legislation of the 1920s and 1930s, marking the final acceptance of payment technologies centred around the bank account, occurred when experimentation of the fiat standard had been under way for some time. Probably, we have now entered a fourth phase, in which electronic systems, and the consequent possibility of intra-day credit, determine the how and when of a new wave of institutional adjustments, spilling over national borders for the first time.

The neo-institutionalist approach has several implications that should be highlighted. First, monetary institutions are viewed as the result of a continuous adaptation, the form of which is dictated by contingent problems and by the existing political and institutional heritage. A crucial role in this process is played by the concept of 'crisis'. A crisis occurs when an innovative payment method shows itself to be precarious and a demand for institutional reform takes shape. The link between crisis of confidence and reform process is a macroscopic phenomenon of monetary history. Yet economists, being theoreticians, have accorded it only passing attention, primarily to minimize its real practical relevance. Instead, this essay takes the view that a crisis is an inevitable step in the process whereby society learns the potential and limitations of a given payment technology.

A demand for reform is not necessarily matched by a supply of reform. This is because the concept of supply of reform involves the political sphere. Thus not only must the demand for reform have reached such proportions as to engage the political sphere, but there must also be a class of political entrepreneurs able to promote and formulate an institutional answer and gather sufficient consensus around it. It is at this point that the problem of collective action comes into play, which Broz studied in relation to the United States. My theory in this regard is that producers of an innovative payment technology play a major role in shaping political supply and need the quasi-rents associated with their investments to be safeguarded in times of instability. In other words, in no way does regulation tend to punish spontaneous market innovation, indeed it is often a way of reducing the likelihood that the producers will behave opportunistically. This is why in most cases it leads to a decrease in competitive behaviour and to the introduction of entry barriers in the monetary sector of the economy.

The important criterion for establishing the point where demand and supply of reform meet is not and should not be the criterion of efficiency, but that of effectiveness. In economic language the word 'efficiency' is often used randomly, as if it expressed an unambiguous concept. While this way of thinking may cause little damage in other fields, in the analysis of institutional processes it can be dangerous. Every institution is an answer to a problem of incomplete contract caused by Keynesian uncertainty or by prohibitive transaction costs. Given this, judging efficiency with respect to an ideal that does not exist is not an approximation, it is a serious logical error. Harold Demsetz has called the tendency to judge an actual situation with reference to an idealized situation that cannot happen the 'nirvana fallacy':

The view that now pervades much public policy economics implicitly presents the relevant choice as between an ideal norm and an existing 'imperfect' institutional arrangement. This *nirvana* approach differs considerably from the *comparative institution* approach in which the relevant choice is between alternative real institutional arrangements.[10]

A more useful notion of efficiency, according to Demsetz, would refer to situations of scarcity and to individuals' knowledge and preferences as they really are, not as they should be. For instance, it is only meaningful to refer to a suboptimal state if it is possible to achieve a situation that is effectively better than the present one. However, as we know, there are no theoretical instruments beyond Pareto improvement that allow such a comparison to be made in abstract terms. In other words, there is no way of evaluating the 'naturalness' of a monetary system or its efficiency. In the monetary field, too, the only proof of the pudding is in the eating. That is why this study never refers to the concept of efficiency, preferring that of effectiveness in respect of the problem perceived to be socially significant at a given point in history and in the light of existing information and institutions. It is because of the structural uncertainty of the outcomes that monetary reforms tend to operate on the fringe of existing systems without overturning them. The history of monetary institutions offers striking examples of what the neo-institutionalists call 'path-dependence', the tendency of present choices to reflect those of the past.

This consideration leads to another of a more general nature. Putting the concept of effectiveness first means broadening the analysis beyond the strictly economic sphere because the feasibility of a given institutional situation depends on the legal and political order – in neo-institutionalist jargon, on the 'institutional environment'. Many examples of this can be offered but here they are confined to two. The spread of banknotes, which sparked the evolution of central banking, would not have been possible if the legal system had not accepted the concept of the bearer security, granting it the same degree of protection as the registered security. It was because of the lack of a suitable legal superstructure that payment technologies with a credit content (already circulating widely among merchants since the fourteenth century thanks to the protection afforded by customary mercantile law) did not become current among large sections of the population until well into the eighteenth century. It would be hard to understand how the concept of legal tender could gain worldwide acceptance without considering the intervening change in the role of parliaments, from bodies overseeing the deeds of the prince to depositaries of popular sovereignty expressed by universal suffrage. The examples abound.

Finally, by stressing effectiveness over efficiency it is possible to explain why the necessary phases in the evolution of central banking were marked by waves of reform, leading to the reproduction of the same institutional model in a multitude of countries, with lesser or greater adjustments according to the local context. This phenomenon would be impossible to explain otherwise, as pointed out earlier in connection with Broz's interpretation of the institution of the Federal Reserve.

At this point, having outlined the essential features of the analysis that follows, it would be appropriate to define the aim and limits of the present exercise. The book does not have historiographical ambitions because its author has neither the training nor the interests of a historian. Most of the sources quoted are secondary sources and the history of central banking is not examined in its entirety – spatial, temporal or functional – but only insofar as it affects the illustration of theories. If a label has to be found for the present approach, then a suitable one would be 'theory of history', of which an authoritative example can be found in some of the works of John Hicks and which has been revived on several occasions even in recent years.[11]

A theory of history, the boundary line suggested by Hicks, deals with general phenomena not specific events and it is obliged to use abstractions, with which specialist historians are often unable to identify. Its usefulness, however, should be judged according to whether it is able to shed light on phenomena that recur in different places and times, and not according to its accuracy of description. As Hicks himself pointed out, however, the main risk of a theory of history is that it may be guilty of determinism. Once the mechanism for reproducing comparable institutions or events has been identified, it is easy to succumb to the temptation to view its operation as inevitable. Although this would be seriously wrong for any historical phenomenon, it is particularly dangerous in the case of the history of money. The 'technology' embodied in a payment technology is largely social because of the role played by trust: therefore, it is evident that its diffusion and the events affecting it, including the fact that it might degenerate, reflect the larger vicissitudes of the community adopting it. If there is 'progress' in the monetary field, it is progress in the sense of 'progressive' affirmation on a vast scale, from the Industrial Revolution on, of payment technologies with a highly flexible supply and that are consequently easier to manipulate. Whether they are then manipulated in the collective interest or for private interests, or in the long term maybe in the interest of no one, will depend on the soundness of the institutional environment and its juridical and political components.

Put differently, the history of money and its management is anything but linear. In order to emphasize how the social aspect takes precedence over the merely technical side, Chapter 2 discusses the credit payment technologies in use in Europe long before the industrial revolution, and which disappeared once the economic and institutional bases for their use no longer existed. From this standpoint, current payment technologies owe their progress to the institutions of the liberal and democratic state, founded on concepts of the division and limitation of power. Nominalism aside, the central bank and the liberal and democratic state are joined in a truly symbiotic relationship: the same origins, the same development, and in all likelihood the same future, whatever it may be. Without liberal and democratic institutions, capitalism would probably be unthinkable, a central bank certainly so.[12] That is why Keynes's dream of a world central bank collapsed at Bretton Woods. It is also why in Europe in the 1990s the creation of a central bank that transcended national borders was only possible because it was part of a much broader project to institute a federal political structure.

Benjamin Cohen may be right that the geographical future of money will see an increasingly clear dissociation between the state and the institutions responsible for the management of that money.[13] However, it is still too early to say whether this is an established tendency or just a stage in the process of redefining the scope and structure of the multinational state. It is present history and much of it has yet to be written. The next stage in the evolution of central banking will very likely depend on its outcomes and its teachings.

PART I

Preliminary issues

1. Money between state and market: the concept of payment technology

1.1 INTRODUCTION

The origins of money will probably remain forever wrapped in mystery. Scores of historians, anthropologists and archaeologists have tried to solve the problem, but it is not easy to trace a phenomenon that pre-dates the invention of writing and thus any documental evidence of human thinking.

But why should such ignorance be of any concern for economists? After all, we do not need to know when, why or by whom the notion of paid work was introduced in order to understand the labour market. Nor do we need to go back to the first time the budget of some ancient monarch failed to balance in order to understand the meaning of sound public finances. Where money is concerned, however, many people believe that things are not so simple. John Hicks, probably the greatest expert on monetary matters of the twentieth century, was among them:

> One of the chief things which monetary theory ought to explain is the evolution of money. If we can reduce the main lines of that evolution to a logical pattern, we shall not only have thrown light upon history, we shall have deepened our understanding of money, even modern money, itself.[1]

Hicks does not tell us why this is so. It is interesting to note, though, that the passage quoted is really a palinode. Thirty years earlier, Hicks himself, under the battle-cry of 'let's spread the marginalist revolution to money', called on the economic profession to give up the historical and sociological diatribes that had characterized monetary debate in the nineteenth century and apply to money the same logical and deductive reasoning that successfully solved the main stumbling block faced by economic theory at the time: the theory of value.[2] What had happened in the meantime? Hicks's call had been enthusiastically taken up by a large group of hard-line theoreticians, who made it their battle-cry. For the next 30 years, the monetary debate and its many ramifications – the formalization of the famous IS-LM model, the discussion of wealth effects, the analysis of the optimal money supply – were nothing but a large gloss on Hicks's study. A gloss that eventually evolved into such a great temple of neo-classical synthesis as Don Patinkin's *Money, Interest and Prices*, whose second and definitive edition appeared in 1965.[3] But in the same year Frank Hahn published an unassumingly titled essay destined, however, to shake the very foundations of the Hicksian edifice.[4] With iron logic Hahn shows that in general equilibrium models, of which Hicks's and Patinkin's are but applications, money has no reason to exist: it is inessential. The most that money can do in a general equilibrium model is build a bridge between present and future, helping the various generations round the constraint of the passage of time. However, this can also be done by any durable commodity in the economy, and possibly with better results. Money is therefore not only inessential, it is also inefficient.

Paradoxically, the neo-classical synthesis could have ended by consigning money to the fringe of economic debate. We now realize that the problem was not the marginalism imported by Hicks into monetary theory, but the implicit assumptions concerning the exchange process underlying the general equilibrium model. If we assume that exchanges are settled and managed centrally by an omniscient auctioneer and that there is perfect trust among agents in the economy, the monetary issue becomes meaningless because there is no need for any medium of exchange, or *quid pro quo*, to conclude transactions. In order to study money we must start from decentralized exchange structures, in which concepts such as risk, imperfect information and transaction cost have a meaningful role to play.

Once the theoretician has left the main route of general equilibrium, his path becomes much rockier. Although the new models are analytically very complex, they all revolve around a simple intuition. Let us assume that a decision-maker has a finite (and known) probability of coming across a counterparty willing to exchange with him a commodity having positive utility (for the decision-maker). Let us also assume that there is a finite probability of encountering someone willing to accept money in exchange for his goods. If the consensus perceptions in the economic circuit are that the second probability is greater than the first one, then a monetary exchange regime will prevail, otherwise it will not (a mixed equilibrium is also possible when the two probabilities are equal). The chief merit of these models is their insistence upon the importance of individual perceptions: the social choice of the medium of exchange depends crucially not on some objective characteristic, but on a system of beliefs whereby in the end individuals will hold for transaction purposes the particular good or object they expect will be accepted by a large number of counterparties. In other words, money is borne out of a set of compatible expectations that make it socially acceptable.

What processes lead the expectations of individuals that operate independently in a system of decentralized exchanges to converge towards a compatible configuration? What is it that determines the social acceptability of money in a world of imperfect confidence and positive transaction costs? Is monetary theory really destined to become a huge tautology, unable to do more than observe that everything commonly accepted is acceptable?

This is where Hicks's observation comes in, that if monetary theoreticians want to move forwards they must first look backwards, building a vision of how money has evolved, of how we have reached our present point. This is not because history is the teacher of life, but because every theoretical construct that aims to tell us something useful about today's monetary facts must also give us a plausible explanation of yesterday's. In sum, it must offer us a theory of history.

The plausibility test, however, is a naturally weak test. It is almost always possible to recount at least two plausible histories of any phenomenon, and often more. Monetary history is no exception. Aristotle, the West's first complete monetary theoretician, reminds us of this. In *Politics*, he outlines what could be called, echoing von Mises, a 'catallactic' theory of the evolution of money (from the Greek καταλλάττειν, to exchange). The existence of a non-communal society (the reference is to Plato's theory, which Aristotle often opposes) implies the exchange of goods, which, at the beginning, naturally takes the form of barter. With time, however, the person who wants what another has, but cannot offer what this other person wants, will realize it is worth accepting in exchange something he does not want, in order to obtain what he really wants by means of another barter. At this point, Aristotle remarks that some goods, such as metals, have features that make them more suitable to perform this function of temporary *quid pro quo*, thus explaining the reason for coinage. Briefly, it is the market that 'invents' money. It is a pity that in *Ethica Nichomachea* Aristotle presents us with a completely different theoretical story, equally plausible at first sight. Money owes its name (in Greek νόμισμα) to the fact that it exists not by 'nature' but by convention or law (νόμοσ). The law sanctions its acceptance in payment. There is little doubt that we are in the presence of a 'statalist' theory of the origin of money.[5]

The catallactic view and the statalist view of the origin of money have accompanied the monetary debate through 2000 years of history. Aristotle's statalism gave rise to the feudal theory of money, chartalism, the weighty theories put forward by the German jurist Georg Friedrich Knapp in *The State Theory of Money*,[6] a book that had a wide impact in the 1920s, and even the present belief, with regard to the European experience, that monetary union without political union is destined to fail in the long run. On the other hand, Aristotle's catallactics can more easily be linked to the metallists of antiquity, to Nicholas Oresme and *De Moneta*, and right up to Carl Menger and the modern theoreticians of free banking.[7]

As always happens when opposing positions are very rigid, the argument between proponents of statalism and catallactics ultimately proved sterile. In real monetary systems state and market have coexisted since ancient time, often sustaining one another, sometimes in more or less open conflict. Until recently, however, the analytical tools available to monetary theorists were not flexible enough to capture such a complex and restless reality. Consequently, there was rarely any proper dialogue between exponents of the two schools. More often than not they just announced their views of things, as a postulate of analysis rather than a theory to be argued and empirically tested. From this viewpoint, it comes as no surprise that the main monetarist debates not only produced a lot of hot air but almost always ended with the collapse, as it were, of both sides, rather than with the victory of one or other school of thought. The history of major conflicts on the monetarist issue is punctuated with episodes of déjà vu.

Today, we are able to look differently at monetary issues because a true theory of institutions has evolved in the meantime. This is something that economic science never had before, not even in the years when the German historical school dominated in Europe and major institutionalist economists such as Thorstein Veblen and John R. Commons were gaining prominence in the United States. The modern theory of institutions, or neo-institutionalism as it is often called to distinguish it from early nineteenth-century American institutionalism, sprang from the seminal work of Ronald Coase on transaction costs and of Herbert Simon on the limits of rationality. According to Richard Langlois,[8] neo-institutionalism rests on three assumptions:

1. the recognition that, in the description of reality, economic activity is coordinated not by market prices alone but also by several other institutions, whose origins and functions should be the object of theoretical analysis;
2. the adoption of an operational concept of bounded rationality instead of a narrow view of rationality; and
3. the principle that economic explanation should be dynamic, or evolutionary, in the sense that the economy should be studied as a process of historical change rather than in terms of optimal states.

Oliver Williamson, together with Douglass North the leading exponent of neo-institutionalism, added to these basic assumptions three methodological and operational precepts: regarding the transaction, not the individuals involved, as the basic unit of analysis; investigating the specific nature of the investments needed to finalize the transaction;[9] and studying the reasons why the contracts used to regulate transactions are 'incomplete' (that is, do not allow the parties to specify reciprocal duties under any possible future state of nature), as well as the form and cost of rectifying that incompleteness.

The vision that emerges from this approach is one of institutions as: 'structures that govern transactions [arising out] of an effort to craft *order*, thereby to mitigate *conflict* and realize *mutual* gains'.[10] In this approach, institutions develop and evolve not necessarily because they are 'efficient', as efficiency is not clearly definable under bounded rationality, but according to the 'best remedy criterion', whereby: 'a mode of organization for which no superior *feasible* alternative can be described and *implemented* with expected net gains is *presumed* to be efficient'.[11]

If we look at money through neo-institutionalist glasses – as in the theory developed in the course of this chapter – the dichotomy between state and market loses much of its interest. The evolution of monetary institutions appears to be above all the fruit of a continuous dialogue between economic and political spheres, with each taking turns to create monetary innovation, to menace the stable value of money, and to safeguard the common interest against abuse stemming from partisan interests.

1.2 MONEY AS AN INSTITUTION: THE CONCEPT OF PAYMENT TECHNOLOGY

Three conditions must be satisfied before one can talk of a monetary economy. First, there must be a common measure of the value of goods, that is, a unit of account. Second, there must be goods or procedures that extinguish any obligation deriving from the exchange of goods, that is, one or more means of payment. In the case of goods, the act of payment is completed when they change hands. In the case of procedures, when a document certifying the start of the procedure (a cheque, for example) changes hands, this is only the first step in a chain of operations that ultimately leads to the transfer of ownership of a certain amount of money, that is, of a means of payment that is socially recognized as such. Third, some form of arithmetic relation must be established between the unit of account and the means of payment (whether one or several), a relation that need not be rigidly fixed but must at least be predictable. We call the set of goods, procedures and conventions that allow these three conditions to be satisfied, 'payment technology'. We are used to simplified monetary economies in which unit of account and means of payment are the same (for example in the euro) and their arithmetic relationship is one to one. In this context, the utility of a concept such as payment technology is unclear. However, for much of history this was not the case. Until the advent of the fiat standard, unit of account and means of payment were separate and the main objective of monetary policy was to maintain a given exchange rate between the two. If we go back in time it is not unusual to find situations in which multiple means of payment were matched by multiple units of account.[12]

The key element of a payment technology is without doubt the possibility to complete an exchange when there is no 'double coincidence of wants' in such a way that no further legally binding obligations exist after the exchange is completed. In other words, the key element is the existence of a means of payment or, in a word, of money.

It follows from this simple definition of the role of money that a necessary, though not sufficient, condition to have a monetary economy is that there exist at least three goods – if only two existed, barter would be an efficient method of exchange; and three separate individuals – if there were only two, it would be possible to have at most a credit economy. Under these circumstances, if the act of handing over money effectively cancels the payer's obligations, then there must exist a tacit or explicit agreement to that effect among all the agents in the economic circuit in which the payment technology operates, not just among the parties directly involved in a given exchange transaction. It follows that money is not a commodity like others but a social institution. In the words of Robert Clower, the first scholar after Patinkin to draw attention to this aspect: 'what matters is the existence of social institutions condoned by either custom or law that enable individuals to trade efficiently *if they follow certain rules'*.[13]

In the literature, money is frequently likened to language or to other social conventions, such as driving on a particular side of the road.[14] The analogy is misleading. Once a social convention has developed, it is self-supporting because it is in the interest of all the members in the society to observe it. This is not true of money. The stock of money can be likened to a durable good that produces a flow of services for the person holding it, whom we shall call the consumer. However, as Benjamin Klein argues in an important article published in 1974, the difference between money and any other durable good resides in the fact that the quality of money, that is, the real services it can render, is a function of the future supply of money, as well as of the demand by other consumers.[15] A sudden increase in the supply of money can greatly reduce the flow of services associated with a given monetary stock. Similarly, monetary services will disappear if the other consumers reach the conclusion that the money circulating up to that time has no value. Put differently, the quality of one nominal unit of money depends on its price at the moment it will be spent.

Rationally, all consumers should adjust their monetary stock until the marginal cost is equal to the marginal gain. The marginal opportunity cost of money – or, as we might say, the price of monetary services – will be given by the difference between the nominal interest rate *(i)* and the rate of return on the money itself *(rm)*. The real demand for money will therefore be an inverse function of the difference *(i − rm)*. However, it will also be a direct function of b, symbolizing the consumer's confidence in the currency. This will depend on the variance of the expected rate of change of monetary prices. If the consumer thinks the future rate of price variation can be accurately anticipated, the value of β will be high, otherwise it will be low. If there are several monies circulating in the economy, the competition mechanism will ensure that those in which confidence is greatest will eliminate the ones of doubtful stability.

Let us suppose that consumers do not have perfect information and that it is costly to obtain information about the future behaviour of money-producers. The quality of a given form of money will therefore be uncertain. One way of representing this situation can be found in contract theory.[16] The decision to build up a certain monetary stock can be likened to investing in a highly specific capital asset (it is specific because the stock would completely lose its value if it cannot be used as money) with an incomplete contract (because it is impossible to negotiate today the future behaviour of money-producers and the demand for money of other consumers). The consumer who decides nonetheless to hold money is therefore in the position of having a quasi-rent (the flow of monetary services) that can be expropriated at any time, because of either a sudden increase in the money supply or a sudden decrease in demand.

No rational consumer could agree to a similar risk unless the money-producers devised some mechanism to increase β, that is, to create confidence in their future behaviour and hence in the quality of the money they produce. It is this that makes money an institution, not just a convention: confidence in its quality must be constantly sustained or the payment technology based on it will deteriorate. For every payment technology there must therefore be a body of rules, conventions and institutional mechanisms designed to sustain the confidence of the people using it. Rudolf Richter calls this the 'purchasing-power-securing order'.[17] More simply, in what follows we will use the term 'confidence-creating mechanisms'. The purpose of a theory of money as an institution is precisely to study the confidence-creating mechanisms that evolved in order to support the acceptability of money as *quid pro quo* in a world of imperfect information or, put another way, of potentially fraudulent agents.

A corollary of the proposed approach is that an analysis of monetary facts cannot leave out an investigation of the legal aspects of payment. The quality of each payment technology will depend crucially on the soundness of the underlying property rights, that is, the reliability of the law. Many means of payment are in fact title to the performance of a service, that is, juridical constructs. The fact that the person with such title can call on the law for enforcement and protection in extreme cases is what makes it a potential currency.

In principle, there are three conceivable confidence-creating mechanisms under incomplete contracts.[18] It is possible, for instance, to choose a capital asset with low specificity, that is, one that can be reused for other purposes at little cost. Alternatively, one can ask the strong party to the contract, in our case the producer, to give the weak party a 'hostage' – a pledge, a legal constraint, or other – in guarantee of future behaviour. Finally, one can imagine some form of vertical integration that joins producer and consumer under a single 'corporate' governance structure.

The history of money offers examples of all three solutions. Commodity money is a payment technology whose low specificity becomes nil if a non-perishable commodity, such as the bronze bar of Roman times, is used as means of payment. Convertible money, on the other hand, is a form of guaranteed money as the holder obtains from the producer a right to have his monetary stock converted into a reserve asset, usually at a fixed rate of conversion. It is harder to imagine a form of vertical integration applied to money. However, on close examination we see that vertical integration of the monetary sector is actually obtained by nationalizing the production of money, or at least subjecting producers to constraints and forms of oversight under the direct responsibility of the state. It was no chance that this form of monetary organization developed with the spread of a means of payment, inconvertible money, with the highest degree of specificity, being without intrinsic value and not guaranteed by any contractual right except that of influencing the decisions of the state through the ordinary mechanisms of political representation, like the right to vote or the rules of political responsibility.

1.3   PAYMENT TECHNOLOGY COSTS

The institutionalist approach opens new perspectives for monetary analysis. In particular, it sheds light on an old paradox: the persistence of commodity money through the ages and in very diverse cultures. Payment technologies based on commodity money appear to be inefficient. At the beginning of the twentieth century, treatises on monetary theory still contained lengthy descriptions of what makes a commodity particularly well suited for use as money. Analysis focused on such features as portability, indestructibility, homogeneity, divisibility and recognizability. However, these were and are secondary aspects. However 'physically' suitable the chosen commodity may be, commodity money will always have two major disadvantages compared with payment technologies based on intrinsically useless means of payment. The first disadvantage is the cost of producing the money-commodity and its unavailability for other uses. This may seem to be a small disadvantage at first, but in fact it is not so. In the last 20 years for instance, if the velocity of circulation had been constant it would have been necessary to increase the money supply by some 3 per cent a year to keep the average price level in the leading countries stable. Since the money supply (M1) amounted to about 30 per cent of gross national product in that period, it would therefore have been necessary every year to allot around 1 percentage point of gross domestic product (GDP) to increase it. In addition to this there would have been the social cost of subtracting these resources to alternative, more productive, uses. Clearly, a cost by no means negligible. Obviously, it can be argued that technologies based on 'pure' commodity money have not been in use for a long time and that a fractional reserve system would produce substantial savings. But such a payment technology would be fundamentally different, being based on convertible money rather than commodity money.

There is then a second disadvantage, less evident than the first but related to it and probably more important on the social level. As Milton Friedman notes in what remains the classic text on commodity money: 'The vices of strict commodity standards are the other side of their virtues. Being automatic, they may not provide sufficient flexibility or adaptability to prevent substantial swings in prices or in income.'[19]

What sort of adaptability is this? The whole argument could be framed in terms of the well-known exchange identity. If the money supply is rigid and the velocity of circulation is also heavily conditioned by the characteristics of the means of payment, the economic system will evidently be exposed to a deflationary drift or a stagnation or both. Conversely, unexpected surges in the supply schedule as a result, say, of the discovery of new ore deposits or the opening of new markets could lead to sudden upward adjustments in the price level when there are bottlenecks in the real sector of the economy. However, this would be a very narrow view; the problem is a much more complex one. As Clower points out,[20] the real difference between money and any other commodity is that money does not have a proper market of its own. When we talk of the money market we are talking about something with a greater degree of abstraction than the market for any other good, although, even in that case, we are not usually referring to a 'physical' market. The fact is that the price of money is simply the inverse of an average of all the other prices quoted in the economy. The money market is therefore made up of all the markets in which money is used. It follows that if the money supply cannot be manipulated at will, any imbalance between money supply and demand can be eliminated only through an extremely decentralized process, involving the renegotiation of many if not all contracts stipulated in the various markets forming the economic circuit. If transaction costs were negligible, none of this would matter. However, as we have seen, we must postulate the existence of substantial transaction costs if we want money to make economic sense. And when there are transaction costs, any monetary imbalance is bound to prove socially costly.

How costly will it actually be? Arthur Okun, writing in 1975,[21] was the first one to draw attention to the fact that precisely because of the magnitude of transaction costs, particularly those due to imperfect information, many markets rely on implicit contracts, in which what is not stated prevails over what is expressly written. These are markets – Okun calls them consumer markets – in which the long-term relationship between producer and consumer takes precedence over short-term profit. When a monetary imbalance occurs unexpectedly in such markets, the parties face a dilemma: they can either explicitly renegotiate their contract, which is by assumption extremely costly, or they can tacitly agree to pretend nothing has happened and continue to observe the existing agreements, although this implies accepting a change in the relative price of the goods traded with respect to all the others. In any case, a monetary imbalance will have real effects. In a world of consumer markets it is socially suboptimal to adopt payment technologies based on a means of payment whose supply is rigid or at least not very flexible with respect to changes in the price level. Institutionalists like Williamson have suggested a name for these costs, which are often neglected in economic theory: they call them maladaptation costs. They are costs caused by the rigid organization governing a given category of transactions so that, when unexpected events occur, the contract among the parties turns out to be insufficiently articulated to prevent opportunistic behaviour.

In the 1951 article cited earlier, Friedman maintains that high production and opportunity costs provided the main incentive to move beyond commodity money. However, there is reason to believe that, historically, maladaptation costs have been just as important, if not more so. For instance, Carlo Cipolla writes in conclusion to an influential reconstruction of monetary events in the Middle Ages:

Progressively, throughout the Middle Ages, everywhere the supply of precious metals proved clearly insufficient, in the long term, to cope with the ever-increasing demand for monetary and industrial uses. The nations that would keep a stable weight and alloy for the money on which their internal price system is based, would suffer a secular deflationary drift, with potentially disastrous consequences.[22]

Carlo Cipolla's interpretation is essentially the same as the one Marc Bloch gives to the development, from the thirteenth century, of 'imaginary money', an institutional mechanism entailing the separation of unit of account and means of payment. This was an ingenious attempt, fruit of progressive adaptation more than a conscious decision by some sovereign, to create an artificial market for money that would reabsorb any demand and supply imbalances by altering the rate of exchange between unit of account and means of payment. In reality, the system was destined to fail in the long term because although it eliminated the need to recoin currency when the rate of exchange varied, it did not stop the prices of circulating goods being renegotiated. Eventually, separating unit of account and means of payment proved to be just a technical subterfuge and so became superfluous with the switch to convertible money. Carlo Cipolla's interpretation is the same as the one underlying Rondo Cameron's comparative studies of the evolution of banking in the eighteenth and nineteenth centuries.[23]

Leaving aside differences of opinion on the relative importance of the various cost categories, the fact is that the two disadvantages of commodity money – call them microeconomic and macroeconomic – should encourage the adoption of somehow more abstract payment technologies. For many centuries this was not the case, however. Of course, forms of token, that is, intrinsically useless, money have been known since antiquity, but there is almost unanimous agreement that until the Industrial Revolution all the predominant payment technologies were based on particular forms of commodity money. We can call this the 'inefficient money paradox'.

In the institutional interpretation offered by Benjamin Klein, however, this paradox is immediately revealed for what it is: a pseudo paradox that owes its endurance solely to the inadequacy of the analytical categories long used in the study of money. In reality, commodity money tends to predominate in all institutional contexts in which confidence is in short supply. It is a way of overcoming the incompleteness of the monetary contract without the need for continuous large investments by a non-party to the exchange – the money-producer, the community or the state – to bolster confidence in the chosen means of payment. The most important thing in a situation of incomplete contracts and imperfect information is

to curb the degrees of freedom of the stronger party to the contract, that
is, the one that can engage in opportunistic or, in the language of contract theory, 'expropriatory' behaviour. Payment technologies do this by
placing more or less direct constraints on the supply of money. In the case
of a physical commodity, the constraint will be physical as well and will
be linked to that commodity's production technology. Such a payment
technology does not need much confidence (is low confidence-intensive)
and once it is in existence it may even prove to be self-enforcing. This is
because the commodity becomes a 'hostage', to use Williamson's term,
in the hands of the individual economic agent. Moreover, the hostage
has low specificity because: (1) it is a commodity that lends itself to non-
monetary uses without much adaptation; and (2) the rigidity of the commodity's supply schedule safeguards it against price fluctuations due to
opportunistic behaviour of the producer.

As soon as one moves away from 'pure' commodity money to 'partial'
commodity money, as Friedman calls it, confidence-creation becomes
a problem without an obvious solution. For example, the all-important
recognizability of coined currency proves illusory on closer examination
because coined metal can never be pure. In fact, one of the greatest monetary problems of the Middle Ages was the relationship between currency
by tale and currency by weight. As the means of payment becomes more
abstract, and hence as the specificity of investment in monetary stocks
increases, confidence-creation costs will inevitably rise because money
is transformed from a set of objects into a set of rights, which must be
socially recognized and protected in order to be enforceable. With intrinsically useless but convertible money, the constraint is a legal one because,
as the supply of money increases for given demand, it will become more
difficult for the producer to honour his convertibility obligations. In the
case of token money the only constraint is political, that is, control over
the executive in its various, more or less democratic, forms.

We are therefore faced with a logical, not historical, process consisting of six stages associated, respectively, with pure commodity money,
partial commodity money, convertible paper money (banknotes), convertible deposit money (bank accounts), inconvertible fiat money, and credit
(Table 1.1). This is without forgetting forms of inconvertible deposit
money based on the issuer's reputation, of which history offers few but
significant examples.

The salient aspects of each monetary form are the payment technology
itself (its characteristics as means of payment, medium of exchange and
unit of account) and the associated set of confidence-creating mechanisms
(the system safeguarding the rights associated with the use of that particular money and the institutions set up to protect its purchasing power).

Table 1.1   Synopsis of payment technologies

Payment technologies	Examples	Confidence-creating mechanisms
1. Pure commodity money	Cattle; pepper; non-coined metals	Self-enforcement
2. Partial commodity money	Coinage	Coinage stamp Methods of verification (money-changer)
3. Convertible paper money	Private banknotes	Exchange rules or issuance requirements Legal safeguards for bearer securities
4. Convertible deposit money	Bank accounts	Exchange rules Property rights Banking supervision Lending of last resort
5. Inconvertible paper money (token money)	Fiat money	Legal tender Independent central bank Parliamentary control Anti-counterfeiting mechanisms
6. Credit	Letter of credit circuit; infra-day overdrafts in netting and gross settlement procedures	Reputation Entry restrictions

Only by taking into account all these components is it possible to analyse and compare the various payment technologies. Thus, for example, while token money has no alternative use it may, depending on the strength of the institutional environment, entail confidence-creation costs that exceed the production and opportunity costs of a commodity such as gold. In other words, the efficiency of a given payment technology can only be judged in relation to the institutional environment in which the economy is embedded.

Of course, we are talking of ideal payment technologies. There have been forms of political responsibility (like the centralized control of the mints) even with payment technologies based on commodity money. Even today, the official reserves held by central banks have the role – actually just psychological – of reassuring holders of token money regarding the future value of their monetary stocks. These elements complicate the issue, however, and it seems right to set them aside for the time being in order to focus on the fundamentals of each payment technology's operating mechanism.

At this point we can draw two major implications from the argument. First, a logically irresolvable tension lies at the root of the 'monetary question'. On the one hand, it would be socially desirable for the money supply to be perfectly adaptable so that the costs of maladaptation would be nil. On the other hand, there is no better protection against the risk of monetary expropriation than to choose a commodity money with very rigid supply or to impose legal restrictions on the creation of money. This is a typical trade-off: the more adaptable the money supply, the greater the risk of opportunistic behaviour by producers, but also the greater the scope for an active monetary policy aimed at the collective interest. In this context, the debate between advocates of rules and advocates of discretionary measures appears in a new light, as the expression of a technical not a political problem at the root of the working of a monetary economy. Naturally, if we start from a position that stresses the role of confidence in the monetary contract, we will end by emphasizing the importance of physical, statutory and legal constraints on the supply of money. Instead, if we start by analysing the costs associated with monetary imbalances caused by exogenous shocks coming from the monetary or the real sector of the economy, we will end by denouncing what John Kenneth Galbraith called: 'the dangerous *cliché* that in the world of finance everything depends on confidence.'[24] As often happens, the truth lies somewhere between the two.

Second, it should be recalled that in an analysis with a long time horizon – the only meaningful horizon to understand the evolution of payment technologies – the institutional environment cannot always be assumed to be exogenous. Indeed, it can change, and often has, following an attempt to shift the trade-off between confidence and flexibility upwards. Explaining how and why this is possible is a separate problem, and will be discussed in the following section.

1.4   THE EVOLUTION OF PAYMENT
TECHNOLOGIES: THE PROBLEM OF
CREATING CONFIDENCE

Every institution is a constraint on the individual's freedom of choice. Explaining how rational individuals, dedicated to maximizing their own utility, can resolve to create an institution and then alter it with time has always constituted a great challenge for economic theory. There has always been a very strong temptation to abandon methodological individualism for a form of holism – the preferred route of sociologists – or to leave every theoretical pretension behind in favour of mere historicist descriptivism, as in early twentieth-century American institutionalism. The new institutionalism, whose prophets are Douglass North, Oliver Williamson and Mancur Olson, differs from all the other earlier 'institutionalisms' precisely because of its insistence on the processes of institutional change.

The point of departure of current thinking on institutional change is the analysis of a nineteenth-century scholar, Carl Menger, who probably would never have described himself as an institutionalist. Menger made a distinction between 'organic' and 'pragmatic' institutions. The first are the accidental result of individual actions to maximize the utility of the individual, not the group. They are the outcome of a long and possibly tortuous convergence towards certain rules, whose observance is shown *a posteriori* to be in the interest of everyone. In other words, they are a product of history. In contrast, pragmatic institutions are the fruit of a conscious choice, of an explicit attempt to limit the options available to every individual in order to reduce the uncertainty of economic processes.

Menger was one of the founding fathers of the neo-classical school and his interest naturally focused on 'organic' institutions, as those represented to his mind a real challenge to his liberal and fundamentally anti-statalist thinking. It is significant that Menger chose money as his main example of an organic institution. He returned to the subject on several occasions, but his thinking on the evolution of money is most clearly expressed in an article published in 1892 in the *Economic Journal*.[25] Menger's theory revolves around the concept of 'saleability'. Someone looking for a counterparty with exactly the right good will learn to replace his endowment of goods with others that are more saleable and thus more liquid. As a measure of saleability Menger proposes the differential between selling price and purchase price that each person is prepared to accept (the bid–ask spread). The most saleable goods – this is the crux of the theory – will have a correspondingly smaller spread. Money will emerge at the end of the process through the unconscious convergence of everyone towards the most saleable good in the economic circuit.

This is not the place for a detailed analysis of Menger's theory and the many attempts to formalize it that have been made in recent years.[26] However, for our purposes it is important to emphasize two points often neglected in the theory. The first is that the most saleable goods are not necessarily the best-suited for monetary use and that the saleability of a good may vary in space. If these assumptions are accepted, as Robert Jones demonstrates, it follows that various equilibria are possible, each based on a different commodity money. Efficiency of the convergence process cannot be guaranteed in a decentralized scheme.[27]

The second point is that for money to be the most saleable commodity it must first of all be saleable, that is, it must be a commodity, and therefore intrinsically useful. The money Menger refers to is therefore commodity money. This is not a minor limitation because, as we saw in the previous paragraph, commodity money in its pure form ceased to exist virtually everywhere at least with the invention of coinage, that is, more than 2500 years ago. Menger himself was fully aware of this and was therefore anxious to conclude his 1892 study with the following clarification:

> Money has not been generated by law. In its origin it is a social, and not a state institution. Sanction by the authority of the state is a notion alien to it. On the other hand, however, by state recognition and state regulation, this social institution of money has been perfected and adjusted to the manifold and varying needs of an evolving commerce, just as customary rights have been perfected and adjusted by statute law. Treated originally by weight, like other commodities, the previous metals have by degrees attained as coins a shape by which their intrinsically high saleableness has experienced a material increase. The fixing of a coinage so as to include all grades of value (*Wertstufen*), and the establishment and maintenance of coined pieces to as to win public confidence and, as far as is possible, to forestall risk concerning their genuineness, weight, and fineness, and above all ensuring their circulation in general, have been every where recognised as important functions of state administration.[28]

In this passage Menger offers an interesting interpretation of monetary events: the market produces and the state perfects. Of course, this is not always true. There are and always will be cases of conscious innovation or counterproductive state intervention. Again, what Menger proposes is an ideal process that should be treated as such.

The problem is the passage from unconscious processes to conscious processes, possibly in the collective interest. As Viktor Vanberg cautions,[29] it is easy to explain the appearance of relatively simple conventions or even of some rules of good conduct in terms of unconscious processes. It is questionable, however, whether the appearance of complex institutions such as money or law can really be explained without any reference to a conscious design. Where does the conscious design come from and how is it created?

There are two dangers to be avoided when tackling this problem. First, we must avoid falling into the trap of functionalism, which consists in assuming that an institution only emerges because it is socially useful. Every act of institutional innovation has a resource cost and, as Mancur Olson tells us,[30] even when a group has a clear interest in establishing common rules there is no guarantee that the free-riding problems associated with any collective action can be overcome. Second, we should not start by postulating the existence of an omniscient state capable of imposing a solution which is *ex ante* inconceivable to market operators.[31] The point is to avoid circular reasoning when considering institutional innovation to be the fruit of a continuous search for efficiency. In fact, in the typical conditions in which institutional innovation takes place – that is, with positive transaction costs and imperfect information – efficiency cannot be defined a priori without falling into what Harold Demsetz calls the nirvana fallacy. The institution, once it has been created, will define what is efficient and what is not, and therefore this cannot help to explain how that particular institution was arrived at.

According to Douglass North, the scholar who contributed more than any other to bringing the subject back into the limelight, studying processes of institutional change involves isolating four separate components: why the process starts; the agents of change; the motives and methods of institutionalization, that is, the passage from the informal agreement stage to a structure with defined features and powers; and, finally, the long-term evolutionary path on which a given institutional innovation is located.[32]

Technically, every pause in economic life can be classified in one of two main analytical categories: changes in relative prices – be they the result of technological innovation, accidents of history such as war or natural disaster, or the opening of new markets – and changes in preferences.[33] However, singling out changed preferences is often an uninteresting route to follow. It is probably true that preferences do change in the long term, but they are less likely to do so in the short term. Convincing explanations can often be found without resorting to theories that are so destructive for the analysis (think of the concept of bounded rationality). In any case, even if economic history were driven by changes in preferences, it would be necessary to explain how and why those changes occur. Often, changes in preferences may themselves be regarded as the fruit of changes in relative prices. Therefore, it is the latter that should receive the most attention.

The monetary field offers many examples of technological innovations or unexpected events that have altered relative prices in favour of this or that means of payment. Take, for example, the invention of coinage. Nowadays, we can say without doubt that technological innovation has played a crucial role in fostering the development of e-money. However, it is difficult to imagine that technological innovation itself could encourage the adoption of payment technologies with a greater degree of specificity and more flexibility of supply. In reality, the prime mover of monetary change has been the needs of trade. All the major monetary innovations have taken place during a sharp growth in trade, particularly international trade.[34] This is obviously how things should be. A rapid expansion of trade, particularly where there is a predominance of deferred transactions and long-term relations between the parties, raises the appreciation of the

maladaptation costs of existing payment technologies, thereby creating
the right incentives for the development of new, more adaptable technologies. As Hicks noted: 'To the merchant, in any age, financial dealings
are a natural extension of trade dealings'.[35] Carlo Cipolla,[36] for example,
draws attention to the continuous deflationary effect of imperfections in
coined money on economies in the late Middle Ages and interprets the
monetary instability that marked much of the period in this light. The
letter of exchange was, among other things, a way round the shortage
of coined money and the problems of transportation. The same is true
of other payment technologies. The banknote is very much the daughter
of the Industrial Revolution; bank money finally established itself in the
industrial countries at the height of the gold standard; awareness of the
potential of token money was only achieved while the Bretton Woods
agreements were in force, one of the longest periods of GDP and world
trade growth that history has known. If changes in relative prices are what
drives monetary history, they are changes that occur outside the monetary
sector of the economy; they often have nothing to do with the costs of producing money but highlight the restraint on profit growth that can come
from an inelastic payment technology.

The most awkward problems from a theoretical viewpoint probably
arise when identifying the agents of change and studying the processes of
institutionalization. In every theory based on methodological individualism, as in the case of neo-institutionalism inspired by the works of North
and Williamson, the agent of change can only be the individual entrepre-
neur. In North's view, the process is started by entrepreneurs when they
realize that, due to some exogenous change, it is better to invest in altering
the existing institutional structure than in maximizing profit for a given
structure. How to solve the problem of free-riding, though? One answer
lies in the work of Avner Greif and his attempt to analyse some major
mediaeval commercial institutions using the tools of game theory. The
theory of non-cooperative games has shown that in repeated games cooperative strategies will tend to prevail if there are few players, they have
accurate information on the actions of other players in previous plays,
and they can reckon precisely the costs and benefits of any defections. In
the vast majority of real-life situations these conditions will not be met and
cooperation can be rationalized only by making additional hypotheses. It
is not always this way, however. Throughout history, the activity of great
merchants has often come close to these conditions.

To explain how cooperative agreements not only came about but also
were actually honoured for long periods without state intervention, Greif
introduces the concept of 'coalition', which he calls 'a non-anonymous
institution based on a multilateral reputation mechanism' and informal

flows of information.[37] A coalition is a solution to problems of incomplete contract and imperfect information whenever the state is unable to provide a means of safeguarding property rights. Basically, it is a way of enabling private agents in a given sector to enter into credible commitments: in games theory jargon it is a 'commitment technology'. Coalitions of this type tend to emerge whenever an external event (a sharp rise in relative prices or the opening of new markets) makes it convenient, for a small group of agents engaged in an activity with large specific investments, to converge towards a cooperative strategy. Two conditions must be met if a coalition is to prove strong. First, the threat of punishment for anyone disobeying must be credible, because inflicting punishment is itself a collection action and *ex post* it is in the individual interest of every coalition member not to bear its cost. Second, the punishment must effectively discourage expropriatory behaviour by participants to the agreement. These conditions will be met only if private agents in the sector share the same view of their long-term interests and if they can exclude any deviator from the sector.

The Commercial Revolution of the late Middle Ages produced many examples of this type of coalition. Greif examines closely the case of the commercial network that formed in the southern Mediterranean in the eleventh century, although a better example for our purposes is the advent of the letter of exchange, a credit-type means of payment that was generated spontaneously by the market between the thirteenth and fourteenth centuries (de Roover[38]). In the next chapter we will look at how, at the beginning of the sixteenth century, the letter of exchange evolved into a true credit-based payment technology, therefore with a high fiduciary content, although its circulation was limited to mercantile spheres.

The problem of informal mechanisms based on reputation is that they become fragile when competition suddenly increases. As soon as the participants in an agreement become replaceable and can therefore be substituted by rival entrepreneurs, the tacit collective action needed to ensure compliance with the rules may be jeopardized. This entails a greater likelihood of opportunistic behaviour. When that happens, only institutionalization – that is, the introduction of explicit rules overseen by a magistrate authorized to inflict punishment – can prevent the break-up of the coalition. At this stage of the argument the theoretical literature tends to be pessimistic because it is one thing to agree on the need for a set of rules and another to subject oneself to them spontaneously when there are no coercive mechanisms. However, looking at the history of commercial and financial relations, it appears that market mechanisms are surprisingly capable of producing conscious attempts to institutionalize tacit agreements even without public intervention. The merchant guilds, studied from the neo-institutionalist angle by Greif, Milgrom and Weingast, are a classic example of this.[39] As Francesco Galgano explains in his history of commercial law,[40] even the *lex mercatoria* can be interpreted as an attempt by the merchant class, first, to protect its reputation against unscrupulous merchants, and then to safeguard its own interests against the absolute monarchs of the seventeenth century. Countless examples can also be found in the history of money, starting with the exchange fairs of the late Middle Ages (proper payment-clearing mechanisms with settlement deferred by weeks, if not months) and going right up to the clearing houses operating in the United States in the decades up to the inception of the Federal Reserve System.[41]

Two remarks are called for at this point. The first is that although these forms of organization result in a restraint of competition and hence a greater degree of monopoly in the reference market, originally most of them were intended to increase the collective welfare. To use the terms of international trade theory, they tend to make possible forms of trade expansion, not just trade diversion.[42] Second, there is ample evidence that in many cases the state, far from discouraging such forms of organization, which somehow substitute the sovereign's powers, actually encouraged them and occasionally even actively promoted them.

The market, thus, seems able to develop spontaneously even complex forms of organization, in some cases with the tacit encouragement of the state. And the monetary sector is no exception in this matter. Actually, Menger was unintentionally overpessimistic in limiting the market's potential to 'organic' institutions alone. In given conditions, payment technologies, including ones with a large fiduciary content and even those based on token money, can become widespread because their producers are able, through informal mechanisms based on multilateral reputation or formal institutions established ad hoc, to create sufficient confidence to support their use, even for fairly lengthy periods.

Payment technologies, however, have two features that tend to prevent the creation of confidence on a completely private base for a protracted period. The first is network externalities, a particular form of economy of scale. Once a given payment technology has become established among a sufficiently wide circle to provide a reference model for other economic agents, almost automatically its use will extend beyond the confines of that circle because the utility of a form of payment – and in this the analogy with language is illuminating – increases with the number of agents using it. It is open to question whether the economies of scale are large enough to create a natural monopoly for the money, since reality, in which the coexistence of multiple forms of payment is a virtually universal norm, tells us that this is not so.[43] Nonetheless, the circulation of a given form of money is undeniably subject to large network externalities. If a given monetary form is not produced in a monopoly but there are a number of issuers, these will naturally compete to expand their market share as the total circulation increases. This is where the second feature comes in. As emphasized earlier, with the increasing abstraction of the means of payment, that is, with the passage from commodity money to monetary forms in which the fiduciary component becomes progressively more marked, the problems of distinguishing between brand-names increase. As it becomes harder for holders of money to distinguish the quality of the issuers, that is, their reliability, it also becomes harder to sustain coopera- tive equilibrium, however institutionalized it may be. In the limit where the brand-names are completely indistinguishable (in other words, if there is no effective protection against the risk of counterfeiting), the cooperative equilibrium will collapse.

On this issue the state can have a comparative advantage over the market. This is because the state can safeguard both the rights of holders of money and the rights of producers of the most reliable brand-names by using its power of coercion, in practice the administration of justice. In fact, it is the state's comparative advantage in confidence-creation that Benjamin Klein, Milton Friedman and Anna Schwartz use to explain its universal and persistent involvement in monetary matters.[44] It is no acci- dent, as Friedman and Schwartz in particular maintain, that all known forms of monetary competition outside state control, except for minor epi- sodes limited in time and space (such as the 'mini-cheques' circulating in the Kingdom of Italy after the declaration of inconvertibility of 1866), are hinged either on commodity money or on money convertible into metal, that is, payment technologies with low confidence-creation costs.

The state can have, but does not necessarily have, a comparative advan- tage. The instances of monetary abuse by the sovereign are too many and too well known to list here. The state that Klein, Friedman and Schwartz have in mind is really a liberal state based on a clear definition of property rights, division of powers and democratic control. Even a state such as this can encounter credibility problems in safeguarding the payment technol- ogy, as the inflation of the 1970s has shown. However, there is little doubt that, in principle, a state with liberal institutions will have a comparative advantage over the market in creating confidence.

The analytical difficulty is to explain the passage from 'social' to 'state' management of payment technologies. How does the move from the eco- nomic sphere to the political sphere come about?

This brings to mind an empirical regularity that is often neglected in theoretical analyses of institutional change: the fact that the main reforms of the monetary structure are associated with phenomena widely perceived as 'pathological' by contemporaries, that is, crises. As the area of circulation of a means of payment broadens and competitive tensions are heightened, the risk of a confidence crisis also increases. To use Klein's terminology, a monetary crisis can be depicted as a sudden fall in β: a macroeconomic phenomenon linked to spreading fears about the selling price of the means of payment and hence about the actual quality of the monetary services that the given monetary form can provide. A crisis does not necessarily lead to direct state intervention as other responses are possible in the short run. Money-producers, faced with the risk of the payment technology collapsing, can collectively introduce institutional innovations to restore the original β. Alternatively, they can intervene individually on the opportunity cost $(i - rm)$ of the money produced so as to offset the poorer quality of the monetary services. However, if the crises tend to recur because conflicts of interest between producers are so great as to make a cooperative arrangement impossible, or for any other reason, the state's intervention will eventually become a focal point, an obvious solution, for two major social categories. These are: (1) users of the payment technology, that is, people who have built up large monetary stocks or based their exchanges on a given technology and are therefore more exposed to the risk of expropriation of quasi-rents or of a sudden rise in transaction costs if the existing payment technology is no longer legal tender; and (2) the original producers, that is, the ones who made investments that cannot be completely recouped and therefore have an interest in protecting their brand-name from opportunistic behaviour by new market entrants.

The demand for reform directed at the political system will be more pressing, the larger the payment technology's area of circulation and the more organized and influential the money producers' lobby. It is worth noting that the two categories do not have the same interests. Money-holders are interested in the stability of the payment technology because only a stable technology can ensure a predictable flow of monetary services. Money-producers are only interested in being protected from outside competition, regardless of the quality of their brand-name. These interests coincide sufficiently, at least in the aftermath of major pathological phenomena, to allow the possibility of a political 'supply' that at the same time pursues the public good of monetary stability and the private good of safeguarding the investments of organized producers. It is an application of the principle that:

> A broad and diverse group of individuals who share interests in the provision of a public good may actually benefit from the rent-seeking activities of a narrow segment of society.[45]

In the language of the theory of collective action this mechanism is known as joint production of a public and a private good. It is important for users' and producers' interests to converge in order to avoid the problems of collective action; this is because the state may have difficulty in devising actions solely designed to meet the demand for protection of a public good, because consumers tend to be less organized, or because they may refuse to be taxed to finance the desired collective action. By contrast, the presence of a powerful pressure group in the background, willing even to make concessions to obtain safeguards for its private interests, may be crucial in shifting the balance towards monetary reform.

The degrees of freedom of political 'supply' are not unlimited, however, and this brings us back to the question of the state's real capacity to sustain confidence in the payment technology. In the short term, and at every given moment in history, a country's joint political, judicial and military apparatus can be likened to a form of exogenously given capital, which I will call institutional capital.[46] To give an example, direct state control over production of a token money under absolute monarchy and with imperfect taxation mechanisms can be rationally explained, at most, as a form of hidden taxation, if not an actual expropriation for the sovereign's own private reasons; it certainly cannot be explained as a manifestation of the state's superior ability to create confidence. Many other examples can be given, such as the development of commercial law, the system of limited liability, the juridical regulation of legal tender, or the establishment of universal suffrage and the concept of authority politically independent from the executive. All these phenomena alter a country's institutional capital and hence the strength of the political response to the demand for monetary reform by pressure groups seeking monetary stability. In some cases, monetary disorder may be so serious or involve such a broad section of the population as to become itself the source of an increase in institutional capital. There is a traditional school of thought that attributes the development of parliamentary democracies to the efforts of the emerging bourgeoisie to protect itself from monetary expropriation by the sovereign.[47] Moreover, a given monetary reform, once completed, can itself lead to the creation of new institutions, which at that point may represent additional capital useful in pursuing other public good. Central banks are a cogent example of this. In the short term, however, institutional capital is exogenous and should be treated as such, at least as a first approximation.

The need to satisfy the constraint of institutional capital, the payment technology producers' interest in safeguarding personal investments, and the cognitive and organizational limits of payment service users are all factors that combine to drive processes of institutional change towards high path-dependence. The vast majority of monetary reforms are just that: reforms. They are hardly ever revolutions. When they appear to be revolutions it is because some radical change – a revolution in fact – has occurred in the meantime in the country's institutional capital, creating a hiatus in the evolutionary path of the payment technologies. In such cases there is often a regression to technologies with lower confidence-creating costs precisely because the institutional capital has somehow diminished, not increased, as a result of the revolution. Moreover, parsimony is the driving force in the field of reforms as well. This is partly because the larger the number of changes, the larger the number of subjects damaged and hence the stronger the opposition; and partly because when negotiations stall it will be easier to focus attention on what are judged to be the most malleable margins of the institutional structure.[48]

A further aspect of path-dependence observed in monetary reforms is the high frequency and international scope of imitative processes. Once a particular reform action has proved worthwhile in the first country to face a progressive erosion of confidence in a given payment technology, it will tend to become a model for reform in other countries, since agents operate in a context of bounded rationality and there are broad and potentially entrenched interests at play. It is in this sense, as we will see in later chapters, that we can talk today of the English 1884 Bank Charter Act model or the post-1914 Federal Reserve System model or, more recently, the Bundesbank model. Monetary reforms tend to come in waves and be inspired by a single model that changes from one wave to the next. Its international dissemination may necessitate local adaptations to take account of each country's institutional capital. However, in some cases dissatisfaction with the existing monetary system may be so great as to prompt individual countries to introduce reforms that will conform to the existing institutional capital. Such was the case, for example, of the reform introduced by the Meiji dynasty in Japan in the 1860s or of the reform introduced by the Allies in Germany after the Second World War. They are risky and rare operations, at least in countries with a large and well-established institutional capital. When it is decided to follow this route for contingent reasons such as military conflicts or revolutions, the success of the operation will depend on the local political system's ability to undertake specific actions to adapt that institutional capital. Without this ability the likelihood of rejection will be considerable.

1.5 A SUMMARY OF THE MAIN THEORIES

The moment has come to draw the various threads together. The point around which the whole argument revolves is that money is a social reality, as the French sociologist François Simiand said.[49] It works by virtue of a configuration of 'compatible expectations', a technical term meaning that whoever holds money must have confidence in the fact they will be able to reuse it at a price that remains stable over time, or at least predictable. Money is therefore always fiduciary, irrespective of its physical form. How is a system of compatible expectations created? Economists have long viewed sociologists such as Simiand with suspicion, fearing that their analyses of monetary phenomena would merely be the prelude to abandoning the methodological individualism that played such a major role in shaping modern economics. Carl Menger's attempt to explain the emergence of money as the unconscious result of the interaction between atomistic, rational and maximizing individuals (as a product of the market) can indeed be interpreted as a way to salvage the concept of methodological individualism, although the concept as such was developed only later by Joseph Schumpeter.

Despite its undoubted merits, however, Menger's analysis has obvious limitations in that it says little about all the conscious attempts to move beyond commodity money and towards payment technologies with a greater fiduciary content and hence greater risk of misuse. Money may indeed originally have been an organic institution, to use Menger's term. However, it has not been one for a long time and instead has become a pragmatic institution that lives, suffers, evolves and sometimes dies as a result of conscious attempts by economic agents to bend it to their will and their needs, whether collective or individual.

Neo-institutionalism has the merit of having broadened the array of analytical tools available to the economist, who can now go beyond Menger's analysis without renouncing methodological individualism. It is enough, on one hand, to recognize that individuals have bounded rationality in the presence of complex problems, for which it is not only difficult to formulate probabilities linked to the various states of nature, but individuals may not even know all the states of nature possible and only learn of their existence by experience. On the other hand, we must focus the analysis on the fundamental incompleteness of the monetary contract, so as to be able to capture all its implications and possible institutional solutions.

What emerges is a view of monetary facts that emphasizes transaction costs and confidence-creation. The lower a payment technology's fiduciary content, the higher the associated transaction costs will be, particularly the specific category of costs that I call, borrowing from Williamson, 'maladaptation costs'. By contrast, the more abstract the payment technology, and thus also its fiduciary content, the more expensive it will be to support its use because a considerable effort will be required in order to create the needed confidence among users in the future value of monetary stocks. The whole history of money has actually played out along this trade-off between maladaptation and confidence-creation costs. The whole succession of great institutional innovations in the field of money, from the invention of coinage to the introduction of milled coins and ending with the creation of central banks, can be interpreted as an attempt to push forward the possibility frontier and increase collective welfare by creating payment technologies that combine highly flexible supply (low maladaptation costs) and low production costs.

Interpreting the history of money in this way, far from negating the market's role in favour of that of the state, as Menger may have feared, actually leads to a reappraisal of any sharp distinction between state and market in monetary matters. On the one hand market forces may prove capable of generating pragmatic institutions, as borne out by countless examples from the history of money. At the same time, the state has, in principle, a comparative advantage over the market in creating confidence and can therefore play an active role in supporting the circulation of payment technologies with a high fiduciary content. Neither proposition, however, can be assumed to hold universally. Everything depends on the configuration of the financial markets and the institutional capital with which each country is endowed. And that is not all. Monetary regimes that emphasize the role of the market may deteriorate and collapse as a result of exogenous shocks or a sudden increase in competition within the monetary sector itself. Conversely, once the state is established as the preferred creator of confidence, it can turn into a predator of monetary rents, as many examples in history have shown. Nothing is deterministic or irreversible in monetary phenomena.

Leaving aside these general considerations, the foregoing analysis gives a set of hypotheses (or stylized facts) about the evolutionary path of monetary institutions that can be empirically tested. First, pressure to choose the most flexible payment technologies tends to increase with the acceleration of economic development and, above all, with the formation of markets on which long-term relationships are of primary importance. Large-scale retailing, especially at international level, and high finance are two such markets that historically have proved to be a continuous source of monetary innovations.

Second, crises play a special role, which we can describe as catalytic, in the transition from the phase of informal experimentation of new payment technologies to their institutionalization. A crisis has a cognitive value in that it directs the attention of money-holders and money-producers to the need for conscious political action to protect their quasi-rents. In other words, the crisis creates a demand for reform of monetary institutions – a demand whose strength depends on the diffusion of the payment technology and the influence of the pressure group formed by the money producers. With their greater homogeneity, substantial financial resources and better organization, money-producers will often be the ones to take the initiative of shifting the battle-front from 'market' to 'politics'. A corollary of this approach is that much of the ensuing regulation will be in line with the interests of those subject to it; but only because, at the time, those interests converge and sometimes coincide with the interests of the general public using the payment technology.

Third, the characteristics of the political supply of reform will be determined by the country's institutional capital. Institutional evolution is incremental and not governed by the search for efficiency but by the search for solutions that appear effective precisely because they are rooted in the local institutional context. The transition to highly flexible technologies can be made, even rapidly, if there is sufficient institutional capital to minimize the likelihood of the state abusing its role as guarantor of monetary stability. The inverse is also possible, that is, the return to payment technologies with less fiduciary content, and thus higher transaction costs, owing to an impoverishment of the country's institutional capital as a result of war, revolution or foreign invasion.

Finally, the evolution of money operates in models. Because learning the characteristics of payment technologies and of the institutions that sustain confidence takes place with their use, once a given reform proves effective in a key country of the international economy it will tend to become a focal point for other countries going through the same processes. This produces international waves of reform inspired by a limited number of models, sometimes only one, with secondary aspects adapted to local traditions and institutions.

APPENDIX: BENJAMIN KLEIN'S MODEL

In one of the most original contributions to post-war monetary analysis, Benjamin Klein considers the role of confidence in monetary matters starting from three very simple questions: can a public good such as money be produced in a regime of private competition? If so, under what conditions? What role do social institutions play in these conditions? Klein overturns historical and sociological analysis: instead of studying the evolution of monetary forms as a gradual fine-tuning of monetary exchange, he tries to isolate, in a logical, atemporal dimension, the conditions under which a money, whatever its nature, can establish itself. This allows him to devise a method that can be used to study the various monetary forms that have emerged in the course of history as given solutions, rooted in the broader economic and socio-political context, to the logical problems posed by the particular nature of the commodity 'money'. It is worth looking closely at his model, to which frequent reference will be made in the course of this book.

If money is considered a durable good producing a flow of services, the stock of money held by an individual must be distinguished from the flow of 'monetary services' that it generates. It is the market for these services that should be the focus of attention. The utility of money depends on the possibility of spending it and hence on the exchange rate between money and real commodities. The real flow of monetary services, N, obtained by an individual holding M_j units of money produced by the jth firm is negatively related to the price level P_j of goods and services in terms of the jth money and positively related to the confidence that the holder of the jth money has in its future value, which is summarized for the moment in a parameter β_j and will be further defined later; assuming homogeneity of degree zero in nominal prices, we have:

$$N = N\,((M/P)_j, \beta_j) \tag{1.1}$$

The jth money yields an interest r_j; there are also bonds, that is, claims to a future unit of the jth money, yielding a rate of interest equal to i_j, so that the opportunity cost of holding the money is $(i_j - r_j)$; in equilibrium the opportunity cost should equal the value (or rental price P_{Nj}) of the monetary-service flow from a marginal unit of the jth money. Therefore, in equilibrium the real rental price will be:

$$P_{Nj}/P_j = (i_j - r_j)\,/\,[(\partial N/\partial M_j)P_j] = (i_j - r_j)\,/\,[\partial N/\partial\,(M_j/P_j)\,] \tag{1.2}$$

where the second term reflects the hypothesis that the individual demanding monetary services is a price-taker.

On the supply side, every firm producing monetary services is assumed to face a perfectly elastic demand for those services; to obtain equilibrium in the market for monetary services the rental price of jth monetary services in (1.2) must equal the jth firm's marginal costs of producing monetary services. Deriving the cost curve

$$C_j = C_j\,(N) \tag{1.3}$$

and differentiating with respect to the arguments in $N(\cdot,\cdot)$ in equation (1.1) we obtain:

$$(i_j - r_j) \, / \, [\partial N/\partial \, (M_j \, /P_j)] = \mathrm{d}C_j/\mathrm{d}N$$
$$= \partial C_j/\partial \, (M_j \, /P_j) \,][\mathrm{d}(M_j \, /P_j)/\mathrm{d}N \,] + [\partial C_j/\partial \beta_j) \,] \, [\mathrm{d}\beta_j/\mathrm{d}N \,] \qquad (1.4)$$

which is the core equation of Klein's model. Assuming all firms to be identical, equation (1.4) determines in equilibrium the quantity of monetary services produced and the number of firms in the market.

The best starting point for a discussion of the implications of introducing confidence in the monetary-service production function (1.1) is the analysis of the case in which confidence is irrelevant. Assuming that consumers can perfectly anticipate the future value of every money, creating confidence has no cost and $\partial C_j/\partial \beta_j = 0$. In this case the equilibrium market condition will be:

$$(i_j - r_j) = \mathrm{d}C_j/\mathrm{d}(M_j \, /P_j). \qquad (1.5)$$

The literature on the origins of money usually assumes also that the production of money is costless. In this case the equilibrium interest rate on monetary stocks will be equal to the interest rate on bonds, i_j, and hence there will be an indeterminate number of firms in the market: the market will be shared between firms present on the basis of some non-pecuniary factor that the model is unable to capture.

If the costs of producing money are positive, (1.5) will yield the quantity of real balances each firm provides to the market, but not M_j and P_j separately. This means that the growth rate of supply of the jth money and associated rate of inflation will be indeterminate within the model. If consumers can perfectly anticipate the future value of each money they will be indifferent to differing combinations of the rates of price change and nominal supply of money as long as they produce the same quantity of real balances M_j/P_j. Put simply, monies with high inflation rates (that is, of poorer 'quality') must pay a higher rate of interest r_j on balances, making the opportunity cost $(i_j - r_j)$ constant.

Abandoning the assumption that confidence-creation is costless, so that $\partial C_j/\partial \beta_j > 0$, let us now attempt an explicit analysis of the role of confidence in monetary matters. We assume that although consumers can distinguish costlessly between different brand-names (and hence between monies in circulation), they are unable to anticipate precisely how the supply of each money will evolve. Let the expected quality of a nominal unit of the jth money be identified with some negative function of the expected rate of inflation in that money. The lower the mean probability distribution of the expected rate of inflation of the jth money (determined by that money's expected rate of growth), the better its quality. We are now in the position to state precisely what β_j is supposed to measure. Since the actual price variation may differ from the expected one, the confidence in (or the brand-name value of) the *j*th money captured by β_j will be a function of the anticipated predictability of the price level in terms of the money; it can therefore be assumed to be negatively related to the variance in the *j*th money's anticipated rate of inflation.

Once the possibility of unanticipated changes in the supply of each money is allowed, an increase in the predictability of a money's future value will increase the flow of monetary services from a given real quantity of money and lower their rental price. It should be noted, however, that the information cost assumption does not imply that demand for monetary services faced by firms is less than perfectly elastic, and that the rental prices of monetary services are therefore not perfectly identical in equilibrium. Although the existing firms produce monies of different quality, in equilibrium they will apply the same rental price for their monetary services, trading lower quality (confidence) for a higher interest rate.

Introducing parameter β in the problem of consumer choice opens up some interesting analytical possibilities. Creating confidence is costly and firms might resort to various means to do so. Supplying commodity money, for example, is the same as creating confidence by placing a physical constraint on money production, while convertibility places a juridical constraint. Instead, producing an inconvertible money requires other forms of investment in confidence, such as advertising, expenditure on balance sheet certification and others. What is important for consumers is that these expenditures should be sufficient, for a given monetary interest rate, to keep the monetary-service rental price constant at the level set by the market. Assuming the physical production cost of money is equal to zero, the firm's pure profit in equilibrium must be nil, hence:

$$(i_j - r_j)\,(M_j/P_j) - \rho\beta_j = 0 \qquad (1.6)$$

where ρ is the real rate of interest, which approximates the opportunity cost of investing resources in the production of confidence. This yields:

$$\beta_j = [(i_j - r_j)/r\,](M_j/P_j). \qquad (1.7)$$

The ratio between the opportunity cost of holding the *j*th money and the real rate of interest can be interpreted as the quantity of brand-name capital needed to sustain confidence in a unit of the *j*th money. Of course, if confidence-creation is costless, the optimum condition (1.5) will hold and brand-name capital will be totally valueless.

If information has a cost, then firms might be tempted to deceive their consumers by increasing money faster than anticipated. A distinction must therefore be made between anticipated inflation and observed inflation. If there are lags in the adjustment of expectations given opportunistic behaviour on the part of firms, a simple comparative static exercise will show that the profit-maximizing rate of inflation is infinite. The only limit to the firm's profit could be a cost element that increases with the jth money's rate of expansion. This mechanism can be incorporated by assuming that brand-name capital diminishes with the difference between the anticipated and the effective rate of inflation: the larger the gap between the two, the greater the degree of opportunism and hence the larger the negative impact on β_j. Since β_j is a factor in the production of monetary services, the opportunity cost of holding money must decrease to keep the rental price of the jth money constant, which competition keeps equal to that of all the other monies. It will therefore be up to consumers to decide how far they will accept pecuniary compensation in exchange for a less predictable value of monetary services. In equilibrium there will be both a finite quantity of brand-name capital for each money and a finite value of the unanticipated rate of inflation.

This leads us to the main result of the model: if consumers and producers share the same estimate of the potential gain from a higher than anticipated rate of inflation, then in equilibrium the need to create sufficient confidence will imply that a firm's actual profit-maximizing rate of inflation is not infinite. The competitive model has no degenerative tendency.

In Klein's model, therefore, it is possible to obtain a market equilibrium in which: (1) different monies produced in competition coexist; (2) a socially optimal quantity of brand-name capital is endogenously produced; and (3) the various payment technologies (commodity money, convertible money, legal tender, credit) can be interpreted as different methods, equivalent in equilibrium, of creating confidence in the future predictability of the money supply. Klein observes that this last result is equivalent to stating that, if confidence-creation costs are taken into account, then every money is a form of commodity money.[50]

There are two aspects of the model worth highlighting. First, the competitive equilibrium that Klein obtains, in which several competing monies are produced, is based on two very strong assumptions. The first is that brand-names are perfectly distinguishable. The second is that money-producers and consumers share the same estimate of the profits from increasing the money supply. If just one of these assumptions fails, the production of brand-name capital will tend to be below the social optimum, possibly setting in motion an institutional innovation mechanism designed to strengthen confidence creation. Klein makes the first assumption because he does not consider the problem of imperfectly distinguishable brand names particularly interesting as its consequences are common to every industry. However, he also notes that while imperfectly distinguishable brand-names lead to progressively poorer quality in every industry, the problem is particularly serious in the monetary sector because money is a public good. Since money can also be a mere financial liability, assuming brand-names to be distinguishable means assuming the existence of a legal system to enforce property rights. When property rights are imperfectly enforced a tendency will develop to adopt payment technologies based on a physical rather than a legal safeguard, so as to protect against the risk of imperfect distinguishability of brand-names. The same consequences would come from eliminating the assumption of identical estimates of the possible gain from issuing money, which is not plausible, particularly while the characteristics of a new monetary form are being learnt. In this case the production of brand-name capital would be suboptimally low and consumers would tend to prefer payment technologies with physical constraints on the money supply, such as commodity money or, at most, convertible money.

In other words, the confidence-creation technology – this is the second interesting aspect of the model – becomes crucially important as soon as we move away from the very restrictive assumptions on which Klein bases his results. For instance, Klein notes that, plausibly, the production of information about the reliability of money-producer, and hence of their monies, is subject to large economies of scale, partly because the total cost of spreading information decreases with the number of producers, and partly because the more homogenous are products in a given industry, the lower will be the anticipated variance of quality distribution. With imperfect enforcement of property rights (an institutional constraint) and economies of scale in the dissemination of information (a technical constraint) there will be a tendency not only to adopt payment technologies based on physical rather than legal constraints, but also for the competitive model to degenerate into forms of oligopoly or even monopoly. All this will come about as a result of the role of confidence in monetary matters. Klein explains that it would be senseless to study money without taking this aspect into account.

Klein simply raises the problem of the consequences of eliminating the assumptions underpinning competitive equilibrium without tackling it completely. The 'hows' of transition from one payment technology to another and the 'whys' of the state's role in monetary events thus remain unexplored. However, almost all the key concepts needed to take this further step have been identified.

2. Fluctuations of trust: pre-industrial credit payment technologies

2.1 INTRODUCTION

The institutionalist approach described in the previous chapter puts trust at the centre of monetary analysis. But, as shown, not all payment technologies are fiduciary, in the sense of requiring external institutions to support the trust of those who use them. We have seen, for example, that commodity money is a payment technology that can be self-supporting because the guarantee against monetary abuse is provided by the value of the commodity it contains. But as soon as an element of credit is introduced into the payment technology, the fiduciary aspect comes immediately to the fore because a credit instrument is no more than a right to a future benefit and as such is uncertain.

Credit payment technologies were not born with central banks. Their history goes back over many centuries and have their roots in the Roman age, if not even earlier. It is with the revolution in trade of the late Middle Ages that the technologies began to become more refined and to spread. Until the beginning of the age of central banks, they nonetheless remained circumscribed to large-scale trade transactions owing to the difficulty of sustaining trust in credit payments in a context in which the legal order had not yet developed institutes capable of protecting the rights of holders of credit instruments. Commercial law gained ground starting from the commercial revolution of the thirteenth century as a law reserved to the community of merchants, as distinct from civil law, to which all citizens are subject. Originally it was a 'class law', according to Francesco Galgano's felicitous phrase,[1] the result of merchants' attempts to develop legal concepts and institutes that gave priority to the circulation of wealth compared with the law of property, which was connected with the holding of wealth. But 'private' commercial law, precisely because of its precarious nature and the latent conflict with civil law, offered credit payment technologies only partial protection. It was only with the 'nationalization' of commercial law, and its improvement thanks to the introduction of the concept of bearer securities, that credit finally turned into money. When this step is completed, the prehistory of central banks comes to an end and their real history begins.

In this chapter it is the prehistory that interests us, however, for two reasons. In the first place, this is because the concepts and institutes developed in the centuries that preceded the Industrial Revolution are still in use today. In other words the nature of credit payment technologies has not changed since then. The only changes concern the institutional arrangements that supported them and the ways in which credit instruments are standardized. To examine these developments is therefore a way of introducing the terminology that will be found in the subsequent chapters. In the second place, re-examining how the pre-industrial wholesale payment sector functioned serves also to highlight the limits of the mechanisms for producing the trust existing at the time, going beyond which was the *sine qua non* for the adoption of credit payment technologies on a major scale.

2.2   CREDIT CHAINS AND FINALITY RULES

Let us imagine that banks do not exist but that economic agents can issue debt instruments (IOUs) and transfer them among themselves.[2] Let us assume that three economic agents exist: a producer, a merchant and a final consumer, which for the sake of convenience we will denote by P, M and C. P provides M with a certain quantity of goods that will have to be sold to the final consumer, C. The problem however is that C does not have money immediately available, although he knows that he can count on future earnings. Since there are no banks, the only alternative to waiting is the issue of credit instruments. M can 'pay' P by issuing an (IOU) instrument in his favour while C will 'pay' M by doing the same in his favour. The transaction can thus be completed through the creation of a 'credit chain'.

Obviously, however, in this way it is only the real part of the transaction that is completed. The financial part, that is, the payment, will be completed only with the extinction of the credit chain and the actual transfer of money from C to M and from M to P. The problem is that in a context in which creditors' rights are not adequately protected the risk of M proving to be an unreliable economic agent is high. Since at the time of the transfer of money M will no longer possess the good sold to him by P (it will be held by C), P will have no leverage over M. If C's payment to M occurs before M's payment to P, M will have an incentive to cut and run with C's money. The credit chain can thus be brusquely interrupted or never be created because the various economic agents involved are fully aware of the risks to which they would be exposed by taking part.

Let us assume now that credit instruments are transferable. Instead of money, M can use the credit instrument issued by C in his favour to settle the transaction with P. There are two differences with respect to the previous situation: first, *M* no longer issues an instrument; second, *M* has no need to hold the instrument issued by *C*. He can simply pass it to P, who can proceed to settle the transaction directly with *C* on a bilateral basis. If certain conditions are satisfied, transferability improves the risk aspects of the underlying transaction. But what are these conditions? In the first place *C* must be a more reliable economic agent than *M*, or in technical jargon must be more creditworthy. In the second place *M* must have an incentive to pass the credit instrument received from *C* on to *P*. This will be the case if *M* knows that if he refuses to deliver the instrument to *P*, the latter can block *C*'s settlement in favour of *M*, thereby interrupting the credit chain created.

The credit chain could be further complicated by introducing the possibility of the credit instrument with which *M* pays *P* not being issued by *C* but by another economic agent extraneous to the transaction, which we can call *B* or 'bank'. *B*'s debt might be more acceptable to *P* because the latter does not deal directly with final consumers and is therefore not able to assess their creditworthiness while it has direct knowledge of *B*, which specializes in the issue of instruments that can be used to make payments. Here again, however, there is a need for rules to allocate losses in the event of an interruption in the credit chain.

We have thus highlighted a general condition: in every payment system based not merely on bilateral credit instruments, but on a credit chain, there is a need for rules that govern the allocation of responsibilities and losses if the chain is broken for any reason (fraud, death of one of the economic agents, negligence, and so on). We will call these rules 'finality rules'. Fundamentally a finality rule establishes when a payment is to be considered completed, in the sense that the buyer is relieved of any obligation deriving from the purchase to which the payment refers. This is a legal concept, because the rule presupposes the identification of a legitimate obligation and actions that lead to its discharge.

The search for broadly applicable finality rules marks the passage from the economic concept of 'transferability' to the legal concept of 'negotiability'. A credit instrument is considered to be negotiable if it is issued in accordance with certain rules established by the legal system, so that the effects of particular forms of non-performance are foreseeable.

In the history of negotiability two legal institutes have played an important role: endorsement and the concept of 'holder in due course'. Initially, a credit instrument could be transferred only if it contained an endorsement, that is, the signature of the transferor (the drawer). An endorsement establishes a joint responsibility of the drawer and the original issuer of the instrument (the drawee). If the original debtor proved to be insolvent, the drawer's obligation would not be considered discharged. It would therefore be up to the drawer, in view of his signature, to honour the debt vis-à-vis the owner of the credit. In other words the principle introduced by endorsements is that payment with an instrument issued by a third party can be considered final only if the latter honours his debt. This mechanism may appear paradoxical in our day and age, because it is equivalent to limiting the degree of finality of a payment to make the credit chain underlying a specific payment technology more acceptable. Kahn and Roberds note, however, that the mechanism can be justified on the grounds that a person who uses an instrument issued by another is better placed to assess its creditworthiness than the recipient of the payment and is therefore also better placed to assess the cost of non-performance. In other words the endorsement is a mechanism for limiting the risk of fraud by the buyer, who would otherwise have an incentive to make payment using instruments issued by parties with a low, or even non-existent, creditworthiness. This is why endorsements, even though they limited the finality of payments with respect to simpler credit chains, fostered the development of payment technologies with a large fiduciary content.

The principle underlying the second legal institute that gained ground with the concept of negotiability, that is, that of holder in due course, is that the debt contracted as a consequence of a purchase cannot be void if the good purchased subsequently proves to be defective. To return to the credit chain described earlier, if P has received from M as a payment an instrument issued by C as a consequence of a legitimate transaction, then P will be a holder in due course of C's debt. P's rights must be respected regardless of the quality of the good he supplied to M. By contrast to endorsements, the principle of holder in due course had the effect of extending the degree of finality of the payment with respect to possible failures or incidents involving the real part of the transaction. The purpose in this case is again to make the use of credit in payments more acceptable by creating an incentive for the buyer to select the seller with care, so as to reduce the possibility of fraud.

As Kahn and Roberds note, the drawback of these finality rules is that they make it very difficult to adopt credit payment technologies outside firmly established merchant communities with relatively few members of solid reputation. A system based largely on the perceived value of a signature was bound to be restricted to individuals whose wealth and reputation were well known within the merchant community.[3] In effect this is what happened in the period between the thirteenth century and the end of the sixteenth century. From a monetary standpoint, the history of these centuries can be described as a prolonged attempt to invent legal and institutional rules that would allow trust to be maintained in credit-based payment technologies, so as to extend their use beyond the wholesale merchant sector. An attempt that was to lead to the creation of a vast and primarily credit-based intra-European payment circuit, which, however, owing to the characteristics of the institutional structure and the divergent interests of the various categories of economic agents involved, proved fragile, to the point that it collapsed within a few years, with the consequent return to favour of metallic money.

2.3   DEPOSIT BANKS

Among the possible credit chains, the most obvious is that which involves the use of a liability of a third party known to both the buyer and the seller. Historically, this role was played by money-changers, who, having become omnipresent in the exchange mechanisms of the late Middle Ages owing to the coexistence of currencies of different coinage and uncertain quality, gradually came to perform the function of 'deposit bank'.[4]

So-called 'payment in bank', which spread from the thirteenth century onwards, replaced money changing hands with the simple change in the ownership of the same money. This practice was particularly attractive for large payments.[5] An interesting aspect of payment in bank is that for most of the pre-industrial age making a payment in this way required the presence at the bank of both the payer and the payee. Technically, the latter's presence was not necessary. However, until payment in bank became legal tender, which occurred in Venice in 1526 and elsewhere much later, the mercantile convention remained that payment in bank could not be considered final without formal acceptance by the recipient.

Payment in bank offered three advantages compared with the transfer of a normal credit instrument. In the first place, bankers, specialized in the role of third parties in payments, could offer greater guarantees of reliability compared with the general run of merchants. In the second place, the use of bank accounts for a whole series of payments gave the parties more opportunities to offset inpayments and outpayments without actually transferring the ownership of claims on the bank or delivery of minted money. Lastly, and this may have been the most attractive aspect, banks were in a position to provide well-known customers with a 'settlement' credit in the form of an overdraft. In this latter respect it is interesting to note that Italian merchants, among the leading actors of the period, do not appear to have made prior deposits at the banks. In large part payment transactions were based directly on credit lines granted by bankers to the leading merchants in the market.

As a consequence of these three mechanisms, in principle it was possible to create the quantity of liquid balances that each merchant had to hold for settlement purposes. The mechanism had a defect, however, that greatly reduced its advantages. Both the fact that the parties had to be present in the bank at the time the deposit was transferred, and the need for the banker to establish a solid reputation, tended to limit the territorial extension of the payment mechanism based on bank deposits. And in practice, for most of the pre-industrial period deposit banks remained local institutions that refrained from undertaking activity on a broad scale and from acting as money-changers. For example, in Venice and in Bruges deposit banks remained firmly rooted in the local market. The volume of bank payments therefore remained quite small compared with today's practices. In the Venice of the fourteenth century, a major importer of cotton effected 25–30 transactions on average per year;[6] comparable volumes of business were to be found in Bruges in the same period.

There were three exceptions to the rule according to which deposit banks restricted their scope to local payments: Barcelona, Valencia and Genoa, cities in which banking received special public recognition that allowed it to increase the range of its activities, both geographically and sectorally.[7] The most interesting of these cases, for its analogies with the subsequent development of central banking, is that of the Casa di San Giorgio (originally the Ufficio di San Giorgio), which was founded in Genoa at the beginning of the fifteenth century. This entity was set up to manage the city's debt, but as early as 1408 it had also obtained the right to engage in banking. In 1444 it renounced this right, however, because the activity was making a loss. It was only in 1586, when the Casa had come to control the management of the city's entire public debt, that banking was revived. At that date the Casa di San Giorgio looked very much like one of today's central banks, except for the issue of banknotes, which was to begin about a century later.

But, apart from these exceptions, the activity of taking and managing deposits remained primarily local throughout the pre-industrial period, although in some cases it involved deposit banks in cities where fairs were held; this did not mean that volumes were always small, because fair banks soon became important settlement agents. But before talking about these banks it is best to introduce the payment technologies based on bilateral credit chains, such as exchange contracts, letters of exchange and obligatory coupons.

2.4   CREDIT PAYMENTS AND PAYMENT FAIRS

While the exchange of coins and bank payments were valid ways of making local payments, for transactions at a distance, which imposed the use of different currencies, subject in turn to different usages and rules, the lack of appropriate payment technologies was a major obstacle to commercial transactions. During the commercial revolution of the thirteenth century, the merchant class overcame the problem by developing three different payment technologies, with very different legal bases. The use of one or another technology thus came to depend on the institutional characteristics prevalent in each country, as well as the size and heterogeneity of the merchants operating in each centre.

The first widely used instrument was the exchange contract, which was a promise to pay formulated, as a rule verbally, before a notary public. The contract provided for one of the parties to recognize that it had received a payment in local currency from the other party, and to undertake to make a payment to the same party at a future date and in a different centre in the currency in use in that centre. Both the parties, or their agents, had to appear for the transaction to be able to take place.

Compared with exchange contracts, letters of exchange were a more complex instrument that involved four actors but offered much greater flexibility. In fact a letter of exchange was not a promise to pay but an order to pay. A merchant wishing to send money abroad, the giver, paid it to a local counterparty, the taker, receiving from the latter a letter of exchange that contained the order to an agent of the taker operating in another centre, the payer, to make a payment in another currency to the fourth actor, the beneficiary. Often the beneficiary was no more than an agent of the giver, but this was not a fixed rule. On receiving the letter, the giver would send it to the beneficiary, who would then present it to the payer for settlement. At the same time the taker would notify the payer of the completed transaction. Naturally, the payer could refuse to accept the entire transaction, which entailed a payment at his expense. In this case the letter that was not accepted was stamped 'SP' (*sous protest*) and the matter became the subject of a dispute. Unlike exchange contracts, which normally expired at the next fair, and therefore involved a settlement lag that varied with the time they were executed, letters of exchange had a fixed expiry, depending on the usage of the centre in which they were issued. In Florence the settlement interval was 20 days, in Bruges it was two months and in London it was three months.

The greater flexibility of letters of exchange lay in the fact that, unlike exchange contracts, they were not notarial acts but merely private agreements between merchants; this reduced the related transaction cost, but also meant that they were not protected by the law. The only protection possible was a tribunal of merchants acting as judges on an informal basis to defend the new payment technology from the risk of abuse. The defence was based on three pillars: first, the requirement that letters of exchange should not only be signed but written entirely by the taker; second, the eligibility in the capacity of takers exclusively of local managers of large, internationally recognized merchant houses; and third, the use of letters of exchange only in relation to periodic trade fairs in a limited number of leading commercial centres, where the presence of important merchants permitted settlements and the resolution of disputes in an orderly manner recognized as legitimate by the whole merchant community. The *lex mercatoria* is largely the fruit of this complex action to protect letters of exchange, the effect of which was that as early as the end of the fourteenth century letters of exchange had already replaced exchange contracts in all the areas in which the leading merchant houses operated, above all in Italy, France, Spain and Flanders.

Outside these areas, however, letters of exchange continued for a long time to be a payment technology that was too legally precarious to take hold. As an alternative, local merchants developed a third credit instrument, obligatory coupons. Like letters of exchange, these were informal instruments written by the taker. The coupon, however, like the exchange contract, was a simple promise to pay, generally referring, moreover, to a single currency, so as to avoid exchange rate complications. As time passed, the simplicity of this instrument permitted it to extend its penetration to areas such as France, the Netherlands, England and Spain, where letters of exchange were also in use. However, its application remained limited to small and medium-sized transactions and in the Netherlands it was used experimentally in the sixteenth century to spread consumer credit.

Of these three credit payment technologies, the letter of exchange was undoubtedly the most innovative and important in terms of its economic and institutional implications. Once the complex network of institutional protection needed to support trust had been set up, the letter of exchange rapidly ceased to be an instrument serving merely to make payments and became a financial instrument in its own right, often unrelated to any commercial transaction. The archival research of Mueller,[8] for example, showed that between 1336 and 1340 the Compagnia dei Covoni in Florence carried out 433 transactions of this kind, of which only 70 were connected with commercial transactions while the remainder were mainly aimed at exploiting arbitrage opportunities between the various financial centres of the day.

From the very beginning the use of letters of exchange in relation to exchanges at fairs raised the question of how to settle the payments connected with commercial transactions. This problem was solved with the establishment of a highly detailed ritual, which reached its most complete form in the Lyons fairs. On the occasion of such fairs, which were held four times a year, 15 working days were devoted to commercial transactions, after which financial transactions held the stage. This phase opened with the 'day of acceptances', when all merchants, regardless of their nationality, possessing a 'daybook' collected and compared their positions as givers, takers, beneficiaries and payers. Two days later was the 'day of exchanges'. At the beginning the merchant-bankers belonging to a narrow circle of nationalities met to agree on the date of the next fair and the procedures for settling the letters regarding cities that did not have a fixed usage. Subsequently, the merchant-bankers from Florence, Genoa and Lucca would meet to determine the exchange rates at which to settle transactions (the so-called 'reckoning'). The two days following the determination of the reckoning were devoted to new financial exchanges, totally unrelated to the previous ones. To conclude the whole process, there was the 'day of payments', that is, the real settlement. The ways in which settlement was made can be classified under four headings: the offsetting of debts; the granting of an overdraft by the creditor merchant to the debtor merchant until the next fair; the assignment to another creditor of a credit held by a merchant who was the debtor in a specific transaction; and payment in metallic money.

The ways in which settlement was made give rise to two considerations of importance for our purpose. In the first place, settlement in metallic money appears to have been decidedly marginal compared with the other methods, evidence of the fact that payment technology is primarily of a credit nature. In the second place, in the context of the Lyons fairs, and even more in the subsequent Bisanzone fairs, which were devoted exclusively to financial transactions and dominated by the Genoese bankers, the use of payment in bank for settlement purposes appears to have been extremely limited. This is hardly surprising insofar as the procedure resembles a centralized mechanism with powerful entry barriers much more than the free competitive market of economics manuals. In this context the production of trust is not a problem. As Kohn notes:

> In such inside markets, because participants were few and of known reputation, there was no advantage in netting and assigning the debt of a deposit bank (its deposits) in settlement. Participants could just as easily net and assign each others' debt.[9]

It is interesting to note that things developed differently in other contexts. For example, the fairs in Champagne in the thirteenth century had much lower entry barriers. Settlement via local deposit banks, commonly known as 'fair' banks, was thus a valid alternative to direct settlement, which suffered from decidedly high counterparty risk. This practice became the rule in fact, except in the Lyons fairs and later the Bisanzone

fairs. As Kohn notes: 'By the fourteenth century, in all the centres of international trade and finance, whether they were fairs or commercial cities,
payment in bank predominated.'[10]

The reason why these complex payment technologies fell into disuse
is still an open question for historians. Boyer-Xambeu, Deleplace and
Gillard[11] attribute responsibility to the upsetting of the oligopolistic equilibrium between the two major merchant 'nations', Florence and Genoa.
Towards the end of the sixteenth century, Genoa's financial policy became
increasingly aggressive, to the point that the Genoese organized a series of
fairs (the Bisanzone fairs referred to above, so called because they were originally held at Besançon, though they were quickly moved to Italy) in open
competition with the Lyons fairs. The open rivalry between Florentines
and Genoese, confirmed by the interruption of the unitary mechanism for
settling letters of exchange, finds an echo in the words of the Florentine
Bernardo Davanzati, one of the most acute observers of monetary affairs in
the sixteenth century, who noted, not without a polemic strain:

> the Genoese have invented a new exchange that they call for the Bisanzone
> fairs, where one went to at the beginning; now they are held in Savoy, in
> Piedmont, in Lombardy, at Trento, at the gates of Genoa, and wherever the
> Genoese like. So that it is better to call them Utopias, i.e. fairs without a place.
> Nor have they anything in common with fairs than the four names, borrowed
> from those of Lyons, because they do not have people to buy goods but only
> fifty or sixty moneychangers with a daybook to deliver the exchanges made in
> almost the whole of Europe and return them with the interest they merit, not
> settled, so that the debt can last.[12]

Another factor contributing to the downfall of the letter-of-exchange
circuit was the monetary policy of the French monarchs, who suddenly
changed course between 1575 and 1577 by imposing the gold escudo as the
unit of account, banning the circulation of foreign currencies and suppress-
ing seignorage, all measures aimed at establishing a national monetary
policy in which metallic money is assigned a priority role. Caught between
the Scylla of the French authorities' nationalist attitude and the Charybdis
of the rivalry between the main groups of private bankers, the 'credit international', based on fragile trust, could only dissolve. And it did so, as was
suitable for such an ethereal payment technology, almost without leaving
any trace. The period from the end of the sixteenth century to the middle
of the eighteenth century saw the triumph of metallic money. The credit
payment technologies continued to survive, in less striking forms, only at
local level, where a favourable institutional environment allowed them to
avoid the abuse of the newborn absolute monarchies. This was the case,
for example, of the giro banks.

2.5 GIRO BANKS

With the waning of the fair payment circuits and related credit mechanisms, the efficiency of the infra-European payment system declined significantly. A large proportion of the coins in circulation was of very bad quality, partly because the technique of milling the edge of coins had not yet been invented. As Fodor noted: 'Until the end of the 17th century, the very poor state of coins often resulted in the strong taking advantage of the weak when payments were made.'[13]

In cities such as Amsterdam, Venice and Hamburg, marked by very large volumes of trade and consequently by the circulation of coins from many different countries, the public sector responded to the needs of merchants by creating a new type of bank, the public giro bank. These banks accepted deposits of coins of any kind, which were valued at their intrinsic value and accredited in a special unit of account, bank money. Payments between merchants were carried out by transferring the ownership of this fictitious money of account. In some cities this practice became obligatory for large-value payments. On the other hand giro banks were not allowed to grant loans, a prohibition that was complied with in large part, although not completely. In this respect a very interesting phenomenon can be observed: the purely fictitious money of account, with no material connotation, was often quoted at higher values than the metallic money it replaced. On this phenomenon Ferdinando Galiani, for example, had this to say about the Venetian money market: 'Thus the money of Banco di Venezia, since it was more necessary to trade than cash and considered to be more secure, was valued with a premium that made it more expensive than cash.'[14]

The phenomenon can also be observed elsewhere. It is a further demonstration that it is not metal that makes good money, but trust. Where the political and legal institutions, and possibly the barriers to entry to the banking sector, were considered sufficient protection against the risk of abuse of the currency, payment technologies flourished. When these conditions were lacking, there only remained metal as the last bulwark of monetary rigour, although this bulwark did not always prove to be robust, as centuries of monetary mutations show. It does not seem an accident that the giro banks were born and flourished in city-states of a republican nature, that is, free from the abuse of monarchs. This aspect is well expressed in the following memorable passage by Montesquieu:

> The erecting of banks in countries governed by an absolute monarch supposes money on the one side, and on the other power: that is, on the one hand, the means of procuring everything, without any power; and on the other, the

power, without any means of procuring at all. In a government of this kind, none but the prince ever had, or can have, a treasure; and wherever there is one, it no sooner becomes great than it becomes the treasure of the prince.[15]

2.6   CONCLUSIONS: THE PASSAGE TO THE 'AGE OF THE CENTRAL BANKS'

This chapter had three objectives: (1) to introduce terms and concepts that are still in use today with reference to credit payment technologies, such as 'clearing', 'settlement' and 'payment finality'; (2) to stress the indissoluble link between credit technologies and law, because any form of payment based on credit cannot do without rules that confirm the legitimacy of the instrument and reduce the uncertainty associated with the possibility of default; and (3) to show how the evolution of payment technologies is not a linear process, going from concrete monetary forms to increasingly abstract forms, but moves along a tortuous path with sudden advances and equally rapid backslidings. The key to the evolution of money is not its physical aspect but the characteristics of the economic and institutional environment in which it is inserted, because what counts is the ability of that environment to sustain the trust in the prevalent payment technology. This aspect was given masterly expression by Boyer-Xambeu, Deleplace and Gillard when they argued that:

> In the middle of the 16th century there was a modern money, based on the unit of account, the relationship between public and private, the integration of the European space, and the hegemony of a social group that exercised its control on the exchange rate; and it was the crisis of the monetary relationships to determine the falling back on metal, the appearance of a monetary policy, the prevalence of the national dimension, and the rise of financiers. And the subsequent history of money will, in turn, have to abandon this phase, in which gold *became* money: the bank of Amsterdam is not the heir of the Lyons exchange fairs, rather it was the indirect consequence of their ruin.[16]

It is with the ruin of the exchange fairs and the monetary crises of the following century that the prehistory of central banks comes to an end. It is at this point, driven by the industrial revolution, that the age of central banks begins. The passage from prehistory to history is marked by the invention of bearer securities, of which the banknote is the main example. The process of institutional adaptation proceeds with the development of bank money on a vast scale and reaches its peak with the nationalization of the central banks in connection with the advent of legal tender. The second part of this book is devoted to the three phases of this process.

PART II

The rise and fall of convertibility

3. The convertible banknote and the 'English model'

3.1 INTRODUCTION

The development of the banknote laid the foundation for the history of central banking. It was not an easy start and definitely not one whose outcome could be taken for granted. The century roughly spanning 1650 to 1750 is, from the monetary standpoint, a trial period during which the most varied solutions were tested to promote trust in a new payment technology that, despite its extraordinary flexibility, proved extremely fragile.

In principle, as Vera Smith remarks in her classical text on the origins of central banking, there are three possible set-ups for issuing notes: (1) by a centralized public body; (2) by a private institution subject to specific surveillance; and (3) by a multiplicity of competing private banks, subject, in the most liberal arrangement, only to commercial law and, in the least liberal, to a series of ad hoc controls limiting their issuing capability.[1]

A certain liberalist vulgate that developed in the 1880s preferred the first solution right from the beginning, for the simple reason that it was the only one guaranteeing state control of a form of hidden taxation, the inflation rate, implemented by issuing more banknotes than the economy required.[2] At first glance, this seems plausible. The main forerunners of today's central banks, namely the Bank of Stockholm, the Bank of England and the First Bank of the United States, were all established with the specific intent of facilitating state funding at a time of large regime gaps, that is, slow fiscal structure and uncertain results. However, providing the means for state funding is quite different from proposing to exploit the power of note issue in order to apply hidden taxes. From this standpoint, which is the one that interests us here, the thesis of today's supporters of free banking is a simplification bordering on misrepresentation.

In reality, as Marc Bloch observed, it is hard to imagine how the convertible banknote could have developed in the eighteenth century if the state had not 'granted its guarantee, to a greater or lesser extent, giving [the issuing institutions] a privilege or a monopoly'.[3] What was missing then, and what would not appear before the 1850s, was an adequate body of company law, protecting the holder of banknotes from abuse by the issuer. The main aim of the legislation establishing the first national banks was to create a legal framework in which the new payment technology, whose flexibility would soon be clear even outside the limited circle of the traders and dealers, could spread and prosper. It is true, however, that at this early stage mishaps, even significant ones, occurred. This was the case, for example, in Sweden in 1661, when banknotes were introduced for the first time on a vast scale. Note issue came to a halt after just three years due to the serious difficulties that the Bank of Stockholm met in honouring the demand for conversion. Another well-known example is the fiduciary system conceived by John Law in France at the start of the eighteenth century. The outcome of these experiments served as a warning for other countries. It was no coincidence that the Bank of England was established as a company with only private capital, over which the Crown had no direct control. Or that, about a century later, Alexander Hamilton, Secretary of the Treasury under George Washington, and one of the most ardent supporters of a national bank for America, emphasized that in the interests of sound management, banknotes would have to be issued on the basis of mainly private capital and that 'the ordinary rules of prudence require that the Government should possess the means of ascertaining . . . that so delicate a trust is executed with fidelity and care'.[4]

The history of the first national banks can, however, be viewed from a completely different angle. Douglass North and Barry Weingast, discussing the reforms introduced in England after the Glorious Revolution of 1688, the most important of which was the establishment of the Bank of England in 1694, witnessed the attempt to replace a chaotic, arbitrary and often inefficient regime with a rational and transparent system that could be controlled by the emerging bourgeoisie, with funding from the coffers of the state. Seen this way, the Crown's irresponsible financial behaviour had driven the reform of the monetary institutions, not vice versa.[5]

The reality, if we intend to remain objective, is that the development of the convertible banknote, which was driven in the eighteenth century by the expansion of trade and industry, represented a formidable challenge to companies at that time, both because of the poor institutional framework, especially legally, and because of the increasing need for state funding for: (1) military demands (the affirmation of the nation-states); (2) social provisions (the need to smooth out the undesirable side-effects of early industrialization); and (3) administrative requirements (the expansion of the role of state bureaucracy).

A prolonged period of experimentation ensued, in the course of which the three frameworks described by Smith were tested, accompanied by minor variants incidental to the country and the historical moment. For a long time, opinions were split about the relative merits of each solution, mainly because of frequent instability. In some countries, the most famous example of which is the United States, sudden changes of direction took place, and not just from the decentralizing to the centralizing solution, but also vice versa.

The definitive convergence on a centralized management dawned only at the turn of the twentieth century. This came about not so much because people had become convinced of the superiority of centralization as a way of managing the convertible banknote, but because by then it was clear that, alongside the banknote, another innovative payment modus operandi had arisen, the bank deposit, which stood to gain considerably from a centralized issue system, in particular as 'lending of last resort'. These developments are not directly related to the banknote and will be dealt with in the next chapter. The stage in the history of central banks when the convertible banknote was the mainstay had ended earlier, with the triumph and spread of a model merging pure decentralization and pure centralization. This was the 'English model', which took shape in 1844 with the adoption of the Bank Charter Act. The English model was based on two principles. First, the faculty of issuing banknotes was assigned to private profit-seeking institutions with an explicit state charter and was therefore under the direct control of the executive. Second, the faculty of issuing banknotes had to be subjected to strict rules which, by restricting the discretion of the issuing banks' management, were intended to protect convertibility and promote trust in the circulation of paper.

The experience of the English model was somewhat paradoxical. Judging by the number of imitations, the success of the model cannot be challenged. To the end of the century, various versions of the English model were adopted in France, Italy, the United States, Belgium and Japan, to name just the main countries to follow suit. Nevertheless, as Morgan commented: 'the surprising thing about the Bank Charter Act is its persistence'.[6] In fact, because the model excised the problem of the overissuance of banknotes, it had obvious limitations, since it deprived the new payment system of its main attraction, that is, a supply more flexible than that of minted coins. Only three years after the adoption of the new framework, it was necessary – even in England – suddenly to halt its implementation to allow the Bank of England to deal with a liquidity crisis, a practice that would suffer several relapses, until the model was eventually abandoned. Nor can it be said that people were unaware of the model's faults at the time. In 1848, Thomas Tooke, one of the most authoritative nineteenth-century monetary economists, expressed a final judgement, defining the 1844 Bank Charter Act: 'the most wanton, ill-advised, pedantic and rash piece of legislation that has come within my observation . . .

an ugly excrescence . . . a total, unmitigated, uncompensated, and, in its consequence, a lamentable failure.'[7]

Tooke, as a prominent exponent of the Banking School, rival to the Currency School, which rightly saw the English model as an application of its own ideas, may be suspected of bias. Not so Sir Robert Peel, the Prime Minister, originator of the Bank Charter Act who, in a confidential letter addressed to the Governor of the Bank of England, revealed his own doubts about the durability of the Act:

> My confidence is unshaken that we have taken all the precautions which legislation can prudently take against a recurrence of a pecuniary crisis. It may occur in spite of our precautions; and if it does, and if it be necessary to assume a grave responsibility, I dare say men will be found willing to assume such a responsibility.[8]

This proves that pragmatic solutions to the unprecedented problems arisen by the new monetary forms produced by the industrial revolution were being sought on a trial-and-error basis. These progressive institutional adjustments would soon have to accommodate the introduction of the cheque and the bank deposit.

3.2   BEARER SECURITY

As a means of payment, banknotes are now so common and rooted in the collective psyche that it is hard to imagine a time when they were viewed with hostility, first and foremost from the legal standpoint, and secondly from the economic perspective. This is because the principles on which the banknote is based, that is, negotiability and bearer security, were still foreign to most legal systems even as late as the early eighteenth century. It is true that the merchant class, from the fourteenth century, had tried to get around the problem by establishing practices and conventions, in some cases backed and even actively promoted by the Crown. However, as pointed out in Chapter 2, these practices and conventions formed a body of 'class' rules, in constant conflict with the civil law ruling the nation's affairs in general. Behind this conflict, there were the sectarian interests of the merchants, aiming for a smoother circulation of wealth, and on the other hand, the interests of the landowners, directed to maintaining the status quo upholding the privileges of rightful owners. As long as the scales of the structure of the economy were tipped towards the agricultural sector, the conflict, whenever it set forth openly, could only be resolved by favouring ownership rights to the detriment of the rights of circulation. Basically, the very development of commercial law can be viewed as the attempt of the emerging merchant class to carve out a legal space for itself that would encourage trade. It was therefore quite natural that the extension of merchant customs to the rest of the population was perceived with hostility, and strenuously contested.

The obstacles to the extension of commercial law, and as a consequence also of the development of the banknote, can be traced back to three main categories: the constraints of holography; the primacy of the equity principle; and aversion to the concept of bankruptcy.

For the whole period of the Middle Ages, contracts were mainly verbal notarial acts: written contracts were the exception.[9] As we saw in Chapter 2, the merchants tried to get around these practices by using letters of exchange. However, in order to control the risk, commercial law initially provided that documents had to be holographs, that is, written entirely by the contractor assuming the responsibility. It was only in the later fifteenth century, with the vast expansion of dealings, that signatures began to gain importance as, previously, contractors did not sign documents because they had written them themselves. At the beginning of the eighteenth century there was a move towards preprinted documents, with a blank space for the signature. In the meantime, merchant practice increased the number of people who were authorized to sign documents. The evolution of commercial law was not, however, simply adopted by the civil law without a fight. For example, de Roover noted that in 1730 the French monarchy was still insisting that promissory notes and receipts had to be written and signed by the same person, an obligation that, interestingly enough, was not extended to letters of exchange, the main instrument for large international exchanges.[10]

However, an even greater obstacle was the primacy accorded by civil judges to considerations of 'equity' as opposed to the mere observance of what had been agreed in the contract.[11] Contracts considered unfair could be simply annulled by the judge, and the possible grounds for injustice included the price or the quality of the goods being exchanged, even if these had been clearly specified in the contract. One aspect of this judicial approach of direct importance for the development of bearer security was the responsibility for default. In the Middle Ages, outside the merchants' circle, the prevailing assumption was that the bearer of a security was a de facto agent of the original lender. But this not only implied that the bearer had, at all times, to be able to prove the legitimacy of his role as an agent; it also meant that the agency contract could be revoked at any time, either by will of the original lender, or by his death. Under these conditions, the credit security of a loan could not be transferred. Any agreement between the bearer and the final debtor could be challenged as unfair. This state of affairs lasted into the eighteenth century. Bearer securities, for example, were still considered illegal in France in 1716.[12]

The last obstacle to the creation of a universally applicable commercial law was the judicial aversion to the idea of bankruptcy. In the eighteenth century, only merchants could be declared bankrupt and not entrepreneurs, artisans or landowners.[13] In England, the prevailing assumption was that bankruptcy could not be the result of events that were accidental or in any case beyond the control of the debtor, but was rather the result of the debtor trying to defraud his creditors or in some way hold up the collection of monies owing; unless, of course, the debtor was a merchant, a category whose practices were tolerated but, at the same time, clearly restricted.

Overall, the image that remains, in the words of O'Brien, is that of: 'a body of law, which existed to protect against fraud, restrained the extension of a network of debt, credit and risk-taking upon which economic growth depended.'[14] But under pressure from economic interests, and the gradual rise of the merchant class, legal practices and doctrine began to change, smoothing the path for the wider use of banknotes. The country leading the way was England: in the aftermath of the Glorious Revolution of 1688 came the first large-scale affirmation of the bourgeoisie, soon to provide the testing grounds for the Industrial Revolution. Before the Glorious Revolution, some early signs of the new trends were already present. In 1666, if a common citizen refused to honour a bill of exchange on the grounds that he was not obliged to respect what he considered to be a mere practice of merchants, the courts would find against him because: 'the law of merchants is the law of the land, and the custom is good enough generally for any man, without naming him a merchant.'[15]

This was the first sign of recognition of the universal value of mercantile law, whose consequence grew thanks to the importance of case law within the common law system. But this judgment did not get to the root of the conflict between mercantile law and civil law, shown in a judgment dated 1703, in which a judge refused to apply the judicial protection afforded to bills of exchange to a note from a goldsmith, a promissory note, the real precursor to the banknote.[16] This grave decision created a sort of legal limbo for promissory notes which were, by then, a commonly used instrument in the City of London and one that was indispensable for the development of trade. But this time the merchant class, by then in power, reacted at the political level. The following year, Parliament enacted a law to grant promissory notes and inland bills of exchange the same standards before the law.

From that moment on, the road towards bearer securities in England was clear. The legal system finally recognized commercial customs towards the middle of the century, the years when Lord Mansfield, one of the great figures in British legal history, was Lord Chief Justice, the equivalent of today's Minister of Justice. He encouraged the English courts to start giving more importance to the promises and intentions of the contractors than to abstract considerations of equity. But the crucial judgment on the theft of a Bank of England banknote was made by Lord Mansfield in 1758. The legitimate owner of the note reported the theft to the Bank, which consequently refused to exchange it for cash to the bearer who had in the meantime accepted it in good faith. It was the bearer who started legal proceedings and whose right to collect was recognized, despite the defence maintaining that the ownership of the banknote, as in the case of any other good, could not be transferred by theft. Lord Mansfield unambiguously rejected this reasoning, explaining that:

> The whole fallacy [put forward by the defence] turns upon comparing bank notes to what they do not resemble and what they ought not to be compared to, viz., to goods or to securities or documents for debts. Now they are not goods nor securities nor documents for debts, nor are so esteemed: but are treated as money, as cash, in the ordinary course and transaction of business by the general consent of mankind; and it is necessary for the purposes of commerce that their currency should be established and secured.[17]

In a country that was preparing to be the centre of world finance in the following century, this judgment sent a clear signal that the interests of the merchant classes had definitively prevailed over those of the landowners. Banknotes were now fully recognized by the law.

3.3 THE CONVERTIBLE BANKNOTE AS A PAYMENT TECHNOLOGY

One of the characteristics of pre-industrial monetary systems was the chronic lack of small-denomination coins. The age-old tendency towards monetary devaluation, seen in Europe since the fourteenth century, can mostly be attributed to a lack of flexibility in the supply of metallic money.[18] Difficulties for trade increased during the eighteenth century because of the plethora of small mints across the European continent. Repeated attempts to rationalize the minting of coins during the eighteenth century were mostly unsuccessful. However, in the key countries of the European economic system and, *in primis*, in England, the combined action of newly boosted population growth and the expansion of manufacturing and trade created the need for new ways of payment.

The main innovation of the convertible banknote compared to metallic money consisted in its contractual nature as a payment means. While the value of metallic money was guaranteed by its content, the banknote was a

debt payable to the bearer, its value depending on the convertibility clause
being respected. Since banknotes could change hands any number of
times before being converted back into metallic money, there was the risk
that the issuer could behave imprudently, if not fraudulently, safe in the
knowledge that the banknote had uncertain legal status and, in the more
developed legal systems, was protected by the limited liability regime. This
risk involves two factors, as Smith explains in a passage in which she summarizes the criticisms of free banking by its opponents:

> A large proportion of such notes is likely to be in the hands of those who are
> either too ignorant, or by reason of their subordinate position, unable, to refuse
> to accept the notes of a bank which a more informed or better-placed person
> would reject because of suspicion attaching to the affairs of that bank. In other
> words, there is placed on the community the burden of discriminating between
> good and bad notes, and it falls especially hard on those sections of the com-
> munity who are least able to bear it . . . [Moreover,] in a free-banking system
> competition among the banks would provoke a constant tendency to the lower-
> ing of discount rates and increases in the volume of credit. It would be followed
> eventually by an external drain of gold, but this was a check which operated too
> late, because by the time the drain began to affect the banks' reserves the seeds
> of the depression had already been sown, and the crisis would only be made
> more intense by the sudden contraction of lending forced on the banks by the
> urge to protect their reserves.[19]

The first type of risk is the one referred to in the Introduction as the risk
of opportunistic behaviour on the part of single issuers, due to the fact that
it was not possible to make out perfectly the trademarks on the banknotes
in circulation. This was mainly a risk of a microeconomic nature. The
second risk was the possibility of a macroeconomic failure in case of an
excessive expansion in note issuing, following an attempt, on the part of
single issuers, to maintain their own market share in the face of aggressive
behaviour on the part of competitors.

In principle, it was possible to avoid these risks – or at least to reduce
them significantly – in three different ways:

1. By strengthening contractual defences (and therefore the degree of
    legal protection) in favour of the owner of the notes.
2. By nationalizing banknote production, thus removing this sector of
    economic activity from the free market and its drive for profit.
3. By subjecting the issuing banks to prudential rules, with the state
    supervising compliance.

Strengthening contractual defences basically meant that note issue was
to become subject to the legal regime of unlimited liability similar to that

of the credit payment systems of late mediaeval fairs. This solution may seem obvious today and, in fact, many recent proposals to reform the monetary framework advocate the reintroduction of unlimited liability in banking.[20] At the time, however, the solution must have seemed less obvious, or perhaps too drastic, given the scant attention it received, compared to alternative solutions. In England, even the supporters of free banking did not go beyond taking on the monopolistic privileges of the Bank of England as a joint-stock company with limited liability. Not many voices rose against limited liability per se and they had little influence. We can only guess as to why this was, since the indications about the effectiveness of unlimited liability as a protection against the risk of overissue were ambiguous. Around mid-eighteenth century the Scottish banking system, which was incontestably more stable than its English counterpart, was made up of a dozen or so medium-sized banks operating with unlimited liability, and three large banks established as joint-stock companies with limited liability.[21] The behaviour of the two groups of banks does not, however, seem to have been affected by the different legal regimes since, all things considered, stability depended on both groups of banks. Conversely, in England, the so-called 'country banks' – which, as we shall see, quickly earned themselves a very poor reputation – used to operate with unlimited liability.[22]

On the other side of the Atlantic, where limited liability had been the norm since the start of banking, various attempts were made, although not very successful ones, aimed at redressing banking instability by changing the liability regime. To start with, priority was accorded to credit in the form of banknotes in the case of bankruptcy. Then a system of 'dual liability' was tested, by which stockholders were responsible for the bank's debts in proportion to the shares held by each one, even beyond the actual amount of capital invested. The third and most ambitious experiment involved a system of obligatory insurance for uncovered liabilities, the New York Safety Fund System. However, none of these projects proved effective in limiting banking instability, and the idea of stockholders being held liable was, in the end, abandoned.

The most radical alternative to the 'contractual route', nationalization, was never seriously contemplated in the political and doctrinal debates at the turn of the nineteenth century. If one basic trend can be traced back to this period, it was that of removing the note issue system from direct state control. In Sweden, for example, the Riksbank was owned and supervised by Parliament from its founding in 1668. But a century and a half later, public opinion in Sweden held that: 'the needs of industry and commerce could be met better by the creation of private [banking] enterprises'.[23] In 1824, in fact, a decree authorized the establishment of private issuing banks. In Denmark, the transformation was even more radical: the Rigsbank was owned by the state and had a legal monopoly over note issue until 1808, when it became the National Bank of Denmark, a bank which was privately owned. Much later in the century, the state-owned Prussian issuing bank was replaced, following German unification, by the Reichsbank, a company that, though subject to controls and governed by a board of political appointees, was private. There are numerous other examples.

It is not difficult to see why the idea of nationalizing note issuing was unpopular at the time. The prevailing ideology, as seen in the work of Adam Smith, was that the state should keep to a few essential functions that did not include the active control of money. In the field of economics, following the decline of the mercantile system that dominated the 1600s, an almost unanimous support for laissez-faire policies prevailed. Furthermore, even from a purely monetary standpoint, the idea of entrusting the state with the management of the new payment forms did not seem very reassuring in a century that had witnessed the financial disasters that John Law caused in France under Louis XV, the hyperinflation produced by issuing *assignats* during the French Revolution, and the unfortunate outcomes of many instances of colonial note issue. As mentioned earlier, and as we shall see in more detail below, even in the United States Alexander Hamilton, a strenuous defender of centralized note issue, recommended that the state should not be involved in managing the institution, and that, in order to avoid any abuse of power, it should not be possible 'to own the whole or a principal part of the stock',[24] although he did stress as one of the main advantages of this set-up that the establishment of a national bank would give 'facility to Government in obtaining pecuniary aids'.[25] It is significant that the only authoritative supporters of nationalizing note issue, namely David Ricardo and James Mill, highlighted the need to remove any margin of discretion from note issuers. Ricardo adopted this position in the first edition of his *Principles of Political Economy and Taxation*, returning to it in a specific study, published posthumously in 1824, in which he proposed the creation of a national bank under government control.[26] We will return to Ricardo's proposal in Chapter 5 because it contains a well-argued description of what is now called 'the principle of central bank autonomy', that is, that the central bank must be guaranteed and controlled by the government but free of operating restrictions. However, in the monetary debates in England in his day, Ricardo's proposal, despite its authoritative source, did not gain much approval and his brother Samson's attempts to repropose it in the years prior to the adoption of the reform in 1844 did not have an impact. The same destiny was shared by the theses of James Mill who, since 1821, had been arguing that: 'The issuing of notes is one of that small number of businesses, which it suits a government to conduct; a business which may be reduced to a strict routine, and falls within the compass of a small number of clear and definite rules.'[27]

The thesis of Ricardo and Mill must have seemed paradoxical even to their own converts, because it was not clear what was to be gained by putting such a sensitive activity as issuing banknotes directly into the hands of the executive powers – the main authors of the monetary 'crimes' of the eighteenth century – rather than adopting a system of rigid rules imposed under the supervision of the state on private note-issuing institutions. When later, in 1844, the monetary doctrine proposed by Ricardo in his *Principles* was transposed into law, controls and not nationalization were called for. Once the two extreme hypotheses had been dropped, only the difficult 'middle way' remained – a way that soon proved just as rocky.

3.4 MONETARY CONTROVERSIES IN THE EARLY NINETEENTH CENTURY AND THE 'ENGLISH MODEL'

The association between the industrial revolution and the spread of the banknote is common to many countries, as shown in particular in the research of Rondo Cameron.[28] England, thanks to its role as precursor of industrial development, was to play an important part in the history of the new payment means. Throughout the eighteenth century, England, as a result of silver being undervalued at the Mint, suffered a constant shortage of small-denomination coins. As noted by Alfred Marshall, by mid-century this had become such a big problem that consumers and tradespeople were forced to improvise coins. It was in this context that note issue, which had been a practice restricted to the goldsmiths in the City and around the Bank of England, began to expand outside the London area.[29] Marshall described the expansion of the circulation of the banknote in the following terms:

> The new activities of business were demanding increased facilities for the quick granting of credits, and the prompt discharge of obligations . . . Of course, bills of exchange could do part of the work without the aid of any formal agencies of credit. But their scope was limited; and there remained a great opening for any paper currency issued by people known in each neighbourhood; and which everyone would accept in payment, at all events for small sums; not so much because he was certain of the permanent solvency of the issuer, as because he felt sure of quickly passing it to his neighbours.[30]

Since the Bank of England enjoyed the privilege of being a public limited company and issued banknotes that were in any case unsuitable for the retail trade, the task of satisfying the growing demand for coins for trading purposes fell to the country (provincial) banks, banking institutions operating with unlimited liability and subject to the constraint of a maximum of six partners. In 1750 there were still only a dozen or so country banks; by 1784 they numbered 120 and by 1810 had reached 650.[31] Until the end of the eighteenth century the English note-issue system comprised two circuits that were quite distinct but with functional connections: the Bank circuit that dominated the heart of the British economy – that is, the City; and the country banks circuit with its medium-sized or small institutions, operating far from London.

English monetary debate in the first half of the nineteenth century turned to the rationality of this set-up. The course of the debate and its legislative consequences were naturally dictated by circumstances, and by two very important events in particular. First, the convertibility of the Bank of England notes was suspended for quite a long period, from 1797 to 1812, as a result of the crisis of confidence that hit the English financial market when the war with France, declared in 1793, began to hit the skids. During the non-convertible period, the Bank could only use its own good sense to guide note issuing, which nevertheless increased greatly. Banknotes in circulation increased from £10 million in the years 1790–97 to £16–17 million in the period 1802–08, to £22–23 million in 1810–13, and to £26–27 million in the 1815–18 interval.[32] Second, repeated episodes of instability marred the country bank circuit. In the two years 1816–17, some 90 bankruptcies were recorded, with a further 70 in 1825–26, and innumerable others at the end of the 1830s.[33]

Two questions were being asked: had the Bank profited from non-convertibility by issuing such large quantities of banknotes to determine an increase in prices and the devaluation of the currency? and: were country banks unstable for internal reasons or due to the Bank of England's policies?

As previously mentioned, there were two important and opposing schools of thought. In time, they came to be called respectively the Currency School and the Banking School, names that only came into common use in the 1830s. To understand the terms of the controversy, it is useful to take a step back, according a brief look at the ideas of Adam Smith on the subject of note issue. In his *Wealth of Nations* Smith, while recognizing the role of the Bank of England, 'this great engine of the State',[34] as to the management of the public finances, stood for free competition in banking. The model he had in mind was the Scottish system, and his conclusion was unambiguous:

> If bankers are restrained from issuing any circulating bank notes, or notes payable to the bearer, for less than a certain sum; and if they are subjected to the obligation of an immediate and unconditional payment of such bank notes as soon as they are presented, their trade may, with safety to the public, be rendered in all other respects perfectly free.[35]

However, Smith was writing in 1776, in a context in which banknotes and the country banks had not experienced the explosive growth seen later at the turn of the century, at which point his theories were attacked by Henry Thornton in his *Enquiry*, which stands as a classic work on central banking to our days.[36] For our purposes, what is most relevant in Thornton's work is that he contested the self-regulatory nature of competition in banking. In his opinion, the supply of banknotes had to be closely regulated, especially in the presence of outflow of specie abroad, in order to achieve 'superintendance of general credit', what we call today 'credit management'. Therefore, not only did competition not guarantee stability, but it was also counterproductive since it hampered a management of loans consistent with the interests of the country. Thornton did not go so far as to call for the abolition of the country banks: he thought that the Bank of England was regulating the circulation of their banknotes too. He was, however, worried about the possibility that the Bank's monopoly on joint-stock banking might be removed.

The ideas of Thornton on the advantages of a single note issuer were shared by the Currency School, whose main exponents were David Ricardo and Lord Overstone. Thornton's ideas about the advisability of discretionary control of credit were not so popular. For the Currency School, since the banknote was a form of money, it should also have served as a simple substitute for a certain quantity of coins. The banknote, therefore, not only had to be convertible, but it had to correspond exactly to a previous deposit of specie. For this purpose, a monopoly over note issue was essential, and we have already seen that Ricardo actually called for the nationalization of note issue together with James Mill, who was the only one to agree with him among those debating the English monetary controversies of the day. On the other hand, the Banking School held that the whole monopoly versus competition debate was misconceived, since note issues were dictated by the needs of trade and, therefore, had to be adjusted passively or – as we would say today – determined endogenously. As long as banknotes were only issued in the face of 'real bills' tied to production and in the short term, convertibility ensured that note issue would increase and decrease in accordance with the needs of the economy. Despite this radical divergence with the Currency School, the Banking School exponents, and in particular Thomas Tooke, the most authoritative among them, agreed on the usefulness of having a note issue

monopoly to prevent frictions in note circulation adaptability to the needs
of trade. Nevertheless, the original Smithian ideas in favour of free competition in banking were not completely abandoned, supported by some
minority exponents of the Banking School who participated actively in the
debate, especially after the 1830s.[37]

Besides the analytical disputes, the first public act connected with the
monetary controversy was the publication in 1810 of the Bullion Report,
a parliamentary report to which Henry Thornton also contributed. The
report was very critical of the work of the Bank of England in the period
of non-convertibility:

> The Directors of the Bank of England did not at once attain a very accurate
> knowledge of all the principles by which such an institution must be conducted.
> They lent money not only by discount, but upon real securities, mortgages
> and even pledges of commodities not perishable; at the same time, the Bank
> contributed most materially to the service of government for the support of the
> army upon the Continent. By the liberality of these loans to private individuals,
> as well as by the large advances to government, the quantity of the notes of the
> bank became excessive, their relative value was depreciated and they fell to a
> discount of 17 per cent.[38]

Essentially, the accusation was of incompetence, associated with an
excessive readiness to fund the government. However, since the government was committed to a war with a trading rival such as revolutionary
France, the severity of this judgement was somewhat tempered by other
considerations. The return to convertibility in 1820 closed the question
temporarily. The repeated crises of the country banks, in particular in
1816–17 and 1825–26, had great political impact, leading to important legislative innovations. The main criticism of the country banks was the issue
of excessive amounts of small-denomination banknotes and the stuctural
fragility of their assets, the latter being the inevitable consequence of the
regulation limiting the maximum number of partners to six. In February
1826, a new law authorized the establishment of 'joint-stock banks', but
only outside a 65-mile radius from St Paul's Church in London. The Bank
of England, on the other hand, was allowed to open branches. A separate
law established £5 as the minimum face value for banknotes. But the
Bank's position was still not perfectly secured, since the controversy surrounding its role in the London market continued. In 1832, approaching
the expiration of the Charter granted to the Bank, Parliament established
a secret commission of enquiry with a mandate to explore 'whether a competition of different Banks of Issue, each consisting of an unlimited number
of partners, should be permitted'. The commission, even if 'secret', worked
with alacrity, carrying out extensive hearings of bankers and scholars. The

verdict reached was almost unanimously in favour of renewing the Bank of England's Charter which, in 1833, was in fact renewed. Presenting the bill to Parliament, the Chancellor of the Exchequer, Lord Althorp, underlined that his intention was to resolve once and for all the choice between monopoly and competition. With the help of the commission formed a year earlier, he had reached the conclusion that:

> if you can contrive an adequate check upon the conduct of a single bank, it will be more advantageous that such a single bank should manage the circulation of the country, than that it should be left to the competition of different and rival institutions.[39]

By adopting the law, Parliament sent a clear signal that the choice between one or many note issuers had now been made. The 1833 law provided further innovations whose importance would manifest in time. First and foremost, Bank of England banknotes were recognized as legal tender as long as they continued to be convertible and carried a face value of at least £5. Furthermore, it was made clear that the monopoly granted to the Bank only referred to banknotes, and did not extend to the collection of deposits, an activity that was becoming increasingly popular at that time. Consequently, joint-stock banks that did not issue notes were allowed to establish themselves in London. Many bankers took up on this opportunity: between 1826 and 1836 about a 100 new joint-stock banks opened, over 70 of these between 1833 and 1836.

However, Lord Althorp's declaration of intent was only a partial solution for it still left one unanswered question: what was the 'suitable control' to guarantee that note issuing would not cause inflation? This the 1833 legislation did not specify.

In retrospect, this was exactly the main bone of contention between the Currency School and the Banking School and it concurred, as we have seen, to the victory of monopoly over competition in the note issue debacle. The supporters of the Banking School never tired of repeating that convertibility was sufficient protection against the risk of excessive issue. From the analytical point of view, this was an objective point of weakness:

> Over-issue . . . had manifestly taken place on several occasions, and the Currency School maintained that this state of affairs endangered the convertibility of the note. Instead of showing that this was not so, the Banking School simply asserted that, so long as notes were convertible over-issue was impossible.[40]

Since the suspension of convertibility, the directors of the Bank had been practising their own interpretation of Adam Smith's doctrine of real bills:

paper money would only be issued on the basis of the legitimate needs of commerce. But how could the 'legitimacy' of the need be established? The Bank of England decided that any request to discount short-term assets at the rate of 5 per cent was legitimate, a rule which guided its conduct for the entire duration of the Napoleonic Wars and beyond, despite the criticisms it received via the Bullion Report. But with the return to convertibility, the unreliability of the rules soon became apparent even to the directors of the Bank. Thus the doctrine of the 'legitimate needs of commerce' eventually came to be regarded as the main cause of the 1825–26 banking crisis. In the following years, this doctrine was replaced by 'Palmer's rules', named after the then Governor of the Bank of England, who listed them before a parliamentary commission. The first rule was that the Bank's discount rate should constitute a sort of ceiling for rates determined by the markets, so that the Bank of England would not be in direct competition with ordinary banks. In the presence of tensions in the market, rates would gradually rise above the ceiling, thus enabling the Bank to reinforce trust. This rule did not presume any active intervention on the part of the Bank, since it would fall on the market to determine any change of regime. The second rule was that, in normal conditions, the Bank would hold two-thirds of its assets in securities and one-third in bullion.[41]

In practice, however, Palmer's rules proved to be misleading. The increase in precious metal reserves could be the result of either an increase in deposits or a decrease in securities. In critical situations, it was reasonable to expect that the increase in discounts would not lead to a large enough increase in deposits to activate the accommodating policy theorized by Palmer in his first rule. On the contrary, the Bank would have to ration its discounts to prevent precious metal reserves falling below the decisive one-third limit of overall liabilities. The problem lay in not distinguishing between paper circulation and deposits on the liabilities side. The Bank should really only have fixed the ratio of reserves to circulation, allowing the other budget items, including the total of assets and liabilities, to adjust themselves to the demand.

The exponents of the Currency School, Lord Overstone in the lead, did not hesitate to point out the incongruity of the two rules. So by the end of the 1830s, Palmer's rules had also been discredited. The result was widespread distrust of any rule that did not directly limit the quantity of banknotes to be issued, which is exactly what the Currency School had proposed. Proposals for reform began to reappear that were more or less viable, starting with Ricardo's old plan to nationalize the note-issuing bank, reproposed by his brother Samson, to that of Robert Torrens to make it obligatory to affix stamps on banknotes. The stamps would be distributed by the different institutions on the basis of their gold deposits at the Mint.

Palmer himself, in a publication in 1837, showed that he had noted the attack, and called on the Parliament for action:

> If there exist any well-founded reasons for supposing that the principle acted upon by the Bank is not sound, it merely remains for Parliament to express an opinion upon either of these points, and there can be no question that the Bank will immediately regulate its course accordingly.[42]

In the following two years, the Bank only survived a new crisis thanks to the help of the Banque de France, which lent its own good offices so that the private houses of Paris and Hamburg intervened with funds in support of sterling.[43] Several dozen country banks were forced to close down. The proximity of the renewal date (1844) for the government charter spurred Parliament to take another look at the question of note issue. The majority of those questioned by the 1840–41 parliamentary commission maintained that it was necessary to make radical changes to the current monetary template, promoting a stricter note issue control. This was achieved when Parliament passed the Bank Acts (1844–45), strongly backed by the Prime Minister Sir Robert Peel and equally endorsed, if not exactly promoted, by the Bank of England itself.[44]

With the Bank Acts of 1844–45 the English model found its definitive form. The circulation of the Bank of England was limited, initially, to €14 million. Notes could not be issued beyond this amount unless they were backed 100 per cent by metallic reserves. This facility was not granted to the other joint-stock banks, however, nor to the country banks. On the contrary, under the new arrangement, if a country bank failed, two-thirds of its permitted circulation would be added to the Bank of England's upper limit. Furthermore, no new note-issuing institution of any kind could be established.[45] To complete the reform, the bank was subdivided into two departments, one to issue notes and the other to manage the bank's portfolio, thus ensuring no operational crossover between the two functions. As noted by Vera Smith, this was an indisputable victory for the Currency School.[46] The explosive increase in bank deposits, itself an effect of the English model for the most part, proved to be a short-lived victory in the years to come.

3.5 FROM PRECURSOR TO LATECOMER: THE STRANGE CASE OF THE UNITED STATES

The monetary history of the United States in the nineteenth century is crucial to understanding the difficult relationship between the development of central banking and the political–institutional environment. A fully fledged central bank was only established in the United States in 1913, with the constitution of the Federal Reserve System, by which time all other countries had already had a central bank in place for decades, some for over a century. And yet, by the beginning of the nineteenth century, through its experience of the First and Second Bank, the country was already aware of the potential of central banking which was at the time unknown elsewhere. Nicholas Biddle, the president of the Second Bank from 1822 to 1836, could certainly contend for the position of the first central banker with J. Horsley Palmer, since he had recognized and theorized about the function of the central bank in a way that now shows considerable foresight and that was certainly extremely modern. Biddle's main mistake was perhaps to underestimate the importance for a central banker not to be too far ahead of his time. It might even have been the very frankness with which he recognized the special status of the Second Bank that led him to lose what history now refers to as the Bank War. This conflict left such deep scars that the United States was deprived of a central bank for the entire second half of the century and the expression 'central bank' – used for the first time during the Bank War itself – was no longer used by the legislators in setting up the Federal Reserve System. We will now look at this more carefully.

As is often the case in questions regarding the history of the United States, the Constitution is a useful starting point. In Article 1, Section 8, the American Constitution states that Congress has the power 'to coin Money, regulate the Value thereof, and of foreign Coin, and fix the Standard of Weights and Measures'. Further down in Section 10 of the same article, the Constitution rules that: 'no State shall . . . coin Money; emit Bills of Credit; make any Thing but gold and silver Coin a Tender in Payment of Debts'.

These provisions can be interpreted as follows. The states were explicitly forbidden to coin money and the federal government was equally explicitly entrusted with this activity. As regards paper money, the states were clearly forbidden to issue notes (or even bills of credit) but a total silence enshrouded the powers of the federal government. Nor was it clear whether the federal government could assign legal tender to any form of money or not, since no mention was made of this either. The interesting question is whether these omissions were deliberate and, if they were, whether the intervention was to make the omitted activities illegal or to leave the door open for later developments in doctrine and practice. In his monumental history of banking in the United States up to the Civil War, Bray Hammond describes the debates leading to the adoption of the definitive text and convincingly shows that the omissions were intended to indicate that those activities were prohibited.[47] Remembering the inflation during the War of Independence against England, the delegates at the Convention purposed to close the door forever on any possibility of issuing banknotes, convinced that this was in the long-term interests of the young federal nation.

But the needs of the economy often require transcending the letter and spirit of the law. The issue is then whether the new interpretation will gain a political consensus sufficiently broad to appear legitimate. The American experience shows that this is by no means a foregone conclusion.

The man who dared to go beyond the constitutional rules was Alexander Hamilton, a very important figure in American history. As George Washington's Treasury Secretary, he proposed the establishment of a national bank in consideration of the fact that the American banking system was extremely underdeveloped – towards the end of the 1780s, there were still only three banks working on the basis of a state authorization with limited liability – and also in consideration of the federal government's tax problems. The intention was that the proposed First Bank of the United States would act as State Treasury agent, issue standard paper money at national level, and provide funds for the government. Despite the spirited opposition of Thomas Jefferson, the motion to give a 20-year charter for the First Bank was approved by Congress in February 1791.[48] The banknotes issued by the First Bank were legal tender but only for payments to or by the Treasury.

The First Bank used its powers with discretion. The special nature of the American banking system was bound to be a source of friction, balanced unevenly as it was between a large national bank and a small number of local 'state banks' in rapid expansion. In the 20 years of the First Bank's activity, the number of state banks rose from 3 to 250. However, most of these institutions were more interested in supplying credit than in collecting savings, and the expansion of this activity was based on a parallel increase in note issue. In its role as Treasury agent and with its national network, the First Bank naturally found itself taking on a structural creditor position vis-à-vis the state banks, whose activity thus came to depend largely on the quantity of notes that the First Bank redeemed for metallic money. This characteristic objectively placed the First Bank in the uncomfortable position of credit regulator in a rapidly expanding economy hungry for credit – a function that Hamilton had not foreseen when formulating his proposal:

> With the private banking system engaged in furnishing credit expansively and liberally, the task of the central bank was performed by pressing the private banks for redemption of their notes and checks and thereby restraining their extension of credit.[49]

Despite the fact that the First Bank's years of activity could be considered extremely positive for the American economy, when the moment came to discuss the possible renewal of the Charter, the opposition of the banking lobby, on that occasion aligned with the interests of farmers, the traditional enemies of the financial world, proved fatal for the institution. Congress rejected the Charter's renewal by the vote cast by the Vice-President in the Senate to break a tie.

It could not have happened at a worse time, since in 1812 there were fresh hostilities with England. War-related activities led to a chaotic increase of the paper money in circulation. Then, when the English burned Washington, a crisis of confidence led to the first generalized suspension of convertibility in America's history, which increased the disorderly circulation of state banknotes. It is therefore not surprising that, as soon as hostilities ceased in 1816, Congress decided without too much difficulty to establish a new national bank, the Second Bank of the United States, with headquarters in Philadelphia and, once again, a 20-year charter. Significantly, the question of the constitutionality of such a bank was not even raised, even though in 1810 it had weighed heavily in the decision not to renew the mandate of the First Bank. The following year, convertibility was also restored.

In its early years, the Second Bank's activities mirrored those of its predecessor without any particular innovations, but things changed when Nicholas Biddle took over the helm in 1823. Biddle, a 47-year-old businessman, had been appointed Director four years earlier. He brought to the Bank his profound and innovative conviction that the Bank should act in the public interest. As early as 1819, in a written reply to a question from Congress, Biddle stated frankly:

> I think that experience has demonstrated the vital importance of such an institution to the fiscal concerns of this country and that the government, which is so jealous of the exclusive privilege of stamping its eagles on a few dollars, should be much more tenacious of its rights over the more universal currency, and never again abandon its finances to the mercy of four or five hundred banks, independent, irresponsible, and precarious.[50]

As President of the Bank, Biddle implemented his ideas by developing a system of credit control based on the discretionary exercise of the faculty of converting banknotes issued by the state banks. The principal indicator used was the exchange rate of the dollar. A fall would spur an immediate increase in requests for conversions and a contraction in discounts, the two tempered by the opening of credits in foreign currency in London.[51]

This kind of regulatory action was not well received by the state banks, which complained about the Second Bank's improper use of its privileged position, creating problems for the state banks for purely competitive reasons – a complaint we will meet again while discussing Italy's post-unification period. Hammond summarized the complaint in the following terms:

> The federal Bank preyed on the state banks, and the federal courts defended it. It received the notes of the state banks and demanded redemption. It made the state banks pay, when what they wanted to do was lend. To the state bankers, most of whom were politicians themselves, this was oppression, and they readily convinced their fellow citizens that it was these measures of the federal bank that drained wealth from the West and prevented them from being as generous as they wished; the Bank was an alien corporation which entered the individual states against their will and went about in them scot-free.[52]

This serious accusation was tenaciously and determinedly championed by Andrew Jackson, a populist leader who was elected President of the United States in 1828. Much to the surprise of Biddle, who had been reassured in private only days earlier that the new President appreciated his work, in his inaugural address Jackson commented that the constitutionality of the Second Bank was 'well questioned by a large portion of our fellow citizens'.[53] Jackson, a man of arms who had won his immense popularity on the battlefield, was not the type to waste his words and that 'well questioned' spelt trouble. Congress immediately set up a commission of inquiry, but the majority verdict, surprisingly, completely exonerated Biddle and the Second Bank. The commission not only supported the constitutionality of his mandate but also remarked on the practical nature of the Bank's operations in regulating a monetary system based on the obligatory convertibility of banknotes. The report used the term 'central bank' for the first time, although it referred to a banking institution under direct government control, something that the Second Bank clearly was not.

Andrew Jackson, however, was nothing if not tenacious. At the start of 1832, when the Congress began to consider the possible renewal of the charter, he raised some doubts about the Bank's compliance with its mandate. A new commission was appointed to investigate the matter and its members were selected more carefully than previously from the Democratic majority. On this occasion, the majority report was openly critical of the Second Bank, accusing it both for being too liberal in its own discount policy and hostile to the state banks, and for its insistence on convertibility. Even today, Biddle's defence is striking for its lucidity and modernity. However, it was probably a tactical error because in this way he was implicitly admitting that the Bank had infringed its original mandate. In reply to the question on why the Bank had acted with liberality during the 1830–31 crisis, for example, Biddle replied that there was:

no connection whatever between the bank and the demand for money, except that the bank has supplied the demand . . . Now, if there was a demand for money, and the bank had the means for supplying it, why should it not? The object of its creation was precisely that . . . It seems a singular objection to a bank, that, finding a demand for money, and having the means of supplying it, it did supply it.[54]

A little further on, he went so far as to remark, with an undoubtedly unfortunate choice of words, given the circumstances, that: 'There are very few banks which might not have been destroyed by an exertion of the Second Bank.'[55] As Timberlake observed, Biddle wanted to vindicate the Second Bank's role as supporter of the state banks. However, to the ears of his hostile interlocutors, what remained was only the phrase 'might . . . have been destroyed'. At this point, it was not even reassuring to hear the claim that the actions of the Second Bank: 'had a natural tendency to control local banks, and thus prevent, rather than excite excessive issue, [and hence the Bank was] the enemy of none, but the common friend of all'.[56]

This was evidently a friendship that the state banks could do without and, what is more, one that Biddle had no right to indulge in at the time of legislation. Still, when Congress voted on the proposal to renew the 20-year charter, a large majority voted in favour. However, Jackson was not intimidated on this occasion either and, in July 1832, he vetoed the decision. The fate of the Second Bank was thus decided. Giving the reasons for his veto, Jackson raised three questions. First, he said: 'The President of the Bank has told us that most of the State banks exist by its forbearance.'[57] This was not acceptable because, and this was the second point, the Constitution did not give Congress the power to delegate its own monetary responsibilities to anyone. Thirdly, the need to keep a national bank had evaporated because, in the meantime, public debt had been almost entirely repaid. For reasons ranging from questions of principle to reasons of economy, the experience of the national banks had been dismissed once and for all. The Bank War became one of the main issues of the election campaign and Jackson's triumph was seen as a vote of support for his stance vis-à-vis the Second Bank. The war was over.

It is not possible to deny the sensation that the fate of the Second Bank and all that followed was at least partly decided by the enthusiasm with which Biddle had taken upon himself the responsibility to 'regulate credit' in a climate of extreme diffidence towards any centralization of powers. Timberlake is probably right when he suggests that:

The Bank of England . . . was perhaps tolerated because of its self-effacing character and its self-styled commercial emphasis as 'just another bank'. By contrast, the Second Bank of the United States was denationalized because of its more purposive attitude toward monetary policy.[58]

The gap left by the disappearance of the Second Bank in 1836 was partly filled by state banks and partly directly by the Treasury which, from 1837, began to issue its own banknotes regularly, which were legal tender for fiscal purposes. This framework was institutionalized in 1846 with the creation of the Independent Treasury, whose operations were not, however, on a very large scale. The notes issued by the Treasury were mainly used by the banks as a reserve instrument held until expiry, because their legal tender status was not extensive enough to make them suitable for retail trade.

A full reform of the banking system had to wait for the Civil War. The first important consequence of the conflict was the issue of 'greenbacks', non-convertible banknotes with a universal legal tender status for the first time in American history. This was in apparent violation of the Constitution, which stated that only coins were legal tender, but was justified on the basis of the 'implicit' powers that the Constitution conferred on the government of the United States in situations of emergency.[59] However, the real reform came only in 1863 with the introduction of an 'Americanized' version of the English model. The National Bank Act was adopted by Congress in 1863 as a war measure, but enacted only in 1865, when the hostilities were over. On the basis of the new law, all state banks meeting the requirements could join in the national system. Every bank in the system would operate on the basis of a federal government charter under the jurisdiction of the Comptroller of the Currency, an ad hoc office in the Treasury. Member banks had to fulfil a reserve requirement of 25 per cent for banks in the main cities and 15 per cent for provincial banks. The overall total issue limit was fixed by law at $300 million. The allocation of this total among member banks was decided by the Treasury. For all banknotes issued, with legal tender status for fiscal purposes only, each bank had to hold US Treasury securities as a guarantee.[60] Banks in the national system also had to hold at least one-third of their capital in Treasury securities.

The severity of the federal laws compared to individual state laws acted as a deterrent to participate in the new system, which risked failure. In March 1865 Congress established a prohibitive 10 per cent tax on banknotes issued by state banks. This created an artificial, functional distinction between national banks, which were encouraged to concentrate on increasing note issue up to the legal limit, and state banks, which in practice were forced to focus on deposit business. Most state banks preferred to forgo the privilege of issuing banknotes, but many decided to enter the national system. At the end of 1864 there were only 638 national banks, but one year later there were 1582, and in 1866 there were 1648.[61] As had already happened in Britain, adopting the English model boosted the development of a new payment system based on bank deposits. The American national template, despite its ups and downs, remained in place with very few important changes right up to the eve of the First World War.

3.6 THE SPREAD OF THE ENGLISH MODEL AND NOTE ISSUE IN ITALY

Experiences similar to those of England or the United States are common to many other countries. In all the economically advanced nations, the first half of the nineteenth century was a period of intense experimentation with the various note issue regimes. Heated doctrinal and political debates speculated on the best way of preserving society's confidence in the new payment instruments based on the convertible banknote. However, it would be of little interest here to analyse this period in great detail, especially since there are already many excellent studies available.[62] For our purposes, it is important to remember that, from 1844 to the end of the century, the way the English note issue system was organized following Sir Robert Peel's reform became not one of many models but *the* model adopted in other countries. From that moment, discussion in Europe was about the details, not the principle that discretion in the management of the paper money supply had to be strictly limited by law. This principle was introduced in France in 1848, in the United States between 1863 and 1865, in Italy in 1874, in Germany in 1875, in Sweden in 1897 and in Japan immediately after the Meiji Restoration in 1868.[63] The principle was also introduced at around the same time in many other smaller countries.[64]

The English model, even though it provided for restrictions to free competition, did not presuppose a definitive choice in favour of either monopoly or pluralism for note issue. Once it had been accepted that competition between note-issuing institutions had to be controlled, the question of one or many note issuers became secondary or was in any case resolved on the basis of other considerations. As a result, three different versions of the original model arose, depending on whether the privilege to issue notes was reserved to: (1) a bank with a monopoly; (2) a group of banks, one of which was in a dominant position because of size or privileges; or (3) a group of competing banks of similar size and status.

Obviously many factors influenced the choice of one or the other version, ranging from public finance needs to the fragmentary nature of the existing payment system at a time when banknotes were beginning to be used more widely, to purely incidental factors. In all instances, however, the political situation of the country played a significant role, confirming the importance of the state actions in creating confidence in payment technologies. As a rule, nations with a strong state tradition, such as France, Britain itself, Prussia (and all of Germany after unification in 1871), Austria and Sweden, quickly began to unify note issue, even if for different reasons. In France, for example, state funding needs played a decisive role from the start of the Napoleonic era, when great-power politics required access to the substantial resources of a strong, centralized note-issuing institution like the Banque de France, founded by Napoleon himself in 1800 and soon after subjected to strict state control, in spite of retaining the structure of a joint-stock company. In Germany, on the other hand, the need to standardize the payment system was of primary importance, in that before 1871 there were more than 30 diverse note-issuing institutions working in extremely different monetary systems because of the highly fragmented political situation. Federally structured countries, torn by latent tensions between the federal government and local authorities, like the United States, Switzerland or Canada, opted for a pluralist solution while still adhering to the English model. The experiences of the First and the Second Bank of the United States were indeed a deterrent against the risks of a 'creeping' unification of note issue. It would therefore be mistaken to conclude, on the basis of the experience of the twentieth century, when the unification of note issue became universal, that the abolition of pluralism was already written between the lines of the English reform of 1844. The truth is that it was not, and it would be anachronistic to contend otherwise. Certainly, the regime of limited competition required the fine-tuning of market incentives and institutional controls; not an easy task.

In this context, the sequence of events regarding note issue in post-unification Italy was particularly important. The newly constituted Kingdom of Italy was modelled on France as regards its political and institutional arrangements, and it shared with Germany the status of a new nation emerging from a revolutionary process. After some hesitation, Italy took the road towards pluralism in banknote issue, given the important economic differences between the Italian regions and also the multiplicity of administrative and financial traditions inherited from the pre-unification states. Whatever the reasons for choosing this system, pluralism of note issue proved a failure in Italy, causing a series of collapses that led, amidst the ruins of the entire banking system, to the reform of 1893–94. This did not eradicate pluralism, given that two banks in southern Italy retained the power to issue notes until 1926, but with the establishment of the Bank of Italy it ratified a clear choice in favour of the gradual concentration of note issue. What makes the Italian experience even more interesting is its role – a negative one – in the debate that began in the United States after the 1907 crisis, which eventually led to the establishment of the Federal Reserve System, a real turning point in American economic and institutional history.[65]

At the time the kingdom was unified, Italy had only two official note-issuing banks, the Banca Nazionale nel Regno d'Italia (established a few years earlier with the merger of Banca di Genova and Banca di Torino) and the Banca Nazionale Toscana. The two traditional banking institutions working in southern Italy, Banco di Sicilia and Banco di Napoli, were not really note-issuing banks in the proper sense of the term because under their by-laws they could not issue notes payable to the bearer on demand. Nevertheless, they did issue registered deposit receipts (the so-called *fedi di credito*) that often served as banknotes. Initially, these issues were limited in volume. After the suspension of gold convertibility in 1866, the circulation of deposit receipts gained momentum, to the point where Banco di Napoli and Banco di Sicilia were, unofficially, on an equal footing with the official note-issuing institutions. The establishment of a second bank in Tuscany was approved in 1860 and it began its operations in 1863. A sixth note-issuing bank, Banca Romana, was added to the group in 1870, when Rome was annexed to the Kingdom of Italy.

From the time of political unification, the government showed its intention to get quickly to a note-issuing monopoly. The Banca Nazionale was authorized to open branches in the centre and south of the country and there was also an attempt to assign the Treasury Service exclusively to them. Lastly, two bills were presented to Parliament in 1863 and 1865, proposing a merger with Banca Nazionale Toscana. The new bank was to be called Banca d'Italia (Bank of Italy). This proposal was soon shelved because of parliamentary opposition, which grew stronger in time. The merger proposal was brought up again, briefly and unsuccessfully, in 1869, and the idea of an exclusive charter for state treasury services was not proposed again until after the 1893–94 crisis. In the course of only a few years, the establishment of Banca Toscana di Credito, the inclusion of Banca Romana's operations in Banca Nazionale nel Regno d'Italia, and the increasingly sizeable monetary operations of the southern banks drastically changed the terms and fundamental tendencies of the question.

The first real piece of legislation on note issue passed by the Kingdom's parliament was an emergency measure for non-convertibility in 1866, to address the growing financial strains produced by the difficult international situation and the conflict with Austria. Banca Nazionale was coerced to give the Treasury a loan of 250 million lire at the preferential rate of 1.5 per cent. In exchange, the bank's notes attained legal tender status and were non-convertible. Under the same legislation, note-issuing institutions were required to obtain the prior agreement of the Treasury before applying any changes to discount rates.

The period from 1866 to 1874 was a time of monetary chaos because of the rapid growth in the outstanding notes of the group of five banks (six from 1870), the direct issue of banknotes by the state and, lastly, the rise of a surfeit of non-legal monetary tokens that had sprung up to meet the need for small-denomination money. On 1 May 1866, 249 million lire were circulating as banknotes in Italy. Seven years later, the sum had reached 1500 million, aside from the unofficial currency, estimated at 30 million lire.[66]

In 1873 the government decided it was time to take care of the currency issue and prepared a bridging measure to be valid 'in the period and only in the period of inconvertible currency', as Prime Minister Marco Minghetti spoke of his proposal to Parliament, which enacted it in April 1874. Compared to the unifying forces of only a few years earlier, this was a Copernican revolution and effectively introduced a pluralist version of the English model. Minghetti himself called the new framework 'regulated pluralism'. Each bank was allowed to issue notes for up to three times the value of equity or capital paid in on 31 December 1873. Notes issued were legal tender, but were not non-convertible. It should be emphasized that the discount rate could not be modified without government authorization. Besides the autonomously circulating notes, totalling about 750 million lire, the consortium of six banks could issue notes on behalf of the state up to a maximum of 1 billion lire, notes which were non-convertible.

The early years of the new note-issue regime were encouraging. The outstanding notes of the consortium remained stable for several years at around 940 million lire and there were no significant infringements of the issue limits on the individual banks. However, this stability was more apparent than real, depending as it was on the slack international economy, falling raw materials prices and the achievement of a balanced national budget in 1875, followed by a series of surpluses that lasted until 1881. The new system was first really tested with the return to convertibility in 1881 and the economic recovery in Italy and abroad. The original intention to review the regulation of note issue on return to convertibility was shelved – a very serious mistake. From the economic point of view, the 1880s were years of excesses, even on the part of the issuing banks, which not only outreached their issue limits – mostly to fund building speculation in Rome and Naples – but also reduced the specie reserves backing the currency. At the same time, the public finances were deteriorating again, mainly because of increased spending on arms.[67] In the second half of the decade, the cycle was inverted: another trade war broke out with France and, as a result, the financial conditions of the note-issuing institutions rapidly worsened. In 1889 an inspection of the banks showed serious and widespread irregularities which, in the case of Banca Romana, took the form of outright fraud by management. The government decided to suppress the inspectors' final document, the Alvisi–Biagini report, and intervened with marginal measures to gain time rather than taking drastic action. The situation came to a head in 1893, when Parliament was informed of the existence of the report. The scandal that followed, which led to the appointment of a parliamentary commission of inquiry that could only confirm the existence of the abuses discovered by Alvisi and Biagini, which in the meantime had become even more serious, overwhelmed the note issue and the banking system and even the government itself, which was forced to resign at the end of the year. Before it fell, however, to dam the wave of mistrust and prevent the collapse of the lira, the government took responsibility and declared that the state would guarantee all notes with legal tender status, even those issued illegally, and quickly prepared a radical reform of the note issue system that led to the establishment of the Bank of Italy with the merger of Banca Nazionale nel Regno, Banca Nazionale Toscana and Banca Toscana di Credito.[68] The newly established Bank of Italy was soon exclusively assigned the State Treasury Service and entrusted with the liquidation of the Banca Romana. For a further 20 years the right to issue banknotes was granted to the two southern banks, but the ceiling set on their issues put them in a clearly subordinate position to the Bank of Italy.[69]

In order to understand the reasons for such a ruinous collapse of Italy's note issue system, it is worth underlining two procedural aspects that characterized it in the international panorama at that time. The first aspect, which we have already mentioned, was government control of the discount rate. The fact that any changes had to be authorized had a braking effect on requests because the banks could not know in advance if they would be allowed to proceed. As Paolo Pecorari notes in his monograph, much stronger deterrents were uncertainty about whether it would then be possible to change the discount rate back to the previous level, and the fact that the government ruled that any profit deriving from an increase had to be paid to the Treasury. Given these premises, it is not surprising that there were only about a dozen changes in the discount rate in the years between the end of non-convertibility and the final collapse of the system. In the other leading countries, as Pecorari shows, there were sometimes as many variations in a single year.[70]

The second procedural aspect, less well known but no less important, was the constraints on the mutual redemption of notes among the issuing banks (the so-called *riscontrata*). Since their operations were characterized by rigid discount rates and territorial divisions, the smooth running of the interbank conversion mechanism was the only possible brake on excessive note issue. It was an unpopular deterrent with the smaller banks, which accused Banca Nazionale of using it as a means of unfair competition. This, as we have seen, was basically the same accusation directed at the Second Bank of the United States by the American state banks. Mutual redemption was not a problem in the early 1880s, while the economy was expanding, but it quickly turned into one when the trend changed. In 1887, when Banca Nazionale presented what were thought to be enormous quantities of Banca Romana notes for redemption, the problem became urgent.[71]

The outcry following the complaints of the directors of Banca Romana and the other, smaller banks forced the government to prepare a bill, proposing two important innovations for the mutual redemption system, namely: (1) the reduction in the frequency of redemption operations from weekly to fortnightly; (2) the possibility for banks that were structurally creditors to issue notes not backed by specie, for a sum not exceeding the total of notes from the smaller banks not presented for redemption. The aim was clearly to reduce the volume of mutual redemption transactions. However, this proposal was not enacted, basically because the smaller banks opposed another part of the bill, that which upheld the validity of the overall limits to note issue set by the 1874 law. The directors of Banca Nazionale nel Regno, however, read this as a clear signal that the mutual redemption system should be used sparingly because the parliamentary majority supported the smaller banks. In the years that followed, Banca Nazionale adopted the dual strategy of limiting note conversions and launching an energetic public awareness campaign to gain support for the system. The results were not encouraging.[72] The 1888 bill had not progressed due to the winter adjournment of Parliament and so the mutual redemption question only returned to its attention in June 1889, when Minister Miceli presented a new bill limiting mutual redemptions to one-tenth of the debtor bank's outstanding notes. However, this bill also failed, but the supporters of the mutual redemption system had no grounds for rejoicing, because the law eventually enacted in August 1891 was even more draconian. Note conversion was limited by law to the total amount of the creditor bank's notes held by the debtor bank. For notes in excess of this amount, the creditor bank had to withdraw them from the mutual redemption session for later use in normal credit operations, or present them in a later session. This provision came two years after the confidential Alvisi–Biagini report on the abuses of the note-issuing institutions, and effectively marked the end of the mutual redemption system. To the directors of the smaller banks and, in particular, to the directors of Banca Romana, the 1891 law must have seemed an objective endorsement by the government of the behaviour criticized in the inspectors' report.[73] With conversions on the part of the public having been suspended for so long in practice if not by law, banknote issue was no longer subject to any kind of control.

There has never been a thorough and convincing investigation of the reasons that directed the newly formed Kingdom of Italy of the 1860s to what even the academics of the time, looking at other countries' experiences, considered to be the road to ruin. We can only guess and wait for confirmation by more detailed historiographical investigations. However, it is hard to disagree with Valeria Sannucci when she maintains that:

> The sometimes inconsistent behaviour of the government, the lack of determination on the part of the banks and the limits on the operation of market forces led to a note issue regime that, if it did not enjoy monopoly benefits, such as greater clarity in defining the relationship between the government and the bank and the latter's accountability to the former, neither did it derive any advantage from full competition and the effective specialization offered by the multiplicity of note-issuing banks.[74]

This judgement largely reflects Tito Canovai's blunt invitation to the US National Monetary Commission to broaden its knowledge of Italian banking history in order to learn 'about the ruinous effects that bad banking systems inevitably cause'.[75]

4.   Bank money and instability: from Bagehot's principle to financial regulation

4.1   INTRODUCTION

One of the guiding principles of the English model was that an issuing institution, whether operating as a monopoly or not, should behave like any other bank, freely seeking maximum profit, as long as it respected the legal limit on the quantity of banknotes issued. Sir Robert Peel, presenting the bill that would later become the Bank Charter Act of 1844, had explicitly exhorted the Bank of England to only serve the interests of profit, while the law would safeguard public interest. The reason for separating the Bank of England's note issue and banking departments was to protect paper currency from the operations that the banking department would legitimately undertake, not in the public interest but solely in that of its own shareholders, in competition with the other banking houses in the English market.

The various versions of the English model all observed this guiding principle, despite many differences of other kinds. Indeed, in some cases, such as that of the Second Bank of the United States, it was precisely the overly paternalistic attitude of the main note-issuing institution towards the rest of the banking system that tipped the political balance in favour of a system of regulated competition.

However, the aim of reconciling public and private interests, enshrined in the 1844 law and in all other legislation it inspired, was not achieved in practice. The mechanism could have worked if the needs of the economy had not called for a steady increase in the money supply. Such needs could not be satisfied by the English model per se and, according to the philosophy underpinning the model itself, they actually represented a threat. But even when the model was adopted in England, key country at the time in the international financial system, this assumption was decidedly anachronistic because a new payment system was already being developed, based on a form of money, the bank deposit, that only existed in the account books and was therefore even more abstract than the banknote. The obsession of the 1844 Act makers and their imitators with an excessive flexibility of banknote supply had produced an institutional structure in which the dangers of issuing too many notes had been removed, but at the price of an unnatural tightening of the money supply overall. This created an incentive to improve payment techniques based on bank deposits, such as cheques and transfers. In other words, from the mid-nineteenth century on, restrictions on note issuing encouraged the rapid expansion of deposit collection.

The cause-and-effect relationship between the universal adoption of the English model and the affirmation of the bank deposit is historically proven, above all thanks to the studies of Rondo Cameron and his colleagues.[1] Until the middle of the nineteenth century, even in England, 'book' payments were restricted to the interbank transaction circuit, although, quantitatively, they were fairly substantial. After 1850, however, cheques rapidly became the main instrument of payment. In 1900, banknotes represented just 4 per cent of the money supply, while bank deposits accounted for 84 per cent. The situation was even more remarkable in the United States: following the introduction in 1985 of a 10 per cent tax on banknotes issued by state banks – as we have seen in the previous chapter, this measure was intended to encourage the adoption of a national system – there were fears for the survival of the banks that decided to stay outside the national system and to give up issuing banknotes. However, such fears proved to be unfounded since state banks discovered that, as a fund-raising instrument, deposits were very profitable. In 1870, there were still 261 state banks and 1612 national banks in business in the United States. In 1910, these figures had risen to 15000 and 7000 banks respectively.[2] The banknote was being increasingly marginalized in countries such as France, Germany, Austria and Japan, where the growth of the financial superstructure arrived later than in the Anglo-Saxon world.[3]

Nevertheless, bank deposits proved even more fragile than banknotes as a payment technology, because of the technical characteristics of bank money and banking activity in general. The non-transparency of bank assets, principally non-negotiable loans, made it difficult for individual depositors to assess the solidity of the capital and reserves of the bank to which they had entrusted their savings. At the same time, the nature of the deposit as a financial instrument with a preset nominal value and the technique, stipulated in the deposit contract, of sequentially reimbursing clients allowed for the possibility that the deposit would not be reimbursed, either because the value of the asset might turn out to be lower than that of the liability (insolvency), or because an individual bank might not have sufficient liquidity to reimburse more than a part of its depositors (illiquidity). Depositors' eventual awareness of this possibility could provoke a run on the banks that, given the non-transparency of bank assets, could rapidly spread to many other banks or even across the whole banking system. This was not just a theoretical problem: the history of financial systems in the second half of the nineteenth century is peppered with similar events.

And so a new phase of doctrinal debate and institutional reform began, centred on how to maintain depositors' confidence in the new payment technology. It soon became clear – although shifting from awareness to action would be more difficult – that the main obstacle to ensuring sufficient confidence was the private nature of issuing banks, which were tied to maximizing profits. In order to maintain confidence in the banking system, an action to counter the trend was necessary; in particular, the bank at the centre of the financial system had to be willing and able to adopt a liberal lending policy when all other agents on the market would try to recoup liquidity by cutting back on lending operations and rebuilding their own money reserves. Only a body with no obligation to maximize profit in the short term could do this adequately in the common interest.

As Goodhart, Capie and Schnadt observed, modern central banks were born when issuing banks recognized and accepted the responsibility of promoting the stability of the banking system first, and then their own profitability.[4] However, it is difficult to put an actual date on the event for at least two reasons. First, because once again each country followed a timetable dictated by the level of development of its own financial system, by its traditions, and by its political as well as institutional framework. Second, because when an issuing bank assumed a central bank responsibility, this was attested more by its managers' perception of their changing role and of the legitimacy of their action in the eyes of the population, than by formal Acts.

Regardless of individual differences in timing and method, the process of institutional adjustment that accompanied the introduction of bank deposits had one dominant feature that was common to all countries: the replacement of the pluralist model of note issue with the unitary one. During the previous phase of convertible banknotes, it was still a matter of opinion whether the unitary or the pluralist model was better, so much so that the authorities in various countries opted for one or the other on the basis of contingent considerations, dictated by history and local traditions. However, the recognition of the importance of public interest in relation to banking stability led to an almost unanimous preference for the unitary model, in both doctrine and public perception. Every now and again, (more or less) authoritative voices were raised in support of the advantages of the pluralist model. But they were isolated voices indeed, unable to dispel the doubts raised by memories of the experience of the United States, a country which was almost forced to opt for the unitary model after decades of vacillation, following the unsuccessful attempts to adapt the pluralist model to the needs of bank money.

There remained, however, two further questions, to which different answers were given according to the institutional context. The first had to do with the level of formalization of the central bank's powers within the banking system. As time went by, the English method, based on custom and informal arrangements, began to represent an anomaly. At the opposite end of the scale was the model taking shape in the United States, following the 1913 law, instituting the Federal Reserve System. Under this system, the powers of the central bank were carefully defined and included a significant new feature that soon became standard practice: banking supervision powers. The framework that gradually established itself in continental Europe at the turn of the twentieth century lay somewhere between the two extremes.

The second question had to do with how the central bank would control the other banks. In England, over the last two decades of the nineteenth century, the central bank sought to increase the importance and value of its own discount rate – the 'bank rate' – as what we now call a monetary indicator. Elsewhere, controlling the money supply by setting compulsory reserve requirements for the commercial banks became of prime importance. In the 1930s, and then again after the Second World War, a whole panoply of instruments was perfected to guarantee direct control of some of the banks' balance sheet items, which was made possible by a heavily interventionist legislation following the Great Depression. At that point, and for several decades afterwards until the liberalist wave of the 1980s, the payment technology based on bank money was truly tamed. But, as in the past, while this was happening other problems emerged, with the arrival on the world stage of a new payment technology: the non-convertible banknote.

4.2   THE PECULIARITY OF THE BANK DEPOSIT AS A PAYMENT TECHNOLOGY

Despite the fact that they both figure on the debit side of the balance sheet of a bank, there are significant differences between a banknote and a bank deposit, giving rise to two completely different types of payment technology. The banknote is payable to the bearer and so, if one has confidence in its convertibility or, as we shall see in the next chapter, in the state's backing, its passage from hand to hand marks the beginning and the end of the payment act. The bank deposit, on the other hand, is merely a balance sheet item representing a personal (nominal) credit of the depositor with the bank. The deposit is not 'physically' transferable; its use as money therefore requires one or more alternative instruments to transfer the legal ownership of the credit to or from the bank. The ordinary cheque is the most typical of these instruments or means of exchange. Other examples are the credit transfer and the banker's draft. Payment using bank money is therefore just the first step in a series of operations that only end when the legal ownership of the deposit has been transferred and, if the operation involves two different banks, when the corresponding interbank transaction has been settled, either by a transfer of reserves or by netting.

In Chapter 2 we saw that the development of the concept of transferability of credit was a long and complicated process, although payment by means of bank money was already in use in restricted circles. This type of payment was called an 'in bank' payment precisely because it required the physical presence at the bank of the two contractors, the payer and the payee. The development of the cheque towards the end of the eighteenth century, with the gradual recognition of the system, greatly encouraged the spread of the bank deposit. Nevertheless, compared with other credit instruments, for a long time the cheque retained a margin of ambiguity as to the responsibility of the parties involved in its circulation. Technically, the cheque is a double credit – vis-à-vis a given individual's deposit at a given bank – and it therefore raises the question of what irrevocability rule it implies. Generally, the law considers a payment by cheque to be final and irrevocable, that is, not contestable, only when the legal ownership of the deposit has actually changed. Until that time, in the event of non-fulfilment, the payee has to try to obtain satisfaction from the payer; how difficult or easy this is depends on the law in force at the time.

The differences between banknotes and cheques are also behind different circulation procedures. Banknotes can change owner an indefinite number of times before returning to be cashed; generally speaking, cheques cannot, for the simple reason that it is difficult for anyone accepting an endorsed cheque to evaluate the solvency of the original issuer. In principle then, even with possible exceptions, after any payment by cheque the transaction has to be cleared, meaning that the cheque has to return to the bank where the deposit is held. While secondary markets for banknotes have often existed, a secondary market for cheques is hard to imagine, except in restricted circles in which all participants are well known to each other.

It is impossible for an excessive amount of deposits to be issued by a given bank in the same way as an excessive issue of banknotes can instead take place, as we saw in the previous chapter. This is because setting up a deposit requires an act of will on the part of the depositor and because any attempt to 'spend' a deposit will give rise to an outflow of reserves. All banks, however, will tend to keep only a part of their deposits in the form of liquid reserves, preferring to invest the funds in more remunerative, not perfectly liquid, assets. In this mechanism, which underlies the famous bank multiplier, lie both the strength and the weakness of bank money: strength because it makes bank money supply extremely flexible; weakness because a sudden increase in money demand could make any bank operating on the basis of this 'fractional' mechanism technically insolvent.

Banking crises recurred throughout the nineteenth and early twentieth centuries. From a technical point of view, this was possible because deposits were credits of a set value, convertible on demand and therefore collectible at any time, and because requests for conversion were usually honoured on the basis of a logical sequence (first come, first served). But for a long time it was not sufficiently clear, from a theoretical point of view, either why there should be a sudden increase in the demand for money nor why deposits had to have such technical characteristics. More recent theoretical reflections have thrown some light on a crucial aspect of the way bank money functions.

A banking panic can be triggered by three different mechanisms. First, it may be the result of a set of self-fulfilling expectations. A random event can raise doubts about a bank's ability to repay deposits and this, in turn, can prompt a reassessment of the banking system as a whole.[5] This explanation is not entirely convincing, however. Since the cause of the first event is unknown, it is not clear why a generalized change in expectations should ensue. The second mechanism is based on the notion of imperfect information: if depositors are unable to evaluate the quality of a bank's assets, they may react unpredictably to partly distorted signals, such as a negative economic result for sectors which the bank is known to finance, or events within the bank itself, that is, changes in senior management. Such signals can provoke a major run.[6] Taking the existence of asymmetric information between depositors and bank management as a point of departure, it can be demonstrated the optimality of the deposit contractual form as it was actually developed in history. Finally, there is a possibility of chain reactions affecting the interbank payment system, which clears and settles payments made against deposits, or even the interbank deposit market.[7]

Whatever its origin, a banking panic is to be feared because it puts the stability of the whole system at risk, together with the soundness of the credit superstructure that underpins capitalist development. As we shall see, the history of bank money is peppered with attempts to hold this phenomenon in check, either by placing restrictions on the exercise of the banking business or by inventing institutional devices to increase the banking system's liquidity, in order to meet the demand for deposit repayments. The problem facing the authorities can be described in the following way. A panic is the result of a dramatic bid by bank customers to alter the ratio of currency (notes and coins) to total deposits in their portfolios. If no action is taken, since deposits are a multiple of currency, the only way to achieve the desired ratio of currency to deposits is by reducing the denominator, that is, through a series of bankruptcies. The alternative is to try to increase the numerator, even only temporarily. Given that the stock of precious metals is fixed in the short term (or can only be altered by raising interest rates, which might then damage the quality of assets of the banks under pressure), this can only be done by stepping up the supply of notes. Historically, an increase in note circulation to counter a banking panic was the first instance of what is now commonly termed 'lending of last resort'.

Lending of last resort does not necessarily require the intervention of the state or the delegation of power to a bank operating as a monopoly. Over the second half of the eighteenth century and in the early nineteenth century two alternative techniques were experimented with: (1) assigning such function to a central institution, under the more or less formal supervision of the state; (2) creating special interbank mechanisms, both spontaneous and cooperative, designed to augment currency in circulation by pooling the available resources of single banks or by issuing special paper, often of dubious legality. Towards the end of that period the two mechanisms were joined by a third, designed to eliminate the need for a lender of last resort: deposit insurance. It was first introduced in the United States in the 1930s (although some precedents of limited impact did exist in the nineteenth century) and remained an American idiosyncrasy until the end of the 1970s.

The basic risk facing lenders of last resort, whether private or operating under the umbrella of the state, was what we now call 'moral hazard': that banks behave less prudently, thereby increasing the probability of a banking panic, just because of the existence of a lender of last resort. Walter Bagehot, writing in the 1870s, believed he had solved the problem by setting out operational rules to restrict lending of last resort to illiquid banks only. However, subsequent events demonstrated that things were not as simple as that, and it is precisely from this observation that modern central banking has stemmed.

4.3   THE 'TREASURY LETTERS' AND THE DEBATE ON THE NATURE OF THE BANK OF ENGLAND: LENDING OF LAST RESORT TAKES SHAPE

Of all the British model versions that have appeared over the years, the original one, set out in the 1844 Act, remains the most rigid. The combination of ceilings on issue, reserve requirements, separation between issue and rediscount operations, as well as financial reporting obligations (the Bank of England was required to publish a fortnightly statement of account) created a framework of draconian restrictions, the purpose of which, as we have seen, was to reduce banknotes to a mere surrogate of precious metal, with no identity of their own. Although many proponents of the system had doubts about its soundness, when asked to contribute to the reform of the issuance system, they preferred to err in the direction of excessive zeal.

Just a few years' experience was sufficient to show that such a model was indefensible in times of financial market tension. However, rather than undertaking a new reform, the government preferred to try a less formal solution. This involved taking responsibility for suspending issue restrictions by sending a letter to the Governor of the Bank of England, exhorting him to lend liberally, without fear of breaking the law because, should that happen, the government itself would put a bill of indemnity through Parliament. The Treasury letter method was frequently and successfully used, allowing the English model to survive intact until 1914. Nonetheless, it obviously was a stopgap measure, which did not quiet the many calls for more courageous action. Criticizing the 1844 Act gradually became almost a national pastime. In 1873, in his influential work *Lombard Street*, Walter Bagehot complained that: 'if you say anything about the Act of 1844, it is little matter what else you say, for few will attend to it'.[8]

In the meantime, far more important events were affecting operating practices. The great merit of Bagehot's book was that it ignored futile political disputes, drawing the experts' attention to the fact that the Treasury letters were producing a sort of genetic mutation before their very eyes: the transformation of a privileged issuing institute dedicated to the private interest into what would later be called a 'central bank', that is, an institution whose primary mission is to pursue the public good of financial stability, if necessary to the detriment of profit. It was a theory that the majority considered heretical at the time, and even Bagehot, as we will see, was not entirely clear about all the elements in the picture he drew. But *Lombard Street* soon became the new point of departure of political and doctrinal debate. It is true that, after experimenting with many alternative methods to ensure a banking system's stability, the model that eventually prevailed was the one formally set down in the United States in 1913 (containing evident traces of earlier European experiments, it has to be said). Yet, many of the operative practices in today's central banks all over the world were conceived and fine-tuned in the two decades following the publication of Bagehot's book. A general review of monetary events in England, from the invention of Treasury letters up to the end of nineteenth century, is therefore essential in order to understand the Copernican revolution that Bagehot simultaneously chronicled and preached.

It all began in 1847, only three years after the passage of the Bank Charter Act. The City was suffering a liquidity crisis triggered by a brusque fall in the price of corn, causing the collapse of a number of provincial banks that had engaged in bull speculation. The Bank of England's reserves rapidly began to dwindle, without slaking the market's thirst for liquidity. During the summer the Bank of England granted over £2 million's worth of 'extraordinary advances', reducing its own reserves to an all-time low of just over £1 million.[9] At that point, the Bank's directors were faced with a dilemma that would cyclically resurface in the following years. On the one hand, they were under pressure to continue rediscounting private paper, increasing the market's liquidity even at the cost of further depleting their own reserves. On the other hand, they met with growing concern on the part of shareholders, who pleaded for precautionary measures to be taken in order to preserve a sound capital base. As a matter of fact, only one solution was possible, since maintaining a liberal discount policy would have led to an infringement of the 1844 Act. Had the Bank of England behaved 'like any other banking house', as Peel claimed, it would have respected the letter and the spirit of the law, but it would also have put the stability of both the City and sterling at serious risk. In such context, the government, in the person of the Chancellor of the Exchequer, resolved to send the Governor of the Bank a letter inviting him to discount letters of credit and other authorized securities at a rate of 8 per cent without considering the consequences, because the government would prepare a bill of indemnity if the currency in circulation exceeded the permitted limits as a result. No one, probably not even the greatest optimists, had imagined how successful this move would prove to be. In a matter of hours the tensions faded and the Bank's cash dropped well within the permitted levels, so that the government's promised bill of indemnity was unnecessary.[10]

Similar episodes occurred in 1857 and 1866. A Treasury letter was used in both cases, with generally satisfactory results. It was only in 1857 that the announcement of the letter failed to prevent a glut, although it was limited and the government kept its promise to the Bank of England, pushing a bill of indemnity through Parliament.

With hindsight, Treasury letters can be described as a merely palliative measure that never tackled the substance of the problem. This was Bagehot's opinion, too, and he dedicated few lines to it. However, we should not forget that such letters represent a very important part of the history of central banking and Bagehot's analysis would have probably had much less influence had it not been founded on the result of that practice. The experience provided irrefutable proof that panics could be overcome even without a sharp increase in money supply, provided prompt and firm action were taken to restore market confidence. At the same time it also convinced the staunchest supporters of laissez-faire that confidence is a public good which market forces are not always able to produce in sufficient quantity.

There certainly was a risk that the success of Treasury letters would cause the problems raised by the new bank payment technology to be undervalued. It was this risk that Bagehot fought, first from the columns of *The Economist* and then in *Lombard Street*. He found a pretext to arouse controversy in the 1866 crisis, during which the Bank of England came under severe criticism for its conduct. The event around which the crisis hinged was the collapse of a leading discounting house, Overend, Gurney & Co., which at one time had controlled more than half the London discount market. Investigations later revealed that for several years the company had been managed with an almost criminal lack of prudence. Significantly, the house had only been made a limited company in 1865, when its owners began to worry that the time of reckoning might be near. In the spring of 1866, when tensions had been running high on the London market for some weeks, its managers decided to ask the Bank of England for financial assistance. After a quick inspection of the books, the Bank of England refused. The next day, 10 May 1866, Overend, Gurney & Co. suspended payments. The panic that immediately spread through the city was the worst since 1825. The Bank of England's reserves decreased by £3 million in a single day. On 12 May a third Treasury letter was issued to overcome the indecision of the Bank's directors, who were more than disconcerted by such a rapid depletion of reserves. Once legal concerns had been put at rest, although not all the economic ones, in the five days that followed the collapse of Overend, Gurney & Co. the Bank of England discounted some £100 million's worth of paper and issued around £3 million of security-backed loans. Panic gradually faded and, though reserves were down to an all-time low of £800 000, the Bank of England was able to manage the situation without breaking the 1844 limits.

Even today the jury is still out on the decision not to bail out Overend, Gurney & Co., whose aggressive behaviour on the market had been a source of frequent irritation for the Bank of England's directors. There was much talk of unfair competition, and the very different response to Baring & Co. some decades later, as discussed below, only rekindled the fires, which still burn in contemporary historiography.

For our purposes, however, the most interesting thing about the Bank of England's management of the crisis is embodied in the words of the Governor of the time, Lancelot Holland, who justified the Bank's conduct before the Board (then known as the Court of Proprietors) in the following words:

> We could not flinch from the duty, which we conceived was imposed upon us, of supporting the banking community, and I am not aware that any legitimate application for assistance which was made to this house was refused.[11]

In *The Economist*, Bagehot welcomed this statement as a belated recognition of the Bank of England's responsibility for preserving the stability of the banking system by whatever means, and therefore even at the cost of damaging its own shareholders or letting its own gold reserves drop below what would be a prudent level in normal conditions. Expressed in these terms, Bagehot's theory could not fail to draw a reaction from the Bank, none of whose directors had ever dreamt of putting public considerations before the owners' interests. Indeed, it was not long before the Bank issued a vehement response. Thomson Hankey, a director and former Governor, called the theory set out in the columns of *The Economist* 'the most mischievous doctrine ever broached in the monetary or banking world in this country'.[12] Hankey's reaction convinced Bagehot that the time had come to set out his ideas more systematically; *Lombard Street* was the result. Vera Smith, writing about the book in 1936, remarked that: 'Bagehot's influence on the shaping of central bank policy must have been more considerable than that of any other single writer either here or on the Continent.'[13] This was confirmation, had there ever been need for any, that today's heresy is often tomorrow's orthodoxy.

But what shocking claim had Bagehot made? He had argued that, whether the Bank's directors were aware of it or not, their actions in some extraordinary situations and especially during the crises of 1857 and 1866, had convinced the City operators that the Bank would always intervene in times of tension, drawing on its own reserves to bolster market liquidity. The expectation of intervention was by now rooted in the market's perceptions and if the Bank had genuinely wished to change tack, it would have had to say so at that time, explicitly and unequivocally. Any other expedient would have proved ineffective. But were the Bank's directors really so unaware of their new responsibilities? Bagehot expressed some doubts on this score, while not resisting a note of sarcasm: if the directors were genuinely unaware of their role, then why maintain a 40 per cent reserve, as against the 10 to 13 per cent that was the norm in an average City bank? Why not try to derive the maximum profit from the new London market structure (that had perhaps gone beyond the original intentions of the Bank and the government)? Hence Bagehot's three prescriptions addressed to the Bank: it should openly acknowledge its own role as a guardian of banking stability, boost its own reserves to have the necessary ammunition to cope with even major crises, and freely lend in times of financial tension, but at a high rate of interest and against good security.

A few years after the publication of *Lombard Street*, Bagehot's theories – which on many points echoed the analyses that Henry Thornton had published as early as 1802 in his *The Paper Credit of Great Britain*, undoubtedly more sophisticated from a strictly economic perspective – were widely accepted and, to this day, they are often cited as the essence of central banking. This judgement is excessive, however, not least because Bagehot is often attributed claims he never made, such as the 'penalty rate' doctrine, but also because his prescriptions soon revealed themselves to be rather optimistic on several important issues, such as the effectiveness of the discount rate in restoring stability and the reliability of ordinary guarantees in situations of financial turbulence. Many additions, therefore, had to be made to his doctrine before it could be fully put into practice. The outcome of this process is that what we now call central banking bears only a passing resemblance to what Bagehot claimed in *Lombard Street*, if we exclude the basic principle of the pre-eminence of public over private interest in central banks' action. Moreover, not all the additions came from the United Kingdom. Several, perhaps the most important ones, such as supervision, were the result of experiences in other countries; I will have more to say on this later. Two particular aspects of what happened in England in the last three decades of the nineteenth century turned out, instead, to be crucial: the development of a discount rate policy and the definition of forms of lending of last resort 'concerted' between the central bank and major private banks.

Bagehot's analysis relied on the assumption that the discount rate applied by the Bank of England, known as the bank rate, governed market rates. By prescribing 'high' rates in situations of financial tension Bagehot's aim was, on the one hand, to discourage applications to the Bank for liquidity that were unjustified by the economy's performance; on the other hand, he wanted to raise the entire structure of interest rates so as to encourage a flow of precious metals into London both from abroad and from the provincial banks. However, the relationship between market rates and the bank rate was anything but fixed, and the lack of reaction by market rates to an increase in the bank rate could only gradually side-line the Bank of England within the discount market. When Bagehot was writing about it, the problem was not yet especially apparent, but it would soon be, thanks to the strong expansion of banking activities within the English financial system. In 1833, deposits in the Bank of England were still valued at approximately £13 million. Deposits in London banks were estimated to be around £22 million, and those in commercial banks between £16 and £20 million. By the early 1870s deposits in the central bank had increased to £28 million while the total funds in the rest of the banking system were estimated to have swollen to around £600 million.[14] The Bank's share of total deposits had therefore fallen from about one-third to around one-twentieth of the market.

As modern banking developed, the payment method based on bills of exchange was also discontinued: the great majority of payments were now made by cheque and at the end of the 1880s most people considered the bill of exchange to be a genuine anachronism. True, its decline had been offset by the development of trade in foreign securities and, from 1877 onwards, by the issue of a new type of Treasury bond. Nevertheless, the contraction in the central bank's discount activities had been extremely severe. A further brake on the development of discounts was the intro-duction of the policy, adopted after the crisis of 1857, of not carrying out transactions with discount houses and bill brokers. Ultimately, the decline of discounts appeared inevitable: in 1875, the latest year about which accurate data are available, discounts amounted to £4.4 million, an almost negligible sum. Having de facto lost the role of market price leader, the central bank pursued a passive rate policy in normal conditions, with the immediate aim of preventing the creation of an overly large gap between the bank rate and market rates to the detriment of the former one. This was the only way to safeguard shareholders' profit, which at that time was consistently less than what could be earned investing the same capital in ordinary banks. When it needed to, the Bank was still able to influence market rates through what we now call open-market transactions, in other words selling securities on the market. But these were costly for sharehold-ers, and the Bank preferred to avoid them as much as possible.[15]

Over time, however, the Bank's directors realized that, while a rise in the bank rate had little impact on market rates, it was extremely effective in replenishing reserves, thanks to the inflow of capital from abroad and from provincial banks.[16] The problem for the directors lay in identifying appropriate uses for the deposits that a high bank rate was attracting. The solution was found in a more aggressive credit supply policy. It was some-thing that had not occurred to Bagehot and which might appear to clash with his ideas about the fundamentally public nature of the central bank.

However, its effect was that of greatly enhancing the signalling function of the bank rate and thereby actually making the policy of accumulating gold reserves, supported by Bagehot, superfluous. The first action of the new strategy was the Bank's decision in 1878 to apply the market rate to its regular customers, instead of the bank rate, which was generally higher. Thus, the discount rate strategy could be freed from considerations regarding the protection of the central bank's share in the discount market. As a result of this decision, the bank rate took on the traits of a penalty rate, because by then it was consistently higher than market rates.[17] But in itself the 1878 decision further eroded the importance of the bank rate as an indicator of market liquidity conditions. Accordingly, as part of the new strategy, it was decided to resume the provision of rediscount facilities for brokers, in particular for discount houses, in order to make them more dependent on injections of liquidity by the Bank. The last element of the new strategy was added later, when the Bank announced that it would also accept securities that were very close to their expiry dates, provided they were of good quality.[18]

As might have been expected, the new strategy resulted in severely strained relations between the Bank of England and the rest of the banking system, which lasted for almost the entire decade. From 1889, however, the climate began to change for a number of reasons. The first was a new crisis, involving this time round one of the major city banks, Baring & Co. Like other London banks, Baring had played a very active role as an underwriter in funding South American states, Argentina first and foremost. In the summer of 1889, however, a revolution broke out in Argentina and Baring found itself with a portfolio full of securities that few people wanted to buy. The difficulties increased in the autumn, due to a general slump in trading on the London Stock Exchange. After trying in vain to shore up its position by selling over £4 million of other securities in its portfolio, Baring applied to the Bank of England for financial support. The Bank's Governor, Lidderdale, decided that Baring ought to be helped, perhaps because it was deemed able to stay solvent in the long term or because of its importance on the London market, but the necessary sum was enormous, in the order of at least £15 to £20 million. Accordingly, he turned to the Government, asking Chancellor Goschen to guarantee Baring's liabilities. But Goschen refused, offering at best to issue a new Treasury letter guaranteeing the bank. At that point, Lidderdale decided to appeal to the main London banks, following the examples of Italy's Banca Nazionale in 1887 and of Banque de France in early 1889. The London banks' response was more positive than expected. In just a few days, they made a guarantee fund of approximately £18 million available. The Bank did not even have to contribute to it, but was able to confine itself to the role of coordinator and manager of the collected funds. At the same time, it passed a series of measures to safeguard its own reserves, anticipating the tensions that would follow the public announcement of the entire affair. Such measures included the sale of Treasury coupons worth £1.5 million to Russia and the taking out of a loan in gold valued at £3 million with the Banque de France. When the news of the crisis was announced on 15 November, just one week after the initial contacts between Baring and Lidderdale, the market remained relatively calm and the hypothesis of another Treasury letter aired by Goschen was not even taken into consideration.[19]

The Baring crisis ended the practice of Treasury letters, which had been so important in previous years, and made the Bank's directors aware of how important it was to have good relations with the major banks in moments of acute tension. The bail-out of Baring was the first in a long series of 'concerted' bail-outs on behalf of central banks the world over, carried out with the help of the banking system, in the following 100 years and more. Two other events helped reinforce, if not actually cement, these new relations in the following decade.

First, after the US crisis of 1893, which we will say more about in the next section, economy and finance experienced a period of great prosperity. After a decline in the first years of the decade, indices of raw materials remained stable for several years; the Bank's discount rate settled for over five years at 2 per cent and market rates were even lower. Moreover, the substitution of gold with silver, under way in the United States, tended to generate copious inflows of surplus gold from across the Atlantic into the Bank's coffers, soothing the fears of its directors, who always paid great attention to the volume and fluctuations of metal reserves, as required by their legal mandate. In these conditions the aggressive practices of the previous years could be markedly softened.

The last event of those years – perhaps also the most significant from a structural point of view – consisted in bank concentration. Then known as 'amalgamation', nowadays as 'consolidation', the scale of this process was remarkable. In 1886–87 there were around 370 banks in the United Kingdom: 250 private associations and 170 public limited companies. Twenty years later, only 32 remained in a clearly dominant position; 20 of them had over 100 branches each. At the same time, private associations had almost entirely disappeared, with no more than a dozen left across the country.[20] By greatly simplifying the banking structure, the concentration process also had two important consequences for the fulfilment of the Bank of England's tasks. First, it almost naturally led the Bank to take on the role of depositary of major banks' reserves. When it suspended the publication of detailed data on its debt, in 1875, interbank deposits amounted to less than £10 million. At the beginning of the twentieth century, they were estimated to have risen well beyond £20 million. This increase in the reserves held on behalf of the banking system was a timely development, not only due to its obvious implications for profit, but also because it gave the Bank a new monetary policy instrument – the regulation of banking reserves – to make up for the definitive decline of discounting, by then occurring in almost negligible quantities.

There was a problem, however. The policy for the reserves was effective only if it allowed influence to be exerted on the lending policies of the major banks, and this was the second consequence of the consolidation process. The effectiveness of the Bank's action no longer depended on the reactions of an anonymous market, which could be influenced simply by increasing discount or lending operations. Now the Bank found itself, so to speak, in the hands of a small group of major bankers. Everything would have been simpler if it had been an established practice within the banking community to maintain a more or less fixed proportion between reserves and total liabilities. The proportion between these two aggregates, instead, was anything but stable. In such conditions, it was necessary to identify other channels to influence overall credit. The 1890s were accordingly characterized by a series of innovations in the techniques employed by the Bank of England, the most important of which were the decisions to operate directly on the gold market and to accept remunerated safe-keeping deposits from several state entities.[21] But the main instrument, albeit the least tangible (it was not traceable in the accounts), became the 'hint from HQ', the allusion clearly being to the Bank of England's headquarters. Nowadays, we would call it moral suasion: influencing the main banks' action through discussion and persuasion discreetly conducted by the central bank's directors, rather than through formal initiatives. There are plenty of indirect indications, but clearly few written accounts, of the effectiveness of moral suasion. The problem, due to the nature of the instrument itself, is that its effectiveness does not only depend on the market's general conditions, but also on the strength of personal relations between the Bank of England's directors and other bankers. That is the very opposite of what the fathers of the 1844 legislation had intended to achieve. Victor Morgan's observation on the issue is enlightening:

> The giving or withholding of co-operation depended on a personal decision, and the help to be expected from each source would constantly vary in response to personal as well as external factors. The directors had, therefore, not only to attend to matters of minute detail, but also to cultivate numerous personal relationships. On their success or failure in this way might depend the smooth working of the whole system . . . About all this, there was nothing automatic, no simple and obvious rule by which all decisions could be tried.

> Some of the sponsors of the Bank Charter Act of 1844 thought they were reducing the art of central banking to a rule of thumb; how great would have been their surprise if they could have sat in the bank parlour on a Thursday morning sixty years later.[22]

It was a method that extracted the maximum benefit from the structure of Victorian society, which was highly cohesive because it was very elitist. The availability of high social capital enabled monetary policy to be very incisive without having to resort to formal measures, and what is more, in the context of a legislative framework that had aimed at removing such discretionary power altogether.[23] In another set of circumstances, the same method would have had disastrous results, as became evident, in those same years when in the United Kingdom the moral suasion method was being developed. As we shall see in the next two sections, Americans and continental Europeans (and finally, the English themselves, once the unique conditions of the Victorian era vanished) would be forced to acknowledge it, too. Contemporary central banking owes its success to these experiences no less than it owes to Bagehot and his Victorian peers.

4.4 THE ESTABLISHMENT OF THE AMERICAN MODEL OF CENTRAL BANKING

The central bank that came into being in the United States in 1913, the Federal Reserve System (now familiarly known as 'the Fed'), was poles apart from the Bank of England of the turn of the century. The definition of its duties, limits and instruments was as formal as possible. And the Federal Reserve was the first central bank to be made formally responsible for banking supervision – a duty the Bank of England would not be assigned until 1980 and only for a short while. Yet the creation of the Federal Reserve represented a definite reversal of the course that had been followed for decades, marked by a deep aversion to the central banking model itself: the dismantling of the Second Bank of the United States had certainly been a symptom and not the cause of it. The creation of the Fed was not an enthusiastic choice of US Congress, an inevitable response to the collapse of the earlier issuance system. Therefore it was only natural that, when the time came to incorporate into the American order what until that moment had been considered as a European aberration, the new institution's functions and powers were carefully circumscribed. Just as naturally, the Fed was heir to the customs and experiences that had arisen on the US financial scene in the previous decades. The consequence was that the Fed represented a new genus among the world's central banks, and one whose influence could only increase along with America's international economic and political power.

The version of the English model that the US had adopted during the Civil War was marked, as we have seen, by two peculiarities. First was the extreme fragmentation of the American banking system, both for issuance and in general. When the Fed was instituted, there were more than 20 000 banks in the United States, including 7000 national banks authorized to issue banknotes. One reason why there were so many banks was branching restrictions: state banks were not allowed to open branches in other states (branching rules within states varied, but southern states were in general more permissive than northern ones). As for national banks, they could only open branches in the locations that their articles of incorporation specified. As a result, many banks outside big cities actually operated under a de facto monopoly and were usually one-branch banks.

The second peculiarity concerned the note issue regime. The requirement placed on national banks to hold Treasury securities to back their notes made issuing strictly tied to the yield on Treasury bonds. Since, for most of the time during which this system held sway, US Treasury securities were considered safer than private issues, their yield was often unattractive. The non-profitability of banknote issue was proved by the fact that the total amount of circulating notes tended to contract for the entire duration of the National Bank system; between 1881 and 1893 it dropped by 60 per cent.[24] The rigidity of banknote supply did not just affect the phases in which an expansion was desirable but also those in which a contraction would be appropriate. A bank wanting to reduce its issues had to follow the same procedure, with the same costs, as for authorization to issue. Besides, there was a legal limit on the amount of notes that could be withdrawn from circulation within a month. Therefore, when a bank was authorized to issue a certain volume of notes, it tended to get rid of them as fast as possible in order to increase its return on assets. But this made it hard for banks to respond to sudden peaks in the demand for notes, unless they reduced their supply of credit at the same time, with the result of highly volatile interest rates in response to the seasonal fluctuations in the demand for money. Hence, the American financial system was characterized by recurring bouts of tension, often resulting in crises of confidence, as in 1873, 1884, 1890, 1893 and 1907. As a matter of fact, in those years banking crises were frequent in other countries too, but in the US they led to much sharper rises in interest rates than in Europe. Furthermore, they often also led to the suspension of convertibility. The American monetary system, as contemporaries diagnosed it, lacked 'elasticity'.[25]

The rigidity of the issue system was no small handicap for deposit banks, such as the state banks, which were subject to a reserve requirement of 25 per cent or 15 per cent depending on whether or not their registered office was in a 'reserve city' – a legal category that included, among others, New York, Boston, Chicago and St Louis – or in a rural locality. This was a minimum, and ordinarily most banks prudently held a much greater amount of reserves. In times of tension, however, they might very rapidly near the limit. As the law prescribed that, when infringing the minimum requirement, a bank had to suspend lending immediately until it came back into compliance, most banks arbitrarily stopped converting deposits before they crossed the threshold. Sometimes such a decision was taken simply as a precaution, well before actual reserves approached the trigger point. Obviously, this was illicit conduct that could technically be considered a declaration of default. Nevertheless, despite the consequent problems for the payment system, it was tolerated by the Comptroller of the Currency in order not to disturb the credit circuit.

The problems were felt most acutely in the reserve cities, which as such were subject to sharper fluctuations in the demand for cash. This prompted the search for mechanisms of cooperation among the leading banks. The main such mechanism was developed within the clearing houses. In 1860 most of the banks doing business in Boston and New York agreed on a procedure to alleviate the reserve needs of the banks that were net debtors within the clearing house. That meant that the debtor bank, instead of settling its debt directly with the creditor bank, would post collateral with the clearing house, in return for a credit certificate it could then use as a payment to extinguish its liabilities. To discourage abuse, such certificates carried a high rate of interest, between 5 and 10 per cent. This was a cooperative way to prevent a fratricidal battle for the control of reserves during times of turmoil. However, it left another question unresolved: the outflow of reserves directly caused by the public's demand for conversion. New York banks tried to solve this problem, too, agreeing on a reserve equalization mechanism whereby the banks mostly exposed to requests for conversion could temporarily draw on the reserves of the more sheltered ones.

Credit certificates, combined in New York with this reserve equalization mechanism, made it possible to stem the crisis of 1860 without suspending convertibility. This success sparked widespread imitation, but only as far as credit certificate procedures were concerned. Reserve equalization was soon abandoned, even in New York, owing to the reluctance of the structurally sounder banks, which found it unacceptable to favour in this way their less scrupulous competitors. Even without reserve equalization, however, credit certificates enabled the system to survive the minor crises of 1884 and 1890 relatively unscathed. But when the first major crisis occurred, in 1893, the mechanism did not work. Despite the issue of large volumes of certificates, convertibility had to be suspended for months.[26]

The lack of a reserve pooling mechanism proved fatal to individual banks, potentially caught between the demands of the public, which had to be satisfied, and the impossibility to exact a payment of reserves from banks in whose respect they were clearing-house creditors, by virtue of the credit certificate agreement. In these conditions, suspension of convertibility, first for one bank and then, progressively, throughout the system, became unavoidable.

The crisis of 1893 rekindled discussion over the malfunctioning of the monetary and credit system, and some timid efforts at reform followed. In 1900 an attempt was made to make banknote issue more profitable by lowering taxation on it and allowing issues for up to 100 per cent of the nominal value of collateral. From then on the Treasury also adopted a broader interpretation of 'eligible collateral', including municipal bonds, too.[27] This measure, however, could affect the level of note issue, not its elasticity. The system remained essentially unchanged.

And so we come to the fateful year 1907, marked by heavy financial turbulence throughout the developed world. In New York the crisis was aggravated by the fierce competition that had arisen in the meantime from a new kind of intermediary: trust companies.[28] The US financial crisis that ensued was of unprecedented severity. Despite the issue of some $500 million worth of certificates (about 5 per cent of the total stock of money, according to Gary Gorton), much of which was placed directly – and in violation of the law – with the public, convertibility had to be suspended for a number of months.

The 1907 crisis turned out to be a watershed. First, it convinced many observers that a purely voluntary, cooperative means for crisis management, such as clearing houses, was unreliable. At the same time, it brought out Americans' latent fear of excessive power concentration in the clearing houses of the main cities, which had had no qualms about breaking the law to issue an enormous mass of illegal notes.[29] An immediate effect was congressional passage of the Aldrich–Vreeland Act, envisaging the institutionalization of clearing houses in the form of Currency Boards, legally recognized bodies that were to consist of groups of national banks. The Boards were to be authorized to make emergency currency issues against collateral, including commercial paper, under the Treasury's oversight.

Clearly, however, this was a stopgap. A much more important consequence of the crisis was the institution of a congressional committee of inquiry, the National Monetary Commission, to study a radical reform of the banking system. Composed of authoritative members of Congress, in four years of activity the Commission gathered an impressive harvest of contributions, studies and testimony on the experience of central banks in other countries. The Commission proceedings ran to over twenty volumes. As Vera Smith observed, the result of these four years of work:

> was to turn the favour of the reformers towards a permanent central organisation which should issue a currency based on gold and commercial paper, act as a lender of last resort and control the credit situation through the bank rate and open market dealings.[30]

Shortly after the termination of the Commission, Senator Vreeland submitted a draft reform bill calling for the institution of a true central bank in the form of a National Reserve Association.[31] But the victory of a Democrat, Woodrow Wilson, in the elections of 1912, revived fears of any plan for centralized power, and Vreeland's proposal was adapted to a federal structure. For months, however, the number of units that would make up the new central bank remained quite uncertain. Advocates of decentralization called for a reserve bank in every state, while centralizers maintained that any more than three or four would be unmanageable. In the end, an agreement was reached on 12, a number conjured up through an ingenious if primitive 'railroad' calculation by Colorado Senator John Shafroth.[32] On the strength of this agreement, in December 1913, Congress passed the Federal Reserve Act, and the Federal Reserve System began operating in August 1914. The banking lobby, which had been decisive in bringing about the fall of the Second Bank of the United States, was now equally decisive in ushering central banking into the American economic system.[33]

Even apart from its federal structure, the Fed did not merely replicate the European central bank model. Kisch and Elkin observe that, given the fragmentation of US banking, the new institution could hardly succeed in its purposes without some degree of coercion.[34] So from the outset the Fed was intended to act as the bankers' bank. It operated on the basis of a pact between the government and the banking system. National banks were obliged to adhere to the Fed (while other banks' membership remained voluntary) and to take a stake in its equity capital (which neither the government nor private investors were allowed to do). But the central bank was prohibited from doing business with the public (though not from conducting open-market operations), in order to prevent competitive frictions with member banks; it was instead mandated to operate on a non-profit basis and given the statutory aims of ensuring an elastic money supply and constructing a more effective banking system.[35] The function of a bankers' bank implied that member banks deposit at least part of their reserves with the central bank. On this matter too, lawmakers took, for fear of misunderstanding, the safest course and established explicit reserve requirements, introducing yet another innovation with respect to European practice.[36]

Finally, this being a contract, verification and enforcement mechanisms were needed. Thus the Federal Reserve Board was formally assigned powers of banking supervision, shared with the Comptroller of the Currency, who remained sole supervisor of the banks that did not belong to the federal system.[37] The system was directed by a Board composed of the Treasury Secretary, the Comptroller of the Currency, and five members appointed to ten-year terms by the President with the consent of the Senate.

With the creation of the Federal Reserve System, central banking was fully instituted in the American legal order, in all but name. In the years that followed, this model, not the hard-to-replicate English one, would serve as a point of reference for countless banking reforms around the world, some successful and others less so.

4.5   THE MAIN CENTRAL BANKS OF CONTINENTAL EUROPE

The central bank model that was gaining ground in the meantime in the main continental European countries was somewhere between the English and the US models. State control over the activity of the central bank preceded the application of both these models, as a direct consequence of the privilege it had to issue banknotes; but the relationship between the central bank and commercial banks remained ambiguous, indeed openly competitive for a long time. In fact, these were countries in which bank money had been slow to develop, partly because the constraints on note issue appeared less rigid than elsewhere; accordingly, the duty of promoting the new forms of banking activity outside the major financial centres had fallen on the main banks of issue. As a result, over time these banks had established a network of branches whose profitability depended on their ability to capture and then defend significant shares of the local market.

The experiences of the Bank of France, the Reichsbank and the Bank of Italy are good examples in this respect. The Bank of France had been set up in 1800 as a bank of issue with privately held capital and totally independent from the state, but as early as 1806 Napoleon altered the legal framework, so as to entrust the head of state with the appointment of the Governor and of the two deputy governors responsible for the Bank's management. His reasoning was perhaps bald, but it was certainly not lacking in clarity:

The Bank does not only belong to its shareholders; it also belongs to the State, since the State itself grants the privilege to coin money . . . I want the Bank to be sufficiently under the Government's control, but not too much.[38]

The law also imposed restrictions on the profits the Bank of France could earn, and in 1808 a new decree established detailed rules for the conduct of the Bank's business. In the early decades of its life, the Bank was more concerned with pushing competitors out of the market than with promoting the growth of deposits and, by the middle of the century, it had acquired the position of a legal monopolist.[39] It continued to be the most important French banking house until well into the twentieth century, with a network of 190 branches in 1900 and 259 in 1928. Its relations with commercial banks were subject, however, to a slow evolution. A first turning point occurred in 1865, when a committee of inquiry was set up to investigate the Bank's conduct in relation to the competitive challenge of Banque de Savoie, which claimed note issue privileges under the treaty annexing Savoy to France. The committee's proceedings were marked by a fierce conflict between advocates of note issue monopoly and competition supporters, which ended with the victory of the former but also had repercussions on the issuing institute's banking policy. The committee absolved the Bank but recommended that it should attach less importance to making profits and, from then on, it ceased paying interest on deposits and focused on discounting commercial paper bearing three signatures. In some cases the Bank intervened in support of banks in crisis. The intervention in 1889 in support of Comptoir d'Escompte served as a model for the rescue of Baring by the Bank of England later in the same year.[40] In the meantime cheques had finally been recognized by law (1857). Shortly afterwards two banks were created that would soon become the most important French deposit banks: Crédit Lyonnais (1863) and Société Générale (1864). The Bank of France continued however to do business with industrial firms, in competition with deposit banks, and this impeded acceptance of its role as the bankers' bank, a role that was fully recognized only after the First World War.

The Reichsbank had a similar history. Founded as a private company in 1875, shortly after the unification of Germany, it was immediately subjected to constraints, concerning both the appointment of senior managers (entrusted to the head of state), and profits, restricted to 3.5 per cent of the capital and 25 per cent of the residual profit. In addition, the Reich Chancellor formally headed the Bank and could participate in the meetings of its board, although ordinary business was conducted by an independent directorate. As regards the Reichsbank's relations with commercial banks, sources are discordant, but many clues suggest that the

Bank, in its early decades, competed fiercely with the other banks. Apart from having a widespread branch network, between 1880 and 1896 it introduced a system of privileged discount rates for customers considered to be the most reliable. But the situation became clearer from the end of the century onwards, thanks both to the establishment of large universal banks that satisfied most of industry's financing needs, and to the banknotes of the Reichsbank being given legal tender status (1909). Public perception of the Reichsbank as a central bank, not aimed at maximizing profit nor mainly guided by commercial considerations, gradually took hold. One contributory factor was the development of a new technique for regulating liquidity, based on open-market operations.[41]

By contrast, the events that marked the first 20 years of the Bank of Italy's life were highly peculiar, owing both to the situation in which it was set up and to the very special role it would soon play in the country's economic modernization. The reform of note issue took place among the ruins of both the 'regulated plurality' system introduced in 1874 and the whole domestic banking system. In 1893, just a few months after the passage of the law setting up the Bank of Italy, the two leading Italian banks, Banca Generale and Credito Mobiliare, failed and dragged several smaller banks down with them. The Bank of Italy itself was met with 'a climate of diffidence, if not downright hostility',[42] that led the government to create a legislative framework in which the Bank was virtually on probation. Not only did the government take upon itself the management of the discount rate, while imposing restrictions on the note issue that considerably reduced its profitability; the Bank was also entrusted with the liquidation of the buildings inherited from the former Banca Romana, a burden that was to weigh on its operations for over ten years. Lastly, the law made the appointment of the Director General (the position of Governor was not created until 1928) by the Board of Directors (which represented the shareholders' interests) subject to government approval.

In these conditions the early years of the Bank's life were inevitably marked by conflict, fierce at times, between shareholders and the government, with the management called upon to perform a difficult task of mediation.[43] Less than one year after the reform, Director General Giuseppe Grillo resigned over disagreements with Treasury Minister Sidney Sonnino, and was promptly replaced by Giuseppe Marchiori, a former member of Parliament more to the Minister's liking.[44] The main problem in the first years of life of the Bank was to ensure its survival, squeezed as it was between a weak balance sheet and stringent legal constraints that left its management very little scope for exercising discretion. The official (so-called 'normal') discount rate, for instance, remained unchanged at 5 per cent from 1894 to 1907 and the authorization, granted by law in 1893, to engage in rediscounting with banks at a 'preferential' rate, one point below the normal one, made little difference, since the preferential rate was equally rigid. In order to allow the Bank, still a private sector company formally required to produce income for its shareholders, to increase its profits, a significant reform was passed in 1895 permitting the Bank to apply an interest rate below the preferential rate to 'prime' bank and non-bank customers, provided it was not below a minimum ('reduced') rate, also fixed by the Treasury Minister. Provision was made for the minimum rate to be revised every three months, and monthly from 1903 onwards.

This decision, however, while giving the Bank some breathing space as regards its operational flexibility, confirmed a regime of open competition between the main bank of issue and commercial banks; a competition the Bank was forced to engage in, order not to sink under the weight of the non-performing assets inherited from the Banca Romana. In 1898 a little less than 80 per cent of the discounts were made at special rates; notwithstanding their names, preferential and reduced rates had become the 'normal' rates.[45] Bonaldo Stringher replaced Giuseppe Marchiori in 1900 as Director General, and became the Bank's first Governor in 1928, remaining in office until his death two years later. He had the great merit of realizing that the Bank's complete legitimization to act as a 'real bank of issue' would call for patient and tenacious work, with the triple aim of loosening the operational constraints imposed by law, strengthening the Bank's capital and creating, as well as maintaining, good relations with the leading Italian banks. All this not only and not so much for the benefit of the shareholders, but to allow the Bank to support the growth that Italy's late entry on the path of industrialization made necessary. Illuminating in this respect is a letter that Stringher was to write in 1907 to the National Bank of Romania, which had asked him for an opinion on the best way to manage a leading bank of issue:

> There are banks of issue that are sustained by national wealth. In that case, they reflect the prosperity of a country, such as France, that has an abundance of metallic money, or England, that possesses highly developed credit instruments and one of the largest volumes of world trade. There are other banks, instead, that, owing to the activity in which they engage, are called upon to rehabilitate and improve the economic environment in which they operate in order to have a favourable influence on the exchange rates and to redeem their notes in metallic money. In this second case, it is essential for the banks of issue to have a solid structure that inspires complete confidence. In fact these institutions − obliged as they are, in those moments of difficulty that never fail to occur, to discount paper that could turn into non-performing assets − have to multiply their ordinary and extraordinary reserves, which can only be done by reducing to its legal minimum the dividend to be distributed.[46]

This view of the role the bank of issue played, in a country undergoing industrialization with a lag, led Stringher to promote the creation of a series of consortia, with the aim of supporting Italy's still fragile financial and industrial infrastructure. The first of these consortia was created in 1907 in response to the crisis affecting the Società Bancaria Italiana. The Bank did not participate directly in the consortium, which primarily had a bank membership, but supported it through rediscounting. Thanks to this intervention, the losses incurred by the Società Bancaria Italiana were entirely borne by the share capital, which was replenished after being written down. That year the same instrument was used, again at Stringher's initiative, to support share values, undermined by the international stock markets' crisis. In 1911 a new consortium was established, in order to support the faltering steel industry, that saw the participation not only of universal banks, but also of some savings banks, so as to underline the general interest of the initiative. Lastly, in 1914 the consortium approach was put on an institutional footing with the creation of the Consortium for the Support of Industrial Securities (Consorzio per sovvenzioni su valori industriali) to support securities and the credit institutions exposed to the risk of runs on deposits before the country's entry into the First World War.[47]

The benefits of this policy can be appreciated both from an economic and from a legal point of view. In fact the crisis of 1907 was overcome in Italy at a relatively low cost, in terms of interest rates, which remained below those of the other main European countries, except for France, and also in terms of its monetary and financial consequences. Again in 1907 a new legislative intervention was made, aiming: 'no longer at keeping banks under control in order to stop them from deviating from the straight and narrow path, but rather at loosening the constraints put in place to prevent that from happening'.[48]

The new law eased the constraints on note issue. It allowed the reduced discount rate to be altered at any time (therefore no longer just monthly) and introduced tax incentives for the use of bills and advances. This was only the first step, followed a short time afterwards by the Consolidated Law of 1910, the first formal legal recognition of the 'Italian way to central banking'. In 1926, the Bank was eventually granted the note issue monopoly, and the existence of a public interest for the 'protection of savings' was recognized. To that end the law of 1926 formally entrusted the function of banking supervision to the bank of issue. Even though it retained its private sector status, at that point it was clear and commonly accepted that the Bank of Italy was a true central bank. The legal framework was enlarged and improved with the banking legislation of 1936, to which I shall come back later. Among the most important innovations of the new legal system was the ban on the Bank carrying out transactions with non-bank customers.

Elsewhere in the world, above all in the countries that were late in achieving industrial and financial development, the American model was adopted because, being basically *dirigiste*, it was easier to apply. In just a few decades many central banks were modelled and remodelled along the lines of the US legislation of 1913. In particular, between the 1920s and the 1930s new central banks constructed on the basis of this model were introduced in South Africa (1920), Spain (1921), Colombia (1923), Chile (1925), Mexico (1925), Greece (1928), Bolivia (1929), Turkey (1930), New Zealand (1933), Canada (1935), Argentina (1935) and India (1935).[49]

4.6 THE BANKING CRISES OF THE 1930s AND THE CONTROL OF CREDIT

One question nonetheless remained open, despite the general acceptance of the concept of the central bank. It concerned the ways in which the central bank should regulate bank money. The English and American models were based on opposite views, whose theoretical bases can be traced back to the two schools of thought that had dominated doctrinal debates in the early nineteenth century: the Currency School and the Banking School. Despite adjustments, the English legal framework was still based on the Currency School approach. Bagehot himself, putting forward his prescriptions on how the Bank of England should act at times of financial tension, only wanted to supplement – not overthrow – that approach. The development of moral suasion in the subsequent decades had made it partly possible to go beyond the rigidities of the 1844 legislation, but it was nonetheless a precarious arrangement, its success depending on the cooperation of commercial banks, which ultimately remained optional. As the events of 1914 showed, fluctuations in the competitive climate of the market could cause malfunctioning or, even worse, outbreaks of instability. The American model, which emerged in response to the lack of elasticity of note circulation, was instead based on the Banking School. The operational criterion followed by the Fed during its first two decades of activity was the real bills doctrine, set out about a century and a half earlier by Adam Smith, and by then conceptually outdated. All told, knowledge about control over the payment technology based on bank money was still rudimentary by the beginning of the First World War.

As was the case on several occasions during the evolution of central banks, it took a major crisis, such as that occurring at the beginning of the 1930s and soon evolving into the Great Depression, to reveal the shortcomings of the existing arrangements and thus to set off a process of reform. In fact it is to the events of the 1930s that we owe: 'a large mass of often extremely detailed and highly technical legislation serving to regulate and control the institutions to which the money of the people is entrusted'.[50]

Bagehot's 'high' interest rate doctrine proved inadequate and, in certain circumstances, counterproductive on the occasion of the 1930s major banking crises. As Ragnar Nurkse argued in an influential paper written for the League of Nations in 1944:

> when the 'psychology of flight' prevails, there is no increase in the discount rate that can prevent it. Rather, an increase in the discount rate could cause a further crisis of confidence and thus produce the opposite effect to that desired.[51]

By contrast, and paradoxically with respect to the intentions of its supporters, the real bills doctrine proved to be an obstacle to the stabilizing action of the Fed. Ultimately commercial banks found themselves with limited stocks of short-term securities eligible for discounting, owing to the boom in long-term investments that occurred during the 1920s, which the Fed had been unable to prevent. Already during the First World War, central banks had been forced to ease the constraints on their activity by broadening the range of securities eligible for discounting and the types of intermediaries admitted. In some cases their statutes had had to be altered.[52] But these were mostly palliatives that did not tackle the underlying problem, that is, how to prevent the formation of widespread instability. Lawmakers in the 1930s, faced with banking crises of unprecedented virulence, could not avoid the problem. And as already in 1844 and in all the reforms based on the English one, in the absence of clear theoretical indications the tendency was to be overzealous and to construct a framework of 'extremely detailed and highly technical' rules, in the words of Allen cited above, so as to curb the new and dangerous payment technology.

The easiest aspect of the reform process consisted in extending the central banks' responsibility to include credit control. In the countries that had adopted the American model this could be achieved simply by inserting the word 'credit' in the central bank's statute. No central bank statute had mentioned the control of credit before the 1920s, but by the end of the decade the central banks that had been established under the auspices of the League of Nations had begun to recognize that function. For example, the Bank of Greece was mandated to 'exercise control on the performance of currency and credit', the Bank of Poland to 'regulate note issue and credit', and the Bank of Romania to 'ensure note issue and credit control'. Later, the central banks of such countries as Canada, India and Germany were assigned the same function.

Apart from the amendment of statutes, there remained three complex problems to be resolved: the legislative method by which to regulate credit, the link between the apparatus so created and the political system, and the instruments of action to promote banking stability. Concerning the question of method, lawmakers had three options: to insert the rules on banks into general legislation, to gather together all the provisions on banks in ad hoc legislation, or, lastly, to enact a 'financial' law extending to all forms of intermediation. The first path was taken by the United Kingdom with the promulgation of the Companies Act of 1929. The second, suited to countries where banking was carried on in a variety of forms, was chosen by such countries as Denmark (1930), Switzerland (1934) and Italy (1936), while the third, appropriate for less financially developed countries, was adopted in Scandinavia and the newly industrialized countries.

Three alternative approaches were also tried with regard to the delicate issue of political control. The first consisted in setting up a special government-controlled body, a banking inspectorate, not subject to the influence of the central bank. The second involved delegating the functions of supervision to the central bank, within the framework of powers and limitations established by the legal system. The third solution, a hybrid of the previous two, was to set up a banking commission composed of technical members (with the central bank in a prominent position) and political appointees. In some cases, second thoughts led to a change of approach. In Italy, for instance, the function of banking supervision was first assigned by the 1926 law to the Bank of Italy and then, with the creation in 1936 of the Inspectorate for Savings and Credit, only de facto delegated to the central bank. Such delegation of powers was formalized with the legislative measures of 1944 and 1977, while a political body, the Interministerial Committee for Credit and Savings, was empowered to set guidelines.

As regards instruments, the prevailing tendency was to hinder access to banking and to introduce reserve requirements similar to those existing in the United States since 1913. In the countries where banking crises had been greatest, steps were also taken to nationalize much of the banking system and to introduce legal limits on bank interest rates. Finally, in the countries where the commingling of banking and industry had led to collusion and fraud, operational specialization was introduced, that is, through the Glass–Steagall Act in the United States and the 1936 Banking Law in Italy. All these interventions drastically reduced the tenor of competition in banking, thereby favouring the emergence of an oligopolistic and collusive market structure.

But along with structural controls the legislation of the 1930s brought two additional innovations, which in the long run proved even more important, as they remained in place even when structural controls began to fall out of favour in the second half of the 1970s, and the tide of opinion turned towards market-based forms of regulation. I am referring to the institutionalization of banking supervision and the special bankruptcy law for banks.

Until the second half of the 1920s the supervisory function had been an idiosyncrasy of the US Federal Reserve, which, for fear of friction with the Comptroller of the Currency, had not performed it with notable alacrity. By the turn of the 1930s it had become evident that supervision constituted a primary function for purposes of banking stability. Inquiries conducted after the crisis showed that the banks' books of financial statements in many countries were literally crammed with false items and imprudent asset valuations. Moreover, the practice of shifting dud loans from one branch to another just before inspections was widespread, as was the granting of soft loans by the banks to their own executives and shareholders.[53] Significant reforms for more effective control on banks' operations had been adopted by Italy as early as 1926 and by Japan in 1928. In 1932 the Federal Reserve Board raised the problem in the United States, arguing that: 'a unified banking system under national supervision is essential for a fundamental banking reform'.[54] However, this did not produce the hoped-for result: although the Emergency Banking Act of 1933 did strengthen the toolkit of supervision, it also created an additional supervisory body, the Federal Deposit Insurance Corporation. In other countries, such as Germany, France, Belgium, Switzerland and even Italy, supervision was put at the centre of the reform process. Among the main countries, the sole exception was once again the United Kingdom, which, consistently with the informal model of central banking, preferred special 'recommendations' made by the government and the Bank of England to commercial banks.

The last important innovation concerned bankruptcy law. As mentioned, commercial law in most countries had not distinguished between banks and other companies. The reforms of the 1930s divided bankruptcy law in many countries into two branches, founded on different principles and institutions. This development still receives little attention from scholars; a systematic study of the reasons for such separation and its practical effects has yet to be made. However, it appears reasonable to argue that three aspects of recent bank crises persuaded lawmakers that it would be useful to have separate banking legislation. One was the difficulty in accurately evaluating bank assets and hence capital adequacy, since the complex necessary examinations presupposed the employment of specially trained personnel. Second, the repercussions of the eventual hurried closure of a struggling bank made a certain degree of flexibility in applying the rules somehow desirable. Lastly, lawmakers thought that, in some cases, it might be socially beneficial for some insolvent banks to be kept afloat, after adequate recapitalization, so as not to disperse the capital of customer information and experience concealed in banks' financial statements (what we may call 'goodwill', which theory today defines as 'information capital'). As Guttentag and Herring remark, crises showed that: 'living banks are usually worth much more than dead ones, even when, alive, their value is negative'.[55]

Though with many adaptations and national variants, the three pillars of the new order – special legislation for banks, structural controls and supervision – formed a consistent whole. Special legislation endowed the supervisory authorities, whose technical autonomy was in many cases increased as a result of the reform, with more powerful instruments for the pursuit of stability as well as a degree of discretion in order to calibrate their interventions. Structural controls established a business preserve for existing banks, facilitating cooperation agreements and reducing the likelihood of a recurrence of the commercial wars that were regarded as one of the primary causes of crises. Lastly, supervision made preventive action possible and gave the lender of last resort access to more detailed and generally more accurate information on the basis of which to decide whether or not to intervene in situations of stress, when the borrower's collateral was often of doubtful value.

Obviously, this is not to say that abuses were impossible, or that the system so devised was not exposed to the risk of a bureaucratic–*dirigiste* drift. The events of the 1970s and 1980s would demonstrate all the risks of an overly prolonged compression of market forces. But in the short run the mix seemed to work, restoring stability to the banking market for several decades and thereby contributing to the definitive success of the payment technology based on the bank deposit creation multiplier.

However, the resulting arrangement was undoubtedly national and unsuitable for integration on an international scale, so much so as to induce the reformers of the Bretton Woods monetary system, several years later, not even to attempt the endeavour. It was national in three respects. To begin with, controls were aimed at achieving objectives whose value was circumscribed to the country where they were applied. But the set-up was national on two much deeper levels, too: on the institutional level, since its effectiveness depended on the functionality and reliability of a series of other bodies, such as courts and financial law enforcement agencies, and other market practices, that is, accounting practices; and on the political level, since the implicit contract between the central bank and commercial banks could only work insofar as the state acted as its executor and guarantor. This implied, on the one hand, that the central bank could count on the government's support in its supervisory action; and on the other, that the state stood ready to use taxpayers' money in order to bail out banks that had become insolvent but whose survival was deemed to be preferable for the common good. As Goodhart and Schoenmaker remark, the implicit contract was very simple and could be summed up in the old English saying: 'He who pays the piper calls the tune'.[56] Despite the numerous efforts to harmonize banking regulation since the 1970s and again, with renewed vigour, in the late 1990s, this principle is still valid today.

4.7 CONCLUSION: CENTRAL BANKING AND THE ASCENDANCY OF THE CENTRAL BANK

The history of the process of formation and diffusion of the payment technology based on bank money ends in the 1930s, with the worldwide adoption of a set-up comprising a central bank, released from the objective of profit-making and subject to a more or less direct control by the state, as well as a dense network of rules and institutions designed to safeguard banking stability.

Was this outcome inevitable? The debate, theoretical more than historiographical, is still open. Advocates of the central bank model such as Charles Goodhart, drawing on and expanding Henry Thornton's theses, believe the answer is yes, because, they assert, there is a 'natural' tendency in the deposit-creation mechanism based on the fractional system to generate a centralization of bank reserves, and because lending of last resort is more effective if it is not exposed to the conflicts of interest that inevitably arise among firms operating in a regime of competition. However, other observers, that as Michael Bordo and Richard Timberlake,[57] judge that this tendency, far from being 'natural', is on the contrary the product of governmental interventions aimed at creating institutions that, having the privilege of issuing money and availing itself of a large market share, would be better at financing the government budget deficit.

Like all disputes regarding the relationship between state and market, this ultimately risks being a sterile one. Neither theory nor empirical analysis will ever offer clinching arguments in favour of one position or the other. Supporters of free banking can argue there are banking systems that have been able to maintain stability over long periods even without a central bank. The best-known example is the Scottish system, cited by Adam Smith as a model of stability and also appreciated by Walter Bagehot. But more pertinent, because closer to us in time, is the example of the Canadian banking system: thanks to the foresight of the Canadian Banking Association and the absence of restrictions on the opening of branches, unlike those that applied in the United States, it was able to do without a central bank until 1935. The opponents of central banking could also point to the fact that the most devastating bank crises occurred in the 1930s, after all the leading countries had already instituted a monopolistic central bank. But the advocates of central banks could respond, not without reason, that the Scottish and Canadian systems had not been left alone to fend for themselves, the former being able to count on the support of the Bank of England, the latter relying on repeated state interventions which ultimately persuaded the government to opt for a central bank in 1935. They could also argue that the blame for the crises of the 1930s did not lie with central banks themselves, but with the policies they were mandated to follow, still harking back to those of the previous century and therefore not sufficiently calibrated to exploit the potential of the central bank model. From this perspective, the crises of the 1930s constitute a critical juncture in the process of learning how to manage bank money.

As can be seen, on merely 'empirical' grounds there is no way out. But what is the truly relevant empirics when dealing with institutional evolution? Do later historiographical analyses or the perceptions of contemporaries count more? And what is the point of considering as imposed by the state an institution that was quickly adopted on such a vast scale and perfected in countries that were well-established democracies rapidly advancing towards universal suffrage? Isn't its widespread success a revealed preference of the taxpayers, a 'vote' of the market in itself? In this sense, it was no coincidence that banking reforms of the early decades of 1900 had been approved by vast majorities in parliaments, often benefiting from the backing of banking associations; the exact opposite of what had happened at the beginning of 1800, when laws establishing privileged banks were often passed by a handful of votes.

To those who lived during the period of ascendancy of bank money, figures in Table 4.1, taken from a study by Michael Bordo, would have surely told more than any theoretical argument or empirical analysis, however refined. They show that in the United States, where there was no central bank, banking crises tended to have higher costs in terms of growth and often involved a suspension of convertibility, whereas in Europe,

The age of central banks

Table 4.1 Banking panics: a comparison between the United States and Great Britain

Cycle		Deviation from the real output growth trend (%)	Inflation differential between cycle peak and trough (%)	Deviation from the money stock growth trend (%)	Notes
Peak	Trough				
UNITED STATES					
1873	1879	0.5	−7.1	−4.7	Suspension of convertibility
1882	1885	−3.2	−12.2	2.6	
1893	1894	−9.5	−9.0	−9.3	Suspension of convertibility
1907	1908	−14.7	−6.1	−1.7	Suspension of convertibility
1920	1921	−7.6	−56.7	−2.5	
1929	1932	−16.7	−12.5	−11.7	
GREAT BRITAIN					
1873	1879	0.9	−7.1	−3.1	
1883	1886	−1.2	−5.4	−2.8	
1890	1894	−0.2	−4.4	−2.5	
1907	1908	−4.7	−13.6	−1.6	
1920	1921	−6.9	−68.0	−5.1	
1929	1932	−3.7	−7.9	−4.3	

Source: Bordo, 'The lender of last resort: alternative views and historical experience', p. 24.

where the central bank model already ruled, this did not happen. A glance at the voluminous proceedings of the National Monetary Commission is sufficient to realize how important these considerations were in prompting the country that had been most hostile to central banking, the United States, to adopt a central bank model that would soon be profusely copied abroad.

5. The fiat standard: monetary nationalism, central bank autonomy and credibility

5.1 INTRODUCTION

The nineteenth century had seen the rise of two innovative payment technologies, one founded on the convertible banknote, the other on bank money, both having the metallic standard as protection against abuse. In the twentieth century, instead, the splitting of money from metal was carried through to completion with the success of legal tender. The new payment technology did not differ from its two forerunners in some tangible characteristic or in the manner of circulation. Legal tender is in fact composed of two different elements, which reproduce the forms of money that had come into their own in the previous century: the banknote, now produced under a central bank monopoly, and the deposit with the central bank. What distinguishes the new form of money, therefore, is only its legal nature: money no longer represents a claim to obtain a quantity of metal, but rather a claim to obtain a performance, the transfer of goods or services, whose price, however, is not fixed. It is an intrinsically useless piece of paper or accounting entry. Its utility depends on its acceptance for payment and on the predictability of the price level, and so its circulation depends on a government guarantee as to its future value. It is legal money in the sense that the state takes it upon itself directly to produce and guarantee it.

This is an astonishing change of perspective from the previous centuries, when the state was frequently singled out as the main enemy of monetary stability. What makes the change even more surprising is that it occurred within the space of a few decades. In fact, in the early twentieth century an eminent American student of monetary questions, Irving Fisher, still remarked: 'Irredeemable paper money has almost invariably proved a curse to the country employing it.'[1] The only theoretical debate of some importance in the second half of the nineteenth century had concerned the merits of bimetallism, or innovative conversion schemes such as Alfred Marshall's symmetalism. But no scholar had dared to propose that the general abandonment of convertibility into metal might be socially useful and politically attainable.

Such a radical change could not take place, and in fact did not take place, through the conscious choice of any government, however influential. Rather, it was the logical outcome of a complex, multiform and largely unconscious process that began in the First World War and culminated in the 1971 declaration of the dollar's inconvertibility. While it may be plausibly maintained, as Kenneth Dam has argued, that the gold standard ceased to exist one morning in August 1914, it does not follow from this that the fiat standard was born fully fledged the following day.[2] It took the Great Depression to convince a large part of the population of the absurdity, indeed the harmfulness, of the efforts to restore gold convertibility, with their acutely deflationary consequences, and it then took the effects of the Vietnam War and Lyndon Johnson's Great Society programme to sweep away the last vestiges of gold convertibility at the start of the 1970s.

As in the preceding phases, the engine of monetary innovation was the need to counter price deflation by making the supply of money more flexible. The concept on which the demand for reform turned was 'managed money': the idea that money, whatever its physical properties and legal supports, does not regulate itself through impersonal market mechanisms, but needs to be managed, with acumen and wisdom, in the public interest. As in other phases of the process of institutional innovation, however, the tempo of the economy and of policy-making did not coincide with the tempo of theoretical reflection. Although the concept of managed money was already known and enjoyed wide support in the 1920s, it was not until the late 1930s, and the publication of Keynes's *General Theory*, that the logical implications were drawn, that is, that monetary management could in principle totally dispense with convertibility. But at that point Keynes's ideas simply reflected the reflationary policies that had already been adopted, with success, in many countries.

The most interesting question raised by the development of legal tender does not concern so much why there was a demand for reform, but how the reform was supplied. How could the state transform itself from being merely a passive guarantor of the arrangement that had taken shape in the nineteenth century into an active producer of confidence in payment technology? To answer this question, we must consider the changes that were occurring in those years in the political and legal sphere: the enlargement of suffrage, the consequent transformation of the role of Parliament in the liberal regimes and of mass parties in the authoritarian regimes, and the transformation of legal arrangements, which saw the apparatus state give way to the regulatory state.

Furthermore, the direct assumption by the state of the task of regulating the currency required, moreover, a massive, highly ramified action of institutional adaptation in which the central banks were conspicuously involved. Like all instances of far-reaching social experimentation, the process was not monotonic, unfolding over seven or eight decades. In a brief initial phase, the attempt to return monetary systems to the pre-war rules and mode of operation assigned a pre-eminent role to the central banks and recognized the usefulness of their having considerable autonomy from the government. This, however, was a tactical expedient more than a genuine institutional innovation: central bank autonomy served solely to shelter monetary policy from the acute political strains generated by that attempt – and to create a handy scapegoat if the attempt failed. That is to say, in this early phase the central banks were tools of deflation, the inevitable corollary of the political decision to restore the gold standard. When that policy proved unsustainable, the principle of central bank autonomy was jettisoned without raising a stir, together with convertibility.

Thus commenced the second phase of the reform process, which saw the nationalization of many central banks and reduction of the autonomy of those that formally remained in the hands of private shareholders. In this phase, which lasted until the end of the 1970s, numerous, significant operational innovations were developed in the conduct of monetary policy, from open-market operations to reserve requirements, ceilings on the growth in bank lending, securities investment requirements, and liquidity swaps, first between central banks, then between central banks and commercial banks. As with the first phase, the curtain was brought down on this phase by a major macroeconomic shock, stagflation, which was interpreted as the consequence of monetary policy's loss of credibility due to its being under the direct control of the executive. In light of this reading, a new, extensive reform of the role and legal status of the central bank was launched; in an attempt to restore monetary policy's inflation-fighting credibility, central banks were granted broad operating autonomy, albeit with the framework of rules that guaranteed democratic oversight and accountability to the legislative power, and in some cases the status of institution recognized and protected by the constitution. But a mechanism of this kind could work only in countries with solid, reliable institutional arrangements. Elsewhere, it was far more arduous to ensure the monetary policy's credibility and it was necessary to try other paths, from pegging the national currency's exchange rate all the way to the extreme solution of giving up monetary sovereignty. In this we have confirmation that the state's ability to produce confidence cannot be taken for granted.

5.2   THE RISE, DECLINE AND AGONY OF THE GOLD STANDARD

Every payment technology based on convertibility presupposes a typically political decision, whatever the actual role of the state in its management. The decision regards the choice of the unit of account and the price of the means of payment in terms of the unit of account chosen. These two elements together configure what is ordinarily called the monetary standard. In the preceding chapters we paid little attention to the question of the standard, since in no phase of monetary developments in the eighteenth and nineteen centuries was it ever doubted that the standard must continue to be metallic. In the early decades of the twentieth century, starting from the First World War, this assumption was increasingly called into question until the link between the means of payment actually in circulation and precious metals was completely severed, though this only occurred much later. The fiat standard is indeed an innovative payment technology, but it is so in the sense that the means of payments no longer represent promises of conversion into metal but, rather, simple accounting items that are guaranteed by the government and the management of which is therefore placed more or less directly under governmental control. The question of the standard is thus crucial to understanding the evolution of monetary arrangements in the twentieth century.

To proceed in an orderly fashion, however, we must take a considerable step back in time and position ourselves ideally around the middle of the nineteenth century, when we find three different metal standards used by groups or blocs of countries. A gold bloc gravitated around Great Britain and included Portugal and most of the British colonies and dominions. Then there was the silver bloc, consisting of most of the small German states, Austria-Hungary, Denmark, Norway, the Netherlands, Sweden, Mexico, China, India and Japan. Finally, a small but influential group of countries, including France, the United States, Sweden and the Italian states (and subsequently the Kingdom of Italy), adopted a bimetal standard.

This tripartite structure had proved surprisingly stable in the first half of the century, but it swiftly dissolved after 1860, with virtually unanimous convergence on gold. The reasons for the ascent of the gold standard are still the subject of historiographic debate. Essentially, four explanations have been offered.[3] Charles Kindleberger and his followers have emphasized that the silver discoveries in Mexico and Nevada and the resulting increase in silver coinage from the end of the 1860s onwards caused a progressive, undesired devaluation of the currencies of the silver standard countries, which made the gold standard 'structurally' more attractive. In addition, with the improvement in living standards and the expansion of trade, the sphere of circulation of gold coins, whose unit value was normally higher, also tended to expand. A third, plainly political factor, was the progressive strengthening, in some silver or bimetal countries, of the position of the industrial and financial bourgeoisie vis-à-vis the agrarian strata, which traditionally supported silver and endemically inflationary monetary policies. In the literature the final defeat of the silver lobby in the United States in the 1890s has been seen precisely as the victory of the creditor classes over the debtor classes.[4] The fourth factor, and perhaps the most important one in the long run, has to do with the economies of scale deriving from the use of a uniform standard at a time of rapid expansion of international trade. For example, Marc Flandreau has shown that in the second half of the century trade between countries adopting the same standard tended to be especially intense, even when other factors such as income level and geographical proximity are taken into account.[5] Moreover, the fact that Great Britain, the industrial pioneer and the leading power, had adopted the gold standard created an almost automatic association between gold and economic progress in the minds of commentators on monetary affairs.

Whatever its ultimate cause, the movement in favour of gold soon attained a global scale, so that by the early 1900s the exceptions to the gold standard could be counted on the fingers of one hand, China being the most important. What is more, between 1890 and 1914 the international monetary system based on gold enjoyed great stability, in the sense that the total supply of money tended to parallel the evolution of the available stock of gold, except for a slight downward trend in the velocity of circulation. The most interesting aspect of these two decades was not the absence of crises, which on the contrary were quite frequent and also intense, especially in the peripheral countries, but rather the diligence (and constancy) with which the countries which were forced to abandon the system sought to restore convertibility at the pre-crisis price as soon as possible. The gold standard, in other words, succeeded in anchoring the expectations of economic agents, despite the fact that the high degree of capital mobility reached towards the end of the century sometimes made it necessary for the authorities to suspend convertibility. As Ronald McKinnon observes, underlying the good functioning of the gold standard there was an unwritten but rigorously applied rule, which went something like this: if exceptional events force a temporary suspension, 'restore convertibility at traditional mint parity as soon as practicable – if necessary by deflating the domestic economy'. This 'resumption rule' de facto kept governments from exerting any long-term influence on the level of domestic prices.[6]

The rigour with which the resumption rule was applied in the years before the First World War cannot but impress observers today. However, along with a series of structural factors, such as the limited voting power of the less-well-off classes, who had to pay the cost of the deflation needed to restore convertibility, it is necessary to recall that at the end of the nineteenth century there was no theory that linked the stance of monetary policy with growth and, more in general, with the state of the economy. The concept of unemployment was itself unfamiliar and not tracked by systematic statistics, and the incidence of trade union membership among the working class was practically nil. No doubt other factors contributed to the success of the gold standard, including the undisputed supremacy of the London financial marketplace, the willingness of the Bank of France to cooperate with the Bank of England at critical junctures, and the still limited diffusion of bank money, but the system would surely have been short-lived if there had not been a definite subordination of other potential policy objectives to the goal of maintaining the gold parity.

All this changed with the First World War. No country could afford to finance a large-scale, modern war entirely through taxation. Britain, the pivot of the gold system, tried hardest to reconcile the war effort with maintaining convertibility, financing about half of its war expenditure through greater taxation of the wealthy classes. This permitted Britain to hold the sterling–dollar exchange rate very close to the pre-war level during most of the conflict. But the stability was a fiction, made possible by gold sales (decreed in August 1914) and by currency market interventions coordinated with the Federal Reserve. Even the United States, which had little trouble in maintaining gold convertibility up to 1917, imposed an embargo on gold exports when it entered the war. From the very outbreak of hostilities all the belligerents opted to finance the war effort largely through borrowing, facilitated in most cases by massive injections of liquidity by the central banks and, in some cases, as in that of Great Britain, directly by the Treasury. The results of these choices are summarized in Tables 5.1 and 5.2. During the war years the increase in the volume of currency in circulation ranged between twofold and fivefold, while the public debt grew by a factor of 5 in Italy and France, 8 in Germany, and 11 in Britain. In the United States, which does not appear in the tables, the public debt grew by a factor of 19, but starting from an extremely low pre-war base.

At the end of the hostilities the authorities faced a drastic choice: to restore the pre-war parities through draconian deflation, or to erode the real value of the debt through monetary inflation. The latter option was unavoidable for the defeated nations, where the depreciation of the currency and the state of the economy precluded any attempt to apply

Table 5.1   *Note circulation of selected central banks, 1913–21 (annual*
              averages of weekly data in millions of national currency)

	Bank of England (pounds)	Banque de France (francs)	Bundesbank (marks)	Banca d'Italia (lire)
1913	28.7[1]	5 665	1 958	1 647
1914	35.6[1]	7 325	2 018	1 828
1915	33.8[1]	12 280	5 409	2 624
1916	35.4[1]	15 552	6 871	3 294
1917	40.2[1]	19 845	9 010	4 660
1918	54.8[1]	27 531	13 681	7 751
1919	76.4[1]	34 744	27 887	10 197
1920	114.8[1]	38 186	52 435	13 525
1921	127.3[1]	37 352	76 536	14 175

Note: [1] Does not include notes issued by the Treasury (€368 million in 1920 and €326
million in 1921).

Source: Kindleberger, *A Financial History of Western Europe*, p. 295.

Table 5.2   *National debt of selected countries, 1913–21 (on specified*
              dates; in millions of national currency)

	Great Britain 1 March (pounds)	France 1 January (francs)	Germany 31 March (marks)	Italy 30 June (lire)
1913	717	32 974	4 926	15 125
1914	708	33 558	5 158	15 716
1915	1 166	38 861	9 736	18 695
1916	2 397	51 250	30 595	23 851
1917	4 054	79 610	56 659	33 694
1918	5 921	124 338	72 275	60 212
1919	781	151 122	92 756	74 496
1920	7 878	240 242	91 710	86 482
1921	7 634	297 368	82 520	92 856

Source: Kindleberger, *A Financial History of Western Europe*, p. 296.

the 'resumption rule'. With his customary acumen, Keynes, in a famous
passage, portrayed the motives pushing the governments of those countries towards hyperinflation and at the same time highlighted the main
weakness of the fiat standard, whose most authoritative champion he
would later become:

A Government can live for a long time, even the German government or the Russian government, by printing money . . . The method is condemned, but its efficacy, up to a point, must be admitted. A Government can live by this means when it can live by no other. It is the form of taxation which the public finds hardest to evade and even the weakest Government can enforce, when it can enforce nothing else.[7]

If this was the alternative, it is easy to see why the victorious nations, with Britain in the lead and with the partial exception of France, clung to the gold standard with an obstinacy that would otherwise be hard to understand. The possibility of abandoning the gold standard for what today we call the fiat standard was simply not even considered. The contemporary debate revolved entirely around the choice between restoring the pre-war parity and attempting to stabilize the exchange rate at a lower parity that took account of the changed domestic and international context. Peter Temin is the historian who has given greatest prominence to this cultural or sociological aspect. The gold standard was swept away as an operating mechanism in 1914, but the monetary regime of reference was still very much alive and rooted in the minds of policy-makers in the early 1920s.

The most striking example of this attachment to the gold standard was the report of the Cunliffe Committee, established in Britain towards the end of the war, whose principal conclusion was as follows:

It is imperative that after the war the conditions necessary to the maintenance of an effective gold standard should be restored without delay. Unless the machinery which long experience has shown to be the only effective remedy for an adverse balance of trade and an undue growth of credit is once more brought into play, there will be a grave danger of a progressive credit expansion which will result in a foreign drain of gold menacing the convertibility of our note issue and so jeopardizing the international trade position of the country.[8]

This position enjoyed a broad consensus, not just in political circles but also among the most influential central bankers of the day, in particular Montagu Norman, Governor of the Bank of England, and Benjamin Strong, the powerful Governor of the Federal Reserve Bank of New York.[9] A passage of Strong's is noteworthy for the light it sheds on the prevailing view among monetary authorities of the time and deserves to be quoted in full:

Mr. Norman's feelings, which, in fact, are shared by me, indicated that the alternative – failure of resumption of gold payments – being a confession by the British Government that it was impossible to resume, would be followed by a long period of unsettled conditions too serious to contemplate. It would mean violent fluctuations in the exchanges, with probably progressive deterioration of the values of foreign currencies vis-à-vis the dollar; it would provide an incentive to all of those who were advancing novel ideas for nostrums and expedients other than the gold standard to sell their wares; and incentives to governments at times to undertake various types of paper money expedients and inflation; it might, indeed, result in the United States draining the world of gold with the effect that, after some attempt at some other mechanism for the regulation of credit and prices, some kind of monetary crisis would finally result in ultimate restoration of gold to its former position, but only after a period of hardship and suffering, and possibly some social and political disorder.[10]

The most interesting thing about this passage is Strong's inability to imagine an alternative to restoring the gold parity; the choice is between sacrifices now (deflation) and sacrifices later, accompanied by political and social upheaval into the bargain. Strong's point of view may have been influenced by the fact that the return to the gold standard was not a problem for the United States, the US having never suspended it, and, on the contrary, it worked in favour of American interests, since the US had emerged from the war as Europe's main creditor. Yet as Strong himself observes, his position was widely shared in Europe, where Keynes's proposal for stabilizing the pound below its pre-war level, though far from revolutionary inasmuch as it was consistent with a policy of restoring the gold standard, was considered heretical even in British government circles.[11] Few raised the question of how to attenuate the deflationary impact of the return to gold on the economies, above and beyond the problems of the transition. This is not to say that monetary scholars were unaware of the deflationary risks inherent in such a move, including beyond the transitional period. Gustav Cassel of Sweden stands out among them for the lucidity of this analysis:

> The gold standard, of course, cannot secure a greater stability in the general level of prices of a country than the value of gold itself possesses. Inasmuch as the stability of the general level of prices is desirable, our work for a restoration of the gold standard must be supplemented by endeavours to keep the value of gold as constant as possible . . . With the actual state of gold production it can be taken for certain that after a comparatively short time, perhaps within a decade, the present superabundance of gold will be followed, as a consequence of increasing demand, by a marked scarcity of this precious metal tending to cause a fall of prices[12]

Only a few years later, however, in 1928, Cassel espoused the view that the problem could be solved by acting on the demand for gold:

> The great problem before us is how to meeting the growing scarcity of gold which threatens the world both from increased demand and from diminished

supply. We must solve this problem by a systematic restriction of the monetary demand for gold. Only if we succeed in doing this can we hope to prevent a permanent fall of the general price level and a prolonged and world-wide depression which would inevitably be connected with such a fall in prices.[13]

Actually, the substance of Cassel's recipe had been adopted by the authorities as early as 1922, with the International Monetary Conference of Genoa, which devised what came to be called the gold exchange standard.[14] The Genoa scheme consisted of two elements. One was the reconfiguration of exchange rates, with a devaluation of the weak currencies, the franc in the lead. The second was the division of the countries participating in the system into two categories: the 'central' countries, which would hold their reserves entirely in gold, and the 'peripheral' countries, whose reserves would consist partly of gold and partly of financial assets denominated in the currencies of the 'central' countries.

Although the Genoa accords were not of a formal nature, their practical impact was far from negligible.[15] In the first place, the agreements led to a strong expansion of monetary reserves. In the 1944 report for the League of Nations, quoted earlier, Ragnar Nurkse estimated that between 1913 and 1928 the share of total reserves in the form of financial assets denominated in foreign currency grew from 12 to 42 per cent.[16] The growth also involved countries, such as France, that had previously shown a marked aversion to replacing gold as a reserve asset. Second, they accompanied the gradual resumption of gold convertibility in the main countries. After the pound's return to gold convertibility in 1925 and the stabilization of the franc in December 1926, the gold standard was again operating on a global scale. An indirect effect of the Genoa agreements was the recovery of capital movements. In the years from 1924 to 1928 transfers between the main countries of the gold system amounted to between $9 billion and $11 billion, 60 per cent of which coming from the United States.[17]

However, the monetary scheme conceived in Genoa had two serious flaws that soon undermined the smoothness of its operation. One was the discretion left to individual central banks to change the composition of their reserves. The logic of the gold exchange standard presupposed the creation of a credit pyramid at whose apex stood the gold reserves of the 'central' countries, which were of limited size. A decision by any country to convert its currency reserves into gold could create considerable embarrassment in the central countries, which would have to react by raising the discount rate and thereby imparting to their own economy the deflationary impulse that the system's architects had intended to ward off at global level. That this was not a purely academic hypothesis was demonstrated in 1927 by the decision of France to convert most of its claims on London into gold, forcing the British authorities to face the unpleasant choice either to abandon the parity that the pound had regained with such effort only two years earlier, or to deflate the British economy, which is what happened. The Anglo-French incident raised a great stir among central bankers, especially within the US Federal Reserve, which had demonstrated little enthusiasm for the gold exchange standard from the start. Moreover, now that requests for conversion could no longer come from private citizens (owing to the substantial implementation of the Cunliffe Committee's recommendation that gold coins be withdrawn from circulation; see below in this section), the conversion of foreign currency reserves into gold represented the main mechanism through which the discipline of the gold system could be maintained. But it was a discipline that the leading countries were finding it more and more difficult to bear. The fear that its role as sole creditor might force the United States to assume direct responsibility for the gold system's stability was the source of Benjamin Strong's opposition to the formalization of the Genoa accords. This fear is apparent in a Federal Reserve internal memorandum concerning a meeting between Strong and Arthur Salter, at the time head of the Economic Office of the League of Nations:

> Governor Strong stated that he had always been opposed to any sort of a formal conference or meeting between the world's central banks, as contemplated at Genoa, for several reasons. In his opinion, it was expecting entirely too much of human nature to think that representatives of the central banks of a great many nations having differences of languages, customs, beliefs and financial and political needs could sit down together and agree on anything at all. Moreover, in the course of his travels he had had occasion to meet a great many of the central bankers, as well as governmental and political representatives, and to learn considerably about the relations between the various banks and their governments, and he was not at all convinced that at a general meeting or in any common organization of central banks the policies of certain banks would not be dictated by the interest of their respective governments rather than by purely monetary considerations. Another point was that in any formal meeting of the central banks, the Federal Reserve Bank would never consent to go to such a conference with the prospect of being outvoted on every issue of any importance which affected the Federal Reserve System. He would have to be sure of having one more vote than all the borrowers combined.[18]

In reality, American monetary policy tended to be procyclical. In 1927 Strong agreed to reduce the discount rate in order to aid the Bank of England at a time when the US economy and stock market were booming, a move, subsequently the target of harsh criticism, which helped to fuel the speculative bubble that burst in 1929. Paradoxically, the decision intended to alleviate the pressure on the pound benefited only the franc, since the near totality of the American capital outflow went to the Paris market.[19]

An error of opposite sign was committed by Strong's successors – Strong died in 1928 – during the Depression, when they maintained a restrictive stance that led to a simultaneous fall in America's imports of goods and exports of capital.[20]

The other economy that tended to destabilize the whole system was that of France. The parity at which the franc had stabilized in 1926 turned out to be too low. The gold reserves of the Bank of France doubled between 1926 and 1929, tripled by the end of 1930 and were four times greater by the end of 1931.[21] In part, this inflow of reserves reflected the difference between the cyclical position of France and that of the other main economies, for the French economy had continued to grow in 1930 and 1931 while the rest of the world was already in recession. But it was also due in part to the rigidity of French legislation, which prohibited the French central bank from lending to the government or carrying out large-scale open-market operations, thus making it impossible in fact to satisfy the growing demand for money that the stabilization had fuelled through any means except gold inflows.

On balance, it is hard to deny that the United States and France tended to build up gold reserves that were excessive for the gold exchange standard to be able to work as its designers had imagined. Towards the end of the 1920s the two countries held 60 per cent of global reserves, a far higher proportion than their share of world output or world trade. On the basis of an econometric exercise, Barry Eichengreen estimates that the effective reserves at the end of the decade were about three times greater than the equilibrium value for the United States and five times for France.[22]

Thus, the system was very fragile, both because the objective of maintaining the parity was no longer perceived as an absolute priority and because dependence on foreign exchange reserves was a double-edged sword: if under normal conditions it was advantageous, permitting greater flexibility in monetary policy management; in critical situations it tended to augment the deflationary impulse required to stem a crisis of confidence. In this context, it could not be taken for granted that central banks would maintain a cooperative attitude.

The task of exploding the gold system's internal contradictions fell to the slump that began in the United States, brought on in part by the monetary tightening undertaken by the Federal Reserve in order to absorb the speculative excesses of the previous years. The history of the Great Depression and the debate on its causes are too well known to require further rehearsal here. A glance at Figure 5.1, showing the trend of industrial production in selected countries, will suffice to recall its magnitude.

Of greatest interest to us here are the purely monetary aspects of the crisis. As the resumption rule was disattended, capital tended to flow out

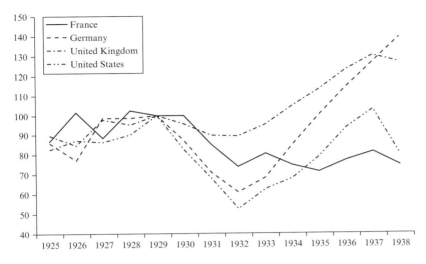

Source: Temin, *Lessons from the Great Depression*, p. 2.

*Figure 5.1   Industrial production indices in selected countries (1929 =
100)*

of a country whose currency was perceived as weak, a mechanism that
Nurkse later dubbed 'destabilizing speculation'. This indeed is what happened as the recessionary tendencies spread. Each central bank sought
to protect its currency by selling foreign currency reserves in order to
buy gold, and by raising rates. Between 1928 and 1931 foreign currency
reserves collapsed from 42 to 11 per cent of total reserve assets but, given
a rigid overall supply of gold, these efforts could only prove vain and, ultimately, deflationary. In these circumstances, and with recession spreading,
the choice was no longer whether or not to stay on the gold standard but
how to escape its clutches. Germany and its main trading partners opted
to introduce stringent exchange controls while formally maintaining the
gold parity throughout the 1930s. By contrast, the United Kingdom, the
erstwhile champion of the return to gold, and the Scandinavian countries took the route of devaluation as early as 1931 and were thus able
to cushion the impact of the world slump. The United States maintained
the gold parity until 1933, resetting it the following year some 70 per cent
lower ($35, as against $20.66). France and the bloc of countries that it led
resisted until 1936, facilitated in this by the undervalued parity established
in 1926. Uncertainty, stagnation and controls combined to dry up capital
flows: between 1932 and 1938 capital outflows from the United States and

Table 5.3   Extension of the franchise (electorate as a percentage of male adult population)

	1880	1890	1900	1910	1920
Great Britain	35.8	62.4	61.5	62.2	62.4
France	86.4	86.6	90.0	91.5	90.5
Germany	91.3	92.3	94.2	94.0	86.8
Belgium	8.2	8.1	90.7	91.6	91.6
Netherlands	12.2	25.6	51.6	62.6	67.0
Switzerland	79.2	80.2	78.1	76.4	75.8
Denmark	78.3	84.2	85.4	87.9	87.8
Norway	23.7	32.2	89.7	95.0	95.0
Sweden	23.5	22.9	27.5	77.5	76.5
Italy	9.0	32.0	26.5	32.2	89.8
Austria-Hungary	24.8	30.5	34.3	94.5	94.5

Source: Peter Flora et al., *State, Economy, and Society in Western Europe, 1815–1975: A Data Handbook in Two Volumes*, Frankfurt, Campus Verlag, 1983, Vol. 1, Ch. 3.

the United Kingdom averaged about $150 million a year. More dramatic still was the slump in world trade, because of massive recourse to protective tariffs and import quotas. Between 1929 and 1933 world trade collapsed to less than a third of its previous value.[23]

Given that real wages rose by an estimated 14 per cent between 1928 and 1931, one may be tempted to trace the Great Depression to excessively rigid labour costs, incompatible with maintaining a monetary standard whose proper functioning depended on a credible resumption rule.[24] Indeed, this was how such authoritative figures as Hawtrey and Robbins read the crisis (only to regret it many years later, at least in Robbins's case). In reality, this was but one aspect of a much more complex phenomenon rooted in the political as well as economic changes catalyzed by the war. Eichengreen and Sussman nicely sum up this transformation with a formula: governments could not send millions to fight (and die) without giving them at least the right to vote. The war did accelerate the enlargement of male suffrage (Table 5.3) and set in motion an analogous process for women, who had had extremely limited voting rights until then. But the broadening of the electorate also implied a gradual expansion of the role of the state, no longer simply 'nightwatchman' but now also supplier of an ever-wider range of social services. In many countries the war also increased the unionization of the workforce, a process encouraged by governments, interested in having a counterparty with which to negotiate the necessary measures for military mobilization and in reducing their economic and social impact. In addition, the immediate post-war years saw the first systematic attempts to gather statistics on unemployment.

This series of political and social changes posed new objectives for economic policy, for instance, insurance against collective risks such as unemployment and workplace accidents, which for the average citizen necessarily came before maintaining the gold parity. Political liberalism had considered Parliament an instrument for controlling the propensity to spend of the sovereign, whether constitutional monarch or republican government. In the new context, in which the state was asked to produce security under the control of the majority of citizens, Parliament was the depositary of the collective will. The tension between alternative objectives, absent during the years of the gold standard, was therefore present before the effects of the Depression unfolded, and it played an important role in the failure of the deflationary policies inherent in the attempt to restore the pre-war gold parities. Monetary policy, that is, had become a political question. What the Depression added to this picture was a widespread lack of confidence in economic liberalism, often accompanied by an equally strong distrust of liberal institutions and a desire to explore new paths in managing the political economy. In this sense the Depression can be considered the turning-point in opinion about the government's role in the economy, what Michael Bordo, Claudia Goldin and Eugene White aptly call 'the defining moment':

> One critical ingredient of this revolution was the decisive shift in public opinion about the appropriate role of government. The apparent failure of capitalism conditioned the public to accept proposed government intervention in markets. Farmers who lost their property, depositors turned away from their banks, the elderly with no pensions, and workers without jobs made the new government programs seem sensible. The question was no longer whether the government should intervene but why it should not.[25]

This shift in perspective concerning the role of economic policy could not be, and indeed was not, painless. Few governments were not turned out of office during the crisis years, the exceptions being those that adopted highly interventionist economic policies. In many countries where institutional resistance to change was especially strong, the reluctant institutions themselves were swept away. Eric Hobsbawm calculates that about 35 countries had electoral constitutional systems in the 1920s; by 1938 the number had dwindled to 17 and by 1944 to 12, out of a total of 64 countries. Hobsbawm speaks of a move to the Right en masse.[26] But if under exceptional circumstances, such as those of the 1930s, the distinction between Right and Left is useful for classifying political institutions, it is a good deal less so for classifying economic policies. Indeed, Peter

Temin has argued convincingly that, above and beyond their often super-ficial labels, post-Depression governments shared a very similar economic programme whose pillars were essentially socialist.[27]

The role of the state was therefore undergoing radical transformation, a process that economists call a 'change of regime'. The idea that the gold parity would be defended whatever the cost no longer was credible. The most striking example of this change of regime was provided by the United Kingdom, which, after championing the return to the gold standard in the immediate post-war years, opted for devaluation in 1931 almost without a struggle; whereas it was other countries, above all France and its satellites, that dug in to defend convertibility.

It is interesting to note, however, that while there was undeniably a change of regime in the government's role, there was no accompanying, conscious adoption of an innovative payment technology. In other words, the fiat standard still lay in the future. This shows us that that payment technologies succeed one another more as the consequence of an accumu-lation of micro-decisions, often taken under the pressure of events, than as a result of a strategic design. Three facts can be adduced to support this view.

First, the gold exchange standard was not explicitly abandoned because of the Great Depression. Although there were successive rounds of devalu-ations, many of them competitive, and the share of reserves assets held in the form of foreign currency diminished appreciably, the main central banks continued to use the gold parity as the reference for their action. In the United Kingdom, despite the suspension of gold payment in 1931, an exchange-rate stabilization fund was established the following year to prevent the pound from floating freely. A similar fund was created in the United States in 1934, in the context, however, of full restoration of the dollar convertibility to meet requests from central banks at the new price of $35 per ounce, the benchmark of the Bretton Woods system after the Second World War. And in 1936 the Americans, British and French reached a tripartite agreement pledging reciprocal convertibility at prede-termined prices.[28] The increasing recourse to foreign-exchange controls, which became the norm after the Second World War and indeed were institutionalized in the treaty establishing the International Monetary Fund, was justified by the aim of reconciling preservation of the gold parity with monetary policy's new tasks. But by now this was a gold system in which gold played a very limited role. The Cunliffe Committee had already recommended that gold coins be withdrawn from circulation, in order to confine transfers of precious metals to the central bank circuit. This was a way to compress the demand for gold and to attenuate the deflationary impact of the restoration of the gold standard. The recommendation was implemented in 1925, when the conversion of banknotes into gold was limited to transactions in amounts exceeding 400 ounces of gold. In subsequent years the principle was adopted by many other countries, and it was perfected in the United States, which as part of the measures to cope with the Depression not only banned the circulation of gold coins but also prohibited private individuals from holding them.[29]

Second, the new margins created by the abandonment of the resumption rule and by the limitations gradually imposed on the freedom of capital movements were exploited with what may strike us as surprising moderation. Throughout the 1930s, in no country was there an aggressive expansion of the monetary aggregates or of the budget deficit. Eichengreen and Sussman identify two factors that may have contributed to this moderation. In the first place, the Keynesian ideas that we take for granted nowadays had just been sketched out and were far from dominant. The change of regime in the 1930s involved the microeconomic more than the macroeconomic sphere. As Temin points out, the new regime was not Keynesian in either form or substance, since the governments that took over during the Depression were grappling primarily with structural problems, on which monetary policy had little bearing.[30] In addition, memories of the post-war hyperinflations were still too vivid for the authorities to yield to the temptation of monetary experiments.

Lastly, the operating arrangements with which central banks managed their liabilities remained unchanged throughout the 1930s. The sole exception was Sweden, which, under the influence of Wicksell's theories, adopted a monetary policy aimed at stabilizing the price level. But Sweden was, precisely, an exception. Elsewhere, central banks continued to follow the old rules and to employ the same instruments.[31] If the changes set in motion by the Great War and reinforced by the Depression were altering the ability of the representative state to produce confidence in the currency and in its circulation, a series of conceptual, institutional and operational adjustments were still needed for the transition to inconvertibility.

5.3 CENTRAL BANKS BETWEEN AUTONOMY AND SUBMISSION

The relationship between central banks and governments (in the European sense of the 'executive') has been immersed in a 'field of tension' from the very first phases of the evolution of central banks. The reason is obvious. When a payment technology becomes universal, its regulation automatically becomes a political question because it has consequences for all holders of money – potentially the whole political corps of a state. In the preceding chapters we have seen that central banks arose precisely when credit-based payment technologies began to spread beyond the narrow circle of merchants, as a guarantee against the risk of monetary abuse. Any action taken by a central bank, regardless of its motivations and its aims, is therefore, inevitably, a political action.

Reviewing the question of convertible banknotes, in Chapter 3 we saw that the origin of one of the oldest central banks, the Bank of England, lay in an attempt to impose a limit, under the control of the legislative power, on the monetary powers of the executive (a constitutional monarch in the case in question). However, this mechanism can function only on certain conditions. One is that the state is not ruled by an authoritarian sovereign able to dominate the other powers of the state. This was the case in France under Napoleon I, and it was he who first argued that a central bank 'too' autonomous of executive power was politically unacceptable.[32] A second is that there is not excessive concurrence of views between the executive and the legislative power concerning the priorities of political action. In wartime, when the very survival of the state may be at stake, or in cases of late industrialization, where there is a broad consensus on the need for a conscious effort on the part of the state to accelerate economic growth, there is no room for discussing the fine points of what is the most suitable degree of autonomy for the central bank in monetary management.

It is hardly surprising, then, that the question of the autonomy of the institution charged with regulating money was clearly raised for the first time in England after the Napoleonic Wars, that is to say, in a country that already had a long parliamentary tradition and had passed through a national emergency. The question was raised by David Ricardo, the most eminent English economist of the early nineteenth century. In his *Plan for the Establishment of a National Bank*, Ricardo observed:

> It is said that Government could not be safely entrusted with the power of issuing paper money; that it would almost certainly abuse it . . . There would, I confess, be great danger of this, if Government – that is to say, the ministers – were themselves to be entrusted with the power of issuing paper money. But I propose to lace this trust in the hands of Commissioners, not removable from their official situation but by a vote of one or both Houses of Parliament. I propose also to prevent all intercourse between these Commissioners and ministers, by forbidding any species of money transaction between them. The Commissioners should never, on any pretense, lend money to Government, nor in the slightest degree be under its control or influence . . . If Government wanted money, it should be obliged to raise it in the legitimate way; by taxing the people; by the issue and sale of exchequer bills; by funded loans, or by borrowing from any of the numerous banks which might exist in the country; but in no case should it be allowed to borrow from those, who have the power of creating money.[33]

In this remarkable passage we already find three pillars of the modern principle of central bank autonomy as formulated, for example, in the Maastricht Treaty, which laid the foundations of the European System of Central Banks in 1992, namely: institutional separation between the power to spend and the power to create money; prohibition of monetary financing of the government budget; and *ex post* political accountability of those entrusted with monetary management.[34]

In Ricardo's time, however, the idea of nationalizing the central bank had few supporters. Considering the weakness of liberal political institutions in most of Europe, most observers felt that a private institution subject to the control of its shareholders and bound by its charter to maximize profit offered more effective protection against the risk of abuse of convertible banknotes on the part of the government.

One might expect that with the spread of bank money and gradual recognition of the function performed by the central bank in the public interest, a lively debate ensued on the principle of autonomy. This was not the case, however. While there was certainly no lack of clashes between the central bank and the government over discount policy in practically all the countries that had instituted strong, centralized banks of issue, the question never held centre stage, nor did it draw the attention of academia. Probably, this was due to the vast consensus that the rules of the gold standard enjoyed among the politically active classes; and in fact, as far as the status of central banks is concerned, the years from the 1870s to the First World War can be considered a phase of independence from governments based on some fundamental rules of conduct, such as those of the gold standard.[35]

The real turning-point in central bank–government relations, as in many other fields, was the First World War. However great the central bank's autonomy in the decades before the war, it was bound to diminish once the decision was made not to finance the war effort with extraordinary taxation (and all the belligerents took this route, albeit in different ways). Central banks were asked to 'pre-finance' war spending by subscribing huge volumes of short-term Treasury bills. Avoiding this commitment was impossible. Although the Governor of the Bank of England, Walter Cunliffe, refused to sign a declaration submitted to him by Prime Minister Lloyd George pledging to support the government's directives to the utmost, after a month of intense political skirmishing he was forced to issue a communiqué of roughly the same tenor so as not to jeopardize the Bank's formal autonomy.[36] The Americans, always distrustful of the United Kingdom's 'informal path' to central banking, preferred to use legislation. In 1918 Congress passed the Overman Act, empowering the President to impose his decisions on all independent governmental agencies, including the Federal Reserve System.[37] Similar episodes also occurred in the other belligerent countries.[38]

The bill for the monetary upheaval caused by the war came due as soon as the fighting ceased, and it now became convenient again to invoke the principle of autonomy in order to facilitate the monetary stabilization that was a necessary prelude to the return to gold. Among the resolutions adopted at the Brussels international conference of 1920 was the following recommendation: 'Banks, and especially Banks of Issue, should be freed from political pressure and should be conducted solely on the lines of prudent finance.'[39]

The text went on to recommend the creation of central banks in countries that still did not have one. Behind the monetary recommendations of the Brussels conference and those of the Genoa conference two years later, which took up and strengthened the earlier positions, was Montagu Norman, the powerful Governor of the Bank of England. Norman had adamantine convictions concerning the role of central banks and the need for them to be suprapolitical institutions, as we can see from the following passage, drawn from his private correspondence:

> Central Banking is young and experimental and has no tradition: it may last and may develop, or its usefulness, to fill a short post-war need and no more, may soon come to an end. On the one hand its sphere is limited by the qualification that no Central Bank can be greater than its own State – the creature greater than the creator. On the other hand, a Central Bank should acquire by external help (as in some ex-enemy countries) or by internal recognition (as in France) a certain freedom or independence within, and perhaps without, its own State. By such means alone can real co-operation be made possible. I cannot define the position thus acquired but it should surely permit a Bank to 'nag' its own Government even in public and to decide on questions on other than political grounds.[40]

The principle of autonomy in this very robust formulation, which Norman 'preached in season and out of season',[41] was inserted into all the stabilization plans upheld by the League of Nations as a prerequisite for obtaining international loans. Even before the Genoa conference the principle had been placed at the centre of monetary reforms in Austria and Hungary. Norman made it a rule not to have relations with countries that lacked an autonomous central bank, and on those grounds he refused to visit Canada and in 1926 resolutely opposed the Italian government's attempts to get an international loan. But Norman's zeal was not shared by the other dominant figure of post-war central banking, Benjamin Strong, who had learned from the Federal Reserve's wartime experience how fragile was the protection offered by a central bank's formal statute when there was a convergence of political interests in favour of a lax monetary policy. In their private correspondence, Strong had warned Norman that the Federal Reserve could never openly oppose the government's policy and that autonomy de facto took precedence over autonomy *de jure*.[42]

In the case of the Italian loan, Strong openly defended Mussolini's government, contending that the Fascist government had displayed far more zeal in the work of stabilization than what any autonomous central bank could have obtained. In reality, Italy's 1926 banking law had substantially enhanced the autonomy of the Bank of Italy. The new legislation unified the authority over the note issue, assigned the powers of banking supervision to the Bank of Italy and abolished extraordinary issues in favour of the Treasury, which had been introduced as a wartime emergency measure. Advances outstanding when the new law came into force would be repaid with the capital gains on foreign exchange reserves made possible by the return of the exchange rate of the lira to 'Quota 90' (that is, 90 to the pound sterling).[43] If this was not a complete implementation of the Genoa recommendations, it came within an inch of it. Although Strong never mentioned the new law, he ultimately succeeded in winning over Norman and the rest of the banking community and Italy received its stabilization loan towards the end of 1927.

Notwithstanding Strong's moderation, Norman's version of the autonomy principle gained a large following and was applied in overhauling the monetary arrangements of numerous countries, even those that did not need to turn to the League of Nations for stabilization assistance. For several years central banks enjoyed such widespread popularity that the early 1920s has even been called their 'golden age'.[44] However, this popularity was to some extent self-interested and would be paid for dearly before long. In fact, if central banks' autonomy under the gold standard had been a little-remarked consequence of the operation of the rules of the game, now the autonomy principle was invoked precisely to restore those rules. When it became clear that the attempt to restore the gold standard, even in the softer form of the gold exchange standard, had ended in an unprecedented failure, central banks had to shoulder most of the blame. Although there is surely an element of exaggeration in Harold James's judgement that 'the peculiar agony of central Europe followed from the combination of strong national banking traditions with new Anglo-Saxon principles of central banking',[45] it is nonetheless true that the Depression was perceived in many countries as the fruit of central bankers' inability to foresee the deflationary impact of their policies.[46]

The outcome was a sudden weakening of the central banks' position. The immediate impact was noticed above all in the countries that had benefited from the League of Nations stabilization loans, which had regarded the autonomy principle more as something forced on them by

international creditors bent upon keeping the monetary lever out of their
debtors' hands than as an institutional advance. Contributing to this
interpretation was the appointment of foreigners to important positions
in the central banks established or reformed under the aegis of the League
of Nations. In a few short years, all the new central banks lost their legally
protected status. But the winds of change hit the creditor countries as well.
Even Montagu Norman, the proud advocate of the autonomy principle,
had to submit to political control. He did this in the British manner, with
an informal statement before Parliament:

> I assure Ministers that if they will make known to us through the appropriate
> channels what it is they wish us to do in the furtherance of their policies, they
> will at all times find us willing with good will and loyalty to do what they direct
> us as though we were under legal compulsion.[47]

The Federal Reserve too fell victim to the wave of distrust of central
banks. The Thomas Amendment to the Agricultural Adjustment Act of
1933 empowered the administration, in the person of the Secretary of the
Treasury, to carry out open-market operations in government securities
without the approval of the central bank, and the Emergency Banking Act
of the same year revived the President's power to assume direct control
over credit policy in an emergency.[48]

In Italy, the 1936 Banking Law, which followed the devaluation of the
lira and came two years after the introduction of the monopoly of the
foreign exchange market – two measures that marked Italy's definitive
abandonment of the gold exchange standard – considerably reduced the
margins of autonomy that the 1926 law had granted the central bank.
The most important changes to the legislative framework concerned the
reintroduction of extraordinary advances to the Treasury, which could
now be granted without limit, 'subject to agreement between the Minister
of the Treasury and the Governor of the Bank of Italy', and the provision
for preferential interest rates in order to facilitate the placement of government securities. As regards credit policy, the new law transferred direct
control over banking supervision from the Bank of Italy to an inspectorate under the control of an interministerial committee chaired by the head
of government. Although the fact that the inspectorate itself was chaired
by the Governor of the Bank of Italy safeguarded some degree of operating autonomy in banking supervision, on the whole the new legislation
marked a decided change of course by the Fascist government in monetary
and financial affairs.[49] The same years saw similar changes introduced in
France and in some minor countries.[50] Norman's dream of an apolitical
central bank able to impose its viewpoint on the government was dead.
In the new era, Ralph Hawtrey observed: 'it is not the independence of

the central bank but its technical competence and insight that will gain a hearing for its protests'.[51]

It was within this institutional framework that countries tackled the problem of financing the new world war, during which virtually no tension erupted in public between central bankers and governments. Essentially, in every country at war, the government resorted to a series of direct interventions on the foreign exchange and credit markets, using the central banks as an operating arm. When the United States entered the war in 1941, it was made obligatory for the Federal Reserve to purchase unlimited quantities of government securities to help the war effort. The other belligerents did no less.[52]

5.4   THE FIAT STANDARD

The international monetary agreements reached in Bretton Woods in 1944 were the birth certificate of the fiat standard. This may seem paradoxical, since the Bretton Woods agreements envisaged not only a grid of fixed exchange rates between participant countries, but also an indirect link to gold, maintaining the dollar's convertibility at the price of $35 per ounce, set when the United States returned to the gold exchange standard back in 1934. On closer inspection, however, there is no paradox at all, or this is an apparent one at most.

The authorities of the countries that emerged victorious from the Second World War had drawn three lessons from the monetary developments of the period before the war. The first was that the gold standard was obsolete as a mechanism for anchoring monetary systems, being too rigid, and therefore had to be avoided at all costs. Keynes and Harry Dexter White, that is to say the two principal negotiators of what became the postwar international monetary system, shared this approach.[53] Second, a regime of floating exchange rates, free to respond to the pressures of supply and demand, was equally pernicious and had to be limited with every means available. The main job of the international monetary architecture was to foster a swift recovery of trade, and the consensus view blamed the collapse of international trade in the 1930s on floating exchange rates, or at least on the competitive devaluations to which the major countries had resorted; for example, Ragnar Nurkse's above-mentioned report took the undesirability of floating exchange rates for granted, containing only a few short sections and scant empirical data on the question, without this drawing critical comment at the time. Third, state intervention in the economy had to be extended from the microeconomic sphere, where most of the effort had gone in the 1930s, to the macroeconomic sphere, in accordance with the rise of Keynesianism. Monetary policy was demoted to being just one among the various tools available to achieve economic policy's objectives, above all full employment.

The architecture of the system that took shape at Bretton Woods faithfully reflects these three lessons, as is testified to by an interesting terminological inversion. Up to then the word 'independence' had been used to describe the central bank's position vis-à-vis the government. As we have seen, its independence had been a simple corollary of the working of the gold standard or, later, a means of returning to gold. Now, instead, independence referred to the relationship between each government's economic policies and the set of supranational rules. The fear, explicit particularly in Keynes and in all the positions taken by the British delegation, was that the international rules could be a constraint on the conduct of 'enlightened' national economic policies. And, in fact, except for the commitment to restore the external convertibility of national currencies in commercial transactions, the text agreed at Bretton Woods contains no reference to rules of sound national economic policy conduct. The key idea is that national economic policy must remain sovereign, not subject to conditions.[54] This is why, among the written and unwritten rules of the Bretton Woods system, Ronald McKinnon awards pre-eminence to the following: 'National macroeconomic autonomy: each member government to pursue its own price level and employment objectives unconstrained by a common nominal anchor or price rule.'[55]

As to the exchange rate regime, while the Articles of Agreement did contemplate fixed parities of the participating currencies vis-à-vis the dollar, they gave national authorities leeway to alter the original parity within a margin of 10 per cent without external approval.[56] The drafters nevertheless did not offer any definition of fundamental disequilibrium. As Harry Dexter White later clarified, this was not by accident:

> In the drafting of the Articles of Agreement no attempt was made to define fundamental disequilibrium. This, as we know, was not an oversight. It was generally agreed that a satisfactory definition would be difficult to formulate. A too rigid or narrow interpretation would be dangerous; one too loose or general would be useless in providing a criterion for changes in currency parities. It was felt too that the subject matter was so important, and the necessity for a crystallization of a harmonious view so essential that it were best left for discussion and formulation by the Fund.[57]

Thus, in the intention of the negotiators, especially the British, the system of fixed but adjustable rates would serve primarily as a mechanism for coordinating currency fluctuations, that is, as an antidote to competitive valuations, rather than as an external constraint on the conduct of macroeconomic policies, as had happened under the gold standard and then under the gold exchange standard until the resumption rule was abandoned. This interpretation is corroborated by the role that the Bretton Woods design assigned to foreign exchange controls. Whereas in the pre-Depression monetary systems recourse to exchange controls would have been considered a violation of the rules of the game, it now became the codified norm. The underlying idea was that the independence of national economic policies could not be ensured if full legitimacy were granted to what Keynes called 'flight capital'.[58] The segmentation of national financial systems was, that is, a way of protecting them against the destabilizing speculation that in Nurkse's opinion had undermined the working of the gold exchange standard. To borrow a metaphor from later macroeconomics, specifically Robert Mundell's work on the effectiveness of monetary policy in an open economy,[59] the 'inconsistent trio' of discretionary policies, fixed exchange rates and full capital mobility was recomposed by totally sacrificing its third component and, if need be, its second too; an excess of zeal which speaks volumes about what was the most important element of the new architecture.

Two other important institutional changes in the years immediately preceding and following the inauguration of the new international monetary system completed the framework of the nascent fiat standard. The first was legislation that incorporated the new objectives of economic policy, assigning monetary role an ancillary role. The second was the nationalization of central banks on a vast scale.

The years just after the Second World War saw the definitive acceptance, at least until the 1980s, of the Keynesian concept of aggregate demand management for the purpose of stabilizing the business cycle. The objective of full employment also made its appearance in legislation. In the United States and Australia, for example, laws were passed making full employment a primary objective of economic policy. In the United Kingdom, Canada, Sweden and South Africa, the laws referred to a high and stable level of employment and income.[60] In Italy and some other countries, the reference to the protection of labour and full employment was inserted into the constitution. Quite apart from countercyclical policy, in many of the countries coming out of the war the demands of reconstruction and the need to lift the pace of economic growth forced the government to make a coordinated effort to support investment and consumption. In addition, some countries emerged from the war as planned economies, with the political and economic liberalism of the early 1920s supplanted by socialist principles. In this context, central banks could only play a minor role in orchestras whose conductors were sceptical of monetary policy's potentialities. The prevailing idea was that, owing to the lag with which it produced its effects and, more in general, the low elasticity of aggregate demand to variations in interest rates, the central banks' task had to be limited to keeping interest rates at the lowest levels compatible with external equilibrium, leaving the lion's share of demand management to fiscal policy.[61] The influential Radcliffe Report in the UK, although dating later, is emblematic of the attitudes already prevailing in official and academic circles towards the end of the 1940s:

> Monetary policy, as we have conceived it, cannot be envisaged as a form of economic strategy which pursues its own independent objectives. It is part of a country's economic policy as a whole, and must be planned as such.[62]

Consistently with this approach, some countries, such as Canada, Australia and New Zealand, amended their central bank's statutes to incorporate the new economic policy objectives.[63] Others passed legislation to establish the framework for the conduct of economic policy, including its monetary policy component. Still others instituted specific committees under government control, such as France's National Credit Council (1945) and Italy's Interministerial Committee for Credit and Savings (1947) and Interministerial Committee for Economic Policy (1967), to ensure effective policy-making coordination.

It was in this cultural climate that there occurred the final step in the central bank's more than century-long transformation from a private institution whose only binding objective was to maximize profits for the shareholders into a governmental body assigned the task of monetary management in the public interest. Before 1936 only a handful of central banks, specifically those of Russia, Bulgaria, Australia and China, were state-owned. Between 1936 and 1945 the central banks of Denmark, Canada, New Zealand, Bolivia and Guatemala were nationalized, while new, publicly owned central banks were founded in Poland, Ireland, Ethiopia and other minor countries. But the height of the wave of nationalizations came immediately after the Second World War, when it extended to major industrial countries such as France, Germany, the United Kingdom and the Netherlands.

The same period also saw the nationalization of the central banks of Norway, Czechoslovakia, Yugoslavia, Hungary, Romania and Spain, and the creation of publicly controlled central banks in many former colonies.[64] Among the main central banks, only the Federal Reserve and the Bank of Italy were not nationalized, confirming the many similarities in the evolution of American and Italian central banking. In both cases, this was due to the specific nature of the institutional changes introduced in the mid-1930s. As we have seen, from its foundation the Federal Reserve had been conceived of as a central bank charged with tasks in the public interest; making profits and competing with commercial banks were not part of its mission.

The 1935 Banking Act had strengthened these characteristics without modifying the ownership structure. Pursuant to the Act, the Board of Governors of the Federal Reserve System was flanked by a new body, the Federal Open Market Committee, composed of the seven Board members and the presidents of five of the 12 Reserve Banks serving on a rotating basis (except for the President of the Federal Reserve Bank of New York, a permanent member). At first sight the change may seem to have been designed to increase the weight of the 'technicians' (the Reserve Bank presidents) vis-à-vis the 'politicians' (the Board members, all appointed by the President of the United States). In reality, and as its name indicates, the new body was entrusted with managing open-market operations, which had become the main instrument of monetary policy and until then had been the exclusive preserve of the individual Reserve Bank presidents. Apart from its form, the change was so radical that an effort was made to temper its effects by replacing within the Board the Secretary of the Treasury and the Comptroller of the Currency, until then *ex officio* members, with two government-appointed members, and lengthening the term of all Board members from 10 to 14 years so as to give them a longer time horizon than that of the US presidents appointing them.[65]

In Italy, too, the banking law issued in 1936 explicitly recognized the objectives of public interest pursued by the central bank. Accordingly, the Bank of Italy, which the new law transformed into a public-law institution, was prohibited from having banking relationships with non-bank customers, so as to reduce its potential conflicts of interest with commercial banks.[66]

By virtue of their particular institutional status, which for some time had already made them an economic policy organ of the executive, both the Bank of Italy and the Federal Reserve were in a position soon after the war to be granted greater autonomy, bucking the trend of events in most of the other industrial countries. As part of the monetary stabilization of 1947, Italy reinstated the rule that extraordinary advances to the Treasury had to be authorized case by case with an ad hoc law of Parliament. In addition, a ceiling equal to 14 per cent of public expenditure was set on the Treasury's overdraft facility with the Bank of Italy. In the United States, the Federal Reserve reached an agreement with the Treasury under which the central bank was no longer obligated to stabilize the prices of government securities. In addition to institutional changes, the nascent fiat standard also required a series of operational adjustments to enable central banks, with their new tasks, to achieve better control over the money and credit aggregates and market interest rates and, through them, over the variables of the real economy.

Up to the end of the First World War, the monetary policy of the central banks had consisted de facto in regulating discounts by modifying the discount rate they charged their own customers. However, the discount channel had been drying up as early as the turn of the century. The supply of private securities to be rediscounted was dwindling, since bank mergers had created an oligarchy of structurally liquid banks able to meet their customers' needs with overdraft facilities. As a result, commercial bills were gradually falling out of use in virtually every country, while a new short-term security was gaining ground, the Treasury bill, whose role was definitively established with the war. Moreover, the effect of changes in the discount rate on the balance of payments and, through it, on the exchange rate was also weakening. Against this background, some major commercial banks began to carry out direct sales and purchases of securities on the market. In truth, in the second half of the 1800s the Bank of England had begun making two types of transaction similar to what we now would call open-market operations: it borrowed on the market and made spot sales of unredeemable government securities (consols) counterbalanced by forward purchases. Analogous transactions were carried out by the Reichsbank as well.[67] In both cases, however, the transactions were sporadic adjuncts to discount rate changes.

The First World War saw generalized recourse to the central banks in order to finance military expenditure, mainly in the form of forced sales to them of short-term government securities. After the war this experience brought some discredit on open-market operations, for it was suspected that, in the best of cases, they cloaked the intention of sterilizing inflows and outflows of gold once the gold standard was restored, and at worst, a forced monetization of the public debt accumulated during the conflict. Thus, for example, upon its reorganization the Reichsbank was forbidden to carry out open-market operations. The same happened to the Bank of France, whose statute did not allow it to buy and sell government securities for own account.[68] At the start of the 1930s the Federal Reserve successfully commenced to carry out open-market operations in order to increase the liquidity of the banking system without using changes in the discount rate and to guarantee the orderly placement of new issues of government securities. The Bank of England adopted similar policies in those same years. The example of the two most important central banks of the time caused a reversal in the prevailing attitude towards the new instrument. In 1933 the Reichsbank's power to carry out open-market operations was restored. In France, a 1938 decree empowered the central bank to make purchases and sales of governments securities with a maturity of up to two years: 'in order to influence the volume of credit and regulate the money market'. Other countries followed suit, and by the end of the Second World War open-market operations had become the chief instrument for regulating bank liquidity.

However, fine-tuning liquidity presupposed the definition of operating objectives or at least of benchmark indicators, a problem heightened in the interwar years by the uncertain fate of the gold parity. The indicator chosen by the Federal Reserve in the late 1920s, significant precisely because of the pioneering use the US central bank was then making of open-market operations, was the level of Federal Reserve System member banks' borrowed reserves. On the basis of experience, Benjamin Strong had determined that a level close to $50 million represented a neutral stance for monetary policy.[69] But after the banking crises of the early 1930s, American banks began to hold significant amounts of reserves in excess of the required minimum, so that attention shifted to 'free reserves', consisting in the difference between excess reserves and borrowed reserves. Controlling excess reserves soon proved to be quite difficult, so much so that the legislation of 1933–35 empowered the Federal Reserve to change member banks' reserve requirements: 'in order to prevent injurious credit expansion or contraction'. This rule marked the transformation of compulsory reserves from a prudential instrument designed to safeguard banking stability into a monetary policy instrument; an instrument that the Federal Reserve Board used on a vast scale in 1936–37, with two successive increases whose purpose was to neutralize some $3 billion of excess reserves held by the banking system. The Board justified its action in the following terms:

> So long as member banks had a volume of reserves far in excess of legal requirements, the customary instruments of credit policy, open-market operations and discount rates, were wholly ineffective . . . Through the elimination of about $3000 million of excess reserves, the Federal Reserve System was brought into closer contact with the market and was placed in a position where sales or purchases in the open market could tighten or ease credit conditions in accordance with the public interest.[70]

The first central banks to adopt the new instrument of monetary policy, before the outbreak of the war, were those of Mexico, Sweden, Australia, New Zealand, Ecuador and Costa Rica. Reserve requirements were introduced in Italy in 1947 and in countless other countries in the following years. In the United Kingdom, always reluctant to use instruments not produced by agreements or tacit accords, they were adopted in 1958. With typical British understatement, a Bank of England press release announced a new interbank agreement by virtue of which: 'the Bank of

England will, if need be, restrict the liquidity of the banking system by calling for special deposits'.[71]

With reserve requirements, direct control of a bank balance sheet item, in this case a liability item, entered the panoply of monetary policy instruments. Two decades later, towards the end of the 1950s, it was the turn of a control operating on the asset side, that is, the ceiling on the growth in bank loans. In general, the ceiling took the form of a fixed limit, based on the amount of each bank's outstanding loans at a given date.[72] Later, use was made of more sophisticated forms based on a growth path, planned on an annual basis, for total loans. All the leading central banks used this instrument between the 1960s and 1980s, especially as part of measures to protect the currency against speculative attacks. The tool was considered brutal and cumbersome and never enjoyed widespread popularity owing to its undesired consequences for the competitiveness of the credit market and its discouraging effects on financial innovation. Nonetheless, many countries continued to use it, however unwillingly, until the wave of liberalization of the late 1980s.[73]

5.5 THE CRISIS OF THE FIAT STANDARD AND THE ISSUE OF MONETARY POLICY'S CREDIBILITY

The post-war monetary set-up had thus been conceived for an indeterminate number of potentially independent currencies. The quantity of each currency in circulation was no longer to be automatically determined by the quantity of gold available, nor were exchange rates to be tied to immutable gold parities – quite a leap from Irving Fisher's strong aversion to legal tender just a few decades earlier. What is most surprising when we look back on the monetary affairs of those years is that none of the monetary system's architects addressed the problem of confidence. What guarantee was there that the new payment technology would not be abused? The Articles of Agreement of the International Monetary Fund, the closest thing to an international monetary constitution ever produced, use the word 'confidence' only to state that one of the Fund's purposes is 'to give confidence to members . . . thus providing them opportunity to correct maladjustments in their balance of payments', a far cry from supporting the confidence of holders of money against the risk of abuse. Nor do the writings of Keynes or White in those years, so farsighted in other respects, contain a single passage at least posing the problem of confidence.

Two factors probably explain this silence. For one thing, memories of the monetary upheaval that had followed the First World War and of the

disastrous consequences of competitive devaluations of the 1930s were
still vivid. The architects of the new monetary order must have thought
it inconceivable that political leaders would want to repeat those experiences, all the more now that a convincing, tested theory of economic
policy management under mature capitalism – Keynesian theory – was
available. The monetary stabilizations of 1946–49, including that in Italy,
brutal yet effective, appeared to corroborate the validity of that approach.
In addition, the Second World War had ended in a climate of widespread
optimism about the abilities of the democratic system, victorious over
dictatorships, to correct its own shortcomings and safeguard the general
interest. The mission of government was to promote the general will; safeguarding the national currency was considered one of the fundamental
tasks of the democratic order.[74]

Nevertheless, the monetary order inaugurated at Bretton Woods did
work, becoming the most long-lived system, and the most successful in
terms of economic growth and the expansion of trade, in the monetary
history to this day. Paradoxically, however, unless we wish to distort
the facts we cannot ascribe that success to the system's original design,
because the international monetary system that took shape soon proved
to be very different from what its architects had imagined. The most direct
way to grasp the difference between the blueprint and reality is to examine
the evolution of exchange rates. After a general realignment of the currencies of the European countries and of those of the United Kingdom's
main trading partners, revisions of parities occurred very rarely. France
devalued in 1957–58 and again in 1969, the United Kingdom in 1967,
while Germany revalued in 1961 and 1969. That is the whole story as far
as the developed countries are concerned. The dollar remained anchored
to the gold price of $35 per ounce as long as the exchange rate agreement
was in effect, and the exchange rate of the Japanese yen likewise remained
fixed at 360 yen to the dollar notwithstanding the great transformation of
the Japanese economy. In essence, the system was a fixed exchange-rate
regime in which the dollar functioned as a pivot vis-à-vis gold.[75]

In this de facto set-up, only American economic policy, monetary
policy in particular, was truly 'independent'. The policy of every other
country was subject to the constraint of maintenance of the national
currency's par value in dollars. For roughly two decades, three factors
ensured the consistency of the whole. In the first place, the main countries
were willing to renounce economic policy-making independence. In a
study of the reaction functions of the monetary authorities between 1950
and 1967, Michael Michaely finds that the domestic channels of monetary
base creation were closely correlated with the external channel during that
period, while the discount rate was inversely correlated with changes in

the reserves, two clear indications that the monetary adjustment mechanism was allowed to operate correctly. On the fiscal policy front, by contrast, the budget balance did not generally correspond either to payments imbalances or to internal imbalances, but conflicts between the conduct of fiscal policy and monetary policy were nevertheless very rare.[76] Secondly, American monetary policy exploited the degree of freedom it had been granted to stabilize the price level, thus anchoring the entire system. Lastly, unlike other countries, after a period of payments surpluses that produced what was called the 'dollar shortage', the United States accepted a structural disequilibrium in its balance of payments that served to fuel an expansion in international liquidity, thereby preventing the rigidity of exchange rates from imparting an endemic deflationary impulse to the world economy.

Why did the monetary authorities of the main countries consider it necessary to distance themselves so markedly from the Bretton Woods design while respecting its form? The only plausible explanation is that they clung to fixed exchange rates for the same reason that they had bound themselves to the gold standard: to give credibility to their action. Fixed exchange rates were, in essence, a symbol of their commitment to conduct sound policies. The most interesting thing is that this symbol was defended as far as possible even in countries, like Germany and the Netherlands, whose currencies tended to appreciate, and that this defence took place in a context in which, because of foreign exchange controls, it was not the financial markets that imposed discipline, as had been the case under the gold standard. It was a question of an unpremeditated response to the problem of confidence that the architects of Bretton Woods had failed to address. The keystone of the mechanism was American economic policy, which reconciled low inflation with a production of liquidity sufficient to fuel the global expansion of official reserves.[77] However, many other factors contributed to its success, from the stability of money demand in the United States, which facilitated the running of monetary policy there, to the wage moderation that characterized the advanced economies until the 1960s and the rapid growth in productivity and national income. In this favourable environment, the commercial convertibility of the individual national currencies was restored in the late 1950s and, thanks in part to this, international capital mobility began to recover.

However, the fixed exchange rate regime to which the Bretton Woods agreements had given rise vanished abruptly at the start of the 1970s. In retrospect, two symptoms of its imminent collapse were the devaluation of the British pound in 1967 and the failure of the 'gold pool', a group of central banks that cooperated to stabilize the market price of gold in order to prevent an unduly sharp rise in the market price with respect to the official price from creating embarrassment for the American authorities. The reasons for the collapse of the Bretton Woods regime are still debated by economic historians. Most of the literature identifies the recovery of capital mobility due to the development of a vast offshore market (the so-called Eurodollar market) and the fragility of an arrangement in which the sole source of international liquidity was America's ever-larger balance-of-payments deficits (the origin of what was called the 'Triffin dilemma'[78]) as the chief determinants of the unsustainability of a regime in which exchange rates, though fixed in the short term, remained adjustable in the long run.[79] Yet on close inspection these appear to have been no more than secondary causes, if not actually consequences of more radical changes in the political and economic context. On the whole, the gold standard had been able to withstand the impact of high capital mobility, and if we look closely at the data it is doubtful that the Triffin dilemma holds up as an explanation for the problems that worried the US authorities towards the end of the 1960s.[80] The fact is that post-war economic recovery in the West, and not only the West, was based on a 'social pact' that called for wage moderation in exchange for high investment and an expansion of social expenditure by the state. Testifying to the pact is the sharp increase in public social transfer payments, whereas in the 1930s the state's role in the economy had grown mainly through the increase in spending on infrastructure (Table 5.4). In the advanced countries, population ageing gradually increased the demand for social services.[81] At the same time, the transformation of the advanced countries from agricultural and manufacturing into service-based economies accelerated (Table 5.5).

Beginning in the late 1960s, this transformation was reflected in sharply slowing productivity growth. In the new context of weaker economic growth and larger trade deficits, honouring the commitment to defend the exchange rate would have meant openly repudiating the social pact that had guaranteed prosperity and growth up to then. Heightened capital mobility and the development of 'hot money' only made the structural change more evident (and painful). What the advanced countries were now seeking was the very independence of national economic policy that they had renounced two decades earlier. But, as the British saw in 1967, this could not be attained without giving up a fixed exchange rate. If the system's pivotal country had remained untouched by the problem, the regime still could have been saved. McKinnon observes:

> If the US Federal Reserve System had continued to anchor the common price level, and if the Americans had not asserted their legal right to adjust the dollar exchange rate as promised by the Bretton Woods Articles, the fixed dollar exchange parities could have continued indefinitely once the residual convertibility to gold was terminated.[82]

Table 5.4   The expansion of public sector expenditure (% of GDP)

	1870	1913	1960	1998
Total outlays				
Australia	18.3	16.5	21.2	32.9
Belgium		13.8	30.3	49.4
France	12.6	17.0	34.6	54.3
Germany		14.8	32.4	46.9
Italy	11.9	11.1	30.1	49.1
Japan		8.3	17.5	36.9
Netherlands	9.1	9.0	33.7	47.2
Norway	5.9	9.3	29.9	46.9
Sweden	5.7	10.4	31.0	58.5
United Kingdom	9.4	12.7	32.2	40.2
United States	7.3	7.5	27.0	32.8

	1880	1910	1960	1990
Social transfers[1]				
Australia	0.0	1.1	7.4	15.4
Belgium	0.2	0.4	13.1	29.7
France	0.5	0.8	13.4	27.8
Germany	0.5	na	18.1	21.2
Italy	0.0	0.0	13.1	24.5
Japan	0.1	0.2	4.0	16.1
Netherlands	0.3	0.4	11.7	31.7
Norway	1.1	1.2	7.9	23.0
Sweden	0.7	1.0	10.8	21.3
United Kingdom	0.9	1.4	10.2	16.8
United States	0.3	0.6	7.3	16.3

Note: [1] Includes spending on pensions, welfare, unemployment compensation and health by national and local governments.

Source: International Monetary Fund, *World Economic Outlook*, Washington, DC, May 2000.

But this was not to be. In the period 1968–72 producer price inflation in the United States averaged 3.5 per cent, compared with less than 1 per cent in the 15 preceding years. Countries that previously had benefited, through the fixed rate, from the credibility of US monetary policy were now led to tighten their own monetary policy in order to avoid importing inflation, but by so doing they accentuated the strains in the system. The inconsistent trio, tamed at Bretton Woods with a skilful attenuation of the claims of all three of its constituents, had become totally unmanageable.

Table 5.5   *The structure of employment in five leading economies,*
              1900–95

	France	Germany	Japan	United Kingdom	United States
1900					
Goods[1]	74.7	78.9	79.3	56.7	66.8
Agriculture	43.4	39.9	64.8	13.0	38.3
Manufacturing	26.0	28.5	12.4	32.1	21.0
Market services	19.5	15.7	16.6	36.4	27.2
Non-market services	5.8	5.4	4.1	6.9	6.0
1950					
Goods[1]	61.6	66.3	68.9	50.9	43.7
Agriculture	28.0	23.9	43.6	6.4	10.5
Manufacturing	25.8	32.6	18.3	33.9	24.8
Market services	21.9	24.2	26.0	36.6	40.1
Non-market services	16.5	9.5	5.1	12.5	16.2
1973					
Goods[1]	48.0	54.5	53.3	44.8	32.4
Agriculture	10.2	7.2	16.1	3.2	3.2
Manufacturing	26.9	36.5	27.1	32.2	21.9
Market services	29.6	30.8	38.9	38.5	43.9
Non-market services	22.4	14.7	7.8	16.7	23.7
1995					
Goods[1]	30.3	38.4	41.1	26.7	21.8
Agriculture	4.6	2.8	7.3	2.1	1.6
Manufacturing	18.1	27.2	22.5	18.7	13.9
Market services	38.4	41.7	50.1	53.1	52.6
Non-market services	31.3	19.9	8.8	20.2	25.6

Note: [1] Includes agriculture, manufacturing, construction, mining and public utilities.

Source: Nicholas Crafts, 'Globalization and growth in the twentieth century', IMF Working Paper, WP/00/44, March 2000.

The so-called Committee of Twenty, formed after August 1971 to restore an orderly exchange rate regime, quickly realized that the patient was doomed and withdrew in good order.[83]

With the exchange rate agreement dead, profuse use was made of the regained independence to stimulate economic growth, a leading role being assigned to the monetary lever. The events of the early 1970s are a useful reminder of the fragility of the fiat standard: when a vast array of political forces favour lax monetary policy, institutional containment policies can do little, especially after decades of underestimation of the risk of abuse of the currency. Federal Reserve Chairman Arthur Burns, accused years later of being overly complaisant towards the Nixon administration in 1972 and thus sowing the seeds of an inflation that soon spread to the other leading countries, defended himself by arguing that it was impossible for central bankers not to be influenced by the dominant ideas of the day:

> What is unique about our inflation is its stubborn persistence, not the behaviour of central bankers. This persistence . . . reflects the philosophic and political currents of thought that have impinged on economic life since the Great Depression and particularly since the mid-1960s.[84]

Bank of Italy Governor Guido Carli expressed a similar concept in a celebrated passage of his address to the Bank's annual meeting in 1973:

> We asked ourselves then, and continue to do so, whether the Bank of Italy could have refused, or could still refuse, to finance the public sector's deficit by abstaining from exercising the faculty, granted by law, to purchase government securities. Refusal would make it impossible for the Government to pay the salaries of the armed forces, of the judiciary and of civil servants, and the pensions of most citizens. It would give the appearance of being a monetary policy act; in substance it would be a seditious act, which would be followed by a paralysis of the public administration.[85]

Other central bankers, such as Olivier Wormser of France, chose the path of open conflict with the political authorities, but they were pushed aside without much ado and without affecting the course of events in the least.[86]

The consequences of the nearly desperate attempt to redress domestic and international economic conditions – these were the years of the first oil crisis – by resorting to the monetary and fiscal accelerator soon proved disastrous, and are summed up in the ugly neologism coined in those years: stagflation. Figure 5.2 depicts its essential terms: high inflation (almost out of control in some countries), spiralling budget deficits, growing unemployment. Exactly how things came to such a pass is difficult to say. Certainly, an important role was played by the conviction that there existed a solid inverse relationship between the inflation rate and the unemployment rate, as observed empirically for the United Kingdom by Alban W. Phillips in a 1958 study referring to a very long time horizon. The 'Phillips curve' was often adopted, as late as the 1970s, as justification for fine-tuning the economy, even when the concept's scant reliability had become clear. Another important factor was the spread of indexation of

Government budget balance (*)
(*as a percentage of GDP*)

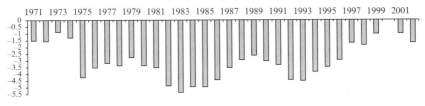

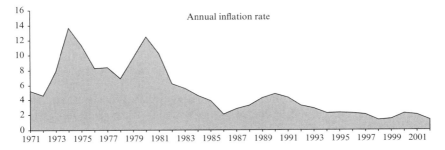

Annual inflation rate

Unemployment rate
(*as a percentage of labour force*)

Note: * Public sector balance.

Source: International Monetary Fund, World Economic Outlook database.

Figure 5.2 *Budget deficit, inflation and unemployment in the G-7 countries*

both wages and securities. From a theoretical perspective, the impact of indexation on equilibrium inflation is ambiguous. In fact, if on the one hand:

> indexation tends to reduce the social costs of inflation, thereby eroding the psychological defenses of money-holders and wage-earners, it also reduces the

government's incentive to use the monetary instrument as a means of levying hidden taxation. But the experience of countries, such as Israel, Brazil and, to a lesser extent, Italy, that relied on indexation in order to cope with the gradual erosion of the real value of their currency leaves little room to doubt that the overall impact on social welfare was negative.[87]

Pulling together the threads of a vast study of the causes of stagflation, Michael Smith reached the harsh verdict: 'Any reasonably plausible explanation . . . will include substantial components of ignorance and error . . . and Government irresponsibility.'[88]

Even more disarming is the report of the US Council of Economic Advisers on 1973. After attempting to trace the causes of the increase in inflation in a setting of rapidly rising unemployment, that body admitted: 'There is no simple explanation for this price behavior, which was the most extraordinary in almost a generation and which confounded the Council and most other economists alike.'[89]

In the history of both economic thought and monetary institutions, stagflation played the same role that in the 1930s fell to the Great Depression: that of indisputable indicator that the existing monetary arrangement was degenerating fast and that the available economic theories offered no ready recipes to put it back into good shape. To save the payment technology based on legal tender, it was necessary to go to the root of the problem and design a credible programme of institutional reform. Against this background, we can understand why the monetary debate, after remaining frozen for decades following the publication of the *General Theory*, experienced an intensification for which there are few precedents.[90] Within the span of a few years the foundations of the fiat standard were called into question and there was even discussion of the advisability of a large-scale return to gold or to some other commodity-based money, an unmistakable sign that the survival of the payment technology produced by the Great Depression was at risk.

A number of distinct schools of thought emerged from the debate on the standard. One argued in favour of restoring some form of convertibility of legal tender into commodities. In the United States, a congressional commission was established to explore the possibility of a return to gold at both national and international level. However, this decidedly retrograde initiative has left only a faint trace in the history of monetary affairs of the past decades.[91] Other prominent scholars proposed mechanisms for anchoring the fiat standard by splitting the means of payment from the unit of account and assigning the latter function to a basket of goods selected in a way designed to discourage the establishment of an effective mechanism of convertibility.[92]

A second school, traceable to Hayek, always a severe critic of the concept of 'managed money' and hence also of the fiat standard, launched a frontal attack on governmental control of money, proposing the total liberalization of the production of money. In reality, the contributions of what became known as the 'free-banking' school are quite heterogeneous. Hayek himself, for example, appears to prefer a monetary regime in which the individual currencies produced by private actors circulate on the basis of exchange rates freely determined by the market, without any convertibility obligation. Lawrence White and David Glasner propose a less radical arrangement, in which each money-producer would be contractually required to guarantee the gold convertibility of its money in a legal regime of unlimited liability. While Kevin Dowd, another prominent member of the school, goes so far as to suggest revising the contractual nature of the bank deposit so as to make it possible for the value of bank money to adjust automatically to the market value of bank assets.[93]

The third school, widely known as the 'monetarist school', was pioneered by the work of Milton Friedman. To avoid the risk of excessive discretion in monetary management, Friedman proposed introducing an iron rule constraining the growth rate of the money supply (or, at the limit, freezing the monetary base). The monetarist proposal found no significant practical application in this extreme version, but it did stimulate the adoption and announcement of annual money supply growth objectives by many central banks, especially those of industrial countries. These targets were often defined as 'intermediate', in that they were functional to the pursuit of the final objective of a given inflation rate (or, in versions still reminiscent of the Keynesian approach, a given rate of growth of nominal income). Hence the term 'two-stage monetary policy', which gained some popularity in the debate on the modus operandi of monetary policy in the 1970s and 1980s.[94]

The fourth school was the least radical, and this is probably why it was the launching pad of the reform process that enveloped monetary institutions throughout the world within a few years. Its analytical foundations were laid by two essays, respectively by Kydland and Prescott and by Barro and Gordon, the latter extending the more general results of the former to monetary policy.[95] The basic insight of these analyses is that the fiat standard is subject to a time inconsistency problem: once a given monetary policy strategy is announced and once agents' expectations have adapted to that announcement, it becomes optimal for the authorities to deviate from the announced commitment, 'surprising' the private sector with a higher-than-expected inflation rate. In this way monetary policy can succeed in affecting the real economy, at least in the short term, whatever the objective that the authorities pursue, that is, whether a higher level of employment, an increase in seignorage, or simply an increase in social welfare. The example is constructed referring to monetary policy, but the same logic could be applied to fiscal policy or incomes policy. The problem with this mechanism, however, is that the private sector will eventually adjust its expectations, based on experience, and will no longer be caught by surprise. At that point, the value of the objective pursued remaining the same, the equilibrium inflation rate will be higher than the socially optimal rate. What prevents inflation from moving to a lower level is the inability of the monetary authorities to commit credibly to not trying to surprise the private sector. In other words, since the government is the ultimate guarantor of all the commitments made within the framework of the economic system, the weakness of the fiat standard is that it lacks mechanisms to oblige the government to honour these commitments.

The papers by Kydland and Prescott and by Barro and Gordon simply reproduce, in a game-theory context, the results obtained earlier by Benjamin Klein in his 1974 study on competitive money supply, except that the concept of credibility has now replaced that of confidence, and the reference to the state monopoly over money is rendered explicit. However, the conclusion does not change: in the absence of mechanisms generating confidence, or credibility, inconvertible money is bound to prove socially inefficient. The trouble is that there is no obvious solution to the problem. If the problem lies in the nature of the government as ultimate guarantor of the commitments, it is not sufficient to employ a contract in order to eliminate the time inconsistency of monetary policy announcements. It is necessary, rather, to initiate institutional reform that limits the government's discretion. But how? It was against this backdrop that theorists and policy-makers rediscovered the principle of central bank autonomy and the usefulness of delegating monetary powers to an independent institution obliged, however, to account for its action *ex post*.

The autonomy principle was revisited, and consecrated, as a result of two developments, one in the realm of theory, the other in that of practice. Kenneth Rogoff demonstrated analytically that the collective welfare can be increased by delegating monetary powers to a person whose utility (or reaction) function incorporates a greater aversion to inflation than that of the government.[96] A natural candidate, suggested by Rogoff himself, is a conservative central banker along the lines of a Montagu Norman or a Benjamin Strong of the 1920s. A conservative banker could succeed in reconciling credibility and discretion in conducting stabilization policies. However, Rogoff's analysis has two important implications. First, the price to pay for having a conservative banker is greater variability of output, and thus, presumably, of employment than would occur otherwise. Second, the central banker may turn out to be too conservative and do more harm than good. A number of significant consequences derive from these two implications. If the collectivity must pay a price for the central banker's conservatism, then a simple delegation of powers is not sufficient; safeguards must be put in place to ensure that the delegation is not revoked as soon as the (short-term) negative consequences of the anti-inflation commitment appear. And if conservatism can prove excessive, mechanisms must be devised to check *ex post* on the policies actually pursued, in order to ensure that the central bank's action is effectively useful for society and thus to defend its legitimacy before public opinion, because in a democratic system monetary sovereignty ultimately rests with the citizens. This is the line of thinking that gave rise to the emphasis placed on the concept of the central bank's accountability.

Obviously, the practical development was of an altogether different nature. For a series of historical accidents, an existing central bank happened to be surprisingly close to the ideal of a central bank endowed with ample autonomy and devoted, almost zealously, to price stability. That central bank was the Bundesbank. The role of the German central bank would deserve a separate study, which is obviously beyond the scope of this book.[97] For our purposes, the significant point is that the central bank's autonomy was only very indirectly the fruit of the German political situation. At the end of the Second World War the idea of a central bank not under the executive's control was strongly upheld by the Allied Occupation Force, determined to avert a new concentration of power in West Germany after the long and tragic conflict. In the late 1920s, in their important survey of central banking experiences in Europe before the First World War, Kisch and Elkin had cited the Reichsbank as the leading example of a bank of issue so thoroughly controlled by the executive that it could be likened to a railway company or tobacco monopoly.[98] The monetary stabilization of the 1920s changed many things, but with the advent of the Nazi regime the Reichsbank's margins of autonomy necessarily remained limited, notwithstanding the influence of Hjalmar Schacht, who was reappointed President of the central bank. After the war the Allies practically invented a central bank with a federal structure from scratch – the Bank Deutsche Länder (BdL), entirely free from control by German political bodies but subject to the directives of the Allied Banking Commission. Many observers, including the chief of the banking section of the Allied military government, doubted that the new institution, completely foreign to the German tradition, had any chance to survive. And, in effect, the German political system ill tolerated the BdL. In 1956, a year before the BdL was replaced by the Bundesbank, Konrad Adenauer complained:

> The central bank is fully sovereign in its relationship with the government . . .
> We have a body which is responsible to no one, neither to a parliament, nor to
> a government . . . It is responsible only to itself.[99]

But at the time the Bundesbank was established, the German government was not in a position to make wholesale changes to the model that the
Allies had introduced a decade earlier and had to make do with a compromise by virtue of which the central bank was 'independent of instructions
from the Federal Cabinet' but pledged to 'support the general economic
policy of the Federal Cabinet'. The new bank was entrusted with 'safeguarding the currency', but was not under specific obligations to account
for its action to the government or Parliament. However, members of the
government were entitled to attend meetings of the Central Bank Council
as observers (Article 13 of the Bundesbank Act).

What made the Bundesbank a model in the reform process triggered
by stagflation was Germany's relative success in containing inflationary
pressures and unemployment. This success was largely ascribed to the
Bundesbank, which on several occasions accepted an open conflict with
the government and came out victorious, thanks to popular support.[100]
In subsequent years empirical studies would attempt, not always
convincingly, to transform the German idiosyncrasy into an empirical
regularity.[101] But the perception that an institutionally autonomous
central bank, with its greater credibility, was able permanently to
improve the trade-off between inflation and unemployment was gaining
ground without any need for particular statistical subtleties. The idea
that the only way to stem the degeneration of the fiat standard was to
rely on the central banks, in the context of a comprehensive revision
of their institutional position, objectives and accountability, prevailed
definitively when in 1980 the new Chairman of the Federal Reserve,
Paul Volcker, proceeded with a monetary tightening that soon brought
the US inflation rate down by ten percentage points, from levels
approaching 20 per cent in the preceding years. From then on, interest in the more radical reform projects began to fade and then quickly
vanished altogether.

The Governor of the Bank of Italy, Carlo Azeglio Ciampi, is to be
credited with having posed the question for the first time in explicit, clear
terms, in his address to the Bank's annual meeting in May 1981:

> The return to a stable currency requires a real change in the monetary constitu-
> tion, involving the functions of the central bank and the procedures for deter-
> mining public expenditure and the distribution of income. The first condition
> is that the power to create money should be completely independent from the
> agents that determine expenditure.[102]

Table 5.6   Central banks' objectives, 1980–89

Description	Number of countries	Percentage of total	Industrial countries
Price stability is the major or only objective in the charter, and the central bank has the final word in case of conflict with other government objectives	2	3	Germany
Price stability is the only objective	6	8	Finland, Greece, Ireland, Netherlands
Price stability is one goal, with other compatible objectives, such as a stable banking system	17	24	Austria, Denmark, Luxembourg, Spain
Price stability is one goal, with potentially conflicting objectives, such as full employment	22	30	Australia, Iceland, New Zealand, United States
No objectives stated in the bank charter	10	14	Canada, Italy, Sweden, United Kingdom
Stated objectives do not include price stability	15	21	Belgium, France, Japan, Norway
Total	72	100	21

Source: Based on Alex Cukierman Steven B. Webb and Bilin Neyapti, 'Measuring the independence of central banks and its effects on policy outcomes', *World Bank Economic Review*, September 1992, Tables 1 and A1.

In the summer of the same year a far-sighted Italian Treasury Minister, Beniamino Andreatta, agreed to grant the central bank a 'divorce', similar to the American accord of 1951, so that the Bank of Italy was no longer required to take up any government securities not sold at auction. This marked the beginning of a reform process that by the turn of the 1990s had enabled the Bank of Italy to acquire a high degree of formal autonomy well before the transition to the euro and the creation of the European System of Central Banks. By that time, however, the tendency in this direction was very widespread.[103] As Table 5.6 shows, at the end of the 1980s two-thirds of the central banks of the advanced countries either did not have an explicit objective or had two or more, not always mutually compatible. The degree of autonomy was, therefore, rather low.

In the following years the picture changed swiftly as regards both the objective, which with increasingly clarity was identified as price stability, and the degree of autonomy in the choice and use of suitable instruments to pursue that objective. The international wave of reform brings to mind the diffusion after 1844 of what we have called the 'English model' and the nationalization of central banks in the period straddling the Second World War.

This process was to receive even greater impulse from the 1992 Maastricht Treaty, which, in outlining the path that was to lead in 1999 to the adoption of the euro and the establishment of the European System of Central Banks (which actually began operations in 1998), marked the constitutionalization of the objective of price stability and the principle of independence in its new and more clearly defined form.

There are some important differences concerning the interpretation of the principle of independence in the new context, as compared with the 1920s. In the first place there is a more precise definition of the task of the central bank, which in fact is to pursue price stability. Secondly, the adoption of the principle is now the result of a reform movement that comes from the political system and is not imposed by creditors seeking to limit the ability of debtors to duck their commitments. Thirdly and lastly, the principle is now set in a broader framework, so as to give adequate publicity to the motives underlying the choices made by central bankers. The latter aspect was magisterially expressed by Governor Baffi in his 1979 Concluding Remarks:

> In the macroeconomic field the actions of central banks are no longer cloaked in silence, and perhaps never will be again. Whereas in the past silence was seen as a guarantee of independence, today this is achieved by giving explicit account of one's action in a way and at a time that do not undermine its effectiveness.[104]

In the years that followed, another major structural change intensified the need for transparency regarding the conduct of monetary policy: the liberalization of the financial markets. The fiat standard, it will be remembered, was born at Bretton Woods at a time of great mistrust of the allocative ability of the financial markets. The dominant idea was that financial activity needed to be considerably constrained at international level and rigidly guided at national level. The result was a regime of financial repression that continued in increasingly pronounced forms until the end of the 1970s. But stagflation, which above all was considered a failure of the allocative mechanism, and the structural lack of innovation that occurred in the countries which had made the most recourse to financial repression, generated a widespread cultural shift with a pronounced revaluation of the role played by competition in the financial field, in growth and in the

allocative mechanism. Contributions to the changed attitude also came
from theoretical developments, especially the essays by Ronald McKinnon
and Edward Shaw, which appeared almost contemporaneously in 1973.[105]
Financial liberalization progressed rapidly in the 1980s and soon spread
beyond the boundaries of the economically advanced world.[106] From the
standpoint of monetary policy, the liberalizing wave implied paying greater
attention to the needs of communication, because *ipso facto* a negative
vote by the markets could cause the failure of a particular monetary action.
If in the meantime the obligation to report to the political authorities has
become a fundamental mechanism for legitimizing central bankers, careful
monitoring by the financial markets has become a 'permanent plebiscite'.

   The new set-up also requires a revision of the operational methods of
monetary policy, both because the concept of price stability must be quan-
tified if it is to provide a useful guide for action, and because in a context
of liberalized financial markets and fully permeable financial frontiers
the old 'two-stage' monetary policy set-up is no longer feasible. With the
disappearance of the intermediate objectives, and given the vagueness of
the concept of price stability, the risk is that the new set-up will lead to an
unjustified increase in the degree of discretion in the conduct of monetary
policy, a sort of 'all's well' that risks undermining authorities' credibility in
the long run. Inflation-targeting models are a response to this need. Apart
from the formal differences between contexts, it is a question of operational
models that provide for: (1) the announcement of a medium-term inflation
objective; (2) a monetary strategy based on manoeuvring interest rates with
the regulation of liquidity through market auctions as the main instrument;
and (3) the use, as a guide to action, of a battery of real and financial indicators made known *ex ante* to the private sector and periodically interpreted
ex post in special publications or during parliamentary hearings.[107]

   It is difficult to isolate what the reformed principle of independence contributed to the return to monetary stability in the advanced countries. As
Figure 5.3 shows, there was undeniably a structural reduction in inflation
in the years the role of central banks was being reconsidered that probably
saved the fiat standard from disintegration. But is there a cause-and-effect
relationship between the two phenomena or is the correlation spurious?
The critics of the theory of temporal incoherence, and hence of the postulate that an independent central bank committed to price stability would
increase the anti-inflation credibility of monetary policy, have two arguments in their favour. In the first place, there has been no reform in the
pivotal country of the world economy, the United States. Excluding the
Humphrey–Hawkins Act of 1978, requiring the chairman of the Federal
Reserve System to report to Congress twice annually on monetary policy,
the Fed of Volcker and Greenspan was the same as that of Burns and

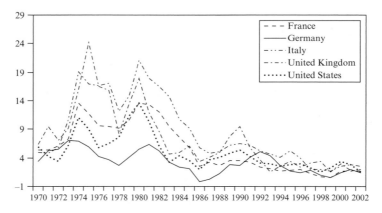

Source: Datastream.

Figure 5.3   Consumer price inflation (percentage changes)

McChesney Martin. Yet the results achieved were very different. Secondly, the success of the new vision of central banking can be attributed largely – or entirely, according to Adam Posen[108] – to the financial deepening of the advanced economies, which led to the formation of large strata of creditors averse to the risk of inflation. It was the changed perception of the costs associated with inflation that led to the reform of the central banks and not vice versa.

Both statements are true, but they do not mean much. It is the destiny of any institution to take form only when a body of opinion develops that is sufficiently broad to produce a political change. But for this to happen, it is necessary for the perception of the shortcomings of the status quo to have shifted in favour of change. And it is undeniable that the changed perceptions owed much not only to the unpleasant innovation of stagflation but also to the changed interests of large strata of the population, which had become holders of net financial wealth. The latter development is shown in Table 5.7. The purpose of institutional change, however, is never, or hardly ever, to provoke a revolution in thinking; rather, it is to crystallize a way of seeing and acting, so as to guide future actions and avoid making the same mistakes as before. This proposition also holds for the independence of the central bank, an institution – a theme repeated in these pages – that can be useful only if large strata of the population consider it to be so, thereby legitimating its existence and action.

These considerations can serve, moreover, as an introduction to another question that is still open. The reform of the role and objectives of central

Table 5.7 *Households' net financial wealth, 1980–99 (as a percentage of*
           total wealth)

	1980	1999 [1]
United States	63.7	77.4
Canada	49.5	61.2
United Kingdom	42.5	62.9
France	28.8	51.4
Italy	35.9	52.2
Japan	30.7	46.1

Note: [1] Italy, 1996; France, 1997; Canada and Japan, 1998.

Source: Laurence Boone and Nathalie Girouard, 'The stock market, the housing market and consumer behaviour', *OECD Economic Studies*, 32, 2002/2, p. 180.

banks did not remain restricted to the economically advanced countries but spread rapidly to the emerging and developing countries and those in transition to market economies. The study referred to above by Cottarelli and Giannini on the evolution of monetary arrangements in 100 countries between 1970 and 1994 shows that between 1989 and the second half of the 1990s between 15 and 20 developing countries adopted the new institutional model. The figure is even more significant when it is considered that for the sake of continuity the sample does not include the transition economies, where the establishment of an independent central bank was often a key aspect of the reform process. The extension of the principle of independence beyond the countries with a consolidated liberal democratic tradition ran up against a major difficulty, however. As I have stressed, the principle of independence does not consist only in the formal assignment of monetary powers to the central bank, but rather requires a system of guarantees and a clear and reliable allocation of responsibilities. It is at times when the costs of the fight against inflation appear that it is possible to test whether formal independence corresponds to de facto independence. But it is well known that the institutional capital of the emerging countries and even more of the developing countries is often inadequate. In these conditions the results obtained may appear to be paradoxical. For example, Alex Cukierman has shown that, far from being negative, the correlation between the degree of independence of the central bank and average inflation in developing countries is statistically null or even positive.[109]

Various explanations have been put forward to justify this result, ranging from the often limited application of the law, to the involvement of the central bank in the financing of development and the national financial markets' lack of depth. But it is a fact that anchoring the fiat standard remains a largely unresolved problem in these countries and that the principle of central bank independence can make only a modest contribution to its solution as things stand today. This explains why the revision of the role of the central bank in these countries has constituted only one pillar of the monetary reform process. The other, more fundamental, aspect is represented by a sort of 'external mandate', whose key features are the fixing of the exchange rate with respect to a leading foreign currency, usually the dollar, and recourse to IMF financing and the related imposition of conditions. In practice the external mandate amounts to renouncing monetary sovereignty with the aim of rapidly acquiring anti-inflation credibility notwithstanding the shortcomings of the national institutional framework. But such a strategy is risky since, unless it involves abandoning the national currency, renouncing sovereignty is a partial step insofar as it can be reversed. The mechanism is akin to fixing the gold parity under the gold exchange standard once the resumption rule no longer exists. Since the markets know that renouncing monetary sovereignty can be reversed, they can withdraw the capital they have invested in the country at the first signs of imbalance, thereby causing a foreign exchange crisis and often a financial crisis as well. The response of some countries to this problem was to make the mechanism for fixing the exchange rate more rigid, for example by introducing an institutionalized currency board, which has the effect of making it more costly to revoke the external mandate. But Argentina's experience in recent years shows that not even this is a crisis-proof mechanism when there are sufficiently deep-rooted domestic economic disequilibria. For some time to come the fiat standard could still prove to be a luxury that several developing countries cannot easily afford. We shall return to this subject in the next chapter, which is devoted to supranational central banking.

5.6 CONCLUSIONS: THE UNCERTAIN BENEFITS OF MONETARY SOVEREIGNTY

The fiat standard is therefore a child of the twentieth century. Its parents are two cataclysms (the First World War and the Great Depression) and the Bretton Woods agreements are the constituent instrument of its payment technology. But it is only in the 1970s, after the collapse of the exchange rate agreement, as a consequence of the resistance to the deflationary discipline implicit in the fixed exchange rate, that the payment technology based on legal tender was faced with the choice between growing and dying. For a time it appeared as though the new technology would die, smothered by stagflation, and reactionary reform proposals re-emerged, ranging from free banking to a return to gold; but then a 'moderate' reform process got under way, the linchpin of which was the principle of independence, in revised forms, with clearer objectives and a broader institutional framework. It was soon found, however, that the principle of independence works as a means of producing trust only if there is adequate institutional capital; where this is not the case, the fiat standard flounders.

This is the main problem today. While the advanced economies appear to have learnt to live with an irredeemable currency, the developing and emerging countries are still measuring the real benefits of monetary sovereignty. For them, as Willem Buiter and Clemens Graf noted, the options are 'anchor, float or abandon ship'.[110] But it is not clear whether there is really a choice because floating generates fear ('fear of floating' according to Calvo and Reinhart[111]) and, owing to the lack of institutional capital, anchoring is always uncertain. This is why a growing number of small countries appear almost to want to commit monetary euthanasia by adopting a foreign currency and accepting the consequences. However, this means definitively renouncing any autonomy for domestic monetary policy without any guarantee that the country issuing the chosen money will take account of the local economy in its reaction function, unless it creates a monetary union. This is an even more rigid arrangement than the most rigid gold standard and raises the problem of what should be the supranational monetary order: the theme addressed in the next chapter.

PART III

Between present and future

6. International money: building trust in an underinstitutionalized environment

6.1 INTRODUCTION

'No central bank can be greater than its own State – the creature greater than the creator.'[1] Montagu Norman, architect of the gold exchange standard and champion in the 1920s of a kind of 'Internationale of central banks', was in no doubt. Central banks were founded on the legitimacy that came from their being part of the state apparatus. For him, the ideal of a supranational central bank was sheer illusion. Yet nowadays the European System of Central Banks (ESCB) is a reality, observed with interest in other geographical areas as a possible model to copy. Indeed there are some who see in the International Monetary Fund (IMF) – in the way it developed after the abandonment of the exchange rate regime conceived at Bretton Woods, above all as a response to the massive increase in international capital mobility in the 1990s – the harbinger of a world central bank. What changed in the duties and prerogatives of the nation-state, in the very concept of central banking, to determine such a radically new perspective?

Post-Second World War monetary history can actually be read as a repeated attempt to refute Montagu Norman's affirmation. True, the fiat standard established itself as a form of emancipation from the economic policy constraints imposed by adherence to the gold standard. What made it an expression of monetary nationalism was its greater flexibility of supply and the fact that it lent itself to being actively managed with collective interests in mind. But already the architects of Bretton Woods, Keynes first and foremost, knew that pure monetary nationalism was impossible; worse, it was undesirable. Just around the corner was the risk that national monetary systems would first degenerate into a hegemonic model in which monetary policies would again be pegged either to a commodity, as in the Middle Ages, or a strong currency, such as the dollar or the pound sterling, but managed for eminently nationalist purposes and therefore without respecting the needs of satellite countries. Then, disenchanted, they would once again turn to autarchic policies, with all the injurious consequences demonstrated by a host of past examples. The plan that emerged from Bretton Woods was very different to the one Keynes had in mind. Its objectives were a lot less ambitious and institutionally speaking it was much more loosely structured.[2] It might almost be defined as a plan aimed at purposefully preventing central banking from gaining an international dimension, in accordance with the views of Montagu Norman. Yet Bretton Woods kick-started a mechanism of integration between national economies, first commercially and later also financially, which over time failed to keep faith with the founding premises of the original plan and led to the emergence of a genuine demand for international money.

The question can be framed in terms of the 'inconsistent trio' mentioned in the previous chapter, otherwise known as the 'open economy trilemma'.[3] If a government opts for fixed exchange rates and full capital mobility, it must renounce the autonomy of its monetary policy. If, instead, it wishes to preserve the independence of its monetary policy and full capital mobility, it must resign itself to flexible exchange rates. At first, Bretton Woods was organized differently: as we saw in the previous chapter, the choice fell on fixed exchange rates, restrictions on capital movements and the autonomy of monetary policies. But the return to commercial convertibility, which was one of the primary objectives of the Bretton Woods agreements, also revived capital movements. Subsequent liberalization measures in the key countries of the world economic system only accentuated the process of commercial and financial integration. This was the point at which the Bretton Woods compromise broke down and it became necessary to pursue alternative arrangements. While economic areas with a low degree of external openness, such as the United States, were able to opt for flexible exchange rates or at any rate a policy of benign neglect for the exchange rate, others could not. Beginning in the early 1960s, therefore, the problem of international liquidity took on unprecedented importance.

But while the demand for international money emerged fully over time, its institutional supply could not be taken for granted. In fact the creation of an international payment technology encountered two non-negligible institutional problems: the issue of control over the quantity of money produced, and that of building trust in the durability of the social convention on which that technology was founded. The concept of international money is not strictly linked to any one payment technology. In principle, any technology can be replicated on a supranational scale. But the fiat standard had developed as a reaction to commodity money, and therefore commodity money could not be a satisfactory solution for the new international monetary architects. International money, if it must be, must be fiat money. But the nature of legal tender makes it especially difficult to generate trust on a supranational scale. The question can be framed as follows. Legal tender is a form of money that implies, as we saw in the previous chapter, a vertical integration of the monetary sector of the economy. This integration is made possible by a political and legal system that defines the legitimate forms of power and guarantees rules of democratic control over the state apparatus. It is these very rules, typical of liberal-democratic systems, that give the state a comparative advantage over the market in the production of trust and made possible the transition from commodity money to fiduciary money, with legal tender being just one form of this. But liberal-democratic states are sovereign, legally speaking, because they do not recognize any entity endowed with superior coercive powers to their own. The state, as the jurists say, is *superiorem non recognoscens*. If this is true, how is it possible to push the vertical integration of the monetary sector beyond the state sector? Which institutions lay the foundation for building trust in a particular political-economic environment, that of the relationship between sovereign states, based entirely on the free will of individual countries to work together for a common goal? In a world of *superiorem non recognoscens* entities, who will guarantee respect for the commitments made?

Only one arrangement avoids these two problems or, better, resolves them without requiring complex institution-building at a supranational level. This is the hegemonic model, by virtue of which the currency of a given nation-state is spontaneously adopted by other states, be it as a reserve currency, or as an actual means of payment. But a genuine international currency necessarily comes up against the problem of the eminently national nature of the institutional capital through which trust is produced – what Dani Rodrik called the 'border effect'.[4] It is here, then, from behind the open economy trilemma that another trilemma emerges, which, given its essentially political nature, is much more difficult to resolve: that between economic and financial integration, mass politics and the nation-state (Figure 6.1).

Thanks to a set of rules limiting the degree of international integration and enabling the relatively painless management of temporary payments imbalances, the Bretton Woods compromise rescued and even bolstered the nation-state, making it compatible with mass politics. The gold standard, instead, had ensured deep commercial and economic integration but only at the cost of keeping the influence of the masses on the nation-state within very narrow confines. Today, in an era characterized by the unprecedented influence of the masses on politics and a high level of economic and international integration, it is the nation-state that must gradually give ground. The creation of international liquidity knowingly managed

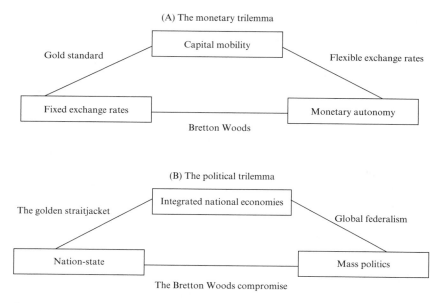

Source: Rodrik, 'Governance of economic globalisation'.

Figure 6.1   The trilemma

by an institution similar to a central bank is one way of attenuating internally the negative social repercussions of the shrinking nation-state and of preventing the emergence of any new form of hegemony, which in many ways would be indistinguishable from a system of monetary dominion, and not only that.

This, with two provisos, is the interpretation we will be giving in this chapter when retracing the evolution of the International Monetary Fund (IMF), the Bank for International Settlements (BIS) and the European System of Central Banks (ESCB). The first proviso is that the two trilemmas just described are merely schemas. In reality, international economic and financial integration is still far from complete. It is therefore possible to have intermediate forms both of monetary systems (fixed, but adjustable exchange rate regimes come to mind, which are still commonplace de facto if not always *de jure*) and of political systems. The second proviso is that political time-frames and mores do not necessarily match those of the economy. In some geographical areas (such as Latin America), viable alternatives to the hegemonic model may not exist, just as in Europe a model of pooled monetary sovereignty was able to assert itself despite coexisting with a still highly fragmented political reality. Monetary internationalism therefore continues to be experimental, characterized by a series of alternative regimes that are not necessarily mutually compatible, coexisting for the time being, but none of which appears to have consolidated its position. All of which makes the beginning of this new millennium a particularly fascinating period for scholars, and a particularly uncertain one for citizens. Everything is in the making. And everything that is in the making may never reach completion. The final outcome depends on a set of factors that are difficult to foresee: the wisdom of the architects, the trust of citizens and the kindliness of destiny.

6.2   THE FORMS OF INTERNATIONAL MONEY: HEGEMONY, COOPERATION AND SHARING

We saw in the first chapter, in our discussion of Benjamin Klein's model, that the production of money is subject to economies of scale due to its intrinsic nature as a common good. The greater the sphere in which money circulates, the greater its usefulness, and accordingly the higher the price its users are willing to pay in the form of opportunity cost. It is therefore in the interest of producers to enlarge its sphere of circulation. However, it does not follow that the production of money is a natural monopoly because, in the attempt to increase its circulation, producers will come up against a special source of cost: the cost of producing trust. In other words, they will have to invest resources to support their own credibility as producers. The technology for producing trust is not a given. It will vary depending on the historical and institutional context as well as on the degree of technical sophistication. In Klein's model, the β parameter determines the equilibrium level in the production of each existing currency. Payment technology is the name we give to the set of monetary forms and mechanisms that producers use to try to influence β, and therefore the trust of potential users.

If we follow Klein's logic then international money is nothing more than national money which, by virtue of investments in the production of trust, has been able to win for itself a sphere of circulation extending beyond the jurisdictional boundaries within which it is physically produced. It is a 'hegemonic currency', in other words it is a currency which, rooted in one nation-state for production purposes, has gained the trust of users living outside its national borders. In principle any payment technology can include a hegemonic currency. However, the transition from the national to the international sphere is not straightforward. The reason has to do with the concept of sovereignty. A state that is *superiorem non recognoscens* is sovereign, meaning it is identifiable as the ultimate source of production and guarantee of law. In a world of equally sovereign states, holders of the hegemonic currency who are not also citizens of the producer-state have no legal instruments to protect their rights from the risk of opportunistic behaviour by the producer. Institutional capital, unless it ends by ceding political sovereignty and therefore redefining the principle of *superiorem non recognoscens* (a possibility that will be explored later on), is effective only insofar as it is recognized as binding by a community of persons: the citizens of the state concerned. It is precisely owing to their nature as legal constructs that credit-based payment technologies struggle to cross state borders, except in the case of just a few, very tightly knit commercial circles, some examples of which we have seen in Chapter 2.

International money, therefore, has always existed. There are even those who view the requirements of long-distance commerce as the fundamental driver behind the invention of minted money and the subsequent invention of a whole series of more sophisticated payment technologies. But more than any other form it was commodity money, precisely because this payment technology was predicated on the lowest institutional capital, that guaranteed against the risk of opportunism since it consisted of the precious metal contained in minted coins.

The historian Carlo Cipolla devoted memorable pages to the history of international currencies, from the Byzantine hyperpyron to the ducat and the florin, demonstrating how at the root of their success was the issuing state's involvement in trade.[5] The 'Mediaeval dollars', as Cipolla called them, were pure metal coins, struck with the specific aim of meeting the needs of international trade. The gradual extension of the sphere of circulation of these coins was due not only to the external trading prowess of the merchant class in the issuing state, but also to its internal political strength, which enabled this class to impose the stability of the value of the money used to govern major trading activities as a priority requirement with respect to any other economic and political consideration. Cipolla shows how in some instances, for example in late Mediaeval Florence, the conflict between the needs of foreign trade and local industry led to an actual duplication of the monetary system in order to safeguard the 'international' currency, normally gold-based coins, from the gradual depreciation of the domestic currency, which was based on silver.[6] The duplication of the monetary system was a way to reduce the 'sacrifice' of resources asked of the issuing state to bolster foreign users' trust in its currency. So long as that duplication was maintained, gold coins enjoyed almost universal trust. But at the appearance of the first cracks in the balance of political power, due to a shift in interclass dynamics, it was inevitable that trust in the currency outside national borders would be affected. What followed was, depending on the circumstances, a more or less rapid transition from one hegemonic currency to another.

For most of known history the international currency was therefore a hegemonic commodity money produced in a competitive system, which owed its ability to gain the trust of leading merchants to the desire and ability of the issuing state to guarantee its value over time. Without these qualities, trust in the international currency was destined to decline, and some new currency would be preferred, produced by a competing state. But the underlying payment technology remained the same, founded on commodity money and the self-regulation of trust.

While it fulfilled the merchants' need for a means of payment that would be accepted outside the issuing state, this arrangement could not fulfil the other need to guarantee flexibility of supply. On the contrary, the rigidity of supply that was typical of commodity money was an essential condition for maintaining trust over time. It was this inflexibility, as we saw in the second chapter, that led to the formation in the late Middle Ages of a payment circuit outside the international mechanism of trade fairs, founded on credit-based payment technologies. This circuit was an exception, and survived thanks to the trust generated by controls on access exerted by the trading states and the gradual development of a customary law. But it remained just that – an exception – destined, as events would later demonstrate, to lead a precarious existence in the fragmented institutional climate of the time.

The first real attempt to move beyond the monetary system inherited from the Middle Ages dates to the end of the eighteenth century, when, as we saw in the second and third chapters, the first credit-based payment technologies became widely established, albeit always within national borders. This development had a series of consequences, which in some senses were paradoxical. For the entire nineteenth century, the need to rationalize the monetary system was one of the main drivers of the birth of nationalism.[7] It was then that the monetary sign became 'national' in a way it had never been before, in other words as a symbol of national unity, of the affirmation of political even before monetary sovereignty. But the fragile nation-states of the time were still not capable of independently guaranteeing trust in the money produced and so all of them, without exception, relied on the convertibility mechanism. As a result of the development of national currencies – and herein lies the paradox – a truly stateless international currency was created for the first time. This currency was gold (which had originally shared this role with silver, although this was quickly supplanted), which through the convertibility mechanism became the ultimate guarantor of the stability of the national currency. In other words, the international currency was gold itself and not the national currencies that were based on it, because the convertibility mechanism could not be safeguarded on an international plane. It was a national legal construct, which did not protect foreign users. The paradox lies precisely in the fact that national monetary policies, in order to protect the convertibility mechanism, were conducted so as to transform gold into a genuine payment technology specialized in the settlement of international trade.

Unlike the monetary system in the late Middle Ages the gold standard was a universal arrangement: the same rules governed both international and domestic trade. This quality, however, heavily penalized domestic trade, which was subject to constant deflationary pressure made even more intensive by the fact that the supply of gold eluded the control of states, being entirely subject to the random discovery of mineral deposits and to technical progress. While this arrangement might have worked in the short to medium term, and even have been helped by the sharp increases in the gold supply following the discovery of new deposits, such as in California in the 1860s, in the long term the brake it put on the expansion of trade risked becoming intolerable. And indeed, we saw in the fifth chapter how the fiat standard became a form of emancipation from the constraints that gold – a 'barbaric relic', as Keynes notoriously called it – imposed on a monetary policy management consciously aimed at optimizing the social welfare. The kind of monetary nationalism that rose from the embers of the gold standard was very different from that which had led in the nineteenth century to the affirmation of national monetary symbols. While the earlier form was an essentially symbolic, nominal development, so much so that it needed to anchor itself to convertibility in order to keep afloat, this one was substantial, the result of an attempt to guide monetary policy towards common goals. In other words, the fiat standard was originally a negation of the concept of international money. In its purest form, which Hayek disparagingly referred to as 'monetary nationalism', it has three defining characteristics: (1) state control over the supply of banknotes; (2) determination of how many are produced (the supply of legal tender) in the pursuit of national objectives; (3) full exchange rate flexibility, aimed at ensuring balance-of-payments equilibrium.[8] In this kind of context demand for international money cannot emerge, except in the limited form of units of account to invoice goods traded with foreign countries.

But in retrospect the monetary nationalism of Hayek's imagination will turn out to have been a historical curio. Already in the Bretton Woods system, monetary nationalism was tempered by an exchange rate agreement, aimed at preventing excessive exchange rate volatility from damaging the recovery of international trade. But, and this is even more interesting, not even after the demise of the exchange rate regime created at Bretton Woods was it possible to say that monetary nationalism had assumed the form so dreaded by Hayek. There were two confirmations of this. The first concerned the exchange rate regimes voluntarily adopted by individual countries, which at that point were no longer bound to a given choice by any international accord. Indeed, contrary to what many expected, flexible exchange rates did not become the norm. Certainly, the number of countries that nominally adopted flexible exchange rates rose significantly. But the significance of this figure is diminished by a number of considerations. First of all, even after 1973 the majority of countries continued to favour more or less rigid forms of fixed exchange rates. In the early 1990s, less than 50 per cent of countries had flexible exchange rate regimes.[9] Second, the switchover to flexible exchange rates was much more marked in industrial countries than in developing ones. In the early 1980s, around 80 per cent of developing countries continued to have fixed exchange rate regimes. Finally, and this is the most interesting point, notwithstanding the official statements of the authorities the flexibility of exchange rates measured on the basis of actual market performance was much lower than expected.[10]

The second confirmation was that demand for official reserves, which should have at least declined with the switch-over from fixed to flexible exchange rates, showed a surprising and markedly upward trend. At the end of the 1990s, global reserves equalled approximately 17 weeks' imports, around double the value reported in 1960 and 20 per cent more than at the beginning of the decade. As a proportion of world output, the trend was even more pronounced: at the century's close reserves amounted to 6 per cent of output, three and a half times the value at the beginning of the 1960s and one and a half times that of 1990.[11] More systematic empirical analyses highlight that the type of exchange rate regime adopted by a country is not the main factor explaining its official reserve requirements, which goes to confirm the results of Reinhart and Rogoff regarding the gap between official rhetoric and the actual performance of exchange rates.[12]

Why this gap? For at least two reasons. The first is that flexible exchange rate regimes resolve the conflicting needs of the economy's foreign and domestic sectors in favour of the latter. This represented a drastic reversal with respect to monetary arrangements during the Renaissance and to the gold standard, that penalizes international trade, which is affected by exchange rate instability, especially when this turns into volatility. As the importance of the external sector grew, this arrangement came to be regarded as increasingly inadequate. The acceptability of flexible exchange rates was therefore, *ceteris paribus*, inversely proportionate to the degree of external openness of an economy. And in fact, after the dissolution of the Bretton Woods agreements, the countries whose economies were most open were also the ones which sought most determinedly to anchor their exchange rates to a guiding currency. Second, as we saw in the last chapter, the ability of the state to produce trust in the absence of convertibility is subject to gradual erosion, leading to fixed exchange rates being identified as a possible external anchor for expectations, aimed at lending credibility to the anti-inflationary initiatives of the monetary authorities.

In this way, and for these reasons, demand for international liquidity was created that the theoreticians of monetary nationalism had failed to anticipate and which was confirmed by the growth of official reserves. Since the international monetary sector, unlike the domestic one, operated under a regime of free access (any currency, without requiring particular institutional expedients, could campaign to become 'international liquidity'), this demand created a latent drift towards the hegemonic system. Whenever the convertibility mechanism fails, national currencies must satisfy two requirements in order to advance their case for becoming the hegemonic currency: first, that the economy of which they are an expression be sufficiently large to provide critical mass to the circulation of money; second, that the issuing authorities' anti-inflationary credibility be on average higher than that of authorities issuing the other moneys. In the post-war period only three currencies proved over time that they were capable of satisfying these requirements: the US dollar, the German mark and the Japanese yen.

But when the dominant payment technology is founded on legal tender, the hegemonic system presents two contraindications. First, it is not a given that the reaction function of the issuing authorities will include parameters of social well-being in the countries that spontaneously peg their currencies to that currency. While the fiat standard ultimately reconciles the stability objective with that of flexibility, it is likely that this happens based on a calculation in which the principal, if not sole, considerations have to do with the national economy of the hegemonic country. This was the experience, for example, of the entire world at the time of the American monetary policy U-turn under the Chairman of the Fed, Paul Volcker, in 1981, and of countries such as Italy and the United Kingdom when, in 1992, Germany's monetary policy turned to primarily internal objectives, thereby contributing to destabilize the European Monetary System (EMS). Second, the hegemonic model tends to produce what is now widely referred to in the literature as 'Triffin's dilemma', which was mentioned in section 5.5 of the fifth chapter.[13] The country issuing the hegemonic currency tends to be characterized by payment imbalances and, from a certain point of view, this is only natural. The hegemonic country must, in fact, satisfy demand for money that extends beyond its national borders. A persistent balance-of-payments deficit is the accounting method whereby a hegemonic country increases the international supply of its own currency. In Klein's words, the seignorage thus earned by a country is nothing more than the demonstration of the price that international users are willing to pay for the monetary services provided by the hegemonic currency: it is the trademark price, higher than that of all the other competitors, which the hegemonic currency has gained for itself. So long as trust in the reliability of the anti-inflationary stance of the monetary authorities in the hegemonic country remains intact, none of this will create problems. However, any deviation from a rigorous anti-inflationary policy risks provoking a crisis of trust, which, given the role of the hegemonic currency and the level of demand it enjoys in normal circumstances, will have devastating consequences, including in the hegemonic country itself.

It was these two flaws in the hegemonic system that gave rise to an unprecedented attempt to improve it through an institution-building initiative (architecture), which would pave the way for a different concept of international money, resting on a more solid basis. At the same time, the attempt raised the problem of moving central banking to an international level, an issue that did not arise in the hegemonic system. The initiative resulted in two alternative regimes, which I will call the cooperative system, and the consortium or pooled sovereignty system. Before pausing to examine these two arrangements more closely, it is worth focusing on the difficulty they faced and which they tried to overcome. This difficulty had to do with the notion of sovereignty. All institutions, given that they curtail the freedom of choice of individuals, must be perceived as legitimate by those who are bound by their rules. Several legitimizing mechanisms exist at national level, from the legal system to the rules of political representation, to religion, in the case of a monotheistic country. But at the international level the principle on which the nation-state is founded, at least from the Peace of Westphalia in 1648 onwards, renders these mechanisms unworkable. The nation-state does not, in fact, recognize any source of legitimization superior to itself. If follows that in a world of formally and concretely independent nation-states any international institution must be able to assert its own legitimacy (to be, in the technical jargon of institutionalism, self-enforcing). This self-legitimization can only be obtained if all the member states of the institution believe it is in their interest to comply with its rules. To say this with greater legal precision: in order to be effective, every obligation deriving from an international accord requires the ongoing agreement of the obligor.

This does not mean, as claimed by the political experts of the 'realist' school, that all international institutions are little more than a smoke-screen for struggles between states. There are numerous examples of international institutions that work well, thanks to the operation of two principles: universality and reciprocity. Universality means that the rules on which the institution is founded apply without distinction and uniformly to all member states. Reciprocity, by contrast, means that there is no predefined division of roles by virtue of which some member states benefit from the institution and others are systematically put at a disadvantage. Each member state must be able to perceive that the institution, on average, distributes costs and benefits equitably, as Milner puts it in an interesting review of the theory of international cooperation.[14] Here, however, central banking raises a special issue. As we have seen in the previous chapters, central banks are established to protect increasingly complex payment technologies from the risk of abuse, often as a result of major crises. Central banks, to put it brutally, are the progeny of crises. But crises have two characteristics that make it particularly difficult to institutionalize their antidotes. First, it is not easy to predict the nature, extent and possible remedies of each crisis. To evaluate the structure of earnings and losses deriving from a particular method of crisis management, the 'pay-offs' as they are called in gaming theory, is therefore an arduous task. Second, if the structural characteristics of several countries mean they are more exposed to risk than others, the likelihood of succeeding, via a careful assessment, in distributing costs and benefits fairly is rather remote. Some will benefit more than others from the activities of the institution. In theory there could be forms of compensation between members and, as we will see in practice, this technique is often used. But it is difficult to imagine a fair compensation in a context in which benefits and costs are not well defined *ex ante*.

The foregoing description – essentially a problem of institutional governance – means that international institutions active in managing crises do not have it easy. It is in the interest of the member countries to define carefully the discretionary power of the institution, in order to have the final say if specific crises occur, or to limit the resources available to the institution itself, in order to be able at the very least to predict accurately, and curb, potential losses. Both these strategies risk harming the effectiveness of the institution in question. Nonetheless it is as well to clarify that given the nature of the problem and the institutional environment, these are rational reactions and not aberrations caused by political shortsightedness. The problem can be overcome only if there is another way, via a different channel, to boost trust among the institution's members – never an easy enterprise in the structurally underinstitutionalized environment typical of international relations – or by limiting the sphere of action of the nation-state through a permanent surrender of sovereignty. The two systems I will now speak of aim to achieve precisely this objective.

The 'cooperative regime', of which the Bretton Woods system remains the highest expression, is characterized by the more or less formalized attempt to make available ad hoc mechanisms for the creation of international liquidity with which to loosen the external constraint weighing on individual economies, in order to increase the credibility of the external anchor of a fixed exchange rate regime. In this case currencies remain national, and issuing authorities remain sovereign. The importance of limiting the exchange rate fluctuations of single currencies is recognized, however, and to this end procedures and criteria for the international management of payments imbalances are defined.

The 'consortium regime', sometimes also called 'pooled sovereignty', is much more ambitious. It consists in the permanent transfer of monetary sovereignty to a supranational level, through the abolition of national currencies and the establishment of a centralized system for managing monetary policy. The most advanced example of the consortium regime is, of course, the Economic and Monetary Union (EMU) among European countries.

Both systems presuppose the resolution of important collective action issues. In the first case, when sovereignty remains national, the thorniest issue is how to define the spheres of authority. What is the domain of cooperation and what is that of national policy-making? In the Bretton Woods system there was an attempt to resolve this problem via a legal mechanism, the treaty that defined the statutes of the International Monetary Fund and the World Bank. But as we saw earlier, even if on a strictly legal level an international treaty is equated with a constitutional law, its application depends on the unqualified agreement of the parties, since there is no *super partes* authority that can ensure compliance. As soon as a sufficiently powerful signatory, or the entire community of signatories, demonstrate their reluctance to follow its dictates, it is very unlikely that the law can prevail over practice. This is why the cooperative regime runs the risk that an even moderately strong economic shock may disable its operations. This is why most efforts to institutionalize the cooperative regime are often aimed at simplifying both the economic environment and the objectives pursued, in order to reduce the risk of conflicts of interest emerging that are detrimental to the cooperative attitude on which the model is based. The 'reductionist' approach adopted in Bretton Woods is a typical example and consisted in leaving full sovereignty to national policies and in imagining a world of geographically immobile capital and segmented financial systems, so as to make the duties of international institutions less complex. We shall be looking at this aspect of the issue in more detail in the next section.

The consortium regime works in a decidedly different way. Sharing sovereignty implies the creation of mechanisms of political legitimization and definite legal rules for resolving eventual conflicts. It is more robust than the cooperative system, but only to the extent that its advent was preceded by a widespread collective initiative aimed at building a supranational institutional capital. This means that the consortium regime also presupposes giving up a certain amount of political sovereignty. How much exactly, is a matter of debate. There are those who believe that a monetary union not supported by a political union is destined to lead a precarious existence, and that therefore the greater solidity of the consortium regime with respect to the cooperative one risks being illusory. I will return to the merits and limits of this thesis when I talk about EMU in section 6.4.

One objective difficulty that both regimes inevitably encounter, however, is the coexistence in the current monetary system of two different payment technologies with very distinctive characteristics: legal tender and bank money. In the case of legal tender, the pooling of sovereignty is facilitated by the principle of central banking autonomy, one of the basic assumptions of which, as we saw earlier, is that central banks must not participate in the financing of the state sector. In other words there is no longer any direct relationship between the state budget and monetary policy. In the case of bank money, instead, the prevailing conception even today is that banking stability must be pursued not only through the action of the central bank but also through a wider safety net, which comprises deposit insurance schemes, special bankruptcy procedures and, in some cases, recourse to taxpayers' money. But if responsibility for banking stability lies squarely with the state and in the final analysis with national taxpayers, and not with the central bank as in the case of monetary policy, it is much less likely that this aspect of sovereignty can be pooled.[15] And in fact, all the monetary treaties, from Bretton Woods to Maastricht, are much more vague when it comes to addressing the issue of banking regulation, limiting themselves to defining procedural aspects rather than the substantive issues. The fact remains, however, that monetary union is also a powerful incentive to deal differently with political integration issues. In this respect, the consortium regime seems more powerful than the cooperative one, precisely because it appears capable of setting in motion an endogenous process to address the issues that originally limited its scope and significance. It is perhaps no coincidence, for example, that debate on the 'hows' and 'whens' of European integration of financial regulations only really took off after the introduction of the euro.

The hegemonic, cooperative and consortium regimes, whose key characteristics are summarized in Table 6.1, are the three possible kinds of monetary internationalism. In the following sections, I will review the attempts to move beyond the hegemonic system, first globally and on a

Table 6.1 International currency regimes

	1. Hegemonic	2. Cooperative	3. Consortium
Monetary regime	Dominant national currency	National currencies and ad hoc mechanisms for the creation of international liquidity	Supranational currency
International institutional requirements	None	Rules (formal or conventional) for the division of tasks between national and international authorities	Supranational central bank; legal and political legitimization mechanisms
Limits	The reaction function of the authorities in the hegemonic country does not incorporate international variables; Triffin's dilemma	Slow response in the face of unexpected developments; low resistance to macroeconomic shocks	Need for supranational institutional capital (limits on national sovereignty); tension between monetary and fiscal authorities over decentralized state budgets
Examples	Mediaeval currencies; the dollar standard	Original Bretton Woods system; European Monetary System	European Monetary Union; Communauté Financière Africaine (CFA)

cooperative basis, later regionally and via a consortium arrangement. And we will also see how today the question of the most appropriate regime is more open than ever, because in many countries the degeneration of the fiat standard has reached a level that requires the solid external anchoring of expectations, in some cases through the spontaneous abandonment of the national currency in favour of a foreign currency. The review will focus on the three major questions posed by monetary internationalism. Who is responsible for making adjustments in the event of payments imbalances? How is international liquidity produced to reduce the burden of adjustment? What are the rules that govern the institutions in charge of managing international liquidity and how cogent are they?

6.3   THE INSTITUTIONALIZED COOPERATIVE REGIME: THE ORIGINS AND DEVELOPMENT OF THE INTERNATIONAL MONETARY FUND

In the last chapter I made a thorough analysis of the philosophy of the Bretton Woods agreements, whose aim was to reconcile the highest possible degree of autonomy of national economic policies with a high degree of order in international monetary relations. However, I only briefly touched on the International Monetary Fund as an institution, despite the fact that it was undoubtedly the most innovative outcome of Bretton Woods. You could say that, from the outset, the IMF was a rough outline of a supranational central bank, almost naturally destined over time to broaden its functions in order to substitute national central banks. One passage in particular in the Articles of Agreement (the statute of the Fund) seems to authorize this interpretation. Indeed, Article I states that one of the purposes of the new institution shall be to:

> give confidence to members by making the general resources of the Fund temporarily available to them under adequate safeguards, thus providing them with opportunity to correct maladjustments in their balance of payments without resorting to measures destructive of national or international prosperity.

But the question is much more complex than that. Certainly, it was Keynes's intention that the IMF would closely resemble a supranational central bank, at least from a monetary perspective. His plan envisaged that the institution would be able to create liquidity *ex nihilo*, the 'bancor', within previously set but nevertheless broad limits, and that this liquidity could have been used by member countries automatically, again within certain limits, to finance their current account imbalances. Keynes never specified the exact amount of bancor he had in mind, but Joan Robinson calculated that the figure had to be around $36 billion.[16] The mechanism would have to be perfectly symmetric: both the lender and the borrower country would have to take all necessary steps to redress the imbalances in their bancor account, whose normal level should have been equal to zero for all members. The idea was based on the banking practice of granting overdraft facilities, a practice that was commonplace in the United Kingdom but not well known in the United States. Harry White's plan, by contrast, was decidedly less ambitious. White also envisaged the establishment of a new unit of account, the 'unitas', but he never saw it becoming a means of payment: more simply it would be an accounting device to facilitate international settlements. Moreover, under White's plan, the IMF would be granted its own self-financing capacity aimed at stabilizing the exchange rates between member states, but the unitas would not have played any role in this (except, that is, as the unit of account for IMF operations). In any event, the quantity of resources envisaged was far less than that attributed by Robinson to Keynes's proposal: $5 billion as against $36 billion. Finally, White's plan made no mention of the symmetry of responsibility between lending and borrower countries, which was a key characteristic of Keynes's. What the two plans had in common, as we saw earlier, was the expectation that in the new monetary system speculative capital movements were to be discouraged by means of administrative controls.

The main problem that had to be resolved in the transition from abstract planning to the practical realization of the plan was the strenuous and, for a long time, united opposition of the American financial sector to the very idea of an international financial body. The widespread concerns in the United States were essentially of three kinds. First, since there was a general expectation that after the Second World War the United States would continue for a long time to be the only creditor country, it was feared that an excessive share of responsibility for operating the mechanism would fall on its shoulders, not only on a strictly financial level but, if Keynes's proposal won the day, also on a macroeconomic one. Second, the American financial establishment opposed the idea of letting borrowing countries use public funds to lighten their debt servicing obligations, fearing that this could generate excessive laxity on the part of governments and a genuine moral hazard. This fear was evident in a document that the main body representing financial interests in the United States, the American Bankers Association, published in 1943:

> a system of quotas or shares in a pool which gives debtor countries the impression that they have a right to credits up to some amounts is unsound in principle, and raises hopes that cannot be realized. Such a system would encourage the impression that credits received may not have to be liquidated, and would invite abuses of the facilities.[17]

Finally, the American financial sectors feared that the emphasis placed as much by Keynes as by White on the segmentation of national financial systems could end up obliging the US authorities to make use of currency controls themselves, thereby discouraging the inflows and outflows of capital to and from Wall Street, and undermining the role of 'world banker' that the New York exchange aspired to in competition with London. This scenario was all the more dreaded since, as readers will recall from the previous chapter, securing this role had been the counterparty that convinced American finance first to accept the establishment of the Fed and later the laws of the New Deal.[18]

Under cover of the official negotiations between the British and

American governments, in the years before the Bretton Woods conference there was intense lobbying within the US political and financial world, resulting in a broad downsizing of the IMF with respect to the original plans. The institution that finally emerged had little in common with a central bank. Both the bancor and the unitas disappeared from the big picture, and the allocation of resources with which the IMF commenced operations, equal to $8.8 billion, was much closer to White's proposal than to Keynes's. In short, as Peter Kenen later pointed out, the IMF was much more like a credit cooperative than a body for the creation of liquidity. To obtain this result, in addition to cutting back on resources a whole series of other tactical ploys were adopted under the influence of American finance. The first and principal strategy was the inclusion, in Article VI of the Statute, of the prohibition on lending funds against capital outflows, regardless of their nature. The second was the adoption of an extremely complex technical language, whose objective was to make it difficult, if only at a lexical level, to assimilate the IMF to a normal bank. The institution's Statute, as Keynes would later complain, was deliberately written in 'cherokee'. Any reference to the idea of supervision or regulation for prudential purposes disappeared along with banking language. The third strategy regarded the obligatory or non-obligatory nature of controls on capital movements. The American private sector succeeded in ensuring that the definitive text of the agreements referred only to the power of governments (and therefore not the obligation) to cooperate in initiatives to curtail capital movements, any obligation being limited to the transmission of information on same to the IMF following a specific request (Article VIII). Moreover, Article VI granted the IMF the power to request the introduction of controls in the context of its own lending programmes; but the proposal to grant the IMF the power of enforcement in this area, or in any event to include the control of capital movements among the obligations weighing on member countries, did not survive. At the press conference held at Bretton Woods, it was White himself who explained that the part of the structure relative to controls had been designed to reconcile the freedom of member countries to use them, with the clear intention of the United States not to.[19]

Another crucial aspect that had to be resolved during the British–American negotiations was the new institution's governance structure. Here again the British plan was more ambitious than the American one. Keynes, with the full support of the UK Treasury, called for an independent body comprised of high-level experts who would meet not too frequently, in order to be able to combine this responsibility with other professional commitments. The Americans, by contrast, insisted on having and ultimately obtained a Board of Directors composed of full-time middle-ranking officials appointed by government, who would have to be permanently stationed at the main offices of the IMF, which after a bitter dispute were headquartered in Washington. This structure objectively placed a further brake on the discretionary power of the new organism, given that at least on paper it stressed political control over the Board to the detriment of its technical authoritativeness.

The result of all these compromises was to make the IMF, as it was originally envisaged, more closely resemble a set of rules than an institution with its own physiognomy and significant scope for action.[20] And yet, it was an unprecedented development, destined over time to take on a much more important role than any reading of its statute would have led one to think.

In its first years of activity, the main problem of the IMF was that of finding a genuine role for itself, given that demand for loans turned out to be rather weak, partly because of competition from the Marshall Plan. The real turning point in the life of the new institution was the return to currency convertibility in relation to European countries' current account transactions, which occurred between 1958 and 1961, and the simultaneous acceptance of the obligations envisaged under Article VIII of the Fund's Statute. This was a truly critical phase, which even changed the nature of the IMF. As James observed:

> There was no longer simply a world of nation-states, and an institution supervising rules of conduct, but rather a system in which nation-states, and the rules affecting their behaviour, interacted with markets, and in particular with fast growing currency and capital markets.[21]

The return to convertibility in Europe was facilitated by another major event that occurred in the same period, that is the formation of a persistent deficit in the balance of payments of the system's pivotal country, the United States. In 1956–57 the 'overall' US balance of payments (defined as the sum of the balances of current items, economic subsidies and government loans, and private investment) was still in substantial equilibrium; in 1958 there was a deficit of almost $4 billion, which rose to $6 billion in 1959. Already in that year, the external liabilities of the United States had matched its gold reserves and would quickly outstrip them in the years to come (Table 6.2) when America's balance of payments persisted in running a deficit. The generalized return to convertibility, if only partial, led to a resumption of capital movements that could be concealed more or less easily behind commercial transactions.

The imbalances caused by the US deficit and increased capital mobility could have been dealt with by changing the exchange rates, in particular

Table 6.2   *US international reserves and liabilities, 1950–71*
             (billions of US dollars)

Year	Total reserves	Gold	Total external liabilities	External liabilities vis-à-vis governments and central banks
1950	24.3	22.8	8.9	4.9
1955	22.8	21.8	13.5	8.3
1958	22.5	20.6	16.8	9.6
1959	21.6	19.6	19.4	10.1
1960	19.4	17.8	21.0	11.1
1961	18.7	16.9	22.9	11.8
1962	17.2	16.1	24.3	12.7
1963	16.8	15.6	26.4	14.4
1964	16.7	15.5	29.3	15.8
1965	15.4	14.1	29.6	15.8
1966	14.9	13.2	31.0	14.9
1967	14.8	12.1	35.7	18.2
1968	15.7	10.9	38.5	17.3
1969	17.0	11.9	45.9	16.0
1970	14.5	11.1	47.0	23.3
1971	13.2	11.1	67.8	50.6

Source: Dam, *The Rules of the Game*, p. 145.

by devaluing the dollar in terms of gold. However, for reasons already mentioned in the previous chapter, this option was not looked on favourably by the governments of the major countries. In the new context, it soon became clear that the resources of the IMF were insufficient to facilitate the financing of current account imbalances, even accepting – something that the Director General at the time, Per Jacobsson, was not inclined to do – that the Fund should refrain from financing capital account imbalances, as envisaged under Article VI. Discussions on international liquidity, which would monopolize the policy debate for over a decade, date from the early 1960s. In reality the label 'international liquidity' concealed three very different problems. The first was how to adapt the total quotas in the Fund to the growth in trade. This was the simplest problem because once there was the necessary political consensus it was relatively easy to increase the quotas, since aside from the gold contribution part of the increase was paid in by each country in its national currency. And in fact, the quotas were increased by 50 per cent in 1959, and by a further 25 per cent in 1966 – two increases that helped curtail the erosion of the Fund's 'weight' as a proportion of world imports. But two, more subtle, problems remained.

First, given the structure of the IMF, which had no monetary creation capacity of its own but simply availed itself of the resources granted it by the members (mostly in national currencies), there was a serious risk that the institution would not have the resources to meet the needs of countries such as the USA and the United Kingdom, whose currencies were structurally scarce insofar as they were universally in demand as reserve currencies. Of course, this problem concerned only a very small part of the Fund membership, although politically they were the members that counted most. The response to the problem took the form of a separate agreement by the main industrialized countries, which set up a stock of virtual and dedicated resources; virtual in the sense that it would materialize only if effectively required, and dedicated because it was reserved to financing payments imbalances of participating countries only. The General Arrangements to Borrow (GAB), as they were called, marked the establishment of the Group of Ten (G-10) in 1962,[22] which in the years that followed would play a vital role in the debate on the international financial architecture. Aside from the purely financial objective already mentioned, the GAB had many aims. The first of these was to establish in advance a sort of store of resources that could be accessed quickly without having to complete the verification process normally required by the Fund's programmes. The second aim was to create a scaled-down credit cooperative in an effort to prevent the IMF's Articles of Agreement from becoming an obstacle in the event of a crisis of confidence regarding the balance of payments on capital account, especially by virtue of the provisions of Article VI. The problem, however, was that precisely because it was not subject to the procedural constraints envisaged under the Articles of Agreement, the structure laid itself open to the risk of abuse.

In the intense debates leading to the establishment of the GAB, the issue of control over the new instrument took on a central role. At the end of the talks, the idea that the agreements could be activated almost automatically was abandoned. By contrast, the French Finance Minister called for and succeeded in ensuring that the GAB had to be endorsed not only by the IMF's Board and a qualified majority of members, but by every single participant whose currency was among those taken into consideration for the draft. This 'double lock' mechanism meant that the GAB ultimately played a modest role in managing balance-of-payments crises in subsequent decades. The golden age of the mechanism was in 1977–78, when the GAB were activated to deal with payments imbalances in Italy, the United Kingdom and the US, albeit for modest overall amounts.[23] After which, despite the adoption in 1983 of the principle whereby the GAB could also be employed outside the circle of participating countries, the instrument was never used again, except for one attempt that was later abandoned during the Russian crisis of 1998.

The last problem under the label of 'international liquidity' was by far the thorniest of the three. This derived from the fact that in the context of international relations as they were structured at the end of the 1950s, the main source of international liquidity was the deficit in the US balance of payments. The international monetary system had long ceased to be, if indeed it had ever been, the symmetric mechanism conceived at Bretton Woods, and had become instead a special version of the hegemonic model, the dollar standard.[24] The weakness of the dollar standard – setting aside the resulting disparities in the status of the IMF members, however inevitable given the countries' differing economic and political status – consisted in the fact that the global supply of liquidity came to depend on the choices of a country operating under a fiat standard regime, and the demand for the reserve currency could, as a result, oscillate considerably depending on the level of confidence in the monetary policy of the anchor country. It was in practice the typical shortcoming of the hegemonic model. As was observed earlier, the issue was put forcefully by Robert Triffin: either the United States would have to correct its payments imbalances, triggering deflation worldwide, or fuel the demand for foreign currency up to the point at which some accidental event, perhaps of a political nature, would generate a crisis of confidence in the dollar serious enough to trigger a 'new 1931', the year in which the gold exchange standard collapsed once and for all. The 'natural' solution to the dilemma would have been to create some form of alternative international money to the dollar as a reserve currency, according to the old recommendations of Keynes.[25] However, as we saw previously, creating a legal international tender is no mean enterprise. The question is how to ensure there is sufficient brand capital for an instrument formally not guaranteed by any state. In the years immediately following the publication of the influential articles by Triffin, the problem did not even arise, because the United States opposed the project for fear that a genuine international currency could damage the dollar's role as a reserve currency. The position changed in 1965, both because the French government provocatively began to air the hypothesis of a return to the gold standard, encouraging its own central bank to convert into gold its dollars held in excess due to balance-of-payments surpluses, and because the price of gold on the free market was permanently higher than the official price, emphasizing that the market believed it possible that the dollar would be devalued.

It was against this background that the decision was taken to create an international currency, given the rather improbable name of Special

Drawing Right (SDR) and approved at the twenty-third annual meeting of the IMF, in 1968, when it was also decided to amend the Articles of Agreement for that purpose.[26] It was immediately clear that this was an international legal tender. The new instrument was not issued against the holdings of reserves of any kind: its existence relied solely on a network of legal obligations undertaken voluntarily by the member countries of the IMF. Moreover, each member country was entitled to participate in the initiative, but there was no obligation to do so. However, SDRs were subject to a series of rules that greatly limited their probability of success. First, their circulation was restricted to central banks and governments of the member countries, thereby preventing the development of a private market in SDRs. Second, a limit was set on the quantity of SDRs that each member state would be obliged to accept. Third, a 'designation' mechanism was created, by virtue of which the IMF would be responsible for establishing which creditor country was in the best condition to collect its credits in SDRs instead of in national reserve currencies. Finally, the decision to issue more SDRs than originally planned was made dependent on a majority vote of 85 per cent of quotas, thereby granting a de facto power of veto to both the United States and the main European countries, if they voted as a bloc.

With these limits, and in view of the fact that the Act formally establishing the SDR came at the end of a decade that had seen a succession of increasingly large US payments deficits, making the problem of international liquidity hardly relevant, it is not surprising that despite its ambitions the SDR turned out to be a massive failure. In 1971, it was the decision to suspend the convertibility of gold into dollars and the subsequent demise of the exchange rate regime conceived at Bretton Woods, that drew the attention of policy-makers to other issues.[27] From then on, the SDR enjoyed a niche existence, playing the part more of unit of account than international means of payment; nor did the reflections made on the IMF's fiftieth anniversary succeed in identifying a useful role for the instrument, demonstrating the difficulty of developing a genuinely international currency in an underinstitutionalized environment.

All in all, the reforms of the 1960s were much less radical than they appeared at first. While they were an implicit acknowledgment of the IMF's role in the midst of systemic crises of confidence, in actual fact as an instrument the GAB had very limited uses and in any event was not subject to control by the institution's management. For their part SDRs, while representing a first form of supranational currency, had been inserted into such a broad mesh of provisions limiting their scope as to almost entirely void their practical impact. If, at the end of the 1960s, the IMF no longer resembled the currency board referred to disappointedly by Hicks in his reconstruction of the talks at Bretton Woods, it was still very far from being a genuine central bank.

More radical changes would have to wait until the last two decades of the century, when the surge in capital mobility – the result of a vast process of financial liberalization that I spoke about in the previous chapter, which began in the Anglo-Saxon countries towards the end of the 1970s and soon spread well beyond the borders of the industrialized world – put the IMF face to face with the same problems that central banks had had to address in the 1930s. There was one difference, though, which again had to do with the different, more limited, room for manoeuvre that an international institution has compared to a body that is fully recognized under national law.

A first taste of what tackling a crisis of confidence in a context of high capital mobility meant occurred at the beginning of the 1980s, when a series of countries in Latin America, with Mexico first in line, found themselves incapable of servicing their foreign debt. Up until that moment the Fund's programmes had been built around the concept of a 'financing gap': on the basis of forecasts of economic performance, the Fund estimated the performance of the debtor country's balance of payments on current account, establishing the quantity of official finance needed to fill the gap between imports and exports of goods and services in the period required to adopt suitable economic policy measures to remove the imbalance. In the context that emerged as a result of financial and currency liberalization, however, the imbalance became more difficult to calculate. As James Boughton explained: 'the old approaches would not work, because new financing from the Fund would quickly be siphoned off as the indebted countries would have to repay other creditors'.[28]

In reality the problem was even more serious than in Boughton's description, because in a system of free movement of capital a crisis of confidence that began among foreign creditors could rapidly spread to resident operators, triggering a flight of capital. Not only could the 'financial imbalance' no longer be taken as a given feature of the problem, but it could become so large (in principle, the entire stock of liquid assets held by residents) as to outstrip even the lending ability of the IMF.

The debt crises of the 1980s were resolved through a mix of pragmatism and inventiveness. The debtor countries suspended repayments. At the same time the IMF began to organize concerted bailouts in which the main international banking institutions were called on to participate. Doubts linger over the effectiveness of these packages. It is, however, undeniable that they allowed a time span of several years during which those same banks were enabled to accumulate adequate reserves to absorb the losses from foreign loans and debtor countries to build political consensus on reform initiatives. Towards the end of the decade, with the Brady Plan, the need to cut the current value of Latin American debt was finally acknowledged and delivered with the help of official and private finance.[29]

The resolution of the crisis in the 1980s, which nevertheless required around ten years to take effect, was made possible by a favourable circumstance: the foreign debt of crisis countries was mostly concentrated in a small number of major banks. This had enabled the monetary authorities of the creditor countries to put pressure on investors not only to accept the suspension of debt repayments without taking devastating legal action, but also to participate in initiatives to lend financial support to the countries in crisis. It was this circumstance that gave the impression that the IMF loans could play a catalytic role, in other words could bolster confidence to the extent that investors would be persuaded to direct new capital towards the crisis countries.

The concept of 'catalytic official finance' (COF) gradually made its way into the lexicon of the IMF and the official community, and was revived and expanded during the subsequent wave of crises, which once again began in Mexico towards the end of 1994, before hitting various Asian countries, Russia, Brazil, Argentina, Turkey and several minor countries between 1997 and 2002. The new crises presented two additional difficulties with respect to the early 1980s. First, this time round foreign creditors were primarily represented by bondholders, who were much more fragmented numerically and less sophisticated financially (as well as less exposed to pressure from the authorities). Second, the crises all had distinctive traits: some were sovereign crises, others primarily banking ones, still others had a high debt exposure to the productive sector. The common element was simply that all the countries involved had had recourse to an external anchor, in the form of a fixed exchange rate, which had led national debtors to make massive use of often very short-term foreign currency loans.

In this new scenario the suspension of debt servicing appeared a high-risk option, because there was no guarantee that this would not trigger a wave of legal initiatives powerful enough not only to bring the country concerned to its knees, but perhaps the international financial system as well, directly or through contagion effects. There was nothing for it but to cling on to the notion of catalytic official finance, refining it on a technical and operational level. The main problem was that, since debt servicing could not be suspended, the official finance quantum had to be increased to suitably 'awe' the markets. This approach, however, raised two problems. The first was that a complete coverage of the risks creditors now faced was unthinkable, because as observed earlier this would have meant putting together loan packages of unprecedented dimensions, equal not only to the foreign debt of the country but also to the liquid assets held by residents. Even setting aside other considerations, without a centralized mechanism for the creation of liquidity, in other words a global central bank, these sums were inconceivable. Then there was the non-negligible problem of protecting the IMF itself from the risk of insolvency and of respecting the statutory limits. There was no immediate solution to the first problem. The second was remedied by establishing an innovative financial window, the Supplemental Reserve Facility (SRF), which was not subject to the usual financial limits on loans by the Fund. The new window was meant to facilitate large and immediate disbursements, albeit at less favourable conditions for the country concerned in the form of a penalizing interest rate, greater conditionality and a faster repayment schedule. In practice it was a 'Bagehotian' facility, adapted to the international context. However, recourse to this facility did not remove the catalytic nature of the interventions, because despite being very large, the official loans were unable to cover the entire theoretical financial imbalance. Forms of 'private sector involvement' – a new expression created especially for the occasion – had to accompany the disbursement of official funds. At the same time, another unprecedented financial window was being prepared at the initiative of the United States, the Contingent Credit Lines (CCL), which aimed at encouraging countries to prevent crises by taking prudential measures, in exchange for a promise by the IMF to provide large quantities of official finance should difficulties arise.

Catalytic packages were prepared for all the countries hit by crises in the closing years of the century, with the sole exception of Mexico in 1994–95. The verdict on their effectiveness, however, remains in doubt.[30] Much caution must be exercised in this respect, both because the crises we are talking about were unprecedented, and because it is impossible to say with statistical certainty what would have happened without packages of this kind. However, setting caution aside for a moment, it is reasonable to state that the packages based on the notion of COF disappointed expectations. A number of elements support this statement. First, while the aim of these packages was to make it possible for the debtor country to limit the economic and social costs of the crisis, it is easy to see how this result fell short of expectations. With the exception of Brazil in 1999, in all the countries that benefited from a catalytic package the real adjustment, measured by the variation in the balance of payments current account, was much larger than originally planned (Figure 6.2), evidence of the tendency to overestimate the catalytic effect of official finance. Second, even in those countries where the crises were promptly overcome, a precarious debt situation persists, as do many doubts over its sustainability in the medium to long term. It is significant, however, that in order to avoid further aggravating the

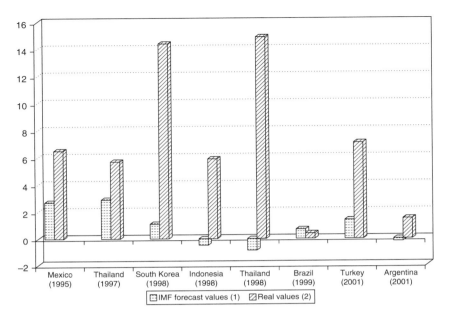

Notes:
1. Difference between the current balance forecast by the IMF for the reference year of the programme and the actual balance of the previous year.
2. Difference between the actual current balance for the reference year of the programme and the actual balance of the previous year.

Source: Atish Ghosh et al., 'IMF-supported programs in capital account crises', IMF Occasional Paper, No. 210, 2002.

Figure 6.2   Balance of payments current account developments in countries hit by crisis (% of GDP)

situation in the country, the anti-crisis facility was often used along with regular windows, which do not have penalizing rates, demonstrating once again the difficulties of applying Bagehot's rules (see Chapter 4). In one particularly prominent case, that of Argentina, despite a series of increases the catalytic package was unable to prevent a declaration of bankruptcy, whose consequences can still be felt today. In the meantime, the concentration of risks in the IMF portfolio reached unprecedented levels (Figure 6.3). To this day three-quarters of IMF lending concern just five of the 184 member countries. For its part, the CCL has remained a virtual facility, since none of the countries that could potentially benefit from the instrument have applied for it.

To understand why the catalytic packages (and the CCL) have met

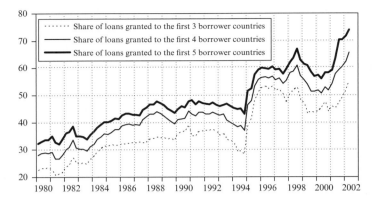

Source: International Monetary Fund, *International financial Statistics*, Washington, DC, various years.

Figure 6.3   Concentration of IMF loans (%)

with so many difficulties despite the extent of funding granted by the IMF, one needs to get to the heart of the limits of the cooperative model of central banking, the maximum expression of which is still today the IMF.[31] In the cooperative model, states remain sovereign. Now, a state is a very special debtor, because the government of a country represents a form of collective action, not a rational individual with clearly defined preferences. The behaviour of governments is determined, amongst other things, by a series of internal political constraints, and can be depicted as the result of a game between multiple 'principals' (pressure groups) and an agent (the government coalition) which, in the majority of cases has its own particular objective function.[32] This is the reason why the IMF ordinarily uses conditionality to safeguard its resources. But the problem is that in the face of a profound crisis of confidence, financial requirements are immediate, while conditionality requires time to take effect. Not only this, but the likelihood of success of a certain initiative is often endogenous, because building political consensus is as important as the quality of the economic policies adopted.[33] Nor can the results delivered in the past by the government of a country be taken as indicators of the likely success of future policies, because each round of voting, in democratic systems, or a change of government coalition, can usher in a change of regime, in other words of preferences. Moreover, some of the information needed to assess the sustainability of the debt of a country (just think of official reserves) are produced by the country itself: there is therefore a potential information asymmetry not just between the country and its private creditors, but also between the former and official financiers, such as the IMF.

The international lender of last resort therefore feels obliged to adopt measures to protect its own resources, such as forms of rationing, penalizing rates and others, thus casting doubts on its effectiveness as an insurer. In other words, why should private creditors feel reassured (thereby setting in motion the catalytic effect) by the intervention of an 'insurer', which in turn feels bound to protect itself from the risk assured, even to the point of taking steps that could aggravate the risk? The problem also arises at national level, but there it is mitigated by legal institutions, ranging from supervision to regulation, to the possibility of introducing a change of management, thereby attenuating its effects. In the context of the cooperative model (I will speak later about the consortium model), these institutions are not present at international level.[34]

The limits that emerged in the catalytic approach convinced the IMF (beginning in 2001 and therefore at the same time as the Argentinian authorities' declaration of insolvency) to pursue other forms of intervention in the event of debt crises which – based on the recommendations of the Rey Report (named after the Chairman of the working group) for the G-10[35] – place less emphasis on loans and more on debt restructuring procedures. The result was the 'two-track' approach embraced by the Group of Seven (G-7)[36] and the former Interim Committee, which later became the International Monetary and Financial Committee (IMFC), at their spring meetings of 2002. The two tracks in question comprised, on the one hand, the so-called collective action clauses proposed by the Rey Group, that is, contractual instruments designed to facilitate the coordination of bondholders if debtors found themselves in financial difficulties; and on the other hand, a new bankruptcy procedure to negotiate forms of debt restructuring, equipped with legal instruments able to impose decisions taken jointly by a debtor and a qualified majority of creditors on any eventual dissenting creditors.

The basic idea underpinning the new approach was that the catalytic model was ill-suited to managing crises of uncertain nature, in which the sustainability of debt is called into question. This is because in reality the catalytic model places responsibility for intervening entirely on the debtor country given that the Fund loans, besides entailing conditionality, that is, a certain amount of macroeconomic adjustment, are provided for a valuable consideration.[37] It is reasonable to argue, however, that for the political reasons mentioned earlier on, the debtor country or rather the taxpayer who ultimately shoulders the costs of economic adjustment and debt servicing is not best placed, in the context of sovereign credit, to implement the measures aimed at curtailing the risk of crises. Among the analytic tools of economic law, the concept of 'cheapest cost avoider' is often employed for allocating accident costs.[38] In terms of international lending, on one level the current practice of letting the costs of managing crises fall on the debtor alone does not reduce the risk of crises, because on the contrary governments have every interest in delaying for as long as possible the admission of a situation of unsustainable debt; on another level, they can result in the creditor – although often an intermediary specialized in information gathering and management – not paying adequate attention to the creditworthiness of the financial sovereign subject. Overall, the result is more crises than probably would have otherwise occurred, and certainly an excessive delay in dealing with what by that time are unavoidable crises, with a consequent rise in social costs.

The aim of the two-track policy is therefore to prepare instruments in advance for the coordination of creditors and to reduce the immediate costs borne by the debtor country, to encourage not only crisis prevention, but also more timely initiatives to prevent the spread of the crises that would erupt anyway.[39] Changing the forms of intervention and financial crisis management is a complex enterprise, comprising not just the creation of new legal structures at international level, but also a credible review of the lending policies adopted by the IMF, to prevent unreasonably frequent recourse to catalytic official finance. This is why the two-track policy was accompanied by much meditation on the operational criteria and procedures of the Fund, as well as on the various financial facilities. It is still too early to say, however, whether the official declarations, which appear to be moving in the right direction, will be matched by concrete and timely action. The fact remains that the reform initiatives clash, as already happened in the years leading up to Bretton Woods, with the strong opposition of international high finance. When the Rey Report was published in 1996, the Institute of International Finance, spokesperson of the main international banking and financial companies, attacked its recommendations, branding them scatterbrained and harbingers of moral hazard. Later, however, this judgement was revised, so much so that nowadays the collective action clauses appear both in the official sector programmes and in private sector ones.

Today the opposition of the financial community is directed above all at the debt restructuring proposals, and the policy for the revision of the financing rules of the Fund. At first sight, this opposition is understandable: nobody likes being indicated as the cheapest cost avoider. To the extent that official action ought to end by reducing the costs of crises paid by the taxpayers of debtor countries, this would necessarily entail an increase in the costs borne by creditors. But this would only be a short-term consequence, aimed at modifying incentives with a view to encouraging greater caution on the sovereign debt market and, in the final analysis, lower costs overall for managing the crisis. All institutional reform initiatives, if put together well and pragmatically implemented, bring benefits for all. This was the case in both the development of central banks and the establishment of the IMF. In both instances, the financial sector fought a rearguard battle, right up to the point when pathological events convinced it that the reform was also in its own interest. Everything points to the same ending this time round too, since the limits of the cooperative model in creating international liquidity are too evident for things to be left in their current state. It is likely that the alternative to reform is not the maintenance of the status quo, so much as a regression towards updated forms of financial and commercial autarchy. International finance, it is to be hoped, will know how to change its stance as it did in the past to ensure this does not happen. When and how, only tomorrow will tell.

6.4 THE INFORMAL COOPERATIVE REGIME: THE BANK FOR INTERNATIONAL SETTLEMENTS AND 'SOFT LAW'[40]

At the time the IMF and the World Bank were established, another institution that shared at least two traits of central banks had been operating for 15 years. The institution in question boasted a highly unusual legal structure and a certain amount of operational and administrative opacity. It was, of course, the Bank for International Settlements (BIS). The BIS was founded in 1930 with the aim of acting as agent for the Young Plan, devised by the victorious powers of the First World War to allow the settlement of German war debts. Although based in Basel, the BIS was not subject either to commercial law or to Swiss banking laws; its legal statute was that of an international body that enjoyed special immunities and privileges.

In the period between the end of the Second World War and the early 1970s, the main activity of the BIS was that of supporting and strengthening the Bretton Woods system.[41] After the oil crises of the 1970s, the focus moved above all to the management of international capital flows. These crises also highlighted the need for better supervision of banks that were more active at international level and, more generally, of the development of international cooperation; something the BIS has made a major contribution to. A particularly important step at the end of 1974, following the failure of several banks with significant international assets,[42] was the creation by the G-10 central banks of the Standing Committee on Banking Regulations and Supervisory Practices, known simply as the

Basel Committee. Despite its informal nature and the fact that it had no legal force, its authoritativeness, technical competence and small number of members made it the most active committee in international financial cooperation.

In its first years of activity, the Basel Committee devoted itself primarily to ensuring that every active international bank had a clearly identified national supervisor, with a precise division of duties between it and the supervisor in the host country. Later on, the Committee obtained important results with the adoption of the principle of supervision on a consolidated basis for international activities, irrespective of the jurisdiction in which the supervision occurred. Finally, at the beginning of the 1980s, following the debt crises in developing countries the G-10 entrusted the Basel Committee with the development, amongst other things, of an internationally applicable system for measuring the credit risk and minimum capital requirements for banks. This effort also led to the Capital Accord of 1998,[43] and the more recent legal structure commonly known as 'Basel II'.

Ever since the Asian crisis of 1997, the issue of financial stability in a context of deeper economic integration and the globalization of finance has been at the centre of attention. In particular, the aim has been to promote a solid regulatory structure worldwide, especially in emerging markets. This signals a major departure from the past, considering that the prevailing doctrine in the run-up to the above-mentioned crisis defined the design and management of the so-called 'safety net' for the banking system as a prerogative of individual nation-states. The safety net is the set of legal and institutional structures set up to safeguard the system with the aim of curtailing the scope and economic consequences of a crisis. This new form of international cooperation constitutes the institutionalization of the approach developed by the Basel Committee, based on the formulation of recommendations and best practices of a non-binding nature: in brief, standards and codes of conduct defined at international level but not legally binding, so that their adoption and implementation are left to the discretion of national authorities, which are in turn stimulated to take action by a system of incentives that is also established internationally.

This is known as the 'soft law' approach. Its precepts do not, in fact, have either the force of ordinary law or the weakness of international conventions,[44] but are, in essence, a process through which informal international agreements are adopted at the level of national jurisdictions. A similar interpretation can be given to current trends in the field of regulation, aimed at forms of action that reflect the need to adapt to diverse institutional contexts, rather than the mechanical transfer of laws already existing in industrialized countries. In other words, soft law is an attempt to reconcile the need to harmonize national financial systems (and the laws that regulate them) with the need to insert international regulatory standards in the political–legal structures of the individual countries (the embeddedness principle), in order to gain the necessary support to attribute legitimacy and flexibility to the standards themselves. This principle reflects the fact that the success of regulatory changes at international level depends on there being adequate national consensus.

Soft law accordingly positions itself as an intermediate regime between centralized global forms of regulation and supervision (up to the extreme of the World Financial Authority proposed by Eatwell and Taylor),[45] on the one hand, and overly simplified and mechanical rules on the other (for example, the idea of making IMF loans subject to a limited number of structural preconditions, along the lines suggested by the Meltzer Commission[46] and George Soros[47]). Contrary to popular opinion, the soft law approach is not the direct result of the Asian crisis. As recalled earlier, in fact, standards and codes of good conduct have influenced international economic and financial relations in various ways since the formation of the Basel Committee in the early 1970s. Besides, the merit of this approach's appeal beyond its normal geographical boundaries can be attributed to the report drawn up immediately prior to the outbreak of the Asian crisis by a working group chaired by Mario Draghi, and established under the aegis of the G-10, albeit including representatives from other countries.[48] It was, however, the Asian crisis that won operational consent and transformed soft law from an approach to a genuine policy strategy.[49]

The conclusions of the G-10 report were taken up again and added to in 1998 in the reports of three sub-groups of the Group of Twenty-Two (G-22) or Willard Group.[50] In early 1999 they became part of the G-7 plan of action, which in the same period established a new body specifically dedicated to strengthening financial supervision and regulation worldwide, the Financial Stability Forum (FSF).[51] The Forum, the only body specially created to improve the coordination and exchange of information between different national authorities responsible for financial stability and identify the actions needed to curb the weaknesses of the international financial system, is the main pillar of the current strategy of cooperation based on soft law. This revolves around three key elements: objectives, governance and incentives.

Regarding the objectives, the aim of the Forum is to gather, internalize and promote the standards devised by specialized bodies, such as the International Organization of Securities Commissions (IOSCO) and the International Association of Insurance Supervisors (IAIS), to ensure they are adopted more swiftly and comprehensively. The first act of the Forum was to compile a list of 69 standards deemed important for international financial stability, summarized in three main categories: macroeconomics, market and institutional infrastructures, financial regulation and supervision. The Forum then identified 12 standards it believed were key for the solidity of financial systems and for which it recommended adoption as a matter of priority. These are minimum requirements of good practice and implicitly presuppose the existence of a reliable legal system and clear rules of political responsibility in the country where they are adopted. But the Forum's activity is not confined to the area of standards and comprises, among other things, the identification of potential weaknesses in the financial system. On this issue it has already published numerous reports, the most important of which concern highly leveraged financial institutions, capital flows and offshore financial centres. Its report in the early 2000s on offshore financial centres that attract investors and financial intermediaries by offering lower taxes and less stringent prudential requirements was particularly important; the result was the publication in March 2001 of a tripartite classification of these centres based on the nature of the regulatory framework. Not surprisingly, the publication of this list caused an outcry.

In respect of governance the soft law strategy faces a kind of trade-off. On the one hand, given that consensus forms the basis of viable informal cooperation, in order for it to work properly the rules it establishes must be perceived as legitimate by the countries bound by them. On the other, the pursuit of consensus implies the need to welcome new members into the cooperative fold. This, however, clashes with the desire of the largest countries, which initiated international cooperation on financial matters, not to overly dilute their decision-making powers. In reality though, in order to boost their chances of success a moderate expansion of membership of the main international fora was inevitable.[52] Broader participation actually lessens the risk that a small group of countries can impose their own standards, and this softens Parliaments' resistance when it comes to the crucial act of transposing these same standards into national law.

The issue of incentives, finally, is of particular importance. The essential characteristic of soft law is the absence of any enforceability requirement using traditional legal means, given that standards are mere recommendations by international bodies and do not have any legal force: the use of incentives are therefore crucial to ensuring their adoption. In theory there are two kinds of incentives: indirect incentives, stemming from market reactions to non-compliance with the standards; and direct incentives, stemming from official community actions. One would expect that in a globalized economy with decentralized governance, the first set of incentives would provide greater stimulus. Instead, in a survey conducted by a working group[53] of the Forum it emerged that market participants were either completely unfamiliar with or only partly acquainted with the numerous standards. One of the most important (and surprising) results of this survey was the fact that these operators assigned greater importance to the existence of a transparent legal and judicial system (as a precondition for an accurate, reliable and effective assessment of risk) than to the observance of the standards themselves.

To a certain extent these results can be attributed to the novelty of the soft law approach, with the implication that over time market participants should learn to attribute greater importance to the observance of the standards. For the time being, however, the success of the strategy is in the hands of the official community, whose first task must be to establish adequate incentives. These fall into three main categories: peer pressure, naming and shaming, and financial incentives. To these can be added the surveillance by international financial institutions.

Peer pressure is the mechanism traditionally employed by the Basel Committee and in other international or supranational contexts, for example the Organisation for Economic Co-operation and Development (OECD) and the European Union. In the international relations lexicon, it is expected to be effective only when the authorities of the countries already form a so-called 'epistemic community', in the sense that they share the same world vision and assign the same value to the advantages deriving from cooperation. Naming and shaming is a more severe instrument and consists in bringing to public attention those countries or financial centres that do not conform to internationally accepted codes of good conduct. In recent times this instrument has been used more frequently than in the past: in addition to the above-mentioned tripartition of offshore centres by the Forum, the main examples concern the classification of the jurisdictions by the Financial Action Task Force (FATF) based on each jurisdictions will to cooperate with international authorities to combat money laundering, and the OECD list of tax havens. The surveillance by international financial institutions lies halfway between peer pressure and naming and shaming, given that it relies on in-depth analyses of the conditions of individual countries whose publication, however, is voluntary. In 1999 the IMF and World Bank introduced two new instruments with this purpose in mind, the Report on the Observance of Standards and Codes (ROSC) and the Financial Sector Assessment Program (FSAP). The first aims to provide a brief overview of compliance with standards by the country concerned; the second, which is broader in scope, is aimed among other things at identifying the strengths, weaknesses and risks of the financial systems, in addition to the most appropriate policy responses.

But the most obvious form of financial incentive is the inclusion of compliance with international standards in the context of 'conditionality': the set of requirements that determines the IMF's decision whether or not to grant financial support to member countries. To a certain extent, the Fund already appears to incorporate conditionality in its daily operations, in the numerous conditions for the financial sector of a country that are generally included in mutually agreed programmes. Another instrument would consist in granting countries that comply with the international standards more favourable weighting for the purposes of prudential capital provisioning by commercial lending banks. However, due to the difficulties raised by this kind of incentive, it is unlikely that it will be widely used in the foreseeable future.

Given this, it is clear that the success of the soft law strategy ultimately depends on the strength of incentives as perceived by the national authorities of the beneficiary countries. Indeed, it is important to avoid the risk highlighted by Giovanoli that soft law turns out to be 'nothing more than the product of "fair weather architecture", without a proper roof', liable to 'crumble like adobe structures with the first heavy rainfall'.[54] In particular, the spreading of standards to emerging countries presents greater difficulties due to the broader differences between these countries' economies and levels of financial development compared with the G-10 nations. This inevitably heightens uncertainty over the results of the process itself, whose success requires: (1) consensus among the group of countries requesting the application of standards; and (2) strong political willpower, within the group as well as within the countries that are requested to apply the standards. It is precisely in this area that progress has so far been slow: soft law still lacks any clearly defined strategy to ensure a reasonably rapid transposition of international rules into national law. In this respect, there are three areas where more could and should be done: the opening of the financial sector to foreign ownership, the strengthening of incentives, and the building of a hard roof for soft law.

Regarding the first point, the strategy rightly does not identify the financial sector structure considered best suited to meeting previously set objectives. This neutrality, however, fails to take into account that a significant presence of foreign-owned financial institutions appears to be a precondition for the rapid transition to a financial regulatory system that reinforces and supports market institutes and instruments. More generally, a greater foreign presence in local financial markets entails both benefits (which are probably less clear in the short term), and risks. The competitive pressures deriving from the entry of foreign institutions appears to stimulate improvements in the national banking system's allocational and operational efficiency. In the event of a crisis of confidence, foreign banks could act as safe havens for national depositors.[55] Furthermore, opening up to foreign intermediaries should enable emerging markets to 'import' both better-quality supervision and better institutions and market practices. On the downside, there is certainly the risk of cherry-picking, in other words that foreign institutional investors might acquire only the most profitable markets and consumers. In the short term, this could lead to a rise in operational costs of national banks, in addition to a higher-risk portfolio and, therefore, in the absence of any strengthening of supervision, a strong temptation for these banks to act imprudently.

On the issue of strengthening incentives, there is broad consensus that in the long term market incentives are the greatest stimulation for the adoption of international prudential standards. In the short term, however, this cannot be taken as given. As we saw earlier, the survey conducted by the Forum demonstrated that the degree of compliance with standards by countries is not a determining factor for market participants when it comes to making decisions. As a result, the official incentives cannot but play a vital role in determining the success or failure of the soft law strategy. Still, the official incentives employed up to now, such as peer pressure and financial support interventions, have highlighted serious defects in the present system. Indeed, peer pressure is not effective when the authorities of countries are heterogeneous or when national interests diverge too widely.[56] In the case of financial support, a mechanical assessment of the degree of a country's compliance with international regulatory and supervisory norms based, in particular, on a small number of criteria, clashes with current trends that instead envisage forms of intervention characterized by an ability to adapt to the conditions of individual countries and by compliance with the embeddedness principle.

For these reasons the international community would probably do well to be less hesitant in allowing the publication of the judgments on countries' compliance with prudential standards. First employed in the financial field in March 2001 for the tripartite classification of offshore centres by the Forum, the naming and shaming instrument is probably the most effective in this respect. It has, however, several limits, such as being ineffective in jurisdictions whose real *raison d'être* is regulatory laxity or support for illegal activities. The problem of providing incisive official incentives could alternatively be dealt with through a stricter use of the 'right of establishment' (known as the access policy): banks lacking adequate supervision structures in their country of origin should not be allowed to conduct international activities. As radical as this might seem, it is actually a simple reiteration of the philosophy underlying the bank Concordat of 1975, the objective of which was to ensure that no bank operating abroad failed to ensure adequate supervision.[57]

The debate on incentives introduces a more general problem concerning the current version of soft law. In a context of sovereign states, multilateral institutions and intergovernmental fora can provide incentives, but not replace national authorities. This is why, given its flexible and practical nature, soft law is particularly appropriate, while an approach based on a set of binding norms (hard law) is probably not. However, this does not mean that the soft and hard approaches must be considered mutually exclusive. Indeed, a hard roof for soft law, capable of protecting the principles of free movement of capital and financial stability as international public goods, actually seems necessary in order to remedy what is soft law's principal defect: the absence of any formal and explicit recognition by the international community of the objectives and principles the strategy intends to pursue. More specifically, the risk that soft law will turn out to be toothless in the long run stems from the omission to mention either financial stability or the liberalization of capital movements in the Articles of Agreement of the International Monetary Fund, the international treaty on which the IMF's legitimacy depends.

It is difficult to achieve and maintain agreement on actions based on official incentives, such as naming and shaming or setting limits on the right of establishment, in a context like the present one, when the principles underpinning the incentives themselves are not clearly recognized or, worse still, can be seen as being in conflict with a certain institution's mandate (in this case the IMF's). This is why the soft law strategy could be interpreted as an attempt to build financial stability into a structure, the Articles of Agreement of the IMF, designed for an economic landscape in which controls on capital movements and financial repression were considered to be permanent features.

Another aspect of the legal problem of soft law strategy has to do with the fact that promoting the liberalization of capital movements, depending on the extent to which international financial stability is protected, puts more pressure on emerging market economies than on industrialized ones. This could be read as a violation of the universality (or equal treatment) and reciprocity principles on which the IMF was founded. Although this argument appears rather weak from an economic perspective, considering that compared to mature markets, emerging market economies need different doses of structural and macroeconomic policies to restore confidence after a financial crisis, it is difficult to contest on a strictly legal level. Accordingly, the real question that needs asking is: what can be done to reinforce the soft law strategy at the level of principles?

The obvious solution would be to amend the Articles of Agreement in order to include financial stability and the liberalization of capital movements among the IMF's objectives. This is an old leitmotif of financial cooperation, on which the international community came very close to reaching agreement, before the talks were ended by the outbreak of the

Asian crisis in 1997. The idea of amending the Articles, however, in addition to there not being general agreement on its desirability,[58] is dubious from a political feasibility perspective in a world of almost 200 nations. Moreover, there is nothing to prevent – at least in theory – a small group of countries from deciding to act according to the principle of leading by example, in other words negotiating and underwriting an international treaty that clearly sanctions principles acknowledged as being essential. In this regard, attention has been called to the significant progress made by the European Union (EU) in the areas of financial integration and regulatory harmonization.[59]

The principle of the free circulation of capital was adopted by the six founding member states of the European Community in 1957, although its translation into concrete action took 20 years. The real turning point for European integration came in 1985, however, when it was realized that the completion of a common market for financial services would not require the harmonization of all applicable regulations. This approach essentially consisted in the single market strategy, which relied on the three pillars of mutual recognition, home country control and minimum prudential standards.

The effectiveness of this new strategy of international cooperation was demonstrated by the fact that in July 1990 eight of the 12 EU countries removed all restrictions on capital movements; having survived the serious currency crises of 1992–93, both the authorities and the public considered this development as being to all intents and purposes irreversible. Despite the need for caution and adaptation implicit in any future attempt to replicate the single market strategy at global level, it seems important to point out how the method adopted in Europe was one factor in the success of the financial integration strategy. This method basically consists in the use of so-called 'Directives', legal documents containing the principles that member states must respect, as an instrument for translating international standards into legally binding rules. At the same time, countries enjoy a high level of freedom in choosing how to implement these principles, and an appropriate transition phase is also envisaged.

Finally, the entire single market structure was built around the idea that, in order for the strategy to work, what ultimately mattered was the will of a critical mass of countries and not unanimity among EU members. It was this principle of leading by example that enabled the gradual enlargement of the Union from its original six members to the current 27 members. The European example demonstrates the importance of specifying clearly the objectives of the process of international financial harmonization and shared principles, in addition to the desirability of a flexible approach, leaving ample room for national preferences and traditions.

This, moreover, highlights how soft law and hard law are ultimately not alternative but rather complementary approaches.

6.5   THE CONSORTIUM REGIME: THE EUROPEAN SYSTEM OF CENTRAL BANKS

The date of 1 January 1999 signals a break in the history of central banking. It marks the renouncement by 11 EU countries of their national currencies in favour of a single currency, the euro, and the unprecedented start of operations of an authentically supranational central bank with a federal structure, the European System of Central Banks (ESCB). It was the first – and to this day the only – example of a consortium regime.[60]

There are at least three interesting things that we can learn from Europe's experience. First, it represented an innovation that was grafted onto a much more ambitious economic and institutional plan for integration, which began in the years immediately following the Second World War and reached its highest expression in the Single European Act of 1986. Monetary union, in other words, was made possible by the building up over several decades of a supranational institutional capital, as well as of a network of intergovernmental relations capable of boosting mutual trust between European states. Second, the European monetary project was originally a response to the decline of the cooperative regime. After it was first formulated in 1970 under the Werner Plan (itself a revival of the cooperative regime, written in response to the strains that would ultimately end in the collapse of the Bretton Woods exchange regime), it was not until the Treaty of Maastricht in February 1992 that the first consciously consortium version appeared. This, to some extent, was a response to the malfunctions of the European Monetary System, also destined to result in the massive currency crisis of 1992–93. Finally, some scholars claim that EMU was an apparent contradiction of the neoclassical theory of optimal monetary areas. In particular, the plans for its institutional structure and system of controls on the public finances, which are still decentralized, did not appear to tally with the prescriptions of theory, which instead envisage that fixed exchange rates should be accompanied by the centralization of public budget at area level and by its greater flexibility, for the purposes of anti-cyclical stabilization.[61]

Hence the scepticism with which most economists greeted the plan for monetary unification. In reality, as we shall see, the institutional fortress that was erected around the euro, and the structure of the European System of Central Banks, which was both complex and unprecedented, could be seen as necessary steps to bolster trust in a currency that was fully supranational for the first time. Steps, that is, towards the realization of an optimal currency area, rather than an expression of inadequate political awareness of the institutional needs of a pre-existing optimal currency area.[62]

The history of European monetary integration is a long one, whose first steps date from the foundation in 1950 of the European Payments Union (EPU) and the Treaty of Rome, which established the European Economic Community (EEC) in 1957. The EPU was a regional response to the scarcity of dollars that the Bretton Woods system suffered from in its first years of operation. The member countries agreed to liberalize commercial transactions in exchange for a system of mutual loans, which allowed them to economize on their dollar and gold disbursements and settle imbalances in their balance of payments through a compensation mechanism. While the EPU's structure was very similar to the Bretton Woods system, its philosophy was not, as it recognized that in the interest of global economic stability intra-European trade liberalization should happen more rapidly than that at global level, which was instead pursued through the Bretton Woods agreements. By supporting the EPU, the United States implicitly acknowledged that the scarcity of dollars was the main problem of the cooperative regime centred around the IMF.[63] The Treaty of Rome, for its part, was also important because although it did not contain any monetary prescriptions, it acknowledged that exchange rates between the currencies of EEC member states were 'a matter of common concern'.

But for so long as the Bretton Woods structure remained in place, there was no reason to move beyond these preliminary steps. The EPU was dissolved in 1958, when general trade convertibility was restored, and the principle adopted in the Treaty of Rome remained long forgotten. Things changed towards the end of the 1960s, when signs of an incipient dollar crisis, and more generally of the exchange system created at Bretton Woods, began to become more evident. In an attempt to safeguard intra-European trade, whose share of total European trade had expanded rapidly in the interim thanks to the customs union and other community policies, especially in agriculture, in 1970 the EEC member states decided to set up a commission to study a European monetary arrangement. The Werner Plan, named after the Luxembourg Prime Minister who was asked to chair the commission, was strongly influenced by the doctrine of the optimal currency areas, which in those very years was being developed by Robert Mundell and his followers.[64] The plan was to complete monetary union by 1980 by progressively narrowing the fluctuation bands of the exchange rates and gradually coordinating economic policies. However, what was most interesting about the plan was the absence of any recommendation on the centralization of monetary policy or the establishment of a single currency, both seen as irrelevant steps once exchange rates had been irrevocably fixed and central bank policies coordinated, and the importance that was instead attributed to centralizing budgetary policy at community level.

The Werner Plan had no practical outcome, unless we attribute to the Plan the obstinacy of the European countries in attempting to fix their reciprocal exchange rates when dollar convertibility was suspended, in 1971, and in later years, despite the quadrupling of oil prices between 1973 and 1974. The result of this quest for intra-European exchange rate stability was the Monetary Snake, which envisaged maximum fluctuation bands of 4.5 per cent, the establishment of short-term lending facilities to combat pressures on the exchange rates of member countries and the creation of a European Monetary Cooperation Fund (EMCF). The history of the Snake was, however, a history of failures: for the entire 1970s stable exchange rates remained a mirage. In retrospect, this reflected, on the one hand, the extremely unfavourable climate in which the Snake found itself having to operate; and on the other, the lack of institutionalization of the structure, as the EMCF was little more than a verbal expression and entirely lacking in any of the conditions needed to coordinate economic policies among European countries. In particular, there was no shared mechanism to allocate the burden of economic adjustment between creditor and debtor countries – the old problem that had forever hindered the working of cooperative monetary regimes.

But by that time the process of European economic and institutional integration had reached a point where any reversal was hard to imagine. This explains how the failures of the Snake led to a new cooperative regime, the European Monetary System (EMS), which in the long run would provide what was needed for the journey to monetary unification. The plan, which became reality in 1979, tried to reconcile the need for symmetrical adjustment in the presence of pressures on exchange rates with maintaining adequate discipline in the economic policies of countries with weak currencies. It did this by advancing institutional requisites more than the Snake had ever done. First, the role of the Monetary Committee of the European Community was strengthened, a body representing all the finance ministries and central banks of member countries, whose job was to assess the economic policies of members, who also agreed to keep their exchange rates within the fluctuation band of 2.25 per cent.[65] To strengthen this assessment, and this was a significant departure from the Snake, quantitative indicators of divergence were agreed on, which were intended to signal the need for corrective measures to safeguard the fluctuation band in both creditor and debtor countries. Given this institutionalized control mechanism, countries whose currencies had been subject to downward pressure were allowed to borrow unlimited currency through the very short-term financial facility that already existed under the Snake.

It is hard to establish to what extent a cooperative monetary regime has been successful or not. The aim of an exchange rate agreement is not to maintain fixed exchange rates, because some macroeconomic imbalances may require variations of the parity. Rather, the objective pursued is that of ensuring an orderly process of macroeconomic adjustment, if necessary including agreed exchange rate adjustments. For example, the design fault in the Bretton Woods system was its overly rigid exchange rates, and it was this and not excessive turbulence which sowed the seeds of the 1971–73 crisis. By contrast, the experience of the Snake can be considered a disappointing one precisely because of the mechanism's inability to guarantee an orderly process of parity adjustments. In this context, the verdict on the EMS should be separated into two phases. In its first years of activity, the EMS was highly successful. Between 1979 and 1983 there were realignments on average once every eight months, and without any major tensions. In the four years that followed, there were increasingly difficult realignments every 12 months. From 1987 to 1992 there were none, and indeed this period is known as the 'hard-EMS'. The apparent stability of the system was instead a sign of weakness. The lack of realignments was not due to the absence of imbalances, but rather to the difficulties involved in achieving an orderly revision of the exchange rates in a context where, as a result of the Single Act of 1986, the member states were moving decisively down the road to currency liberalization. It was this growing capital mobility that paradoxically tended to harden exchange rates, making it more difficult to govern coordinated realignments – a similar problem to the one that had undermined the cooperative regime of Bretton Woods.

In principle, the EMS had a defence mechanism that Bretton Woods did not have, and that is unlimited very short-term loans. But the credibility of the mechanism was subject to the size of the imbalances to be financed. And indeed, on entry into the EMS, the President of the Bundesbank, Otto Emminger, penned a confidential letter to the German Chancellor, wisely affirming the Bank's right to not provide unlimited loans to countries that had suffered exchange rate pressure, if this were to conflict with the maintenance of internal monetary stability, which would in fact have been the case if the German government proved unable to ensure the devaluation of the currency under pressure.

This exchange of letters was kept secret for the entire lifespan of the EMS. Meanwhile in the wake of the Single Act, currency liberalization and the apparent stability of the hard-EMS, the plan for monetary unification returned to the fore. This time round, there was much greater political decisiveness in addressing the issue compared with the beginning of the 1970s. In 1989 the new Delors Plan was published, which was transformed into a binding international treaty in February 1992 in Maastricht. The plan for monetary unification was no longer a working hypothesis; rather it was a political agreement sanctioned by a legislative Act which, once ratified by the respective Parliaments, would attain constitutional status. As to the contents, the Delors Plan differed in almost every way from the Werner Plan.

In the monetary sphere the recommendations included the issue of a single currency and centralization of monetary policy, under the control of a newly established body, the European Central Bank, which would enjoy a high degree of autonomy from the political authorities. In the area of taxation, by contrast, the hypothesis of centralization was rejected. Moreover, it was recommended that national budgetary policies be subject to quantitative limits in order to guarantee adequate discipline in the conduct of national economic policies. Like the Werner Plan, the Delors Plan envisaged the gradual attainment of the objective of monetary unification. But this time round, there were three clearly defined phases to be completed, which would begin with the complete liberalization of capital movements and end with the introduction of the single currency and establishment of the European Central Bank, assuming that a sufficient number of states met several economic requirements (the so-called 'convergence criteria').[66] The middle phase, due to begin in 1994, would be devoted to technical preparation, through closer coordination of the economic policies and the establishment of a provisional body, the European Monetary Institute, charged with preparing the ground for the future central bank.

The substance and in many instances also the form of the Delors Plan were taken over by the Maastricht Treaty, a document whose most interesting feature was, perhaps, the fact that it was signed at all. We saw earlier on how the failed transition from the cooperative regime to a consortium system when faced with a hegemonic drift was what ultimately determined the destiny of Bretton Woods. In Europe a similar situation was beginning to take shape. The growing inflexibility of the EMS meant that European monetary policy was de facto conducted by the Bundesbank, while all the other countries were obliged to take steps to avoid speculative attacks in a context of high capital mobility. Why did the German authorities accept what the American authorities had rejected, that is, to tie their hands by sharing their own monetary sovereignty with other countries?

There are two possible answers to this question. First of all, in a certain sense the plan for monetary unification in Europe was endogenous: in other words, it was the natural conclusion of a process of institutional and political integration that was deeply rooted in the past. It was probably no coincidence that the main champion of German adherence to Maastricht was not the Economy Minister but the Minister of Foreign Affairs, who saw the Treaty as a fundamental step towards the political unification of the EU. Second, an important role was played by the farsightedness of the authors of the Delors Plan, who understood that monetary unification could not be reduced to a technical event, precisely for the relative institutional incompleteness of the European context. It was necessary to nourish and foster the trust of member states in the new currency, and it was precisely on this issue that the Maastricht Treaty was most innovative. From the point of view of its complementarity with the rest of the European edifice, especially regarding the community *acquis* and in its reference to the founding principles of European law – mutual recognition, minimal harmonization, subsidiarity – the Treaty outlined a unique blueprint for the EU central banking model. It also set out the fundamental guidelines for a system of coordination and reciprocal surveillance of economic policies of member countries that would later be implemented under the Growth and Stability Pact, signed in June 1997 by the EMU countries in addition to the Treaty.

The adoption of a single currency got to the root of two problems posed by the cooperative regime: that of ensuring uniform adjustment between member countries, and that of guaranteeing a sufficient and transparent supply of liquidity. A third problem, however, was only exacerbated: that connected with confidence in the new currency and the legitimacy of the body proposed for its management. It could not be taken for granted that the new currency, the euro, would enjoy the same level of trust as the hegemonic currency it had replaced, the German mark. In other words, the euro would be born without its own brand capital. Likewise, it could not be taken for granted that the new central bank conceived in the Delors Plan would be seen as equally legitimate in all member states. Both these problems were compounded by the climate of uncertainty in which the new central bank would have to operate. It was to be expected that, for several years, knowledge of the statistical properties of the data needed for monetary policy purposes and of the transmission mechanism itself would be patchy, or in any event less reliable than average national statistics. The new central bank would therefore necessarily have high margins of discretionary power, and would be more likely to err. The challenge was to prevent the risk that this situation could lead to the outbreak of political conflicts capable of upsetting the enterprise and damaging the process of economic and political integration. The institutional picture that emerged from the Treaty attempted to respond to these requirements, on the one hand, by drawing up a new model of federal central bank; and on the other, by providing, via the Stability and Growth Pact, clear rules for coordinating the economic policies of individual member states through the peer surveillance mechanism.

6.5.1 The European System of Central Banks

The plans for the central bank's structure echoed the traits and experiences of the other two main federal central banks, the Federal Reserve and the Bundesbank. But both these models were extended and refined, in the knowledge that there was a substantial difference between a federal central bank operating in what was also a federal political system, and a federal central bank operating in a system of nation-states. The newer aspects regarded the definition of the bank's purpose and functions, its degree of institutional and operational autonomy, its governance and its working structures. On the first point, the Treaty indicated price stability as its prime objective, adding that other macroeconomic objectives could be pursued only if they were not detrimental to the primary objective. Of the bank's functions, monetary policy was assigned absolute pre-eminence. After this, the central bank was assigned the task of guaranteeing the proper functioning of the payment system. By contrast, it was not given any direct role in banking supervision, in recognition of the fact that not all EU countries assigned this function to the central bank.

This set-up both reflected and confirmed the changes that had taken place in central banking in the interim, due to the decline of the fiat standard in the 1970s, which I dealt with in the previous chapter. Special care was taken to enlarge the new central bank's sphere of independence as much as possible, in order to prevent it from falling prey to political interference. On an institutional level, the central bank was prohibited from soliciting or accepting instructions from any of the member states or community bodies. On the level of instruments, first of all, the Treaty assigned to the central bank the task of 'defining and implementing the monetary policy of the Community'; secondly, the central bank was banned from granting any form of monetary loan to the governments of member countries of the Union. Finally, on a financial level, it was established that the seignorage resulting from the conduct of monetary policy be used to guarantee the financial autonomy of the central bank.[67]

These elements of the Treaty risked putting the newly established central bank into institutional limbo and pushing its autonomy towards genuine political independence, which was unacceptable in a fiat standard regime. Hence the need to legitimize the management of the euro with suitable legal arrangements. The first and most important of these was precisely the federal structure, by virtue of which the 'European central bank' was in reality a composite body, comprising the central banks of the countries belonging to the euro (at that time 12) and a central monetary body located in Frankfurt, which was rather misleadingly called the European Central Bank (ECB). The Treaty called this composite body the European System of Central Banks, transformed in practice into the Eurosystem to take account of the fact that not all EU countries were also part of the monetary union. The governing arrangements faithfully replicated this structure. The Governing Council is the supreme decision-making body, comprising the governors of all the adhering national central banks and the six members of the ECB's Executive Board, nominated for a limited period via a complex intergovernmental procedure and responsible for implementing the Council's decisions and overseeing the day-to-day running of the ECB. The operational structure also helps in the legitimization process. Unlike the American model, which combines decision-making centralization with a high degree of operative centralization, the EU tends towards a model of operative decentralization, whereby broad responsibilities are given to the national central banks. The operational and decision-making link is guaranteed by permanent committees of national experts competent in each area, whose task is to work with all the national central banks to investigate the issues to be brought to the attention of the Governing Council.

6.5.2 The Stability and Growth Pact

One clause of the Treaty envisages that, in addition to meeting the convergence criteria for joining EMU, member countries must also work to avoid 'excessive' public deficits – defined as a deficit exceeding 3 per cent of gross domestic product (GDP), unless it has occurred for 'exceptional' and 'temporary' reasons – and prepares the legal ground for European bodies to check compliance with this objective. The fundamental aim is that member countries be committed to achieving medium-term budgetary positions that are 'close to balance or in surplus', in order to secure margins to allow public finances to respond to cyclical output movements and boost confidence in a healthy economy. The aim of the Stability and Growth Pact, approved by the European Council in June 1997, is to implement these legal measures in a way that they retain the necessary political consensus not only *ex ante*, on the signature of the Pact itself, but above all *ex post*, when a member state finds it must change its otherwise sovereign taxes and public spending decisions to respect the commitments made. The Pact addresses the issue of the substantive transfer of sovereignty from the national to the European levels that these measures entail with a careful mix of preventive and dissuasive elements, which make constant use of the peer pressure mechanism.

First of all, the Pact clarified which circumstances ought to be seen as 'exceptional' and 'temporary' in the context of how excessive deficits were defined in the Treaty; moreover, in order to prevent countries from positioning themselves permanently near the 3 per cent threshold, it commits them to presenting to the bodies of the Union (the European Council and Commission) and to a special body comprising the finance ministers of the member states (the Ecofin Council) a three-year 'stability' plan, in which the medium-term budget objectives are established. This innovative measure introduced by the Pact essentially established a kind of code of conduct for the ordinary administration of the public finances, discouraging an opportunistic management of budget surpluses during phases of cyclical expansion. In the event, however, that a country exceeds the threshold, the decision to define the deficit as excessive is made by the Ecofin Council, following a proposal made by the European Commission and based on the objective parameters established in the Pact. If necessary, it is also the Ecofin Council that launches the complex procedure 'on excessive deficits' envisaged by the Treaty, which begins with the request that a member state take corrective public finance measures and can end with the setting of fines if the deficit has not fallen below the 3 per cent limit of GDP within the two years of the original finding.

It should not surprise us that the Stability and Growth Pact dates from several years after the Treaty, and only a little before the launch of EMU. In fact, between the signing of the Treaty and the approval of the Pact by the European Council, what many were dreading came to pass: the EMS was hit by an unprecedented crisis. Underlying the question was the particular nature of the process of international law-making compared with that at national level: while a national law becomes law the moment it is approved by Parliament, international laws must first be negotiated by the governments and then ratified by national Parliaments. On monetary matters, the time lag between the two may be full of pitfalls. This was the case of the EMS, when Denmark rejected the Treaty of Maastricht in a popular referendum held in June 1992. The markets foresaw in this event the possibility that the Treaty might not have a happy ending. It was followed by a currency crisis that first battered the lira and sterling, and subsequently turned its attention to a currency that many had deemed strong up to that moment, the French franc. The virulence of the crisis laid bare the weaknesses of the EMS. Based on the institutional accords of 1979, Italy and the UK should have had access to credit lines in strong currencies, essentially the German mark, in order to respond to a speculative attack. But the pressures were so great that the Bundesbank decided to make public an exchange of letters between its President and the Chancellor, which had previously been kept confidential, in order to be exonerated from the lending obligation. On the same day, the lira and sterling were forced to suspend participation in the European exchange rate agreements. This was not enough to calm the markets. In the months that followed, Spain and Portugal were forced to devalue their currencies on several occasions, while Finland, Norway and Sweden opted to float. In January 1993 the Irish pound also had to be devalued by 10 per cent. Pressures then shifted to the French franc, while the French and German authorities frantically tried to reach a political agreement for a supportive action. The agreement was not reached: in July 1993 the countries that were still members of the EMS opted to broaden the band from 2.25 to 15 per cent, which meant the de facto suspension of the exchange rate agreement. Once again, as in 1971, a cooperative regime that had been transformed into a hegemonic system was frustrated by market pressures.

The EMS crisis could have marked the end of EMU. Instead, it sparked efforts to acquire sufficient institutional capital to support confidence in the new European currency. At least three factors contributed to this result. The first was the widespread view that the 1992–93 crisis was only partly attributable to the imbalances accumulated by some counties, such as Italy and the United Kingdom, in the period of the hard-EMS. It was indeed felt that the self-fulfilling expectations of financial markets had played an important role, according to a mechanism that could have damaged the working of any formalized cooperative or hegemonic regime: the consortium regime was seen as the only strong response to the otherwise inevitable superiority of the markets over politics.[68] The second factor was the desire of strong-currency countries, and above all Germany, not to squander the progress made on economic, institutional and political integration. Finally, there was the belief in weak-currency countries that the loss of flexibility of economic policies due to the elimination of the national currency would be more than compensated by the benefits, above all for the public finances, implicit in the boost to credibility that authorities would gain by 'tying one's hands' as in the mechanism described by Giavazzi and Pagano in a famous article.[69] And so what we saw happen many times in the history of central banking came to pass: a crisis of greater proportions that instead of leading to a regression in monetary innovation enabled a leap ahead in terms of institutional development. In this instance, the leap ahead consisted not only of the Stability and Growth Pact, which strengthened the defences against excessive divergences in the management of the public finances in the member states, but also in a vast review of national systems aimed at increasing the independence of national central banks and meeting in the shortest possible time the Treaty of Maastricht requirements, especially as regards the convergence criteria and the financing of the budget.

This vast enterprise, which may be compared to a massive investment in brand capital to be given to the burgeoning single currency, is what allowed the EMU to be launched on schedule on 1 January 1999. From a strictly macroeconomic perspective, it is difficult to appreciate the attendant benefits, because the institutional ties devised to buoy confidence in the euro, like the complex governance and operational structure of the Eurosystem, undoubtedly had the drawback of making the conduct both of a common monetary policy and of national budget policies less flexible. Nor was there any shortage of criticisms of the European monetary structure in this respect.[70] But this is, as we have said, a narrow perspective. An investment in brand capital imposes a sacrifice by definition, and we have seen in previous chapters how in all the key phases in the evolution of the central banks, reform ended by temporarily tightening monetary policy to safeguard payment technology from the risk of abuse and to ward off a crisis of confidence. Only with time, by consolidating the brand capital associated with a certain monetary form, was it possible to regain margins of flexibility. The creation of a supranational central bank, an unprecedented historical event which many believed impossible, could not be free of costs, because faith is not an unlimited good: it must be generated and sustained. The problem of the years to come will be how to move beyond Maastricht and the Stability and Growth Pact. But this can only happen by increasing institutional capital outside of the economic sector, with a greater degree of political and legal integration; an enterprise that has resulted in the definition of a European Constitution and the enlargement of the European Union to Central and Eastern European countries. Further proof, if it were needed, that central banking is endogenous to the institutional environment and cannot be analysed independently of it.

6.6   CONCLUSIONS: IMPERFECT BIPOLARISM

Monetary internationalism has been the prevalent regime in history. Monetary nationalism – based on what Benjamin Cohen called 'territorial monies', that is, monies issued in a monopoly regime and in a uniform manner across the national territory by a sovereign state – is a recent invention. As we have seen in the preceding chapters, there are four phenomena underlying monetary nationalism: the search for a symbolic unit that would help to legitimate the emerging nation-state; the reduction of the transaction costs associated with the multiplicity of types of money in circulation; the need to increase state revenue through seignorage; and lastly, the emergence of the concept of managed money and with it the pursuit of domestic macroeconomic goals. But the latter development, by marking the passage from convertible currency to legal tender, also introduced a series of difficulties for territorial money, related essentially to the problem of how to ensure the anti-inflationary credibility of monetary policy, an aspect of the more general problem of engendering trust, which is the thread running through the content of this book. The difficulties met with by territorial monies are directly responsible for a revival in the demand for monetary internationalism, or in other words for a supranational coordination of monetary policy. But meeting this demand implies transposing central bank action to the international level, and it is not clear how this can be achieved. The development of the central bank is itself a result of the emergence of territorial monies: the central bank has its foundations in domestic political institutions and its *raison d'être* in the need to support trust in credit-based payment technologies, insofar as they need the protection of the legal system. This is why for a long time many believed the supranational transposition of central banking to be impossible.

The attempt to blend monetary nationalism and internationalism while safeguarding the national character of central bank action gave rise to what we have called the cooperative regime, the key examples of which are the Bretton Woods Agreements and the EMS. But the cooperative regime has a precarious lifespan because the conflicts of interest between the participating states, which conserved their monetary and political sovereignty, can at any time, especially in the presence of asymmetric macroeconomic shocks, endanger the cooperative attitude of one or more major countries and thereby undermine the functioning of the regime. All things considered, the risk of that occurring is limited as long as capital remains relatively immobile. And in fact the architects of Bretton Woods took particular care to ensure that national financial markets remained segmented. But with the return to international capital mobility, it was inevitable that the cooperative regime would collapse.

Why capital mobility should have increased so much from the 1960s onwards, going against the original intentions of the founders of the cooperative regime, is one of the most interesting historiographic questions of the postwar era. There are two opposing explanations. According to the school initiated by Susan Strange and taken furthest in the writings of Eric Helleiner, the return to capital mobility was an objective consciously pursued by the leading countries of the international system, the United States and the United Kingdom.[71] It was a comeback of the pressure groups that were an expression of the financial sector, on which the cooperative regime had been imposed with a political decision at the end of the Second World War; a comeback made possible by the transformation of the United States from a net creditor nation to a net debtor nation.

At that point promoting capital mobility became a strategic priority for the United States and the United Kingdom: the former, to guarantee itself an easy way to finance its growing external imbalance; the latter to acquire the role of financial intermediary on a global scale, as it did with the financial centre of London. According to the other school of thought, of which Barry Eichengreen was the leading exponent, the increase in capital mobility was the logical consequence of trade liberalization and the return to convertibility of the European currencies towards the end of the 1950s.[72] The achievement of the primary objective of the Bretton Woods Agreements, the recovery on a vast scale of world trade, made it possible to get round exchange controls. From then onwards it became ever more difficult to maintain the segmentation of national financial markets. In the meantime, precisely the difficulties national monetary authorities encountered in acquiring credibility convinced them that the financial markets could impose useful discipline. Instead of fighting a rearguard action that was in any case bound to end in defeat, the authorities began to take a favourable view of foreign exchange liberalization, and not only in the leading countries, but above all in the countries afflicted by endemic problems of inflation and institutional shortcomings. This led to what Tommaso Padoa-Schioppa and Fabrizio Saccomanni called the 'market-led global financial system'.[73]

For our purposes it is not important to take a position in favour of one or the other view, although we shall return to the question in the last chapter. We are concerned, instead, with noting that the decline of the cooperative regime also marked that of the attempt to blend monetary internationalism with territorial monies. A new monetary geography thus developed based on the deterritorialization of money. Two expressions of this are the hegemonic regime and the consortium regime, different in everything except for the renunciation of national monetary sovereignty. The new bipolarism began to emerge in the 1990s, when the international mobility of capital reached its peak, with levels comparable to those observed in the period of the gold standard. The hegemonic regime took the form of a dollarization of the economy, which was sometimes implicit and sometimes explicit. It was implicit in the countries where it occurred as a spontaneous tendency as a result of the redenomination in dollars of monetary liabilities previously denominated in local currency. Implicit dollarization occurred in many Latin American countries and in less evident forms in Asia as well. It was explicit where it occurred with an imperious act, through the adoption of the dollar as a means of payment in place of the national currency, which at that point was suppressed. This was the road taken more recently by countries such as Ecuador and El Salvador, and less recently by satellite countries such as Panama and

Liberia. Analogous phenomena of 'euro-ization', almost always implicit, took place in Central and Eastern Europe during the 1990s and early 2000s. On the other hand, the consortium regime is fully developed in the European Union. But discussions and first steps on the road to a sharing of monetary sovereignty are emerging in other geographical areas, ranging from the American continent to Asia.

The bipolarism that follows is nonetheless highly imperfect, for at least two reasons. In the first place this is because the experience of the European Union does not in itself establish a necessary trend. As we have seen in this chapter, the institutional requirements for the sharing of monetary sovereignty are very demanding. If a single currency and a supranational central bank were created in Europe, it was due to the contemporaneous action of a series of factors outside the monetary sector, from the process of trade integration to the desire of the political authorities to create an integrated market capable of competing with the North American market, to the broader project of political unification.[74] It is unlikely that such a favourable conjuncture will occur again in other areas in the near future, except on a much smaller scale. In the second place, the complete renunciation of sovereignty connected with the adoption of the hegemonic regime appears acceptable for small countries, where sovereignty is in many cases fictitious and the domestic financial sector is so small as to make an active central bank role superfluous or at any rate of little use. Larger and more financially developed countries continue to experiment other ways that are binding to a greater or lesser extent on the authorities. Moreover, in newly formed countries, such as those that have emerged from the dissolution of the Soviet Union, there has been a tardy territorialization of money, moving in the opposite direction to bipolarism.

There therefore remains a wide grey area between the two poles with a range of different monetary regimes. The outlook for this area is uncertain. Two scenarios appear possible. Disappointment with the potential of monetary sovereignty might gradually push many of these countries towards the explicit hegemonic regime, a choice that could be made less painful by the opening of the ownership of local banks to foreign capital, so as to alleviate the problems associated with the prevention of banking instability in the absence of central banking at national level. Alternatively, repeated episodes of instability produced by the high level of capital mobility could push groups of countries to repeat the experience of Bretton Woods and the Basel model on a smaller scale, by reintroducing currency controls to defend new forms of international cooperation on a regional basis. In this case, what these countries would come to be without would not be monetary sovereignty or territorial money, but the action of the 'market-led global financial system', with the related beneficial discipline on economic policy. In the absence of far-reaching action to strengthen national institutions, there would therefore be a resurgence of the credibility problems that undermined the fiat standard between the 1970s and the 1980s. The cooperative regime *à la* Bretton Woods option would thus make sense only if it were the first step towards a gradual intensification of economic, institutional and political relationships, so as to be just the prelude to membership of a consortium regime based on the EU model.

In all probability cooperative, hegemonic and consortium regimes will continue to coexist on the world scene in the years to come because of the differences between the economic problems, institutional endowments and recent histories in the various geographical areas. The universal ideal of Bretton Woods will presumably give way to regional realities, whose consistency is intended to be guaranteed by soft law and the monitoring of the International Monetary Fund.

The three regimes of monetary internationalism nonetheless all face the same challenge, which will be addressed in the next chapter. It is the challenge of what we might call the 'coexistence' of the various payment technologies. To internationalize legal tender, once expectations have been reined in regarding the benefits of monetary activism in the macroeconomic field, appears to be a feasible project today. To internationalize bank money is quite another matter because the banking system is still protected by a safety net that is the responsibility of the nation-state and, ultimately, of local taxpayers. The deregulation that was popular in the 1980s has given way to forms of re-regulation with a return to awareness that bank money has a 'natural' propensity to be unstable, that can be attenuated only through careful supervision and regulation conducted at the most local level possible. How to safeguard the effectiveness of the safety net protecting bank stability and maintain adequate margins for lending-of-last-resort transactions is perhaps the crucial problem in the monetary field today. All three regimes – the cooperative one via soft law, the consortium one via the definition of common rules for the handling of crises, and the hegemonic one via the negotiation between the hegemonic country and satellite countries of lines of credit to use at times of turbulence – are trying to tackle this problem. But it will be difficult to find a solution without a high degree of institutional integration. In the long term it is likely that this problem will produce a strong incentive to share monetary sovereignty on a regional basis and in some cases to look for a new territorialization of money on a broader geographical scale, through the creation of innovative forms of political union.

7. The revolution in the payment system

7.1 INTRODUCTION

The transition to legal tender brought with it an interesting phenomenon, which we could call 'payment system oblivion'. In the nineteenth century and the first few decades of the twentieth the payment system occupied a pre-eminent position in monetary thought. Just think of the amount of space and analysis dedicated to it – even though the term 'payment system' was not yet current – in some of the classics of monetary theory, such as Jevons, Wicksell, Von Mises and Keynes.[1] In the literature produced between the later 1930s and the mid-1980s, by contrast, any search for a systematic treatment of the theoretical and institutional questions raised by the circulation of money would be fruitless.

Theoretical and practical factors probably contributed to this situation in equal measure. On the theoretical plane, starting with Hicks's celebrated 'suggestion',[2] the emphasis in monetary analysis shifted progressively from the function of means of exchange to that of storage of value. This led to an emphasis on the problems connected with the holding of money, and a neglect of circulation.[3] In this light theoreticians directed a good part of their work to comparing the properties of legal tender and commodity money. The two payment technologies, however, share the characteristic that they do not presuppose any clearing and settlement mechanism: in both, the means of exchange and the means of settlement are identical. On the practical plane, the consolidation of a monopoly on the issuance of legal tender and of a collusive oligopoly in the production of bank money eliminated the strains of the transition from commodity money to monetary forms with a large fiduciary component produced under fully competitive regimes, where the payment system was the natural catalyst and amplifier.

As we saw in Chapter 6, the advent of legal tender brought a new set of problems: the relationship between the central bank and the government, the formal assignment of banking supervisory powers, and the design of procedures to guarantee credibility in the conduct of monetary policy. In this context the problems of the payment system were relegated to the rank of mere technical questions for the central bank to resolve as part of its operational and administrative action. And in fact they were resolved, with the gradual development of a pyramid-shaped operational model in which commercial banks intermediate the payments of private customers and the central bank serves as settlement agent for the banking system, offering settlement accounts to banks and banks only.

Once again, the impetus for change came from the pressure generated by a sudden alteration of the economic and financial environment. After the stagflation of the 1970s – partly in response to it, partly as the product of technological innovation – in the major countries the onset of rapid financial deepening and the resumption of economic growth caused an exponential rise in interbank payments and the emergence of new, highly innovative payment instruments such as credit and debit cards and, later, electronic money. As a consequence, there was a revival of interest in payment systems – at first, in subdued fashion, in central banking circles, then also in the academic community, and finally among economic observers generally.

At the beginning attention focused on the retail payment system, because there were those who predicted, and those who feared, that the new payment instruments would supplant legal tender, with repercussions not only on the payment system but on the conduct of monetary policy and the accounts of the central bank. This theme aroused the passions of scholars and in fact generated a particular strand of literature, the 'new monetary economics'.[4] But the banknote, against all expectations, has held out. As Mark Twain would have said, the reports of its death have proven to be exaggerated. Between 1990 and 2000 in five of the 11 G-10 countries, including the United States, the stock of banknotes increased in proportion to GDP, and where the ratio declined it did so only marginally.[5] Surveys in individual countries on the actual use of cash yield another picture: there is a decline, but not so steep as to suggest the complete disappearance of banknotes anytime in the foreseeable future. And even if this were to happen, the effects would probably be much less severe than some people fear, because central banking functions, and monetary policy conduct in particular, would not be affected substantially by a significant diminution in the importance of cash or even, at the limit, by its outright disappearance.[6]

Much more radical have been the changes that have occurred in the meantime in interbank dealings – what is often called the 'wholesale' payment industry. And again the transition from reflections among the initiates to general interest and effective action for reform was marked by 'pathological' episodes, notably the US stock market crisis of October 1987.

The outcome was a series of major modifications in the payment system's institutional arrangements, its mode of operation and its relations with the economy. Today the pyramid model itself, and with it the role of central banks, is being called into question. This may be a true revolution (only the future can tell how far the transformation goes), originating in subdued fashion but gradually and inexorably gathering strength. This chapter traces the origins, patterns and possible future developments.

7.2 THE PYRAMID MODEL OF THE PAYMENT SYSTEM

A payment technology hinging on bank money presupposes deferred settlement, that is, settlement subsequent to the transaction. Where payment by commodity money or banknote is a distinct act that ends in the very moment it is performed, payment via bank money is a process composed of several phases: the exchange of documents attesting the purchaser's obligation to pay (a cheque, say); possibly the clearing (offsetting) of payments of opposite signs; and definitive settlement in monetary base in the form of liabilities, or money, of the central bank.

The monetary system that emerged from the 1930s, in which legal tender and bank money coexisted, thus embodied two different forms of settlement: immediate in the case of legal tender, deferred in the case of bank money.[7] The first of these technologies is particularly well suited to small – or, in jargon, 'retail' – transactions. For larger transactions, in the past considerations of security, convenience and opportunity cost made deferred payment preferable. As we shall see, recent developments in technology and finance have produced the virtually universal elimination of deferred payment for large-value transactions ('wholesale' payments).

The division of tasks between legal tender and bank money is quite uncomplicated and can basically be left to market forces, but the organization of the bank money payment process itself is less straightforward. Three fundamental questions need to be cleared up: one bearing on the relations between the settlement agent and the payment managers, essentially commercial banks; one on the choice of settlement mode; and the third on the length of the process, that is, the ideal amount of time that should elapse between the initiation of the payment and finality of settlement.

Before examining these points in greater detail, let us look at the configuration of the payment system since the 1930s, which can be effectively portrayed as pyramidal in form (Figure 7.1). At the base is the general public of consumers and firms, whose daily 'market' activity generates the flows of retail payments in bank money. At a higher level there is a set of specialized intermediaries, such as brokers and dealers, who operate in the money, financial and primary goods markets as middlemen between

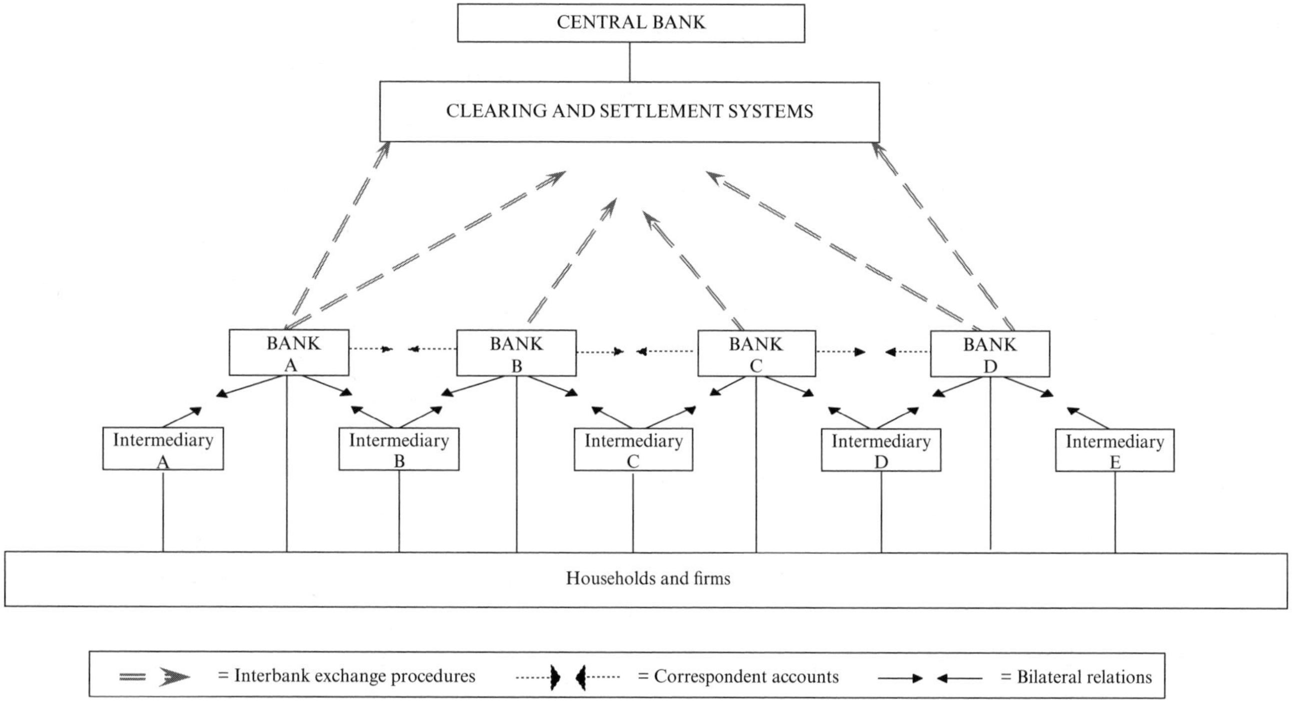
CENTRAL BANK
CLEARING AND SETTLEMENT SYSTEMS
BANK A
BANK B
BANK C
BANK D
Intermediary A
Intermediary B
Intermediary C
Intermediary D
Intermediary E
Households and firms
= Interbank exchange procedures
= Correspondent accounts
= Bilateral relations

Figure 7.1 The pyramid model

buyers and sellers of assets. Both the final users and these intermediaries may resort, at times unwittingly, to the clearing or netting of payments. At the end of the process, though, their operations result in settlement in bank money, that is, a transfer from one bank to another.

This brings us to the top level of the pyramid, interbank transfers. At this level there may be three types of payment machinery. First, banks may agree to settle in legal tender the interbank obligations arising from payments originated lower down on the pyramid. Second, each bank can open an account with each of the other banks within the system to settle their reciprocal payment flows on a bilateral basis. These reciprocal accounts – reproducing the Renaissance *vostro* and *nostro* account practice – are known as 'correspondent' accounts. Third, settlement may be made by transferring title to the deposits held by each bank to a third institution, which could hypothetically be another commercial bank or the central bank.

Interestingly, banks' choice among these alternative modes is unconstrained, but over the years some configurations came to prevail. First, banks have never preferred legal-tender settlement, and since the 1930s settlement has alternated between the other two modes. Second, except in countries where by law or tradition banking is highly decentralized, the importance of correspondent accounts has waned steadily at domestic level (but not, as we shall see, internationally). And finally, in all countries the function of settlement agent has been taken by the central bank.

In most cases, then, commercial banks settle through accounts with the central bank (called centralized accounts), which puts the latter at the apex of the pyramid. What prompted the commercial banks to choose this arrangement? There are two possible reasons. First, with the institutional reform that followed the advent of legal tender, the central bank took on a unique status within the financial system as the sole intermediary with zero credit risk (as a public entity it enjoys the guarantee of the state) and zero liquidity risk (because it can expand the monetary base at its discretion) for those holding its liabilities (for a definition of these risks, see Box 7.1.) In a word, an account with the central bank is risk-free. This is a clear comparative advantage, one that ultimately depends on the fact that the central bank is part of the state apparatus, in the broad sense. Second, with the termination of direct business with non-bank customers and the assumption of an institutional role in the public interest, not constrained to profit maximization, the central bank ceases to be a competitor for commercial banks, which gives it another comparative advantage over private credit institutions.

Settlement on central bank accounts may be effected in either of two main modes: clearing or gross settlement. In the last three decades of the twentieth century, technological advances gave rise to computerized

---

BOX 7.1   PAYMENT SYSTEM RISKS

Liquidity risk: the risk that a counterparty (or participant in a settle-ment system) will not settle an obligation for full value when due. Liquidity risk does not imply that a counterparty or participant is insolvent since it may be able to settle the required debit obliga-tions at some unspecified time thereafter.

Credit risk/exposure: the risk that a counterparty will not settle an obligation for full value, either when due or at any time thereafter.

Systemic risk: the risk that the failure of one participant in a trans-fer system, or in financial markets generally, to meet its obliga-tions will cause other participants or financial institutions to be unable to meet their obligations (including settlement obligations in a transfer system) when due. Such a failure may cause signifi-cant liquidity or credit problems and, as a result, might threaten the stability of financial markets.

Source: BIS Committee on Payment and Settlement Systems, 'A glossary of terms used in payment and settlement systems', Basel, January 2001.

---

payment systems based on these two alternative principles, and today practically all the world's payment systems can still be described as falling into one or the other category.[8] In clearing systems, which are also called netting systems, participants exchange 'IOUs' (promises to pay) for a set amount of time, and when that interval ends they settle the balance (pay-ments owed net of those received) using the liabilities of a third agent as means of settlement. For example, through the 1970s many countries around the world had multilateral clearing systems[9] in which the promises were chiefly paper documents (cheques, various debit claims), the settle-ment interval was the working day, and the means of settlement was gen-erally central bank money (monetary base). In gross settlement systems, instead, each transaction is settled using whatever means of settlement has been chosen, with no previous netting phase.

It should be clear, then, that the main difference between netting systems and gross settlement systems is simply the settlement interval: positive in clearing systems, nil in gross settlement. Deferred settlement makes it pos-sible to offset payments of opposite signs without drawing on means of set-tlement and so reduces the stock of money required for a given volume of trade. But it has a drawback, namely that the longer the wait, the greater the likelihood that some incoming payment will not be successfully completed. As the payments exchanged in clearing systems are mere IOUs, they do not become effective payments until the time of settlement.[10] As the settlement interval lengthens, therefore, there is a heightened risk that one or more payments will be revoked, with potentially devastating repercussions on the subsequent settlement phase. Various kinds of problems may arise: technical hitches (of which examples are given below), problems of liquidity, complications in connection with fraud, even the extreme case of the sudden, unexpected failure of a participant. All this creates risks for the participants: credit risk, liquidity risk, systemic risk.

The optimal settlement interval is derived from the calculation whereby each individual weighs these two opposite forces, transaction costs and risk. This interval does not necessarily correspond to that which is socially optimal, both because different individuals have differing perceptions and because there may be a problem of collective action, since systemic risk is a typical externality, whose magnitude may be regularly underestimated by the individual participants in payment systems. In the long run, however, it is likely that the exchange, clearing and settlement procedures will adapt to social desires, among other things because, assuming there are no asymmetries between individuals in the structure of payments, technical progress will shorten the optimal settlement interval.[11] And in fact, over the centuries there has been a gradual shortening of the settlement intervals entailed by credit instruments. At the Renaissance exchange fairs, the interval was the time between one fair and the next, several months as a rule. By the early nineteenth century the interval had been shortened to a week. With the monetary reform of the 1930s, the convention was that cash settlement was effected every day at the conclusion of the clearing operations. Securities settlement took place at the end of the month (for shares) or after several days (for bonds). Following this line of reasoning, what is probably the most important innovation of the 1980s and 1990s, namely the spread of gross settlement systems, can be seen as the logical outcome of a secular process that has gradually shortened and finally eliminated the settlement interval altogether. Today, this is possible thanks to information technology that allows real-time transfer of monetary base between centralized accounts at extremely low cost.

7.3 EXCEPTIONS TO THE PYRAMID MODEL

Though even today the pyramid offers a good picture of the payment system, there are a number of exceptions to that model. First, payments in legal tender do not go through the pyramid, because there is no need to involve the banking system at all. Banknotes are a retail payment instrument produced and managed directly by the central bank. They come back into the pyramid only insofar as commercial banks use them to settle the balances stemming from interbank payments – a practice that has now fallen into disuse. Second, the pyramid model only really covers domestic payments within each country. In the absence of a supranational central bank, the model cannot handle cross-border payments, which generally involve foreign exchange transactions. For these payments, until the start of 2002 when the Continuous Link Settlement Bank began operations (see section 7.6), there was no alternative to international correspondent banking. But even today, as a rule every bank must have, for its cross-border payments, correspondent accounts with as many foreign banks as there are countries with which it ordinarily does business. The relationship is usually reciprocal (and the accounts are accordingly often called 'reciprocal accounts') and involves banks that are themselves near the top of their own national pyramid.

In countries characterized by a highly internationalized financial system, correspondent banks generally need to have access to a clearing system that specializes in cross-border payments, such as CHIPS in the United States or FXYCS in Japan. The present configuration of the world payment system can thus be represented as a series of pyramids of varying size like that shown in Figure 7.1, bound together by a dense network of 'laces' representing the correspondent accounts. The latter are hooked into the upper part of the pyramids, generally in special nodes constituted by clearing procedures specializing in cross-border transactions.

The pyramid model thus embodies a division of labour between commercial banks and the central bank. The latter, with the significant exceptions of legal tender and, in many countries, payments on account of government, is responsible for wholesale payment management, the commercial banks for retail payments. This division of tasks has stemmed from a series of important operational and institutional decisions over time, most notably non-interference by the central bank in the retail payment market. In other words, as a rule the central bank allows only commercial banks and the like to hold centralized accounts, precisely in order to avoid any direct relations between the central bank and final customers. In the sphere of legal tender as well, the central bank has long taken a passive or at least neutral stance and has not sought to promote this form of payment at the expense of bank money. Central banks have also developed forms of credit for the commercial banks in order to make the use of centralized accounts smoother. All in all, this actually amounts to an implicit contract, which David Humphrey, a student of the matter and former Director of the Federal Reserve Bank of Richmond, describes as follows:

Central banks have typically protected commercial banks and other financial institutions from competition in order to insulate them – and the payment system – from the higher failure rates experienced in non-bank business enterprises generally. The protection accorded to banks from payment competition has focused on excluding non-banks from direct access to central bank settlement. In the recent past, this was justified by valid concerns that allowing open access to central bank settlement could lead to increased risk to the payment system. At that time, intraday credit was being supplied at zero cost to banks and procedures were not in place on large value networks to either monitor or control this risk exposure [for central banks].[12]

The foregoing applies, roughly, to all the main payment systems in the advanced countries. But there are substantial differences from country to country in the effective operational involvement of the central bank at the lower-middle levels of the pyramid for purposes other than settlement strictly speaking. In this field, the extremes are the United Kingdom, where the central bank has traditionally had only very limited involvement in the exchange and clearing of payment flows, and at the other extreme the United States and Italy, where the central banks are present in practically all the 'production' phases in payments. Other significant differences, to which we will return further on, concern the central banks' policies on pricing and on the granting of credit to commercial banks, especially intraday or 'daylight' credit, which with the transition to gross settlement has become of decisive importance.[13]

7.4 THE STORM OF FINANCIAL DEEPENING OF THE 1980s

Few periods of history have experienced financial innovation as intensive as the 1980s and 1990s, involving the breadth of the financial superstructure, the daily volume of trading in the financial markets, and also the types and features of financial instruments. The process carried major implications both for the operation of payment systems and for central banking, in a dialectical process that has not yet issued forth in a new, stable relationship between central banks and payment service institutions. It is worth examining the process systematically.

In 1973, independently, Ronald McKinnon and Edward Shaw each introduced the concept of 'financial repression'.[14] At the time the notion quite faithfully captured the reality of financial systems in the advanced and the developing countries alike. Almost everywhere, albeit to different degrees, there were restrictions on entry into the banking industry, quantitative controls on credit aggregates and, less frequently, constraints on bank deposit or borrowing rates. The authorities often discouraged financial innovation, and many countries had massive state ownership of financial intermediaries. Finally, in keeping with the philosophy of the Bretton Woods system, foreign exchange controls were the norm in the member countries of the International Monetary Fund.

In reaction to the stagflation of the second half of the 1970s, under the impulse of the ideas of McKinnon and Shaw the end of the decade saw a sweeping process of financial liberalization that changed the face of finance within the span of a few years. The analysis of John Williamson and Molly Mahar, though rudimentary, is enough to give an idea of the order of magnitude of the phenomenon.[15] They use a series of qualitative indicators to classify nine advanced and 27 developing countries' financial systems as 'repressed', 'partially repressed', 'largely liberalized', or 'fully liberalized'. They ran the exercise in 1973 and repeated it in 1996. Between these two years there was an abyss. In 1973 only one of the industrial countries qualified as largely liberalized, the rest being either partially or totally repressed, while in the developing world financial repression was practically universal. By 1996 the few remaining restrictions in the advanced countries were little more than nominal and capital movements were totally liberalized. The change in the developing countries is more surprising still, even considering that by construction the Williamson–Mahar sample excludes all the countries that decided not to modify their degree of financial repression.

The changed attitude of regulators is not the only qualitative change over this period. Within the financial industry there was a revolution in investment instruments and techniques, symbolized by derivative products. The key feature of derivatives is the possibility of unbundling and separately contracting the various risks embodied in any investment, whether it is in financial or real economic assets. The literature on derivative products has grown very extensive, and it is beyond the scope of this volume to review its themes and findings.[16] For our purposes, it is enough to note that the development of derivatives made possible the 'commodification of risks', the impact of which on the economy has been comparable to that of the invention of limited liability at the end of the eighteenth century.[17] Just as back then the new concept, once recognized and regulated, permitted the assumption of risk by a growing mass of investors not directly involved in the operation of firms by limiting their potential losses in case of failure to the amount invested, so today the new financial products make it possible to produce 'tailor-made' risk profiles that are independent of the characteristics of the investment that generates the risks.[18]

The speed with which derivatives have become an established fact is impressive. As late as the mid-1980s they were still practically nonexistent. In 1994 the total notional value of derivatives traded on stock

Table 7.1   Financial assets and real wealth (national currencies; billions)

	Year	Gross financial assets (FA)	Real wealth (W)	FIR (FA/W)	Real wealth/ GDP	GDP per capita
France	1980	13 416	12 755	1.05	4.85	80
	1997	70 766	30 495	2.32	3.71	70
Germany	1980	5 426	6 693	0.81	4.55	90
	1998	24 892	17 899	1.39	4.87	71
Italy	1980	1 342 318	1 546 861	0.87	4.05	73
	1998	11 414 730	8 519 888	1.34	4.16	67
Japan	1980	1 102 720	1 373 029	0.80	5.71	73
	1996	4 276 003	3 252 175	1.31	6.49	82
United Kingdom	1980	1 489	1 104	1.35	4.76	65
	1996	8 334	2 914	2.86	3.92	65
United States	1980	13 816	13 007	1.06	4.67	100
	1996	58 267	27 932	2.09	3.66	100

Note: Indices: United States = 100; constant prices of 1995, converted in dollars using purchasing power parities of 1995.

Source: Pierluigi Ciocca, *La nuova finanza in Italia: una difficile metamorfosi (1980–2000)*, Turin, Bollati Boringhieri, 2000, p. 12.

exchanges and in over-the-counter (OTC) markets had risen to some $20 trillion, according to the Bank for International Settlements (BIS), and by the end of 2001 to $85 trillion.

With the liberalization of finance, the development of derivatives, the introduction of the new techniques of active portfolio management, and the development of information technology, in the late 1980s both the dimensions of the financial superstructure in the main economies and the volume of daily trading began to grow with unusual if not unprecedented speed. The conventional indicator of the size of an economy's financial superstructure is the financial interrelations ratio (FIR), proposed by Raymond Goldsmith in 1969.[19] After decades of stability that had led some scholars to hazard the hypothesis that a physiological limit to the ratio between finance and economy had been reached (at about 1), the FIR started to rise again, and very rapidly by historical standards (Table 7.1). The phenomenon embraced financially backward countries, like Germany, Italy and France, as well as the world financial leaders, America and Britain. In fact, between 1980 and 1998 the FIR doubled in the United Kingdom, the United States and France and rose by half in Germany, Italy and Japan.

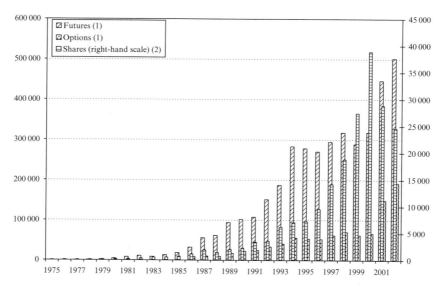

Notes:
1.   Notional value.
2.   Value of trade in the shares included in Datastream's World Index.

Source: Bank for International Settlements for futures and options; Datastream for shares.

Figure 7.2   World trade in futures, options and shares in the main regulated markets (billions of dollars)

Gauged by volume of trade rather than by the accumulation of gross wealth, the phenomenon is even more striking. A study by the G-10 central banks found that during the spring of 1992 the net volume of trade in the foreign exchange markets amounted to nearly $900 billion, or three times as much as in 1986, and on an annual basis some 12 times the aggregate gross domestic product (GDP) of the Organisation for Economic Co-operation and Development (OECD). Between the turn of the 1980s and the turn of the 1990s the number of transactions on regulated markets grew exponentially (Figure 7.2). In the United States it soared from 1 million to 7 million. This growth caused quite a stir at the time but it actually turns out to have been moderate compared with later increases.

The financial deepening of the economy brought with it an unprecedented increase in the volume of payments handled by the gross and net settlement procedures (Figure 7.3). This was common to all the main countries and was most marked between the mid-1980s and the mid-1990s. For instance,

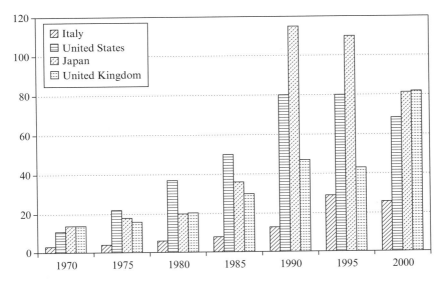

Note: * Payments in transit in wholesale and retail payment systems.

Source: Bank of International Settlements. The data up to 1995 are in relation to GNP and are drawn from the Annual Reports for 1992, 1993 and 1997; the data for 2000 are taken from 'Statistics on payment and settlement systems in selected countries', 2003.

Figure 7.3   The volume of payments handled by banks, 1970–2000 (ratio to GDP)*

in Japan the volume of transactions rose from about 30 times GDP in 1985 to over 100 times GDP in 1995. At the end of the century, for reasons discussed below, these values appeared to stabilize. The demand for money for transaction purposes remained stable if not declining in proportion to GDP in all the leading countries, even though disinflation and low interest rates in the 1990s reduced the opportunity cost of holding money. It was the velocity of circulation, then, that absorbed the impact of the explosive growth in financial transactions. How it did so is the subject of the next section.

7.5   FINANCIAL INNOVATION AND THE PAYMENT SYSTEM

The torrent of financial innovation of the 1980s and 1990s, then, is paradoxical. While there was unprecedented growth in financial transactions and in the volume of transactions intermediated by the payment system, the most specifically transactive monetary aggregates were stable if not declining in proportion to economic output. The paradox is all the more startling considering that derivatives have a distinctive feature with respect to other financial instruments, namely that their widespread use is founded upon the assumption that the relevant markets will always be highly liquid. For example, dynamic hedging presupposes the possibility of selling even very large volumes of securities when prices are falling and of buying when they are rising.[20] In the same way, highly leveraged speculative positions presume a capacity to procure, quickly in the course of a given business day, the liquidity necessary to meet margin calls as market prices fluctuate. In other words, active financial management of a derivatives portfolio is only possible if every investor and the market as a whole have access to cheap and abundant liquidity. A derivatives market that works properly presupposes that agents assign a high degree of finality to transactions. But the sole monetary form that is perfectly definitive in a legal-tender regime is monetary base, that is, the central bank's liabilities. And the demand for monetary base, if it has not contracted as was predicted by the new monetary economics, has not expanded either, as would be expected if the transaction function of money were paramount. And that, in a word, is the paradox of the financial deepening of the 1980s and 1990s.

On closer examination, however, this turns out to be a paradox that we have already encountered, whenever a new payment technology arose. In this case, the new technology goes by the somewhat inelegant name of 'daylight' – or 'intraday' – credit. The expansion of financial transactions, in fact, is made possible by the development of a dense network of credit relations that are instituted in the course of the day and vanish, like a river going back underground, at the end of operations with the final settlement of the balances in monetary base. Essentially, what we have is a payment system based on the circulation of IOUs. In the case of correspondent accounts, the bilateral credit or debit is tacitly, and indefinitely, renewed, without ever actually settling in monetary base. In the case of real-time netting, by contrast, credit is granted freely and automatically during the working day but terminates at its end when the interbank balances are settled via transfers on central bank accounts. An exception to this bipartite scheme is the Federal Reserve's gross settlement system, Fedwire, which provides for the settlement of every single transaction in monetary base (and hence does not involve any bilateral credit between the paying and receiving banks). But Fedwire too is part of the new payment technology; the only difference is that in this case the credit is granted directly by the central bank: to guarantee the fluidity of the payment system, from the very beginning the Fed has had a policy of automatic, cost-free, uncollateralized intraday credit for Fedwire members.

In principle, it should be noted, intraday credit existed even before the 1980s. As we have seen (section 7.2), the credit mechanism that enables the payer to defer settlement underlies the operation of any clearing or netting system in which the settlement interval is not zero. Yet it was not until that decade that banks and the central bank fully realized that the promises to pay (IOUs) exchanged in the interbank circuit were actually a form of credit, and that potentially, therefore, they might have repercussions on the stability of the financial system. In all the industrial countries, in fact, after this financial deepening of the economy, there was explosive growth in the volume of transactions, which was generally associated with a comparable increase in intraday credit. In the United States, for example, the average value of payments settled daily on the accounts of the 12 Federal Reserve banks, which in 1960 was about equal to the average reserves held by members of the Federal Reserve system, rose to 30 times that value in 1985 and 60 times in 1992.[21] And in correspondence, the volume of intraday credit supplied by the Fed became enormous. In a special report on payment system risks, the Fed estimated the amount of credit granted daily through Fedwire at $60 billion and that associated with the operation of CHIPS, the private real-time clearing system for the New York financial marketplace, at $50 billion.[22] During each business day, many large banks have exposures far greater than their capital. As we shall see further on, in response to these developments the policy of cost-free credit on Fedwire was called into question and eventually abandoned.

Another characteristic of the new interbank payment technology, one we have encountered earlier as well, is its 'opacity'. At first, except for intraday credit in connection with Fedwire, about which the Fed is informed (though the data are not made public), very little is known about the actual magnitude of bilateral credit, whether intraday or not. Naturally, data on correspondent account balances are extremely hard to come by. In 1987, in the first comprehensive report on the national payment system by any G-10 central bank, the Bank of Italy estimated outstanding bilateral credit obligations for payment system purposes among the largest five Italian banks at 4 trillion lire.[23]

Central banks' involvement in the payment system, which as noted was quite limited until the end of the 1970s, was connected with retail payment procedures, above all the development of such innovative instruments as credit and debit cards. But these concerns were soon largely overshadowed by the importance of interbank payment circuits, with the steadily heightening awareness of markets and central banks of the potential risks inherent in these systems.

The problem that these developments posed, quite familiar to economic theory, is the typical problem of multilateral credit. What happens if the credit risk in a given bilateral obligation materializes? That is, what if, because of economic problems (default) or merely some technical mishap, the debtor is unable to honour the obligations contracted in the course of the business day? In a settlement system based on intraday central bank credit, like Fedwire, the answer is simple, if disquieting. In these procedures payments are final, because they are accompanied by the transfer of monetary base. Therefore in case of default by a participant it is the central bank that must take on the obligation. At the end of the day it must convert the intraday credit granted to the defaulting agent into monetary base that then, unless sterilized after the fact, circulates normally within the economy. In the case of a typical private clearing system of the 1980s – before the introduction of the risk controls and institutional reforms described below – the answer was not so simple, because the payment messages entering the system in the course of the day were only notifications of future payments. The failure of a member to settle at the end of the day would thus produce a chain reaction of cancellations of payments that could no longer be honoured. This is systemic risk, whose effective repercussions depend on the magnitude of the defaulter's obligations and the degree of concatenation of the credit relations arising within the clearing system.

A worrying indication of the systemic risk harboured within the CHIPS system was generated by a simulation conducted by David Humphrey in 1986. Taking the data from a set of typical business days, Humphrey sought to see what would happen if at the end of the day a large participant was unable to discharge its obligations. The result was the default, in a kind of domino effect, of nearly 50 per cent of all the participant institutions.[24]

As in earlier stages of monetary evolution, however, what captured the attention of policy-makers and triggered radical reform was not academic reflection on the inherent risks of the new practices, but rather a set of grave crises little known to the general public. In 1974 the failure of the Herstatt Bank had already cast doubt on the soundness of the international payment system. At that time, however, the problem was dealt with from the supervisory standpoint, and the result was the institution of the Basel Committee on Banking Supervision.[25]

A different kind of incident occurred in 1985, with potentially even more devastating repercussions. Because of a computer malfunction, the Bank of New York, which was an active trader in US Treasury paper, was unable to settle the balances deriving from the obligations it had contracted during the day, with the risk of a domino effect of payment failures among other intermediaries active in the Treasury security market. Following a series of frenetic exchanges of information, the New York

Federal Reserve decided to guarantee the settlement of the bank's obligations in monetary base, instantly expanding this aggregate by about 10 per cent. As collateral, the Fed took the Bank of New York's entire balance sheet assets. As Garber and Weisbrod noted, the legal principles whereby the Fed could actually have drawn on that collateral in the event of the Bank's failure were not clear.[26]

An even larger problem arose with the American stock market crash of October 1987. In just ten trading hours, between the opening on Monday 19 October and the low on Tuesday morning, the New York Stock Exchange lost 22 per cent, and the futures index 36 per cent – the sharpest contraction in US history. Although, as a series of official reports in the following months made clear, the fall had no connection with the operation of the payment system, the stability of the entire payment circuit was salvaged only by massive injections of liquidity into the banking system by the Fed, with the express indication that it was to be used to ensure the execution of stockbrokers' payments. Similar developments were registered in the leading financial marketplaces all over the world.

7.6 THE PROCESS OF INSTITUTIONAL ADAPTATION

The stock market crash of October 1987 marked the start of action by the central banks of the G-10 countries to attenuate the risks of the new credit payment technology in the upper part of the pyramid owing to the financial boom. This action was postulated on the thesis that financial innovation had produced an excessive build-up of risk within the payment system, owing to the undervaluation by all the participants of the systemic risk created by the increase in the amount of credit risk that each one took on, more or less knowingly, in the course of the business day. The key word in this reform was 'finality'. The problem was how to guarantee the operative and legal irreversibility of the payments entering the system as a result of financial transactions; in other words, how to shorten the optimal settlement interval to zero, completing the secular decline that began at the dawn of capitalism itself. The solution was obvious technically but less than perfectly satisfactory economically: all that would be needed to eradicate systemic risk would be to require simultaneous settlement of every interbank transaction in monetary base, via transfers on central bank accounts.

In this case, however, this solution was unsatisfactory, because it entailed a highly cogent constraint on the volume of transactions that the payment system would be able to handle for a given amount of monetary

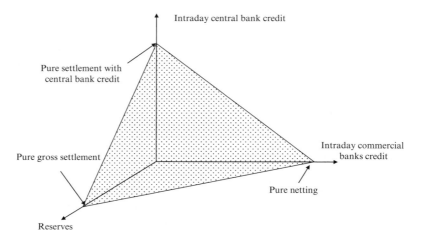

Figure 7.4   Choice of payment systems

base. The error, in conceptual terms, would have been analogous to that
committed by the English Bank Charter Act of 1844, which sought vainly
to resolve the problem of excess issues inherent in convertible banknotes
by setting an administrative ceiling on the amount of paper money in circulation (see Chapter 3). Central banks worked to avoid falling into that
trap. The objective – reducing the risk for a given volume of transactions
– necessarily required institutional adjustments.

The question may be cleared up by the graph originally proposed by
Angelini and Giannini (Figure 7.4).[27] Any volume of financial trading can
be seen as the product of three different payment technologies, each with
its own specific input and its own contraindications. At one apex we put
the clearing systems described in section 7.2, whose input is bilateral credit
between commercial banks. At another apex there are the 'pure' gross
settlement systems, those that require immediate settlement of all payments within the circuit using previously accumulated monetary base. In
this case the input consists in each bank's reserves with the central bank.
Finally, the same volume of payments could be achieved with gross settlement based not on the use of reserves but on intraday credit supplied
by the central bank, as in Fedwire. The intermediate points on the plane
shown in the figure are hybrids, with characteristics common to clearing
systems and to 'pure' settlement systems. For example, in some systems
outgoing payments which cannot be settled due to insufficient liquidity
are put on a waiting list ('queued payments') and transmitted as soon as
the debtor's account has a sufficient balance to cover the obligation. The

Swiss gross settlement system (Swiss Interbank Clearing) was the first to institute this mechanism.

Every one of these solutions has its contraindications. The netting method reduces the need for money to a minimum, and also the direct risks for the central bank, but at the cost of high systemic risk. Relying on central bank credit, by contrast, avoids systemic risk, but at the cost of high credit risk for the central bank. Pure gross settlement, finally, is not subject either to systemic risk or to central bank credit risk, but it is very costly, because it presupposes sufficient stocks of liquidity, with the attendant opportunity costs.[28] To determine the optimal mix of inputs, significant additional information would be needed. First of all, one would have to know the 'price' of each input, so as to calculate substitution ratios. In the figure it is implicitly assumed that these ratios are constant at 1:1, but this is a perfectly arbitrary assumption that serves only for ease of exposition. Second, one would have to have a social welfare function in order to frame and resolve a constrained maximization problem.

Lacking these data, the action of central banks and regulators takes on a composite form which, rejecting drastic administrative intervention, seeks to reconcile the various exigencies of the new context, calibrating the incentives of payment system participants and actively seeking their cooperation. There are four key elements:

1. regulatory action to limit risks in private systems;
2. creation or revision of real-time gross settlement systems, which give participants access to central bank credit but require them either to sustain the related cost, or to post adequate collateral;
3. institution of delivery-versus-payment schemes in the main securities markets;
4. development of an independent payment system oversight function within the central bank.

Before briefly describing each of these elements, let us note the difference between the present period of institutional adaptation and those of the past two centuries. In the past the problem of institutional adaptation was quintessentially national in nature. The fact that reform proceeded in waves depended on the natural propensity of the authorities in each country to draw on the experience of others in order to solve similar problems when they arose on the national plane. Distinctive national paths to institutional adaptation remained possible and in some cases were pursued, and at length. The degree of financial market integration attained in the 1980s and the importance of international payments, however, made the hypothesis of decentralized reform strictly academic.

If there was to be reform, it would have to be internationally concerted and coordinated.

And in fact this is what happened. Shortly after the release of the Federal Reserve's report on payment system risks, in 1988, the G-10 central banks formed a working group to study the international aspects of the matter. In 1990 these same central banks published the report of another working group, which marked the creation of the Committee on Payment and Settlement Systems as a permanent body. In this report the G-10 central banks defined a set of minimum standards with which all private netting systems had to comply (originally, these standards were designed only for dedicated cross-border payment procedures, such as the US CHIPS and the Japanese FXYCS systems, but they were rapidly extended to all netting procedures).

Two aspects of these 'Lamfalussy standards', as they were called after the working group's Chairman, Alexandre Lamfalussy, are especially relevant to our purposes here (Box 7.2). First is the linkage between operative practices and legal principles, which is asserted peremptorily in the first standard. Effective risk control cannot result in an operative practice unless this has a well-founded legal basis. This is the same problem that arose at the very beginnings of bank money, when courts refused to recognize the legal value of the 'endorsement' until a legislative act sanctioned the legitimacy of the practice. In the case of netting systems, the problem was to confer legal value upon the balances resulting from the netting of single payment transactions, so as to facilitate the cancellation, where necessary, of transactions that could not be completed, under the principle of 'netting by novation'. It was only thanks to the application of this principle that the individual transactions could take on the characteristics of finality required to reduce systemic risk.

The second aspect concerns the consequences of default when a payment has already become final through novation. Here, the fourth standard – requiring that the system be capable of completing settlement even when major players are unable to settle – implicitly calls for loss-sharing mechanisms using a predetermined formula and previously constituted funds or collateral.

A detailed account of the changes in the regulatory framework designed to limit payment system risk would go beyond the purposes of this chapter, but a second development that warrants mention is the passage of a series of European Directives to reduce risk in the systems for the management and transfer of assets.[29] As a consequence of these modifications to the regulatory context and also the market's new awareness of the problem of risk, in the 1990s private payment systems underwent a good many changes, including the institution of rules on finality by a number

---

BOX 7.2   THE LAMFALUSSY STANDARDS

Minimum standards for the design and operation of cross-border and multi-currency netting and settlement schemes

1. Netting schemes should have a well-founded legal basis under all relevant jurisdictions.
2. Netting scheme participants should have a clear understanding of the impact of the particular scheme on each of the financial risks affected by the netting process.
3. Multilateral netting systems should have clearly defined procedures for the management of credit risks and liquidity risks which specify the respective responsibilities of the netting provider and the participants. These procedures should also ensure that all parties have both the incentives and the capabilities to manage and contain each of the risks they bear and that limits are placed on the maximum level of credit exposure that can be produced by each participant.
4. Multilateral netting systems should, at a minimum, be capable of ensuring the timely completion of daily settlements in the event of an inability to settle by the participant with the largest single net-debit position.
5. Multilateral netting systems should have objective and publicly disclosed criteria for admission which permit fair and open access.
6. All netting schemes should ensure the operational reliability of technical systems and the availability of back-up facilities capable of completing daily processing requirements.

Source: Bank for International Settlements, 'Report of the Committee on Interbank Netting Schemes of the central banks of the Group of Ten countries', Basel, November 1990.

---

of netting systems. These were self-insurance agreements among system members that established procedures for the sharing of losses in case of failure to settle by a small number of participants.

The second element in the reform action was the promotion of real-time gross settlement. At the start of the 1990s gross settlement systems were uncommon. In Europe, they were to be found only in Switzerland, Denmark, Germany, Italy and the Netherlands. And except for the Swiss SIC system and to a lesser extent the Danish one, they were not highly automated, and thus handled only a small fraction of large-value trans-actions. Towards the middle of the decade, with a view to the launch of Economic and Monetary Union and the transition to the single currency, an extensive review of the role and execution procedures for gross settle-ment got under way. Some countries, including Germany and France, opted for coexistence of gross and net settlement rules, while Britain and Italy, among others, decided on the complete migration of wholesale pay-ments to the gross settlement scheme. The various European systems were then integrated in a trans-European gross settlement system, TARGET.

The new importance of gross settlement immediately posed the problem of reconciling the liquidity requirements of the schemes with the mainte-nance of fluidity in the transactions and markets that used them. 'Pure' gross settlement was deemed impracticable everywhere. At one end of the spectrum, as we have seen, was Fedwire, which made massive recourse to intraday credit, without collateral, from the central bank. Even the Federal Reserve sought to move away from unlimited, cost-free overdrafts by introducing a pricing policy for intraday credit designed to motivate banks to make less use of it by optimizing the entry of their payments into the system or increasing their reserves in the course of the day.[30] The debate thus turned on the best possible hybrid system for reconciling liquidity, fluidity and risk containment (the intermediate points on the plane shown in Figure 7.4). One system in this class is Switzerland's SIC, with 'queues' for payments that have been entered but lack sufficient funds for real-time execution. But this solution too is not without contraindica-tions: the queued payments, in fact, represent a potential source of sys-temic risk in that the debtor might be unable to settle, triggering a domino effect conceptually analogous to that occurring in a netting system. This becomes more probable as the volume of queued payments increases and the waiting time lengthens. And the effects may be magnified if the member banks have access to the information on queued payments and may therefore take on binding obligations in expectations of their success-ful completion by the end of the business day.[31]

The central banks of Europe conducted intense debate on these issues throughout the second half of the 1990s, with the architecture and functioning of the future EU payment system at stake.[32] In the end, the system chosen was midway between the Swiss and the American model. Unlimited, uncollateralized intraday overdrafts were discarded in favour of fully collateralized credit with a predetermined cap, while to ensure flu-idity the queuing of temporarily unexecutable payments was envisaged. As a rule, however, the member banks are not allowed access to the informa-tion on queued payments.

Securities payments display a good many similarities with foreign exchange trading. In both cases the transaction consists of two operations. In one case this is the sale of one currency and the acquisition of another; in the other, the transfer of cash against a counter-transfer of securities. Conceptually, then, the risk is the same, namely that because of non-performance one party will have definitively honoured its obligation before the other has done the same. In this field, central banks have sought to institute the 'delivery versus payment' scheme (DVP), as was suggested by the 1989 report of the Group of Thirty major market operators and academic experts.[33] However, in the securities market the technical difficulties were more severe, for two reasons. For one thing, in the early 1990s established practices in the securities markets of the G-10 countries still differed considerably and were often far from the final objective in any case. A number of exchanges settled securities trades with a lag of two or three days, others after weeks or even months. For these markets, a sudden switch to DVP would have meant a collapse of liquidity, hence trading. The transition to DVP therefore had to be facilitated by the creation of institutions assigned to play the role in securities trading that central banks play in monetary base settlement. These are 'central counterparties', which are interposed between the two parties to a trade, temporarily taking on part of the default risk and thus increasing the liquidity of the market. Secondly, an effective DVP scheme presupposes a real-time, automated link-up between the central bank's gross settlement system and the securities settlement systems, generally run by private operators.[34]

Apart from the operative intervention, as early as the Lamfalussy report a new function for central banks began to take shape, namely payment system oversight. At first the role was only tacit, not enshrined in the statutes of any central bank. But the identification of the substantial externalities of the payment system, such as systemic and gridlock risk and the network economies in handling retail payments, meant it was just a matter of time until legislatures recognized the public interest in the proper working of the payment system. A first act in this direction was the Treaty of Maastricht, which assigned the planned European System of Central Banks to 'promote the smooth operation of payment systems'. In Italy, Article 146 of the Consolidated Law on Finance defines this function in practically identical language. But the abstract recognition of a new function is not enough. It must be infused with content and instruments, and differentiated from the traditional supervisory function. On this terrain the individual central banks proceeded each on its own, with timetables and methods dictated by national needs, traditions and styles of thought.[35]

The financial crises in a number of emerging countries in the later 1990s prompted the G-10 central banks to broaden their sphere of action and lay down a series of standards to guarantee the smooth working of 'systemically important' payment systems and their proper oversight. The final report of the CPSS, with its 'Core Principles', was published in January 2001. It contained a series of recommendations for the substance and efficacy of central banking oversight (Box 7.3).[36]

A problem that the Lamfalussy standards, per se, could not resolve is Herstatt risk, which stems, as we have seen, from the fact that every foreign exchange trade actually comprises two payments, the payment of one currency and the receipt of another, which are generally settled each within its own national payment system. Assuming that the two operations are conducted in the same way and in analogous phases in the two systems (say, by a cash payment at the start of the business day), the time lag in a trade of yen for dollars is 15 hours, that in a trade of euros for dollars 10 hours. Another CPSS document, the 1993 Noël Report, from the name of its Chairman, T.E. Noël, set forth a series of possible solutions. The most radical option was the institution by central banks of a common supranational settlement agent in a position to settle both legs of the trade simultaneously. This was deemed politically unrealistic, however, and shelved. In recent years an alternative approach has gained support, namely the accessibility of central settlement accounts in national currency to foreign banks.[37]

7.7 RECENT TENDENCIES: THE PYRAMID UNDER SIEGE

At the start of the 1980s, then, payment systems still hinged on the clear division of tasks between the central bank and the banking system, a kind of tacit contract. The central bank engaged not to interfere with commercial banks' provision of retail payment services (except for banknote issue and, in a number of countries, payments on account of the Treasury, areas of business in which in any event the central bank's attitude was passive, or not promotional) and to supply liquidity to the banking system to facilitate its intermediation role. For its part, the banking system used its accounts with the central bank to discharge its settlement requirements and engaged to comply with a series of requirements and controls for risk containment. The contract was partly tacit – its philosophy, at any rate, was implicit – but in part it was explicit, in that it rested upon a set of legal norms that specified the central bank's responsibilities and mandate and the obligations of the commercial banks. Internationally, there being no common legal order, links between payment systems were effected via correspondent accounts and informal agreements between the main central banks.

BOX 7.3   THE G-10 CORE PRINCIPLES FOR PAYMENT SYSTEMS

A. Core Principles for systemically important payment systems

1. The system should have a well-founded legal basis under all relevant jurisdictions.
2. The system's rules and procedures should enable participants to have a clear understanding of the system's impact on each of the financial risks they incur through participation in it.
3. The system should have clearly defined procedures for the management of credit risks and liquidity risks, which specify the respective responsibilities of the system operator and the participants and which provide appropriate incentives to manage and contain those risks.
4. The system should provide prompt final settlement on the day of value, preferably during the day and, at a minimum, at the end of the day.
5. A system in which multilateral netting takes place should, at a minimum, be capable of ensuring the timely completion of daily settlements in the event of an inability to settle by the participant with the largest single settlement obligation.
6. Assets used for settlement should preferably be a claim on the central bank; where other assets are used, they should carry little or no credit risk and little or no liquidity risk.
7. The system should ensure a high degree of security and operational reliability and should have contingency arrangements for timely completion of daily processing.
8. The system should provide a means of making payments which is practical for its users and efficient for the economy.
9. The system should have objective and publicly disclosed criteria for participation, which permit fair and open access.
10. The system's governance arrangements should be effective, accountable and transparent.

B. Responsibilities of the central bank in applying the Core Principles

1. The central bank should define clearly its payment system objectives and should disclose publicly its role and major policies with respect to systemically important payment systems.
2. The central bank should ensure that the systems it operates comply with the Core Principles.
3. The central bank should oversee compliance with the Core Principles by systems it does not operate and it should have the ability to carry out this oversight.
4. The central bank, in promoting payment system safety and efficiency through the Core Principles, should cooperate with other central banks and with any other relevant domestic or foreign authorities.

Source: Committee on Payment and Settlement Systems (BIS), 'Core Principles for systemically important payment systems', Basel, January 2001.

The financial deepening of the economy in the 1980s and 1990s brought major changes, notably financial deregulation and the advent of financial derivatives. In response to the pressures generated by the rapid growth of financial transactions and the liquidity requirements of trade in derivative products, a new payment technology was developed based on intraday credit. The extremely rapid expansion of intraday credit, both that granted directly by central banks and that created implicitly in the framework of the netting procedures, triggered concerns on the part of the authorities, concerns whose basis in reality was confirmed by a series of crises and technical incidents that jeopardized the stability of important financial systems. In this way, primarily at the initiative of the G-10, wide-ranging action was undertaken to control the risks inherent in the new payment technology. This was a diversified programme of institutional adjustment that sought to reconcile the recurrent contrast between the need to protect the new payment technology from potential sources of instability and the need not to undercut its most attractive features for users, namely operating flexibility and reserve savings. The objective was complicated, because risk control efforts cannot but result, at least in the immediate term, in higher costs for the banks. In fact, the options at the disposal of the central bank for reducing intraday credit consist in explicit charges, collateral requirements and, for private schemes, operating constraints and mechanisms for the sharing of any losses.

We have no reliable estimates of the costs of the transition to gross settlement and the introduction of payment finality rules in netting schemes, but indirect evidence suggests that they were not negligible. For example, in the first few weeks of explicit charges for Fedwire overdrafts, the average amount of overdrafts and the maximum in a typical business week fell sharply, by 33 and 40 per cent respectively.[38] The cost of posting collateral is even harder to gauge, because there are a multiplicity of relevant risk profiles. It has been estimated that the annual cost of collateral ranges from 20 to 45 basis points in the United States, and from 7 to 31 in the United Kingdom.[39] In any case, these amounts are not negligible, especially considering the volume of business handled by the interbank payment system. Whatever the actual cost, it is a fact that from the very start commercial banks criticized the risk control policies adopted and encouraged by central banks precisely for their costliness, real or presumed. The institution of gross settlement queuing, for example, is an attempt to reconcile the multiple necessities. Another of the banking community's complaints concerned the lack of machinery for coordinating the use of collateral between the various national settlement systems so as to save on the overall costs.

Apart from the dissatisfaction of the commercial banks – predictable, in a way, in that the central banks' action was in response to a perceived externality, systemic risk, that the private banks' operating procedures did not pick up – in the years to come the configuration of the payment system is bound to feel the powerful impact of a sweeping phenomenon that took on particular virulence at the end of the century: consolidation within the financial systems of the main countries.

The pace of mergers and acquisitions grew unusually intensive at the turn of the century, prompting the G-10 to form a group, chaired by Roger W. Ferguson, Jr, to study its origins, causes and implications. The Ferguson Report[40] was very widely publicized. Financial sector mergers and acquisitions increased in number from 324 a year at the start of the 1990s to 887 at the end, and in value from $38 billion at the turn of the decade to $495 billion in 1998. Even more interesting is the breakdown by type of operation: about 60 per cent by number and 70 per cent by value involved banks. Since most of the mergers were within national boundaries, there was a substantial increase in the degree of concentration of the G-10 national banking systems. And if off-balance-sheet assets – generally associated with derivatives markets – are counted, the concentration was even more pronounced.

Turning to the direct effects on the payment system, the immediate

impact of the process of consolidation consisted in a concentration of
payment flows and securities custody at a small group of banks with a
marked inclination for international business. It was estimated that by
2006 the top five or six financial institutions would manage two-thirds of
the entire world market in correspondent accounts.[41] Yet several distinct
facets of the phenomenon warrant special treatment. Three appear to be
particularly important: the tiering of interbank dealings, the creation of
the Continuous Linked Settlement Bank for cross-border settlement, and
the possible development of quasi-systems.

7.7.1 Tiering

Some tiering is an inherent part of the pyramid structure. Financial consolidation is heightening its importance, for at least two reasons. First,
with mergers between banks doing different types of business that in many
cases will retain their own branch networks, many correspondence payments will become intragroup ('on us') payments, as such escaping central
bank surveillance. And second, in many countries consolidation has
created a sharp split between large, internationally active banks and a host
of small and mid-sized banks engaged chiefly in domestic business; this
favours a division of roles between these two components of the banking
system.

7.7.2 Continuous Linked Settlement

The New York-based private settlement scheme operated by CLS Bank
represents a response to Herstatt risk. It obviates the risk by opening local
currency accounts at the most important central banks, thus permitting
simultaneous settlement of the two legs of a foreign exchange transaction.
The mechanism is complex and not worth describing in detail here.[42] Let
us just note that in eliminating Herstatt risk, it creates risks, the effective
magnitude of which depends on the organizational arrangements and the
effectiveness of supervisory action. In particular, as the system settles via
accounts with central banks, the latter take on credit risk insofar as settlement relies on intraday credit. In other words, one leg of the foreign
exchange transaction could be settled in monetary base and the other in
intraday credit, leaving one of the central banks exposed to end-of-day
default risk.[43] In any event, it is estimated that when CLS is fully operational it will reduce the flow of cross-border payments via correspondent
accounts by between 10 and 50 per cent. This should accentuate tiering.
Interestingly, the advent of CLS brought significant change to central
banks' policy on opening centralized accounts. Hitherto the rule had been

that only the banks that they themselves supervised were eligible for such accounts, except in the European Union where, by virtue of legal and supervisory coordination with a view to monetary union, remote access for all EU banks was already in place. With CLS, an American bank – CLS Bank itself – was allowed to open accounts with all the main central banks, thus instituting a form of non-European remote access.

7.7.3 Quasi-systems

This term was coined by the Ferguson Report to designate an institution that in the eyes of the other private agents acquires, as a result of consolidation and specialization in the management of correspondent accounts, operating capabilities and a risk profile making it preferable or at least equivalent to the central bank as settlement agent. If this happened, the pyramid structure of each national system would be maintained but the vertex would no longer be the central bank but the 'quasi-system'.

Financial innovation, changes in the structure of the financial system and especially in the degree of concentration, technological progress, and the risk-control action of central banks themselves have put the pyramid model under pressure. A growing share of large-value payments is migrating from central bank to privately operated procedures or to intermediaries that by size, operating diversification and risk have come, at least in the perception of most agents, to resemble central banks. It is very hard to tell how serious this threat to the established arrangement is. It may be nothing but a minor aftershock or adjustment to a new payment technology – relying on intraday credit – that was totally non-existent just 20 years back. It may also be that the private sector's perceptions of the real risk of private payment systems prove unfounded, as has happened recurrently in the past in connection with various payment technologies.

However, as overseers of the payment system, central banks have the obligation to take these phenomena seriously and to be prepared. In this task, they face severe information gaps. At best, relatively well-founded conjectures can be formulated on the actual extent of tiering, on the existence of quasi-systems, and on the market potential of CLS, but no precise data are available. However, the pressure for change is undeniable, as is demonstrated by the central banks' initiatives to increase the efficiency of the payment services provided by the banking system. All the main central bank payment systems, in fact, are studying or installing operating procedures to reduce the liquidity requirements for member banks. This pattern embraces the German RTGS-plus and the French PNS system. Similarly, among privately operated systems we find a tendency to adopt operating procedures that reduce risk (as in the American New CHIPS system). The authorities are also studying the request of the leading international banks to constitute a common collateral pool in the most important countries that could be used flexibly in the various settlement systems depending on the need to back each one's 'local' intraday credit.

But if the 'privatization' of the payment system were to proceed, other, more demanding actions could well be taken into consideration. Hypothetically, three different central bank strategies are possible:

1. Limiting the sphere of action to oversight and accepting a smaller operating role within the payment system (the 'decapitated pyramid' hypothesis).
2. Actively promoting the present pyramid structure with operational changes to lower the cost of central bank services and with administrative action (the 'strengthened pyramid' hypothesis).
3. Extending access to central bank accounts to all the main financial market participants, including non-financial corporations, and accepting the challenge of competing with the banking system in providing universal payment services (the 'repudiated pyramid' hypothesis).

None of these hypotheses will be easy to realize; each has its advantages and disadvantages. So it is unlikely that consistent action along one of these axes will be undertaken in the absence of some kind of pathology, which naturally no one wants to see. As always in the history of central banks, as in biology, it will be the function that develops the organ, not the other way around.

Epilogue

My intention in this book was not historiographic analysis – since it would have been beyond my abilities, and given that in many countries the history of central banks is still unbroken ground awaiting a competent ploughman – but to conduct a theoretical argument based on historical materials. Following the precepts of John Hicks and Fausto Vicarelli cited at the outset, I have asked whether or not – beyond the forms, which as in every aspect of human society vary from era to era and country to country – there is some consistent logic to the evolution of central banks and central banking, clearly discernable and subject to an economic interpretation. Drawing on neo-institutional theory, I answered in the affirmative. The answer turns on the fundamental contractual incompleteness within which the circulation of money takes place, hence on the necessity for trust if a full-fledged capitalistic economy using credit-based payment instruments is to thrive. What has emerged is what Hicks called a 'theory of history'. Whether or not it is a persuasive one, of course, is for the reader to say.

In this afterword, let me seek to recapitulate the argument and enucleate some thinking points on the future of central banking. My point of departure was the observation that the neo-classical attempt to treat money merely as a commodity, useful though it is in analysing monetary policy and portfolio choices, when it comes to the evolution of monetary forms and institutions actually raises more problems than it solves. In reality, money itself is an institution, with the peculiar characteristic that its exchange price cannot be known when it is stored. There is no way to know in advance the real value of the monetary services associated with a given quantity of money. The monetary contract is fundamentally incomplete. So money exists and prospers only insofar as it enjoys the trust of those who use it. It follows that money cannot be studied apart from its cultural, political and legal context. This is the heart of the message conveyed by the institutional view of monetary matters espoused in this volume.

Trust can spring from what Émile Durkheim called the 'dynamic density of exchange',[1] that is, repeated interaction among a small number of actors. But when the sphere of a currency's circulation broadens, which is to say when the agents who use it increase in number and diversity, so also does the need for the deliberate production of trust by means of institutions. I introduced the concept of a 'payment technology' – broader than that of money – expressly in order to underscore that any monetary economy, even the most primitive, needs a mechanism to safeguard the social convention on which the circulation of money rests. Payment technologies differ essentially in two features: the flexibility, or manipulability, of supply and the institutional requirements for eliminating the risk of abuse; that is, the risk, to use the terminology of institutional theory, of opportunistic behaviour by the producers of money.

I have traced the evolution of central banking within this framework. We have 'read' the formation of central banks as a key element in the institutional response to the problems posed by the transition from payment technologies whose institutional requirements are minimal, because they are hard to manipulate – commodity money – to those with a greater component of trust, because they are based on credit mechanisms and thus necessitate a more sophisticated set of institutional safeguards. The prime mover in the process was identified as capitalistic development, which by expanding the volume of trade, extending the network of markets and increasing transaction costs, generated an endemic upward tendency in the demand for money. This in turn stimulated financial innovation to make the supply more elastic. I have adopted the theses of Keynes and Carlo Cipolla on the importance of the monetary brake as an impediment to economic growth. But my interpretation conflicts with the 'free banking' advocates who see the central bank as nothing but a state imposition for purposes of expropriation, and with Alan Posen's thesis that monetary institutions are merely the crystallization of existing power relations and thus have no effect on collective welfare. In my reading institutions do count, and they count all the more in monetary matters owing to the pervasive role of money in the economy and the great importance of trust in determining the demand for monetary services. What has to be stressed, however, is that the criterion on which institutional change is based is not that of efficiency. Quite simply, where there is no theoretical frame of reference for the adjustment process, efficiency cannot be defined. To postulate as a benchmark a utopian world without imperfections is tantamount to committing the 'nirvana fallacy', in Harold Demsetz's illuminating image. The criterion that drives institutional change is not efficiency but effectiveness, the ability of a prospective solution to overcome a problem perceived as socially significant. It is the effectiveness factor, in my interpretation, that explains why central banks developed in waves of reform that followed a single model in different countries, albeit adapted to local needs in matters of secondary importance.

What made the central bank possible, in fact, was a much broader development, outside the monetary sphere and indeed outside the economic sphere altogether: namely, the rise of the state of law and representative democracy. Central banks were born, grew and will probably die with the liberal state. They are an important part of that state, have suffered its vicissitudes and, in the long run, are destined to share its fate. To consider the central bank as nothing but a technical entity is to make a serious error of judgment. The central bank is an intrinsically political animal, because its choices necessarily have consequences for the distribution of income. If in the long run money is neutral – a proposition that more and more analysts have come to doubt – in the short run it certainly is not. This is why the central bank needs an independent source of legitimacy, which can only derive from the legal order and political institutions.

This point of view enables us to shed light on some regular patterns and some paradoxes in the history of central banking. The patterns include the link between crucial transitions in the formation of central banks and major financial crises and the tendency of these transitions to come in international 'waves' marked by national replications of a single model tuned up by the needs of a country central to the world economy. Financial crisis is the sign of distress for a new payment technology, of difficulty in sustaining trust when the number of producers increases and the sphere of circulation expands. If the crisis is widespread enough, it will give rise to an alliance between the original innovators, who at this point will have acquired an interest in defending their quasi-rents against expropriation by new entrants, and users who want to defend the real value of their stock of money. It becomes then politically easier to overcome the resistance to institutional change from debtors and newly formed financial enterprises. The waves of reform reflect the fact that institutionalization is a trial-and-error process. Every payment technology raises new problems, so it is natural for successful – or apparently successful – reforms to be adopted in other contexts, with minor adaptations. The evolution of central banks is the history of a succession of models some of which more effective than others.

At least two paradoxes also need to be highlighted. First, although the ultimate purpose of the development of central banks is to protect payment technologies that have become steadily easier to manipulate, the immediate impact of reform has often been to make the money supply more rigid, thus having a deflationary effect. I have interpreted this historical fact as a manifestation of what Benjamin Klein calls 'investment in brand capital'. To generate trust, in the various phases of their evolution central banks have had to demonstrate their ability to safeguard the stability of the payment technology against the threat of excessive competition or, in the case of legal tender, debasement by the state. In the short run this made it necessary to subject monetary policy to simple, transparent, and so unavoidably rigid rules. The classical examples are the 'English model' of 1844 and the central bankers' international of the 1920s, which sought to protect the nascent form of legal tender with a heavily deflationary gold exchange standard. Often, however, this was a short-term phenomenon, as the very revival of monetary innovation imposed new forms of discretionary power and operational flexibility.

The second paradox is the strange relationship, generally symbiotic but sometimes conflictual, of the central bank with the state and the financial system. Without the support of the state and the financial system, central banking is inconceivable. But when they are too strong, the state and the financial system grow restive under the discipline imposed by an independent, authoritative central bank. The strains are most evident where the state is authoritarian, as in the Napoleonic era, during the world wars of the last century, or under Fascist or Communist regimes. But clashes have also developed in liberal regimes, such as those of the 1960s and 1970s. The strains with the financial system have often been the product of waves of competition and the reallocation of market shares in situations in which it is hard for the central bank to be truly impartial.

Central banking, today, is the object of a good deal of scepticism. There is considerable backing for the idea proposed, most notably by Barry Eichengreen, that the monetary trilemma leaves little scope for conscious action by central bankers. With perfect or almost perfect capital mobility, in a single country the only possible options for policy-makers are letting the exchange rate float and irrevocably tying their own hands. In either case, the central bank will have a marginal role, at the most as a technical support, and not in setting policy guidelines. However, this position is not convincing. True, many tiny countries have abandoned monetary sovereignty or are on the road to doing so, while other, larger ones, as in Europe, are seeking to share sovereignty. But between these two extremes there is an enormous grey area where monetary nationalism and internationalism coexist, with variable results. And even where the adoption of floating exchange rates is formally total, the authorities are certainly not indifferent to the external sector and confidence in the national currency. Nor is there any lack of countries that have enacted moderate limitations to capital movements.

More interesting than the monetary trilemma, in examining the prospects for the future of central banking, is the political trilemma: the incompatibility among far-reaching international economic integration, the nation-state and mass politics. As a first approximation, we observe that central banking is not bound unequivocally to any particular configuration of these three factors. The three 'golden ages' of central banking – the era of the gold standard (1890–1914), the period of greatest success of the Bretton Woods regime (1958–69), and the recovery from stagflation (from the Volcker policy revolution to the Treaty of Maastricht) – differ radically. The gold standard regime assigned priority to the nation-state and to market integration, sacrificing the popular masses, who were entirely marginal to politics and to policy. The principles of the Bretton Woods regime were diametrically opposite. In the name of mass democracy and maintaining the prerogatives of the nation-state, in some measure the system sacrificed economic integration, especially the movement of capital but also, through the 1950s, that of goods. It is probably no accident, as Eichengreen notes, that the problems began with the restoration of currency convertibility, when the system faced the impossible task of reconciling all three horns of the trilemma. With the financial and foreign exchange liberalization of the 1980s, there was a new inversion. Now the nation-state itself gave way to very strong trade and financial integration (globalization) and a high degree of mass politics.

Of these three periods, the most surprising is certainly the last. One would have expected the 1970s, with the definitive arrival of the masses on the political scene, to mark the end of De Cecco's élite central bank assigned to protect creditors. And this was what happened, basically, but that did not mean the end of central banking – quite the contrary. Central banks emerged from the stagflation crisis not diminished but on the contrary powerfully reinforced in their powers, instruments and institutional status (raised to constitutional status in some countries). The Treaty of Maastricht, though designed for a supranational context, was in a way the manifesto of this transformation. The change was fostered not only by the new awareness of the importance of central banks as generators of trust, implying the need to put them above politics, but also by what we could call 'mass finance'. The people who used to be called the 'gnomes of Zurich' – during the speculative attacks against sterling or the lira in the 1960s – are now just as likely to be your next-door neighbour:

> The de-demonization of finance is part of a democratization of financial activity. We are like the heroes or villains of the past when we tap e-trades into our home computers. As a consequence, we have a completely different concept of financial sin from that which stimulated the nineteenth-century critiques of capitalism . . . Marx's and Wagner's demons are now quite commonplace characters. It is no longer a question of mysterious gods of high finance in top hats: we are all part of the system.[2]

If we are now all 'part of the system', the central bank becomes a bit more 'central', a bit more a common property. But this change is not free of drawbacks, both for its relations with the state and for those with the financial industry. The nation-state is going through a difficult time, between market integration and mass politics. Though now more respected within their national confines, central banks cannot but suffer, because historically their legitimacy derives precisely from the nation-state itself. Which is why, in an effort to weaken this grip, central banks addressed themselves more and more to the holders of money and not to the holders of political power. After the decades of self-imposed silence, central bankers now speak – and often – in an effort, admittedly, to make their actions known and to shape expectations, but also to gain a direct legitimacy of their own, independent of the established constitutional powers. To achieve this they conducted a sophisticated strategy, in many respects diametrically opposed to that of previous eras: no more vagueness on objectives but extreme precision in making price stability the 'main objective'. No longer would they have a steadily increasing number of functions but a definite hierarchy of tasks, headed by the strictly monetary ones, from monetary policy to the sound operation of the payment system. No longer would central banks be abundantly forthcoming in analyses marginal to their actual powers and bare on monetary policy questions; instead, they would engage in timely and explicit discussion of the reasons for the decisions and of alternative scenarios. In many ways this strategy reversal was inevitable, in an era of mass politics, but it did put central banks on a collision course with the nation-state, with its steadily shrinking powers, and will continue to do so. In fact, among the political circles least favourable to globalization, the suspicion is harboured that financial liberalization has been deliberately propagated by central banks as a tool for their emancipation from political control, as a way of making the 'act of sedition' – that so disturbed Governor Guido Carli in the 1970s – politically acceptable. Without the rise of mass finance, none of this could have happened.

Nevertheless, the central banks did have to pay a price. In some countries, including Britain, the true homeland of central banking, this price took the form of exclusion from the sphere of banking supervision. This exclusion failed to become really widespread, and the tenor of this volume certainly casts doubt upon its validity, but it has been adopted in enough countries to suggest that it represents a noble attempt to defuse the conflict with the political system and achieve better control over finance in a context in which central banks are everywhere tending to become 'small' compared with the banks supervised. Whether or not this is an effective move on the institutional plane, only time will tell. And central banks have also paid internationally, as nation-states desperately seek new space in the sphere of intergovernmental relations and appear quite unwilling to share their fate with the central banks, as they had done in the 1920s and under Bretton Woods. The signs of impatience with the central banks have multiplied internationally. If the national central banks belonging to the Eurosystem have managed on the whole to gain a supranational status with the endorsement of the political system, at the single national level they are struggling to retain the roles assigned them in previous eras. For the central banks, consequently, the present configuration of the political trilemma offers a mixed picture indeed: an enviable status at the country level, especially in the eyes of public opinion, which in many countries now perceives them, particularly for the conduct of monetary policy, as a body of constitutional rank; but a latent conflict with the nation-state both in relations with citizens and in relations with other governments, especially as regards other areas of activity, notably banking and financial supervision.

In the years to come, the most interesting developments will probably be precisely in the sphere of supervision and regulation. First of all, the concentration on disinflation in the 1980s and the increased complexity of the monetary policy transmission mechanism have deflected the attention of economists and policy-makers from the banking system as transmission belt. But while inflation has been tamed practically everywhere, we still find, as the series of studies being conducted at the Bank for International Settlements demonstrates, solid links between credit aggregates and speculative bubbles in the securities and real estate markets.[3] Insofar as instability is the key defect of the market-led system, it will very shortly be impossible to avoid facing the problem that tormented scholars at the time bank money was being introduced: how to exploit the 'magic of credit' for growth without inciting banks to imprudent lending practices. The Basel II accords represent a tentative response. It is questionable whether they are sufficient.[4] This is confirmation of the thesis set forth in Chapter 6, namely that a significant feature of the present configuration of monetary systems is the coexistence between the payment technology based on legal tender and that based on bank money (and, looking to the future, electronic money). This is a theme being grappled with by those engaged in designing a new international financial architecture in practice, but it also warrants greater attention in theoretical work, now that the fiat standard has been mastered from that standpoint.

Second, with very few exceptions, in all the main countries the activity of the central bank vis-à-vis the financial system is based on and legitimated by a special body of law whose purpose is to remove banking from the sphere of commercial law in order to ensure swift government intervention in case of crisis and the protection of the banking system as a whole. Each of these codes seeks to reconcile conflicting ends: equal treatment of creditors, the preservation of the value of the troubled bank, and preventing contagion from spreading to other banks. They do so following criteria and procedures dictated by national law, in keeping with local legal traditions and preferences. So there is no assurance that as some banks begin to take on transnational dimensions, there will arise transnational banking regulations that can guarantee a modicum of consistency in the procedures for crisis intervention and resolution on the part of the authorities. This is a task for which cooperation between central banks and nation-states is indispensable, but still to be achieved.[5]

The awareness of a latent conflict with the executive power led central banks to reinforce their relations with the financial industry, seconding its needs and stimulating its growth. The 1980s and 1990s were years of unprecedented expansion for the financial superstructure, and it is unlikely that this could have happened without the concrete contribution of the central banks. As Eric Helleiner maintains, it was the Federal Reserve and the Bank of England that set the process in motion in the 1970s, but in the 1980s the other central banks began to join in, including the Bundesbank, perhaps the most resistant to financial innovation. The development of intraday credit, the extending network of financial markets, and the elimination of many limits on banks' operations were often due to the decisive impetus imparted by the central banks.

Financial development itself created new problems, however. First of all, the conduct of monetary policy is a much more complicated business now than just 20 years ago. The prevalence of inflation targeting was a response to the difficulty of reproducing a two-stage monetary policy in a situation of fast-reacting financial markets. Appearances to the contrary notwithstanding (the market-led system, the removal of regulatory constraints, the auction system for liquidity injection), the scope for discretionary monetary policy increased enormously. But there is always a risk that policy-makers will end up acting according to markets' expectations, in an attempt to minimize negative surprises. An 'expected' money supply, in fact, is the opposite of a 'managed' supply. And it is questionable that today the Keynesian lesson on the financial markets' lack of any self-regulating capability can be dismissed. One aspect of this problem is what role to attribute to the equity markets in the transmission of monetary policy. Charles Bean, for one, contends that it is no use for monetary policy-makers to look at stock market trends; that all they need to do is set the problem with a sufficiently long horizon.[6] The argument is unconvincing, however. For one thing, with mass finance the direct repercussions of a stock market crash on consumer demand threaten to be much more severe than in the past. For another – and basically for the same reason – the relation between stock markets and the instruments of monetary policy can be non-linear, and stock market performance may therefore contain important information for the optimal policy course. However, intervention to discourage, say, a speculative bubble that will eventually affect the prices of goods and services may run counter to the interests of the citizens who now serve as the coalition that supports the central bank. In this context, it is not easy for a central banker to buck the trend, as Paul Volcker could do in 1979 or Antonio Fazio in 1994. Doubtless, it is hard to achieve just the right combination of warning, action and support. The risk that a central banker may sway public opinion thanks to his powers of media communication rather than his analytical persuasiveness is a serious one.

Yet there is another, possibly still more insidious difficulty. Globalization has sharply increased financial concentration. In the banking sector in the main industrial countries (not, of course, the emerging economies), this has created national champions, far out of proportion with the rest of the economy and even the central bank. This was predicted by Fred Hirsch in the little-known article that marked the start of modern studies of central banking, in 1977. Hirsch noted that given informational asymmetries the attempt to subject banking to strict market discipline would result in concentration, as large banks sought the protective umbrella of government.[7]

To be sure, the hypothesis has not yet been proven – just as the others suggested themselves lack demonstration. The Ferguson committee within the G-10 and individual scholars have struggled unsuccessfully to discover economies of scale or scope sufficient to justify such a massive wave of mergers and acquisitions. And moral hazard as an economic mechanism has always been extremely hard to document empirically. But in the meantime a series of financial enterprises, not just banks, have begun to provide customers with cash and securities payment services that were once the exclusive preserve of central banks. This is the payment system 'pyramid under siege', a little-known phenomenon found mainly in the narrow circles of bankers but that has, like the Renaissance credit circuits, the potential to subvert the workings not just of the payment system but of monetary policy itself. For if the central bank is not perceived by citizens as having a comparative advantage in generating trust such as to justify the greater costliness of the money it produces vis-à-vis alternative instruments, the very notion of central banking is impossible. Obviously, we are not yet at this point. But it is precisely the central banks of the countries whose financial superstructure is most developed – the Federal Reserve, the Bank of England, the Bank of Japan – that are subject to the fiercest opposition, including political opposition, from big finance, which is increasingly intolerant of the ties and fetters of regulations seen as largely superfluous. There is nothing wrong with this as such, because the objective of the central bank, as a public agency, cannot be self-perpetuation. But it is hard to believe that the emergence of private payment systems can be a viable solution to the problem of trust, because of the conflicts of interest that would arise, as they did in other eras, between producers whose objective is profit maximization.

Some central banks seem to be tempted to respond to competition with competition; that is, to violate the non-belligerency pact of the early twentieth century, which Charles Goodhart saw as the crowning touch in the recognition of the need to regulate money and lending of last resort. For central banks, competing in this sense would mean opening up their services to ordinary customers, households and firms, ceasing to subsidize some services provided at zero cost, and revising their wholesale payment procedures to make them as smooth as private procedures.

It is doubtful that such a strategy could succeed, however. The time may not be propitious for central banks as a group, because the political problems raised by globalization are too big to be tackled by what are still technical entities, even though over the decades and in the response to stagflation they attained the status of public guarantors. Only three or four world-scale central banks can still play on a par in the world financial arena, and always under the protection of their government. For as Adam Smith said, the comparative advantage of the central bank (the 'bank of issue' as he called it) in producing trust rests on its being part of the 'machinery of state'. The attempt to compensate for the gradual withdrawal of the favours of the nation-state by competing on an equal footing with the financial industry smacks of adventurism. However much the relationship between the central bank and the public holders of money and finance can be strengthened, it will always be too precarious to withstand the combined shock of nation-state and multinational finance. Better tenacious, obscure action than such uncertain adventure. The best example is the 'soft law' strategy discussed in Chapter 6. Created to embody the new attempt by politics to shape financial regulation and supervision, the executor of that strategy, the Financial Stability Forum, saw a 'central banking' approach prevail, little by little, not as the backlash of an institution in difficulty but because in the underinstitutionalized international environment the creation of common values, confidentiality and mutual respect is more important than the announcement of binding constraints, which may have great psychological impact but which are hard to enforce in practice.

Whatever its detractors may say, the central bank has no need to move into new lines of business. Capitalism generated the central bank, and capitalism will come to it again, even if the current infatuation with the financial markets' self-regulating capacity were to endure. And already today this infatuation appears to be threadbare in many areas: the renewed diffidence with respect to stock market fluctuations, doubts about the benefits of short-term capital movements, and fears over the illegal use of financial systems and offshore centres.

The central bank produces an intangible but essential good – trust – of which capitalism (based as it is on a pyramid of paper if not mere electronic signals) has an immense need. We must not forget that trust, or its synonym 'confidence', derives from the Latin *fide*, meaning faith, which cannot be produced simply by contract. In fact the legitimacy of central banks does not lie in their policy activism, or their ability to generate income or even, save in a highly indirect sense, their efficiency. Rather, as Kenneth Boulding taught in a fine essay now over a quarter-century old, it derives from competence, moderation, the long-term approach, and the refusal to take on any tasks beyond their primary role.[8] If, as I am sure, there is to be another phase in the development of central banking, it will spring from these values.

Notes

PREFACE

1. 'Determinazione del livello dei prezzi e politica monetaria in un'economia senza moneta', *Giornale degli Economisti e Annali di Economia*, September–October 1986; 'L'evoluzione del sistema dei pagamenti: una sintesi teorica', *Moneta e Credito*, June 1988.
2. 'Confidence costs and the institutional genesis of central banks', Banca d'Italia, *Temi di discussione No.* 226, 1994; 'Money, trust, and central banking', *Journal of Economics and Business*, 1995.
3. The studies with the most direct bearing on the book are: 'On the economics of inter-bank payments systems', *Economic Notes*, May–August 1994 (with Paolo Angelini); 'Which target for monetary policy in Stage Three? Issues in the shaping of the European Payment System', *Weltwirtschaftliches Archiv*, October–December 1997 (with Carlo Monticelli); 'Dalla finanza alla moneta: il ruolo del sistema dei pagamenti', in Giacomo Vaciago (ed.), *Moneta e Finanza*, Bologna, Il Mulino, 1998 (with Giovanni B. Pittaluga and Fabio Fornari); 'Enemy of none but a common friend to all', *Princeton Essays in International Finance*, 214, June 1999; 'Pitfalls in international crisis lending', in Charles Goodhart and Gerhard Illing (eds), *Financial Crises, Contagion, and the Lender of Last Resort: A Reader*, Oxford, Oxford University Press, 2002; 'Credibility without rules? Monetary frameworks in the post-Bretton Woods era', IMF Occasional Paper No. 154, December 1997; and 'Bedfellows, hostages or perfect strangers? Global capital markets and the catalytic effect of IMF crisis lending', IMF Working Paper, WP/02/193, November 2002 (the last two with Carlo Cottarelli).

INTRODUCTION

1. This inscription was found on an ancient coin from Malta. See Georg Simmel, *Philosophie des Geldes*, Leipzig, Duncker und Humblot, 1900, p. 149.
2. Fausto Vicarelli, 'Central bank autonomy: a historical perspective', in Gianni Toniolo (ed.), *Central Banks' Independence in Historical Perspective*, Berlin, Walter de Gruyter, 1988, p. 1.
3. See H. Geoffrey Brennan and James M. Buchanan, *Monopoly in Money and Inflation*, London, Institute of Economic Affairs, 1981; Friedrich A. von Hayek, *Denationalization of Money: The Argument Refined*, London, Institute of Economic Affairs, 1978; David Glasner, *Free Banking and Monetary Reform*, Cambridge, Cambridge University Press, 1989; Kevin Dowd, *The State and the Monetary System*, London, Philip Allan, 1989; Lawrence H. White, *Competition and Currency: Essays on Free Banking and Money*, New York, New York University Press, 1989.
4. See Douglass C. North and Barry R. Weingast, 'Constitutions and commitment: the evolution of institutions governing public choice in seventeenth-century England', *Journal of Economic History*, December 1989; Patrick O'Brien, 'Central government and the economy, 1688–1815', in Roderick Floud and Deirdre McCloskey (eds), *The Economic History of Britain Since 1700, I: 1700–1860*, Cambridge, Cambridge University Press, 1994.

5. Charles A.E. Goodhart, *The Evolution of Central Banks*, Cambridge, MA, MIT Press, 1988.
6. See, among others, Oliver Williamson, 'The economics of governance: framework and implications', in Richard N. Langlois (ed.), *Economics as a Process: Essays in the New Institutional Economics*, Cambridge, Cambridge University Press, 1986; Avner Greif, Paul Milgrom and Barry R. Weingast, 'Coordination, commitment and enforcement: the case of the merchant guild', *Journal of Political Economy*, August 1994; North and Weingast, 'Constitutions and commitment', op. cit.
7. J. Lawrence Broz, *The International Origins of the Federal Reserve System*, Ithaca, NY, Cornell University Press, 1997.
8. This view of the evolution of money owes much to the historiographical contributions of Carlo M. Cipolla, whose book *Money, Prices, and Civilization in the Mediterranean World: Fifth to Seventeenth Century* (Princeton, NJ, Princeton University Press, 1956) drew the attention of scholars to the deflationary pressures caused by the growth in the demand for money at a time of rapidly increasing trade and rising population. On the theoretical level, the most obvious reference is John Maynard Keynes, *A Tract on Monetary Reform*, London, Macmillan, 1923.
9. John R. Hicks, *A Theory of Economic History*, Oxford, Clarendon Press, 1969, pp. 95–96.
10. Harold Demsetz, 'Information and efficiency: another viewpoint', *Journal of Law and Economics*, April 1969, p. 1.
11. John Hicks, *A Theory of Economic History*, op. cit., and *A Market Theory of Money*, Oxford, Clarendon Press, 1989. See also Nathan Rosenberg and Luther E. Birdzell Jr, *How the West Grew Rich: The Economic Transformation of the Industrial World*, New York, Basic Books, 1989, and Douglass C. North, *Structure and Change in Economic History*, New York, Norton, 1981.
12. The relationship between the formation of nation-states and the creation of national currencies has not yet been analysed in depth from the historiographical angle. So far, the question has only been touched upon, for example by Gianfranco Poggi, *The Development of the Modern State*, Stanford, CA, Stanford University Press, 1978 (see also *La vicenda dello Stato moderno*, Bologna, Il Mulino, 1978), and by Eric J. Hobsbawm, *Nations and Nationalism Since 1780*, Cambridge, Cambridge University Press, 1990.
13. Benjamin J. Cohen, *The Geography of Money*, Ithaca, NY, Cornell University Press, 1998.

CHAPTER 1

1. John R. Hicks, 'The two triads. Lecture I', in *Critical Essays in Monetary Theory*, Oxford, Oxford University Press, 1967, p. 2.
2. John R. Hicks, 'A suggestion for simplifying the theory of money', *Economica*, February 1935.
3. Don Patinkin, *Money, Interest and Prices*, New York, Harper & Row, 1965.
4. Frank Hahn, 'On some problems of proving the existence of equilibrium in a monetary economy', in Frank Hahn and Frank P.R. Brechling (eds), *The Theory of Interest Rates*, London, Macmillan, 1965.
5. This is not the place for a detailed exegesis of Aristotle's thinking. It is sufficient to recall that in *History of Economic Analysis* (New York, Oxford University Press, 1954, Vol. 1, p. 63) Joseph Schumpeter dismisses the contradiction as non-existent and maintains that the passages in which Aristotle stresses that whatever circulates as money must be, first and foremost, a commodity are unequivocal. Modern historians of ancient Greece are not so sure. Crawford, for example, denies that money may originally have been coined in response to the needs of trade, whether internal or external, and suggests that

what Aristotle may have had in mind in the passage of *Ethica Nichomachea* is the link between monetization and state prerogatives, such as payment of mercenaries and collection of taxes (see Michael H. Crawford, *La moneta in Grecia e a Roma*, Rome and Bari, Laterza, 1982, pp. 12–14).

6. Georg Friedrich Knapp, *Staatliche Theorie des Geldes*, Munich and Leipzig, Duncker & Humblot, 1905 (abbreviated English edition, *The State Theory of Money*, London, Macmillan, 1924).
7. On the argument between statalism and catallactics see the introduction by Curzio Giannini and Giovanni B. Pittaluga to *Moneta e istituzioni monetarie*, Milan, Hoepli, 2001.
8. Richard N. Langlois, 'The new institutional economics: an introductory essay', in Richard N. Langlois (ed.), *Economics as a Process*, op. cit.
9. The concept of specificity of an investment refers to a situation in which a given transaction entails tying up assets, which could only be reused in other activities, if the original transaction were broken off early, at substantial cost. See Oliver Williamson, 'The economics of governance', op. cit.
10. Oliver E. Williamson, 'The New Institutional Economics: taking stock, looking ahead', in *Journal of Economic Literature*, September 2000, p. 599.
11. Ibid., p. 601.
12. See Carlo M. Cipolla, *Moneta e civiltà mediterranea*, Venice, Neri e Pozza Editore, 1957.
13 Robert W. Clower, 'Introduction', in Clower (ed.), *Monetary Theory*, op. cit., p. 13.
14. See Karl E. Warneryd, *Economic Conventions: Essays in Institutional Evolution*, Stockholm, Stockholm School of Economics, 1991.
15. Benjamin Klein, 'The competitive supply of money', *Journal of Money, Credit and Banking*, December 1974. Klein's model is discussed at greater length in the Appendix to this chapter.
16. See Benjamin Klein, Robert G. Crawford and Armen A. Alchian, 'Vertical integration, appropriable rents, and the competitive contracting process', *Journal of Law and Economics*, October 1978.
17. Rudolf Richter, 'The new institutional economics applied to monetary economics', *Journal of Institutional and Theoretical Economics*, February 1988.
18. See Williamson, 'The new institutional economics', op. cit.
19. Milton Friedman, 'Commodity reserve currency', *Journal of Political Economy*, June 1951, Vol. 59, n. 3, p. 206.
20. Clower, *Monetary Theory*, op. cit., p. 14.
21. Arthur Okun, 'Inflation: its mechanics and welfare costs', *Brookings Papers on Economic Activity*, 2, 1975.
22. Cipolla, *Moneta e civiltà mediterranea*, op. cit., p. 50 (author's translation).
23. Rondo Cameron (with Olga Crisp, Hugh T. Patrick and Richard Tilly), *Banking in the Early Stages of Industrialization: A Study in Comparative Economic History*, New York, Oxford University Press, 1967; Rondo Cameron (ed.), *Banking and Economic Development: Some Lessons of History*, London and New York, Oxford University Press, 1972.
24. John Kenneth Galbraith, 'Introduction', in Robert Shaplen, *Kreuger: Genius and Swindler*, New York, Alfred A. Knopf, 1959, p. ix. See also Harold James, *The End of Globalization*, Cambridge, MA, Harvard University Press, 2001, p. 34.
25. Carl Menger, 'On the origin of money', *Economic Journal*, June 1892.
26. The most interest formalization of Menger's theory is in Robert A. Jones, 'The origin and development of media of exchange', *Journal of Political Economy*, August 1976.
27. The problem becomes even more complex if we assume, with Hodgson, that the quality of the commodity undergoes variations that are not easy to assess. In these conditions, people may unconsciously converge towards monetary use of only poor-quality versions of the chosen commodity (see Geoffrey W. Hodgson, 'Carl Menger's

theory of the evolution of money: some problems', *Review of Political Economy*, 4 (4), 1992).

28. Carl Menger, 'On the origin of money', op. cit., p. 255.
29. Viktor Vanberg, *Markt und Organisation: Individualistische Sozialtheorie und das Problem Korporativen Handelns*, Tübingen, J.C.B. Mohr, 1982. See also Langlois, 'The new institutional economics', op. cit., pp. 18–19.
30. See, for example, Mancur Olson, *The Logic of Collective Action: Public Goods and the Theory of Groups*, Cambridge, MA, Harvard University Press, 1965, and *The Rise and Decline of Nations: Economic Growth, Stagflation and Social Rigidities*, New Haven, CT, Yale University Press, 1982.
31. This is the main defect of all analyses of state intervention based on the concept of market failure. It is unclear why the state should be able to provide institutional solutions (and predict their outcome) that the market is unable to produce. If we do not wish to assume that the state has a different degree of knowledge from that of private agents, then other theories must be found (Coase, and so on).
32. Douglass C. North, 'Towards a theory of institutional change', *Quarterly Review of Economics and Business*, Winter 1991.
33. See Douglass C. North, *Institutions, Institutional Change and Economic Performance*, Cambridge, Cambridge University Press, 1990.
34. See Douglass C. North and Robert P. Thomas, *The Rise of the Western World: A New Economic History*, Cambridge, Cambridge University Press, 1973.
35. Hicks, *A Theory of Economic History*, op. cit., p. 73.
36. Carlo M. Cipolla, 'Currency depreciation in medieval Europe', *Economic History Review*, April 1963.
37. Avner Greif, 'The fundamental problem of exchange: a research agenda in historical institutional analysis', *European Review of Economic History*, December 2000, p. 266.
38. Raymond de Roover, *L'évolution de la lettre de change XIVᵉ–XVIIIᵉ siècle*, Paris, Colin, 1953.
39. Greif, Milgrom and Weingast, 'Coordination, commitment and enforcement: the case of the merchant guild', op. cit.
40. Francesco Galgano, *Lex mercatoria: storia del diritto commerciale*, Bologna, Il Mulino, 1993.
41. The essential reference for exchange fairs is Fernand Braudel, *Civilisation matérielle, économie et capitalisme XVᵉ–XVIIIᵉ siècles*, Paris, Colin, 1979. See also the monograph by Marie-Thérèse Boyer-Xambeu, Ghislain Deleplace and Lucien Gillard, *Monnaie privée et pouvoir des princes*, Paris, Edition du Cnrs, 1986. The US clearing houses will be discussed in greater detail in Chapter 4.
42. See Greig, Milgrom and Weingast, 'Coordination, commitment and enforcement', op. cit.
43. On this question see Roland Vaubel, 'The government's money monopoly: externalities or natural monopoly?', *Kyklos*, 1, 1984.
44. Klein, 'The competitive supply of money', op. cit; Milton Friedman and Anna Schwartz, 'Has government any role in money?', *Journal of Political Economy*, January 1986.
45. Broz, *The International Origins of the Federal Reserve System*, op. cit., p. 211.
46. North, *Institutions, Institutional Change and Economic Performance*, op. cit., and Williamson, 'The new institutional economics', op. cit., refer to the same concept when they talk of the 'institutional environment'. I prefer the expression 'institutional capital' to render the idea of a stock that may increase or diminish with time according to how it is used by a given community. Institutions are an economic concept, not a fact of 'nature'.
47. See Poggi, *The Development of the Modern State*, op. cit.
48. See North, 'Towards a theory of institutional change', op. cit., p. 6.
49. François Simiand, 'La monnaie réalité sociale', *Annales sociologiques*, série D, 1, Sociologie économique, 1934.

50. Milton Friedman takes up this observation and studies it in greater depth in an essay titled 'The resource costs of irredeemable paper money', *Journal of Political Economy*, June 1986.

CHAPTER 2

1. Galgano, *Lex mercatoria*, op. cit., Chapter 2.
2. This section summarizes the exhaustive treatment of Charles M. Kahn and William Roberds, 'The economics of payment finality', *Federal Reserve Bank of Atlanta Economic Review*, 2, 2002.
3. Ibid., p. 5.
4. See R.S. Lopez and J. Le Goff (eds), *L'alba della banca: le origine del sistema bancario tra Medioevo ed Età moderna*, Bari, Dedalo, 1982.
5. See Meir Kohn, 'Early deposit banking', Dartmouth College, Working Paper 99-03, February 1999 (draft chapter of *Finance, Business and Government before the Industrial Revolution*, at www.dartmouth.edu/~mkohn).
6. See Reinhold Mueller, *The Venetian Money Market: Banks, Panic and the Public Debt 1200–1500*, Baltimore, MD, Johns Hopkins University Press, 1997, pp. 20–21, cited by Kohn, 'Early deposit banking', p. 4.
7. See Giorgio Fodor, 'Ascesa e declino della banca d'emissione: il caso della Banca d'Inghilterra 1694–1913', in *Ricerche per la Storia della Banca d'Italia*, Contributi series, Vol. 6, Rome and Bari, Laterza, 1995, p. 365.
8. R. C. Mueller, *The Venetian Money Market*, Ch. 8, cited by Meir Kohn, 'Bills of exchange and the money market to 1600', Dartmouth College, Working Paper 99-04, February 1999 (draft chapter of *Finance, Business and Government before the Industrial Revolution*, at www.dartmouth.edu/~mkohn, p. 12).
9. Kohn, 'Bills of exchange and the money market to 1600', p. 21.
10. Kohn, 'Early deposit banking', p. 8.
11. Marie-Thérèse Boyer-Xambeu, Ghislain Deleplace and Lu Gillard, *Monnaie privée et pouvoir des princes*, Ch. 5.
12. Bernardo Davanzati, 'Notizia dej cambi' (1581), in *Scrittori classici italiani di economia politica*, Collezione Custodi, Parte antica, tome II, Milan, 1804 (anastatic reprint, Rome, Edizioni Bizzari, 1955), pp. 61–62.
13. Fodor, *Ascesa e declino della banca d'emissione*, p. 367.
14. Ferdinando Galiani, *Della moneta* (1750), in *Illuministi italiani*, Tome VI, *Opere di Ferdinando Galiani*, Milan and Naples, Ricciardi, 1975, p. 264.
15. Montesquieu, *De l'esprit des lois* (1748), Book 20, Ch. 10, in *Oeuvres Complètes*, Tome II, Paris, la Pléiade, 1958, p. 592. (Translated by Thomas Nugent, revised by J.V. Prichard. Based on a public domain edition published in 1914 by G. Bell & Sons, London. Rendered into HTML and text by Jon Roland of the Constitution Society, http://www.constitution.org/cm/sol.txt.)
16. Marie-Thérèse Boyer-Xambeu, Ghislain Deleplace and Lu Gillard, *Monnaie privée et pouvoir des princes*, p. 356.

CHAPTER 3

1. Vera C. Smith, *The Rationale of Central Banking*, Westminster, King & Son, 1936.
2. This is a line of thought that can be traced back to von Hayek's work, *Denationalization of Money*, op. cit., and which, in Brennan and Buchanan, *Monopoly in Money and Inflation*, op. cit., found its most extreme expression. Those who embraced this view were usually in favour of reform inspired by the principle of free banking, that is, of free

note issue. However, free banking takes on different connotations according to different authors. For a collection of more in-depth articles on this topic, see Dowd, *The State and the Monetary System*, op. cit.

3. Marc Bloch, *Esquisse d'une histoire monétaire de l'Europe*, Paris, Colin, 1954, p. 85.
4. Cited in Richard H. Timberlake, *Monetary Policy in the United States: An Intellectual and Institutional History*, Chicago, IL, University of Chicago Press, 1993, p. 6. (Translator's note: original citation in *Annals of Congress*, 1st Cong., 2nd Sess., 14 December 1790, 'Report on a National Bank', p. 2101.)
5. North and Weingast, *Constitutions and Commitment*, op. cit.
6. E. Victor Morgan, *The Theory and Practice of Central Banking, 1797–1913* (1943), London, Frank Cass & Co., 1965, p. 228.
7. Thomas Tooke, *A History of Prices*, vol. 4 (1839–1847), London, Longman, Brown, Green & Longmans, 1848, pp. 354, 401–402.
8. See Charles S. Parker (ed.), *Sir Robert Peel from his Private Papers*, London, Murray, 1899, Vol. 3, p. 140.
9. See, among others, Fodor, *Ascesa e declino della banca d'emissione*, op. cit., p. 371.
10. De Roover, *L'évolution de la lettre de change XIVᵉ–XVIIIᵉ Siècle*, op. cit., p. 142.
11. See O'Brien, *Central Government and the Economy, 1688–1815*, op. cit., p. 231.
12. See Fodor, *Ascesa e declino della banca d'emissione*, op. cit., p. 374.
13. See Galgano, *Lex mercatoria*, op. cit., p. 61.
14. O'Brien, *Central Government and the Economy, 1688–1815*, op. cit., pp. 231–232.
15. This passage is cited by Fodor, *Ascesa e declino della banca d'emissione*, op. cit., p. 378. (Original citation is J.M. Holden, *The History of Negotiable Instruments in English Law*, London, 1955, p. 34.)
16. There was in fact little similarity between the traditional letter of exchange which, as seen in Chapter 2, was an instrument developed for international trade usually involving two different currencies and four different contractors, and the promissory note. However, in English practice, a simplified letter of exchange was used and had been recognized by the courts. This 'inland bill of exchange' did not presume any exchange of money, nor the participation of other contractors besides the two directly involved (the promisor and the promisee). The judgment in question, sanctioning the non-applicability of the law relating to inland bills of exchange to the promissory note, was actually much more debatable.
17. C.H.S. Fifoot, *The Development of the Law of Negotiable Instruments and of the Law of Trusts, Journal of the Institute of Bankers*, 59, December 1938, p. 447.
18. See Carlo M. Cipolla, *Before the Industrial Revolution: European Society and Economy 1000–1700*, London, Methuen & Co., 1976, pp. 187–189.
19. Smith, *The Rationale of Central Banking*, op. cit., pp. 155–156.
20. See Lawrence H. White, *Free Banking in Britain: Theory, Experience, Debate, 1800–1845*, Cambridge, Cambridge University Press, 1984.
21. See Cameron (with Crisp, Patrick and Tilly), *Banking in the Early Stages of Industrialization*, op. cit., pp. 68–69.
22. The instability of country banks may have been exacerbated by the English law prohibiting the participation of more than six people in holding stock. However, it is not possible to single out the influence of this factor.
23. Alfred W. Flux, 'The Swedish banking system', Senate document No. 576, in National Monetary Commission, *Banking in Sweden and Switzerland*, Vol. 17, Washington, DC, Government Printing Office, 1911, p. 30 (cited by Goodhart, *The Evolution of Central Banks*, op. cit., p. 123).
24. Cited in Timberlake, *Monetary Policy in the United States*, op. cit., p. 5. (Translator's note: original citation in *Annals of Congress*, 1st. Cong., 2nd Sess., 14 December 1790, 'Report on a national bank', pp. 2082–2111).
25. Ibid., p. 6. (Translator's note: original citation in *Annals of Congress* as in note 24, p. 2101).
26. David Ricardo, *A Plan for the Establishment of a National Bank* (1824), in Piero Sraffa

(ed.), *The Works and Correspondence of David Ricardo*, Vol. 4, Cambridge, Cambridge University Press, 1951.

27. James Mill, *Elements of Political Economy*, London, Baldwin, Cradock & Joy, 1821, p. 113.
28. Cameron (with Crisp, Patrick and Tilly), *Banking in the Early Stages of Industrialization*, op. cit., and Cameron (ed.), *Banking and Economic Development*, op. cit.
29. It is not necessary to restate here the story of the Bank of England's beginnings. It is sufficient to note that the Bank was incorporated in 1694, with a capital of £1.2 million and 1217 subscribers, including the King and Queen. The immediate aim of the Bank was to rationalize the funding of the Crown's finances under the control of Parliament. The capital paid in was immediately lent to the government and, in exchange, the Bank was authorized to issue banknotes for the same amount. A crucial step in the life of the Bank came in 1707 when, as a result of an increase in capital, the Bank obtained a statute as a 'joint-stock bank' in the terminology of the time. This provision established that no other bank of this kind could be established in England; from then on, all other banks would have to be established in the form of a partnership of not more than six members. However, this privilege did not extend throughout all Crown territories. In Scotland, in particular, the Bank of England had soon to face competition from the Bank of Scotland (founded in 1695), the Royal Bank of Scotland (1727) and the British Linen Bank (1747). In 1751, on the occasion of another renewal of the charter, the Bank was also granted the management of the public debt. It is interesting to note that throughout the 1700s, the banknotes issued by the Bank of England were of very high denominations. Until 1759, no note had a face value of less than £20, at that time a sum equal to five months' salary of a Bank of England employee. It was only in 1793 that, despite the perplexity of its own shareholders, the Bank decided to issue £5 notes, a sum still large at the time, to address a crisis of the regional banks. The basic text on the history of the Bank of England is by John Clapham, *The Bank of England: A History*, 2 vols, Cambridge, Cambridge University Press, 1944.
30. Alfred Marshall, *Money, Credit and Commerce*, London, Macmillan, 1923, p. 303.
31. See Norbert Olszak, *Histoire des banques centrales*, Paris, Puf, 1998, p. 25.
32. See Claudio Rotelli, *Le origini della controversia monetaria (1797–1844)*, Bologna, Il Mulino, 1982, p. 11.
33. See Olszak, *Histoire des banques centrales*, op. cit., p. 50.
34. Adam Smith, *An Inquiry into the Nature and Causes of the Wealth of Nations*, London, Strahan & Cadell, 1776, Vol. 1, p. 387.
35. Ibid., p. 399.
36. Henry Thornton, *An Enquiry into the Nature and Effects of the Paper Credit of Great Britain*, London, Hatchard, 1802.
37. The contribution of the supporters of free banking was ignored for many years in history books. Lawrence White's *Free Banking in Britain*, op. cit., was responsible for giving the necessary weight to this aspect of the monetary controversy concerning the banknote.
38. *Report of the Select Committee on the High Price of Gold Bullion*, London, 1810, p. 17, also cited in W.G. Sumner, *A History of American Currency*, New York, August M. Kelly Publishers, 1968, p. 364.
39. This passage is cited by White, *Free Banking in Britain*, op. cit., p. 67.
40. Morgan, *The Theory and Practice of Central Banking, 1797–1913*, op. cit., p. 132.
41. For Palmer's rules, see Rotelli, *Le origini della controversia monetaria (1797–1844)*, op. cit., Ch. 4.
42. J. Horsley Palmer, *The Causes and Consequences of the Pressure upon the Money-Market*, London, Pelham Richardson, 1837, p. 42.
43. See Olszak, *Histoire des banques centrales*, op. cit., p. 50.
44. On this subject, see White, *Free Banking in Britain*, op. cit., p. 77.
45. The 1826 ban on country banks' setting up in the London area was also confirmed.
46. See Smith, *The Rationale of Central Banking*, op. cit., p. 18.

47. Bray Hammond, *Banks and Politics in America from the Revolution to the Civil War*, Princeton, NJ, Princeton University Press, 1957.

48. It is interesting to note that Washington himself had sufficient doubts about the initiative to ask Madison to prepare the text for a veto in opposition to Congress's decision. According to Hammond's reconstruction, if things went differently it was because of Hamilton's fine arguments when he maintained that: 'every power vested in a government is in its nature sovereign and includes, by force of the term, a right to employ all the means requisite and fairly applicable to the attachment of the ends of such power and which are not precluded by restrictions and exceptions specified in the constitution, or not immoral, or not contrary to the essential ends of political society'. These words must have been music to the ears of a statesman of Washington's calibre. See ibid., p. 118.

49. Ibid., p. 199.

50. Ibid., p. 301.

51. See Timberlake, *Monetary Policy in the United States*, op. cit., pp. 32–33.

52. Hammond, *Banks and Politics in America from the Revolution to the Civil War*, op. cit., pp. 283–284.

53. Ibid., p. 374.

54. Cited in Timberlake, *Monetary Policy in the United States*, op. cit., p. 40.

55. Ibid., p. 39.

56. Ibid., p. 41.

57. Ibid.

58. Ibid., p. 83.

59. The story of how the legal tender status of the greenback was reconciled with the Constitution is one of many controversial episodes in the monetary history of the United States. In 1867 the question was put before the Supreme Court whose Chief Justice at the time was Salmon P. Chase who, as Treasury Secretary during the war, had introduced and affixed portrait and signature. To everyone's surprise, the Court ruled by four votes to three that the legal tender status was unconstitutional. However, the question was then put before the Court again a short time later. In the meantime, another two justices had been appointed, bringing the total to nine, as required by law. This time the constitutionality of legal tender status was defended on the grounds of exceptional needs arising from the Civil War. With a ruling in 1884, the Court recognized the power of Congress to confer legal tender status on the currency even independently of the presence of exceptional circumstances. For further details, see Arthur Nussbaum, *A History of the Dollar*, New York, Columbia University Press, 1957, pp. 118–123.

60. Banknotes were not supposed to exceed 90 per cent of the face value or the market value of the securities held, whichever was the lower.

61. See Nussbaum, *A History of the Dollar*, op. cit., p. 111.

62. A valuable source of information is the volume by Cecil H. Kisch and William W.A. Elkin, *Central Banks: A Study of the Constitutions of Banks of Issue, with an Analysis of Representative Charters*, London, Macmillan, 1928. Very broad and well-researched contributions on the subject have been made in recent years by Charles Goodhart, alone or together with other scholars. See Goodhart, *The Evolution of Central Banks*, op. cit., and Charles Goodhart, Forrest Capie and Norbert Schnadt, *The Development of Central Banking*, in Forrest Capie, Charles Goodhart, Stanley Fischer and Norbert Schnadt, *The Future of Central Banking*, Cambridge, Cambridge University Press, 1995.

63. Japan's experience ran curiously parallel to that of the United States. Immediately after the restoration of the empire, Japan adopted the American version of the English model, literally copying the National Banking System. However, the results were so disappointing that after a few years the Japanese authorities changed tack completely, opting instead for a single note issuer. Thus in 1882 the Bank of Japan was established, following the guidelines of the Belgian legislation. See Goodhart, *The Evolution of Central Banks*, op. cit., Appendix.

64. See Michiel H. de Kock, *Central Banking*, London, Crosby, Lockwood, Staples, 1974, Ch. 1.

65. In his work for the National Monetary Commission of the US Congress looking into the experiences of other countries, Tito Canovai, Deputy Director General of the Bank of Italy, underlined that the Italian experience was a case study on how not to organize the issue of convertible banknotes, maintaining that many of Italy's difficulties in managing the money supply could have been avoided had it been possible to have a single note-issuing bank. Canovai's report was very influential within the Commission and Italy's experience was expressly mentioned by its Chairman, Nelson W. Aldrich, in his final report.

66. See Paolo Pecorari, *La fabbrica dei soldi: istituti di emissione e questione bancaria in Italia, 1861–1913*, Bologna, Pàtron Editore, 1994; Giuseppe Di Nardi, *Le banche di emissione in Italia nel secolo XIX*, Turin, Utet, 1953.

67. See Gino Luzzatto, *L'Economia italiana dal 1861 al 1894*, Turin, Einaudi, 1968.

68. For further details on the events which Gino Luzzatto called 'the darkest years of the new Kingdom's economy', see the previously cited book by Luzzatto, and also Guglielmo Negri (ed.), *Giolitti e la nascita della Banca d'Italia*, Rome and Bari, Laterza, 1989.

69. The 1893 reform did not mark an abandonment of the English model. The maximum limit of notes in circulation was fixed for a four-year period at 1097 million lire, of which 800 million lire were for the Bank of Italy, 242 million lire for the Banco di Napoli, and 55 million lire for the Banco di Sicilia. Provisions were also set for a mechanism to gradually reduce the notes in circulation in equal proportion at the end of the four-year period. Lastly, it was established that within a year the reserves had to be brought up to 40 per cent of notes outstanding, with at least three-quarters of specie in gold. See Pecorari, *La fabbrica dei soldi*, op, cit., pp. 116–117.

70. Ibid., pp. 38–39.

71. See Sergio Cardarelli, *La questione bancaria in Italia, 1860–1892*, in *Ricerche per la storia della Banca d'Italia*, Serie Contributi, Vol. 1, Rome and Bari, Laterza, 1990.

72. Ibid., pp. 157–176.

73. The inspectors' report at the 16 January 1893 sitting of Banca Romana's Council of Regency showed that the fraud by the bank was concentrated in the six years from 1887 through 1892, and that the cash shortfall, about 9 million lire in 1889, had risen to 26 million at the end of 1892. See Luzzatto, *L'economia italiana dal 1861 al 1894*, op. cit., p. 203.

74. Valeria Sannucci, 'Molteplicità delle banche di emissione: ragioni economiche ed effetti sull'efficacia del controllo monetario (1860–1890)', in *Ricerche per la storia della Banca d'Italia*, Serie contributi, Vol. 1, Rome and Bari, Laterza, 1990, p. 217. The text was translated from Italian for publication in this book.

75. Tito Canovai, *Le banche di emissione in Italia*, Rome, Casa Editrice Italiana, 1912, p. 7.

CHAPTER 4

1. Cameron (with Crisp, Patrick and Tilly), *Banking in the Early Stages of Industrialization*, op.cit., and Cameron (ed.), *Banking and Economic Development*, op. cit.

2. See John A. James, *Money and Capital in Postbellum America*, Princeton, NJ, Princeton University Press, 1978, p. 25, and the discussion in Jeffrey A. Miron, 'The founding of the Fed and the destabilization of the post-1914 US economy', in Marcello de Cecco and Alberto Giovannini (eds), *A European Central Bank? Perspectives on Monetary Unification After Ten Years of the EMS*, Cambridge, Cambridge University Press, 1989, p. 303.

3. See Cameron, *Banking and Economic Development*, op cit., and Charles P. Kindleberger, *A Financial History of Western Europe*, London, Allen & Unwin, 1984.

4. Goodhart, Capie and Schnadt, *The Development of Central Banking*, op. cit., p. 65.
5. See Xaviet Freixas, Bruno M. Parigi and Jean-Charles Rochet, 'Systemic risk, interbank relations, and liquidity provision by the central bank', *Journal of Money, Credit and Banking*, August 2000 (Part 2).
6. Historically, this is the most likely mechanism, although it is also the most irksome to formalize. The best-known contribution on the subject of banking panics, by Diamond and Dybvig, completely disregards information problems (Douglas W. Diamond and Phillip H. Dybvig, 'Bank runs, deposit insurance and liquidity', *Journal of Political Economy*, June 1983). This shortcoming has been remedied by Yehning Chen, 'Banking panics: the role of the first-come, first-served rule and informational externalities', *Journal of Political Economy*, October 1999. It is interesting to note that this mechanism was already implicit in Walter Bagehot's theory, as the following passage indicates: 'Supposing that, owing to defects in its government, one even of the London joint stock greater banks failed, there would be an instant suspicion of the whole system. One *terra incognita* being seen to be faulty, all other *terrae incognitae* would be suspected', Walter Bagehot, *Lombard Street: A Description of the Money Market*, London, King & Co., 1873, p. 264.
7. See Franklin Allen and Douglas Gale, 'Optimal currency crises', *Carnegie-Rochester Series on Public Policy*, December 2000.
8. Bagehot, *Lombard Street*, op. cit., p. 2.
9. See Morgan, *The Theory and Practice of Central Banking, 1797–1913*, op. cit., p. 150.
10. An influential banker declared, before the committee set up the following year to shed light on the episode, that: 'The effect [of the promise of a bill of indemnity] was immediate. Those who had sent notice for their money in the morning now sent us word that they did not want it – they had only ordered payment by way of precaution . . . From that day we had a market of comparative ease.' Cited in ibid., p. 151.
11. Cited in ibid., p. 180.
12. In Bagehot, *Lombard Street*, op. cit., p. 169.
13. Smith, *The Rationale of Central Banking*, op. cit., p. 127.
14. See Morgan, *The Theory and Practice of Central Banking, 1797–1913*, op. cit., p. 192.
15. As Richard Sayers observed: 'When the Bank's responsibility, it being the central bank, clearly called for such action, it did bear the expense, but it did so grudgingly'. Richard S. Sayers, *Central Banking after Bagehot*, Oxford, Clarendon Press, 1957.
16. Sayers attributes the phenomenon to three factors. First off, up to the beginning of the 1890s, the years in which the English banking system began to consolidate, provincial banks continued to look at the Bank as a natural point of reference for the investment of excess liquidity. Second, the global output of gold was expanding and London financial market had a comparative advantage as a market for the placement of reserves. Finally, foreign lending activities were also developing and were extremely sensitive to bank rate variations. Ibid., p. 13.
17. This probably explains why Bagehot is often said to have advised that the central bank carry out its own transactions in situations of tension at penalty rates with respect to the market rate. In actual fact, as we have seen, this opinion is totally unfounded, both because Bagehot never talked about penalty rates (on the contrary, the practice adopted by the Bank in 1878 must have surprised him quite a lot), and because the new policy referred to normal market conditions, not to situations of crisis. On the argument, see Charles Goodhart, 'Myths About the Lender of Last Resort', in *International Finance*, November 1999.
18. See Morgan, *The Theory and Practice of Central Banking, 1797–1913*, op. cit., p. 199.
19. On the Baring crisis, see Clapham, *The Bank of England*, Vol. 11, pp. 325–339, and Morgan, *The Theory and Practice of Central Banking, 1797–1913*, pp. 203–206.
20. See John H. Clapham, *An Economic History of Modern Britain*, Cambridge, Cambridge University Press, 1938, Vol. 3, pp. 278–279. See also Morgan, *The Theory and Practice of Central Banking, 1797–1913*, pp. 210–214.
21. It was an established practice at the Bank not to pay interest on deposits. The practice was to some extent bypassed by accepting funds as deposits that were then reinvested

at market rates. The Bank gained a rather handsome commission, while the owner of the deposit received the interest matured. This technique is typically employed by asset management companies.

22. Morgan, *The Theory and Practice of Central Banking, 1797–1913*, pp. 226–227.
23. See Fred Hirsch, 'The Bagehot problem', *Manchester School of Economic and Social Studies*, September 1977.
24. Smith, *The Rationale of Central Banking*, p. 131.
25. For a systematic analysis of the defects of the US system and its propensity for crisis, see O.M.W. Sprague, *History of Crises under the National Banking System*, Washington, DC, National Monetary Commission, Government Printing Office, 1910. For an exhaustive treatment of the developments recounted here, the best source remains Milton Friedman and Anna J. Schwartz, *A Monetary History of the United States (1867–1960)*, Princeton, NJ, Princeton University Press, 1963.
26. See Gary Gorton, 'Clearinghouses and the origin of central banking in the United States', *Journal of Economic History*, June 1985.
27. A more ambitious reform proposal known as the 'Baltimore Plan' was quickly shelved. See Smith, *The Rationale of Central Banking*, p. 134.
28. These were newly formed investment companies which, thanks to a lower reserve requirement and their natural propensity for financial innovation, quickly gained popularity. They were viewed with suspicion by the banking establishment, which saw them as dangerous competitors. In 1903 the New York clearing house decided that they could not be members unless they increased their own reserve deposits. Trust companies took this as a declaration of war, and in retaliation many severed their financial links with the clearing banks. In 1907 the Knickerbocker Trust, one of the trusts still connected with the banking system, applied to the clearing house for a loan to deal with the emerging financial tensions. The loan was denied, triggering the trust's failure. The crisis quickly spread to other trust companies and then to the banks. As the situation degenerated, the New York clearing house announced that it would support any financial institution so requesting, regardless of its nature. But by then it was too late. On this episode, see Eugene W. White, *The Regulation and Reform of the American Banking System, 1900–1929*, Princeton, NJ, Princeton University Press, 1983.
29. The Comptroller of the Currency exerted all his influence and authority for the institution of a European-type central bank. In his 1907 report he maintained that: 'the inevitable and logical conclusion [of the clearing house concept] is that we should have a national central bank of issue and reserve'. A congressman put it in more concrete terms, stating before Congress that: 'Every fair-minded man would prefer control over currency to be vested in seven men selected from different parts of the country rather than leaving it to the five managers of New York clearing house'. Quotations in Timberlake, *Monetary Policy in the United States*, pp. 207 and 210.
30. Smith, *The Rationale of Central Banking*, p. 145.
31. Interestingly, as we saw in Chapter 3, throughout the discussion that led to the institution of the Federal Reserve, there was studied avoidance of the expression 'central bank' – an echo of the Bank War against the Second Bank of the United States 80 years earlier.
32. Shafroth's idea was that in case of need every commercial bank director should be able to get to the nearest Federal Reserve Bank by night train, arrange for emergency lending, and wire the outcome back to his bank's staff before opening time. See Olszak, *Histoire des banques centrales*, p. 78.
33. On the role of the banking lobby in the negotiations, see James Livingston, *Money, Class and Corporate Capitalism, 1890–1913*, Ithaca, NY, Cornell University Press, 1986. For an interpretation turning on international interests, see Broz, *International Origins of the Federal Reserve System*.
34. Kisch and Elkin, *Central Banks*, pp. 100–103.
35. The Act authorized the Fed to conduct open-market operations directly with private

parties. The original wording did not distinguish between two-signature and three-signature bills, which was standard practice in Europe. The banking lobby moved to introduce the distinction, for fear that the Fed might violate its statutory obligation not to compete with commercial banks. The final version of the text banned the Federal Reserve from trading in two-signature commercial paper. Later the Federal Reserve Board interpreted this rule restrictively, ordering that only Treasury securities and bankers' acceptances would be eligible for open-market operations. See Henry P.B. Willis, *Theory and Practice of Central Banking: With Special Reference to the American Experience, 1913–1935*, New York, Harper, 1936, p. 81.

36. The Act required banks to pay in reserves equal to 7 or 13 per cent of their sight deposits, depending on the bank's location, and 3 per cent of their time deposits. Kisch and Elkin, *Central Banks*, p. 103.

37. The Act required the Fed to conduct inspections of the member banks at least twice a year on behalf of the government. Moreover, the Board was given discretionary powers of inspection, while the 12 Reserve Banks could conduct special inspections of member banks under their jurisdiction.

38. Cited in François Crouzet, *La grande inflation. La monnaie en France de Louis XVI à Napoléon*, Paris, Fayard, 1993, p. 544.

39. A law of 1803 had granted the Bank the monopoly for the issue of notes of at least 500 francs in Paris, while outside the capital other banks of issue could be set up with a government authorization and the privilege of issuing notes of at least 250 francs. For an account on note issuing in France, see Olszak, *Histoire des banques centrales*, pp. 52–63.

40. See Marcello de Cecco, *Money and Empire: The International Gold Standard, 1890–1914*, Oxford, Blackwell, 1974, pp. 90–91.

41. See Goodhart, Capie and Schnadt, *The Development of Central Banking*, pp. 70 and 154–159.

42. Antonio Confalonieri, *Banca e industria in Italia (1894–1906)*, Vol. 2: *Il sistema bancario tra due crisi*, Bologna, Il Mulino, 1980, p. 87.

43. See Franco Bonelli (ed.), *La Banca d'Italia dal 1894 al 1913: momenti della formazione di una banca centrale*, Rome and Bari, Laterza, 1991.

44. On the conflicts between government and shareholders in the early years of the Bank of Italy, see Negri, *Giolitti e la nascita della Banca d'Italia*, pp. 71–80.

45. See Confalonieri, *Banca e industria in Italia (1894–1906)*, Vol. 2, p. 140. On the competition between the Bank of Italy and ordinary banks, see Bonelli (ed.), *La Banca d'Italia dal 1894 al 1913*, p. 20.

46. The passage from Stringher's letter was translated from Italian for publication in this book. The letter, originally written in French and translated into Italian by Franco Bonelli for publication in Bonelli (ed.), *La Banca d'Italia dal 1894 al 1913*, p. 60, was the summary of a text written in cooperation with Luigi Luzzatti and Cesare Vivante.

47. On the various consortia devised by Stringher, see Pecorari, *La fabbrica dei soldi*, pp. 164–178.

48. Bonelli (ed.), *La Banca d'Italia dal 1894 al 1913*, p. 28.

49. The only aspect of the US model that remained controversial concerned banking supervision. In the United States as well, supervisory functions remained divided among various bodies; the Fed had a subsidiary role in this field at least until the 1930s (see White, *The Regulation and Reform of the American Banking System, 1900–1929*, Ch. 3). In Europe, where there was no experience comparable to that of the clearing houses, the US model was deemed inadequate, because it was believed that too much power would be concentrated in what at the time was still a private sector institution. Consequently, the banking reforms of the 1930s entrusted banking supervision to the so-called Inspectorates, under the direct control of the Ministries for Finance and Trade (the solution adopted by the Scandinavian countries, Canada, Japan and Italy); or to independent banking commissions, made up of a maximum of six government-appointed members (as in Belgium, Germany and Switzerland, for example). On the development of banking supervision, see A.M. Allen, 'The principles of statutory

regulation', in A.M. Allen, S.R. Cope, L.J.H. Dark and H.J. Witheridge, *Commercial Banking Legislation and Control*, London, Macmillan, 1938.

50. Allen, 'The principles of statutory regulation', p. 7.
51. Ragnar Nurkse, *International Currency Experience: Lessons of the Inter-war Period*, Geneva, League of Nations, 1944, p. 163.
52. See de Kock, *Central Banking*, p. 89.
53. See A.M. Allen, 'The United States of America', in Allen, Cope, Dark and Witheridge, *Commercial Banking Legislation and Control*.
54. See Benjamin J. Klebaner, 'Banking reform in the New Deal era', *Banca Nazionale del Lavoro Quarterly Review*, September 1991, p. 322.
55. Jack Guttentag and Richard J. Herring, 'The lender-of-last-resort function in an international context', *Princeton Essays in International Finance*, 151, May 1983, p. 8.
56. Charles Goodhart and Dirk Schoenmaker, 'Should the functions of monetary policy and banking supervision be separated?' *Oxford Economic Papers*, October 1995, p. 544.
57. See Michael D. Bordo, 'The lender of last resort: alternative views and historical experience', *Federal Reserve Bank of Richmond Economic Review*, January–February 1990; and Timberlake, *Monetary Policy in the United States*.

CHAPTER 5

1. Irving Fisher, *The Purchasing Power of Money: Its Determination and Relation to Credit, Interest, and Crises*, New York, Macmillan, 1911, p. 131.
2. Kenneth W. Dam, *The Rules of the Game: Reform and Evolution in the International Monetary System*, Chicago, IL, University of Chicago Press, 1982, pp. 38–40.
3. See Barry Eichengreen and Nathan Sussman, 'The international monetary system in the (very) long run', IMF Working Paper, WP/00/43, March 2000.
4. Ibid., p. 19.
5. Marc Flandreau, *L'or du monde: la France et la stabilité du système monétaire international, 1848–1873*, Paris, L'Harmattan, 1995.
6. Ronald I. McKinnon, 'The rules of the game: international money in historical perspective', *Journal of Economic Literature*, March 1993, pp. 1–44.
7. Keynes, *A Tract on Monetary Reform*, op. cit., p. 46.
8. Excerpts of the Cunliffe Report are now in Barry Eichengreen and Marc Flandreau (eds), *The Gold Standard in Theory and History*, London, Routledge, 1997. The passage quoted is on p. 242.
9. Cunliffe had been Governor of the Bank of England up to a short time before the publication of the report bearing his name.
10. The passage, from a memorandum drafted by Strong in January 1925, is quoted in Donald E. Moggridge, *British Monetary Policy, 1924–31: The Norman Conquest of $4.86*, Cambridge, Cambridge University Press, 1972, pp. 59–60.
11. Keynes put forward his proposal in *A Tract on Monetary Reform*, Ch. 4. On the reaction to it, see Robert Skidelsky, *John Maynard Keynes, II: The Economist as Saviour, 1920–1937*, London, Macmillan, 1992, pp. 160–164.
12. Gustav Cassel, *The Restoration of Gold as a Universal Monetary Standard*, 1925, cited by Robert A. Mundell in his Nobel lecture, 'A reconsideration of the twentieth century', *American Economic Review*, June 2000, p. 329.
13. Gustav Cassel, *Postwar Monetary Stabilization*, New York, Columbia University Press, 1928, p. 44.
14. The Genoa conference meeting was the second major international gathering convened to deal with the international monetary system. The first conference had been held in Brussels in 1920 with the participation of 39 countries, including all the major powers except Russia. The Brussels meeting did not have ambitious goals and was,

more than anything, the occasion for resuming diplomatic relations in the economic field. Far more ambitious were those of the Genoa conference, carefully prepared by British diplomacy in the two preceding years. An important part of the Genoa accords concerned the role of the central banks, to be discussed in greater detail later in this chapter. On the monetary conferences of the 1920s, see Richard S. Sayers, *The Bank of England, 1891–1944*, Vol. 1, Cambridge, Cambridge University Press, 1976, pp. 153–163.

15. It is worth noting Resolution 12 adopted at Genoa, which requested the Bank of England to: 'call a meeting [of the central banks of the participating countries] as soon as possible to consider the proposals adopted by the Conference and to make recommendations to their respective Governments for the adoption of an International Monetary Convention'. Despite the Bank of England's activism in the following months, the idea was soon dropped. See Sayers, *The Bank of England, 1891–1944*, Vol. 1, pp. 160–163.

16. Nurkse, *International Currency Experience*, p. 29.

17. See James, *The End of Globalization*, pp. 48–49.

18. Quoted in Stephen V.O. Clarke, *Central Bank Cooperation, 1924–31*, New York, Federal Reserve Bank of New York, 1967, p. 40.

19. See Peter Temin, *Lessons from the Great Depression*, Cambridge, MA, MIT Press, 1989, p. 19.

20. See Eichengreen and Sussman, 'The international monetary system in the (very) long run', p. 25.

21. Idem.

22. Barry Eichengreen, 'The gold exchange standard and the Great Depression', NBER Working Paper, no. 2198, March 1987, p. 25.

23. See McKinnon, 'The rules of the game', p. 12; Rondo Cameron, *A Concise Economic History of the World from Paleolithic Times to the Present*, Oxford, Oxford University Press, 1989, pp. 355–357.

24. See Nicholas Crafts, 'Globalization and growth in the twentieth century', IMF Working Paper, WP/00/44, March 2000, p. 32.

25. Michael D. Bordo, Claudia Goldin and Eugene N. White, 'The defining moment hypothesis: the editors' introduction', in Bordo, Goldin and White (eds), *The Defining Moment. The Great Depression and the American Economy in the Twentieth Century*, Chicago, IL, University of Chicago Press, 1998, p. 10.

26. Eric J. Hobsbawm, *The Age of Extremes. The Short Twentieth Century, 1914–1991*, London, Michael Joseph, 1994, p. 112.

27. Temin, *Lessons from the Great Depression*, Ch. 3.

28. See Dam, *The Rules of the Game*, pp. 46–50.

29. Ibid., pp. 54–60.

30. Temin, *Lessons from the Great Depression*, p. 107. Indeed, Calomiris and Wheelock ask whether the Great Depression, instead of fostering an inflationary propensity on the part of the monetary authorities, did not actually create a bias in favour of deflation, as the monetary tightening of 1936 and 1937 would seem to indicate. However, their reply to this question is negative. See Charles W. Calomiris and David C. Wheelock, 'Was the Great Depression a watershed for American monetary policy?' in Bordon, Goldin and White (eds), *The Defining Moment*, pp. 36–37.

31. On the evolution of central banks' use of the different operating instruments of credit control (discounting, reserve ratios and open-market operations), see de Kock, *Central Banking*.

32. See Chapter 4, section 4.5.

33. Ricardo, *A Plan for the Establishment of a National Bank*, p. 282.

34. For a fuller discussion of the principle of autonomy, see Curzio Giannini, 'Confidence costs and the institutional genesis of central banks', Banca d'Italia, Temi di discussione del Servizio Studi, no. 226, May 1994. See also Pierluigi Ciocca, 'Il principio di autonomia nel "central banking"', *Quaderni di economia e finanza*, 1, 1992.

35. See Rolf Caesar, 'Central banks and governments: issues, tradition, lessons', *Financial History Review*, October 1995.

36. See Sayers, *The Bank of England, 1891–1944*, pp. 99–107.

37. The Overman Act authorized the President: 'for the national security and defense, for the successful prosecution of the war . . . to make such a redistribution of function among executive agencies as he may deem necessary, including any functions, duties and powers hitherto by law conferred upon any executive department, commission, bureau, agency, office or officer'. See Caesar, 'Central banks and governments', p. 130.

38. See Goodhart, Capie and Schnadt, *The Development of Central Banking*, pp. 52–53.

39. See League of Nations, *International Financial Conference*, Brussels, 1920, Vol. 1, p. 18.

40. Letter to John Pierpont Morgan, 19 November 1927, quoted by James, *The End of Globalization*, p. 36.

41. The ironic comment is by Sayers, *The Bank of England, 1891–1944*, p. 159.

42. 'We cannot afford, practically or politically, to embark upon a course which ignores the policy of the administration, which would possibly antagonize the administration and place us in the position where we would be quite helpless to resist the repeated efforts which have been made in Congress to effect important and possibly vital modifications in the underlying principles of the Federal Reserve System.' Letter from Strong to Norman, 18 February 1922. The passage is quoted by Clarke, *Central Bank Cooperation, 1924–31*, p. 30.

43. See Cosma O. Gelsomino, 'The Bank of Italy from its foundation to the 1950s: institutional aspects', in Carl-Ludwig Holtfrerich, Jaime Reis and Gianni Toniolo, *The Emergence of Modern Central Banking from 1918 to the Present*, Aldershot, Ashgate, 1999, pp. 170–172.

44. See Olszak, *Histoire des banques centrales*, p. 88.

45. James, *The End of Globalization*, p. 52.

46. See Goodhart, Capie and Schnadt, *The Development of Central Banking*, p. 54.

47. Quoted by Dam, *The Rules of the Game*, p. 53.

48. The Emergency Banking Act echoed the Overman Act, passed in 1918 as a wartime measure and subsequently repealed. See Richard Sylla, 'The autonomy of monetary authorities: the case of the US Federal Reserve System', in Toniolo (ed.), *Central Banks' Independence in Historical Perspective*, p. 30.

49. Gelsomino, 'The Bank of Italy from its foundation to the 1950s', pp. 172–174.

50. See Olszak, *Histoire des banques centrales*, pp. 93–96.

51. Ralph G. Hawtrey, *The Art of Central Banking*, London, Longmans, 1932, p. 268.

52. On central banks and the war, see Caesar, 'Central banks and governments', p. 134.

53. See Dam, *The Rules of the Game*, pp. 60–76.

54. The concept of conditionality would only develop later, as an application of the International Monetary Fund's obligation, laid down in its statute, to protect the resources lent out. The concept of macroeconomic surveillance was introduced with the reforms of the late 1970s. See Harold James, 'The historical development of the principle of surveillance', *IMF Staff Papers*, December 1995.

55. McKinnon, 'The rules of the game', p. 17.

56. The Fund's assent was required for changes greater than 10 per cent. A running argument between the British and American delegations about the proper penalties for unauthorized changes was settled with a linguistic compromise that was open to any and every interpretation. See Dam, *The Rules of the Game*, pp. 88–93.

57. Quoted by Joseph Gold, *Legal and Institutional Aspects of the International Monetary System. Selected Essays*, Jane B. Evensen and Jai Keun Oh (eds), Washington, DC, International Monetary Fund, p. 526. See also Dam, *The Rules of the Game*, p. 91.

58. See Dam, *The Rules of the Game*, p. 98.

59. Robert A. Mundell, 'Capital mobility and stabilization policy under fixed and flexible exchange rates', *Canadian Journal of Economics*, November 1963.

60. See de Kock, *Central Banking*, pp. 137–144.

61. See Goodhart, Capie and Schnadt, *The Development of Central Banking*, p. 24.

62. Radcliffe Committee, *Report on the Working of the Monetary System*, HMSO, London, 1959, section 767.
63. In reality, Canada was a forerunner in this field. When the Bank of Canada was established in 1934, one of its tasks was to: 'mitigate through its influence fluctuations in the general level of production, trade, prices and employment so far as may be possible within the scope of monetary action'. See de Kock, *Central Banking*, p. 138.
64. On central bank nationalizations, see de Kock, *Central Banking*, pp. 305ff., and Goodhart, Capie and Schnadt, *The Development of Central Banking*, pp. 22–27 and 54–59.
65. On the 1935 Banking Act, see Sylla, 'The autonomy of monetary authorities', pp. 21–24.
66. See Gelsomino, 'The Bank of Italy from its foundation to the 1950s', pp. 172–176.
67. See de Kock, *Central Banking*, pp. 177–179.
68. Some scholars see this French institutional constraint as an important factor in the tensions that arose between the leading central banks towards the end of the 1930s and brought the gold exchange standard to its knees.
69. See Calomiris and Wheelock, 'Was the Great Depression a watershed for American monetary policy?' pp. 34–35.
70. Cited in de Kock, *Central Banking*, p. 209.
71. Cited in ibid., p. 231.
72. In reality, a direct form of control on credit had been used widely during the Second World War, namely selective controls on credit whose purpose was to direct credit towards sectors of strategic importance for the national economy and defence. Although selective controls continued to be used by Italy and a number of other countries up to the 1970s, they cannot be considered monetary policy instruments in the strict sense.
73. See de Kock, *Central Banking*, pp. 241–249.
74. See Peter Gourevitch, *Politics in Hard Times: Comparative Responses to International Economic Crises*, Ithaca, NY, Cornell University Press, 1986, Ch. 4.2.
75. Changes of the parity were also quite limited among the developing countries. Between 1949 and 1971 there were 69 devaluations of the currencies of these countries, more than half of them managed by the International Monetary Fund (IMF) through its programmes. See Sebastian Edwards and Julio Santaella, 'Devaluation controversies in the developing countries: lessons from the Bretton Woods era', in Michael D. Bordo and Barry Eichengreen (eds), *A Retrospective on the Bretton Woods System*, Chicago, IL, University of Chicago Press, 1994.
76. See Michael Michaely, *The Responsiveness of Demand Policies to Balance of Payments: Postwar Patterns*, New York, Columbia University Press, 1971, especially Chapter 2.
77. See McKinnon, 'The rules of the game', pp. 20–22, Eichengreen and Sussman, 'The international monetary system in the (very) long run', pp. 29–30, and the essays in Bordo and Eichengreen (eds), *A Retrospective on the Bretton Woods System*.
78. The dilemma, which the Belgian economist Robert Triffin (1911–93) formulated in a series of influential articles that appeared in 1959 and were collected into a book the following year, consisted in the thesis that the expansion of America's payments deficit, necessary to fuel the growth of world liquidity, would threaten to undermine confidence in the convertibility of the dollar, given the growing disproportion between the dollar liabilities and gold reserves of the United States.
79. These are the factors on which Eichengreen and Sussman insist in their often-quoted survey of the evolution of the international monetary system.
80. In reality, precisely because the American payments imbalance served to satisfy a demand for reserves from the rest of the world, the idea that it was a genuine imbalance was debatable. In effect, during the years of the exchange rate regime's crisis there is no trace of a contraction in dollar-denominated liabilities, showing that the regime did not collapse owing to a crisis of confidence in the dollar, as Triffin had predicted. See Paul De Grauwe, *International Money: Postwar Trends and Theories*, Oxford, Oxford University Press, 1989, pp. 22–26.

81. According to Lindert's econometric analysis, the changes in the structure of the population are the main explanatory factors of the expansion of public spending between 1960 and 1980, in the same way as the enlargement of suffrage had been in the early decades of the century. See Peter H. Lindert, 'The rise of social spending, 1880–1930', *Explorations in Economic History*, January 1994, and, by the same author, 'What limits social spending?' *Explorations in Economic History*, January 1996.

82. McKinnon, 'The rules of the game', p. 26.

83. See Dam, *The Rules of the Game*, ch. 7–8.

84. Arthur Burns, *The Anguish of Central Banking*, the 1979 Per Jacobsson Lecture, Washington, DC, International Monetary Fund, 1979, p. 21; also in Pierluigi Ciocca (ed.), *Money and the Economy: Central Bankers' Views*, London, Macmillan, 1987, p. 162.

85. Banca d'Italia, *Abridged Version of the Report for the Year 1973*, Rome, 31 May 1974, p. 189.

86. Wormser was removed a few weeks after Valéry Giscard d'Estaing's election as President of France for having written an article sharply critical of the policy of the government in which Giscard had served as Finance Minister. On this and other episodes of strains between central banks and governments in the early 1970s, see John B. Goodman, *Monetary Sovereignty: The Politics of Central Banking in Western Europe*, Ithaca, NY: Cornell University Press, 1992.

87. What soon became the prevailing judgement on indexation is nicely summed up by Arthur Burns, who, as we have seen, headed the Federal Reserve in a crucial phase of the process: '[Indexation] is a counsel of despair . . . I doubt if there is any practical way of redesigning economic contracts to deal with this problem satisfactorily. In any event, if a nation with our tradition attempted to make it easy to live with inflation, rather than resist its corrosive influence, we would slowly but steadily lose the sense of discipline needed to pursue governmental policies with an eye to the permanent welfare of our people.' Arthur F. Burns, *Reflections of an Economic Policy Maker: Speeches and Congressional Statements, 1969–1978*, Washington, DC, American Enterprise Institute, 1978, p. 148.

88. Michael R. Smith, *Power, Norms, and Inflation: A Skeptical Treatment*, New York, Aldine de Gruyter, 1992, p. 249. In defence of the most authoritative proponents of the Phillips curve, it must be said that they never fell into this error. Paul Samuelson and Robert Solow, for example, in a 1960 review of its merits, stressed that the concept referred only to the short term whereas for the long term it must be considered unreliable, since expectations would adjust to the government's use of the instrument and structural unemployment would probably increase whenever an increase in cyclical unemployment was accepted. See Paul A. Samuelson and Robert M. Solow, 'Analytical aspects of anti-inflation policy', *American Economic Review*, May 1960. From the point of view of the history of economics, it is interesting to note that Hayek, in an early critique of Keynesianism, had predicted that the attempt to alter real wages by manipulating inflation would soon prove ineffective owing to the reaction of expectations: 'The working class would not be slow to learn that an engineered rise of prices is no less a reduction of wages than a deliberate cut of money wages, and that in consequence the belief that it is easier to reduce by the round-about method of deprecation the wages of all workers in a country than directly to reduce the money wages of those who are affected by a given change, will soon prove illusory.' Friedrich A. von Hayek, *Monetary Nationalism and International Stability*, London, Longmans, Green & Co., 1937, p. 53.

89. Council of Economic Advisers, 'Annual report', in *Economic Report of the President*, Washington, DC, United States Government Printing Office, 1974, p. 65.

90. Jacques Rueff, who long served as French President De Gaulle's economic adviser, quipped that anyone who dealt with monetary affairs in the 1950s and 1960s risked being considered mentally retarded.

91. Phillip Cagan remarks with some sarcasm that: 'the Commission expressed such

widely divergent views on the role or nonrole of gold that in the final Report it agreed on essentially nothing'. See Phillip Cagan, 'The report of the Gold Commission (1982)', *Carnegie-Rochester Conference Series on Public Policy*, Vol. 20, 1984, p. 247.

92. See Robert L. Greenfield and Leland B. Yaeger, 'A laissez-faire approach to monetary stability', *Journal of Money, Credit and Banking*, August 1983; Axel Leijonhufvud, 'Inflation and economic performance', in Barry N. Siegel (ed.), *Money in Crisis*, Cambridge, MA, Ballinger, 1984. For a survey of these proposals, reminiscent of the so-called 'phantom money' of the late Middle Ages, see Warren L. Coats, 'In search of a monetary anchor: A "new" monetary standard', IMF Working Paper, WP/89/82, October 1989. For a formal representation of these schemes, see Curzio Giannini, 'Determinazione del livello dei prezzi e politica "monetaria" in un'economia senza moneta', *Giornale degli Economisti e Annali di Economia*, September–October 1996.

93. The free-banking school produced a truly impressive number of essays in just a few years, a sign of the interest aroused by the degeneration of the fiat standard. For two contrasting surveys, see Goodhart, *The Evolution of Central Banks*, Ch. 2, and Glasner, *Free Banking and Monetary Reform*.

94. On Milton Friedman's proposals, which referred back to his famous article 'The lag in effect of monetary policy', *Journal of Political Economy*, October 1961, see 'Monetary policy for the 1980s', in John H. Moore (ed.), *To Promote Prosperity: US Domestic Policy in the Mid-1980s*, Stanford, CA, Hoover Institution Press, 1984. On the role of intermediate targets in the formulation of monetary policy, see Benjamin M. Friedman, 'Targets, instruments and indicators of monetary policy', *Journal of Monetary Economics*, October 1975.

95. See Finn E. Kydland and Edward C. Prescott, 'Rules rather than discretion: the inconsistency of optimal plans', *Journal of Political Economy*, June 1977; Robert J. Barro and David B. Gordon, 'Rules, discretion and reputation in a model of monetary policy', *Journal of Monetary Economics*, June 1983.

96. Kenneth Rogoff, 'The optimal degree of commitment to an intermediate monetary target', *Quarterly Journal of Economics*, November 1985.

97. On the subject, see Goodman, *Monetary Sovereignty*, pp. 58–102; David Marsh, *The Bundesbank: The Bank that Rules Europe*, London, Mandarin, 1992.

98. Kisch and Elkin, *Central Banks*, p. 17.

99. Quoted in Marsh, *The Bundesbank*, p. 57.

100. See Goodman, *Monetary Sovereignty*, pp. 61–62; also, Carl Ludwig Holtfrerich, 'Relations between monetary authorities and government institutions: the case of Germany from the 19th century to the present', in Toniolo (ed.), *Central Banks' Independence in Historical Perspective*.

101. The pioneering study in this field was Vittorio Grilli, Donato Masciandaro and Guido Tabellini, 'Political and monetary institutions and public financial policies in the industrial countries', *Economic Policy*, October 1991, pp. 341–392. For an ample survey, see Alex Cukierman, *Central Bank Strategy, Credibility, and Independence: Theory and Evidence*, Cambridge, MA, MIT Press, 1992.

102. Banca d'Italia, *Abridged Version of the Report for the Year 1980*, Rome, 31 May 1981, p. 181.

103. See Carlo Cottarelli and Curzio Giannini, 'Credibility without rules? Monetary frameworks in the post-Bretton Woods era', IMF Occasional Paper, 154, December 1997.

104. Banca d'Italia, *Abridged Version of the Report for the Year 1978*, Rome, 1979, p. 158.

105. Ronald J. McKinnon, *Money and Capital in Economic Development*, Washington, DC, Brookings Institution, 1973; Edward S. Shaw, *Financial Deepening in Economic Development*, London and New York, Oxford University Press, 1973.

106. See John Williamson and Molly Mahar, 'A survey of financial liberalization', Princeton Essays in International Finance, no. 211, November 1998.

107. See Carlo Cottarelli and Curzio Giannini, 'Credibility without rules?' pp. 17–20. A large literature has developed in the last ten years on inflation targeting. See, for example, Lars E.O. Svensson, 'Inflation targeting as a monetary policy rule', *Journal*

of *Monetary Economics*, June 1999, and Ben S. Bernanke, Thomas Laubach, Frederic S. Mishkin and Adam S. Posen, *Inflation Targeting, Lessons from the International Experience*, Princeton, NJ, Princeton University Press, 1999.

108.   Adam S. Posen, 'Why central bank independence does not cause low inflation: there is no institutional fix for politics', in Richard O'Brien (ed.), *Finance and the International Economy: 7*, The Amex Bank Review Prize Essays, Oxford, Oxford University Press, 1993.

109.   A. Cukierman, *Central Bank Strategy, Credibility, and Independence*, pp. 419–422.

110.   Willem H. Buiter and Clemens Grafe, 'Anchor, float or abandon ship: exchange rate regimes for the accession countries', *Banca Nazionale del Lavoro Quarterly Review*, June 2002.

111.   Guillermo A. Calvo and Carmen M. Reinhart, 'Fear of floating', *Quarterly Journal of Economics*', May 2002.

CHAPTER 6

1.   See Chapter 5, no. 40 (letter to John Pierpont Morgan).

2.   Hicks's comment on this is enlightening: 'What is liable to happen, if there is a failure of international credit, is that nations will turn in upon themselves, becoming more autarkic or more protectionist, impoverishing themselves and each other by refusing to trade with each other . . . The remedy, my old nineteenth-century experience would tell us, would be an International Central Bank, an international bank which would underpin the credit structure, but in order to underpin it must have some control over it. That was what Keynes, who understood this international aspect very clearly, wanted to get at Bretton Woods, but all he got was a currency board (for it is little more than a currency board, being so tied up with rules and regulations) – the IMF. That, we are finding – and Mill could have told us, one hundred and twenty years ago, that it is what we should find – is not enough. But how should the powers, which governments have been unwilling to entrust to their own central banks (once they have realized what is involved) be trusted to an International Bank? That is the dilemma, the old dilemma, to which we have now come back, on the international plane.' John Hicks, 'Monetary theory and history – an attempt at perspective', in *Critical Essays in Monetary Theory*, op. cit., p. 173.

3.   See also Maurice Obstfeld and Alan M. Taylor, 'The Great Depression as a watershed: international capital mobility over the long run', in Bordo, Goldin and White (eds), *The Defining Moment*.

4.   Dani Rodrik, 'Governance of economic globalization', in Joseph S. Nye and John D. Donahue (eds), *Governance in a Globalized World*, Washington, DC, Brookings Institution, 2000.

5.   Cipolla, *Moneta e civiltà mediterranea*, op. cit.

6.   Carlo M. Cipolla, *Il governo della moneta a Firenze e a Milano nei secoli XIV–XVI*, Bologna, Il Mulino, 1990.

7.   See Eric Helleiner, 'Denationalising money? Economic liberalism and the "national question" in currency affairs', in Emily Gilbert and Eric Helleiner (eds), *Nation-States and Money: The Past, Present and Future of National Currencies*, London, Routledge, 1999.

8.   Hayek, *Monetary Nationalism and International Stability*.

9.   See Cottarelli and Giannini, 'Credibility without rules? Monetary frameworks in the post-Bretton Woods era'.

10.   See Carmen M. Reinhart and Kenneth S. Rogoff, 'The modern history of exchange rate arrangements: a reinterpretation', NBER Working Paper, No. 8963, June 2002.

11.   See Robert P. Flood and Nancy P. Marion, 'Holding international reserves in an era of high capital mobility', IMF Working Paper, WP/02/62, April 2002.

12. See Peter B. Clark and Jacques J. Polak, 'International liquidity and the role of the SDR in the international monetary system', IMF Working Paper, WP/02/217, December 2002.
13. See Triffin, *Gold and the Dollar Crisis*.
14. See Helen Milner, 'International theories of cooperation among nations. Strengths and weaknesses: a review article', *World Politics*, April 1992.
15. This is the meaning, as we saw in Chapter 4, of the expression used by Charles Goodhart and Dirk Schoenmaker, 'He who pays the piper calls the tune' in 'Should the functions of monetary policy and bank supervision be separated?' p. 544.
16. See Dam, *The Rules of the Game*, p. 103.
17. American Bankers Association, 'The place of the United States in the postwar economy', Report by the Economic Policy Commission of the American Bankers Association, New York, September 1943, pp. 14–15.
18. See Eric Helleiner, *States and the Reemergence of Global Finance: From Bretton Woods to the 1990s*, Ithaca, NY, Cornell University Press, 1994, pp. 39–50.
19. Idem., p. 49.
20. See Harold James, *International Monetary Cooperation since Bretton Woods*, Washington, DC and Oxford, International Monetary Fund and Oxford University Press, 1996.
21. Ibid., p. 151.
22. The G-10 comprises ten countries (Belgium, Canada, France, Germany, Japan, Italy, the Netherlands, the UK, the US and Sweden) that in 1962 were already members of the International Monetary Fund, and Switzerland, which did not join the Fund until 1992.
23. See Margaret Garritsen de Vries, *The International Monetary Fund, 1972–1978: Cooperation on Trial*, Washington, DC, International Monetary Fund, 1985, Volume 1, p. 590.
24. See McKinnon, *The Rules of the Game*, in particular pp. 15–17.
25. See Triffin, *Gold and the Dollar Crisis*, pp. 87–93.
26. On the negotiations that led to the creation of the SDR and its technical characteristics, see Dam, *The Rules of the Game*, pp. 142–168, and James, *International Monetary Cooperation Since Bretton Woods*, pp. 165–174.
27. However, as observed in section 5.5 of Chapter 5, the devaluation of 1971 could not strictly speaking be considered a validation of Triffin's theses, given that the demand for dollar liabilities remained relatively stable in those years.
28. James Boughton, 'Historical perspectives on financial distress: a comment', in *Carnegie-Rochester Conference Series on Public Policy*, December 2000, p. 171.
29. See James Boughton, *Silent Revolution: The International Monetary Fund, 1979–1989*, Washington, DC, International Monetary Fund, 2001.
30. See also Carlo Cottarelli and Curzio Giannini, 'Bedfellows, hostages, or perfect strangers? Global capital markets and the catalytic effect of IMF crisis lending', IMF Working Paper, WP/02/193, November 2002.
31. For a broader overview, see Curzio Giannini, 'Pitfalls in international crisis lending', in Charles Goodhart and Gerhard Illing (eds), *Financial Crises, Contagion, and the Lender of Last Resort: A Reader*, Oxford, Oxford University Press, 2002. See also Curzio Giannini, 'Enemy of none but a common friend to all?' Princeton Essays in International Finance, No. 214, June 1999.
32. See Avinash K. Dixit, *The Making of Economic Policy: A Transaction Costs Politics Perspective*, Cambridge, MA, MIT Press, 1996.
33. See Omotunde E.G. Johnson, 'Policy reform as collective action', IMF Working Paper, WP/97/163, December 1997.
34. The argument could be expressed in stricter terms. In the sort of model proposed by Diamond and Dybvig (*Bank Runs, Deposit Insurance, and Liquidity*), the intervention of a lender of last resort is socially optimal only when accompanied by a uniform distribution of information. When the information is asymmetric, a policy suspending convertibility (or debt servicing) is, generally speaking, socially superior. See

Kenneth Rogoff, 'International institutions for reducing financial instability', *Journal of Economic Perspectives*, Autumn 1999.

35. Group of Ten, 'The resolution of sovereign liquidity crises: a report to the ministers and governors', May 1996 (also available on the website of the BIS, www.bis.org).

36. Since 1986 the G-7 comprised the United States, Japan, France, Germany and the UK (whose ministers of finance began to meet as the G-5 in the early 1970s), Italy and Canada (on the development of the international monetary system after the demise of Bretton Woods, see also Paul Volcker and Toyoo Gyohten, *Changing Fortunes: The World's Money and the Threat to American Leadership*, New York, Times Books, 1992).

37. Nor in the light of past experience can it be claimed that these were loans granted at subsidized rates, seeing that the Fund's loans enjoyed special treatment upon reimbursement, and could therefore be considered as essentially less risky than private loans. See, in this regard, Olivier Jeanne and Jeromin Zettelmeyer, 'International bailouts: moral hazard and conditionality', *Economic Policy*, October 2001. Whether or not this assumption is still justified, given the high concentration of risks that has materialized in recent years as a result of catalytic packages, is an open question which cannot be resolved here.

38. The concept was invented by Guido Calabresi, *The Costs of Accidents: A Legal and Economic Analysis*, New Haven, CT, Yale University Press, 1970.

39. Described in more detail in Curzio Giannini, 'Toward a sovereign bankruptcy procedure and greater restraint in IMF crisis lending. An interim assessment', *Banca Nazionale del Lavoro Quarterly Review*, June 2003.

40. This section summarizes the article by Curzio Giannini, 'Promoting financial stability in emerging-market countries: the Soft Law approach and beyond', *Comparative Economic Studies*, Summer 2002 (translator's note).

41. See Kristin K. Howell, 'The role of the Bank for International Settlements in central banking cooperation', *Journal of European Economic History*, Autumn 1993, and Gunter D. Baer, 'Sixty-five years of central bank cooperation at the Bank for International Settlements', in Holtfrerich, Reis and Toniolo, *The Emergence of Modern Central Banking from 1918 to the Present*.

42. In particular the Bankhaus Herstatt of Cologne, the British–Israel Bank of London, and the Franklin National Bank of New York. The failure of the Bankhaus Herstatt, a small to medium-sized German bank, which was very active on the exchange market, was the first and most spectacular. It was ordered to shut down operations by the supervisory authority of Germany at the close of trading on 26 June 1974. The abrupt cessation of Herstatt's activity led to the cancellation of around $600 million in payments to banks operating on the New York Stock Exchange, which had already settled the corresponding amount in European currencies (primarily marks). This event, due to the asynchrony of the settlement in dollars and marks, a phenomenon known from that time on as 'Herstatt risk', caused serious turbulence on the exchange market. On this episode see Richard J. Herring and Robert E. Litan, *Financial Regulation in the Global Economy*, Washington, DC, Brookings Institution, 1995.

43. See Basel Committee on Banking Supervision, 'International convergence of capital measurement and capital standards', Basel, July 1988.

44. See Mario Giovanoli, 'A new financial architecture for the global financial market: Legal aspects of international financial stability standard setting', in Mario Giovanoli (ed.), *International Monetary Law: Issues for the New Millennium*, Oxford, Oxford University Press, 2000.

45. John Eatwell and Lance Taylor, *Global Finance at Risk: The Case for International Regulation*, Cambridge, MA, Polity Press, 2000.

46. Meltzer Commission, 'Report of the International Financial Institution Advisory Commission', Washington, DC, Senate Committee on Banking, Housing and Urban Affairs, March 2000.

47. George Soros, *Open Society: Reforming Global Capitalism*, London, Little Brown & Co., 2000.

48. Working Party on Financial Stability in Emerging Market Economies, 'Financial stability in emerging market economies: a strategy for the formulation, adoption and implementation of sound principles to strengthen financial systems', April 1997 (also available on the website of the BIS ww.bis.org).

49. In its turn, the soft law approach developed in the report had much in common with the international banking standard proposed by Morris Goldstein in 'The case for an international banking standard', Washington DC, Institute for International Economics, 1997. While relatively neglected at the time, these two contributions paved the way for the philosophy of the core principles of effective banking supervision, published by the Basel Committee in the summer of 1997.

50. 'Reports on the international financial architecture', Working Groups on Transparency and Accountability, Strengthening Financial Systems, International Financial Crises, October 1998 (also available on the website of the BIS, www.bis.org). Together with some major industrialized countries that were not members of the G-7, several developing countries including the majority of those involved in the 1997 Asian crisis attended the meetings of the Willard Group (named after the hotel in Washington in which some of its meetings were held). The Group was established for a brief period and was the brainchild of the US Treasury.

51. The FSF had over 40 members, representing the economic and financial ministries, central banks and regulatory authorities of several countries (the G-7 countries plus Australia, the Netherlands, Hong Kong SAR and Singapore). International financial institutions, the European Central Bank and the major regulatory bodies (for example the Basel Committee) were also members. In 2009, membership in the FSF was broadened, with its transformation into a Financial Stability Board, open to all G-20 countries, Spain and the European Commission as well. The G-20 countries make up around 66 per cent of the total of IMF quotas.

52. The first step towards boosting membership dates from the days immediately following the Mexican crisis of 1994–95, with the introduction of the New Arrangements to Borrow in which 25 countries participated, selected on the basis of their ability to contribute to international bailout operations. The next step occurred after the Asian crisis with the establishment of the G-22, which as was said earlier comprised the G-7 members plus another 15 countries, including various emerging economy countries. Finally, in 1999, the G-7 established the Financial Stability Forum and the G-20, which had a mandate to hold informal discussions on elements of risk in the international financial system. As noted, membership in the FSF has been broadened to all the G-20 countries.

53. Financial Stability Forum, 'Final report of the follow-up group on incentives to foster implementation of standards', London, September 2001 (also available at www.forum.org).

54. Giovanoli, *International Monetary Law: Issues for the New Millennium*, p. 59.

55. In Korea and Indonesia, for example, the share of deposits in foreign banks tripled between January 1997 and July 1998.

56. Scepticism over the effectiveness of peer pressure was perhaps behind the proposals aimed at making IMF loans subject to the degree of compliance with international standards by a given country, such as those, already mentioned, put forward by Soros and the Meltzer Commission. However, while attractive at first sight, the proposals would prove very difficult to realize; the main obstacle is that assessing a country's adherence to standards is to a large extent more a qualitative than a quantitative affair. The problem is exacerbated by the difficulty in distinguishing between best practices and basic principles. In both cases, what appears most important is not so much absolute compliance with each standard as the ability of individual countries to achieve substantial progress.

57. See William R. White, 'Recent initiatives to improve the regulation and supervision of private capital flows', BIS Working Papers, No. 92, October 2000.

58. See the conclusions of the G-22 in 'Report of the Working Group on International Financial Crises', p. 37.

59. Giovanoli, *International Monetary Law: Issues for the New Millennium*, pp. 54–56.
60. History provides other examples of monetary unions, from the Latin monetary union in the late nineteenth century to the Communauté Financière d'Afrique, which to this day brings together a total of 13 African states, formerly French colonies, split into two groups with two different currencies pegged to the French franc and to other currencies. But these are unions with much less ambitious objectives and institutional apparatuses. In particular, the Communauté Financière d'Afrique, which most closely resembles the European monetary union given that it also comprises two central banks, actually conceals a hegemonic regime; the system relies, in fact, on liquidity provided by the Bank of France. On the history of monetary unions, see Cohen, *The Geography of Money*, op. cit. Regarding the advent of the European monetary union, it should be borne in mind that the actual circulation of euro banknotes and coins dates from January 2002, while the European Central Bank, the central body of the ESCB, was established on 1 June 1998. On these aspects, see Francesco Papadia and Carlo Santini, *La Banca centrale europea*, Bologna, Il Mulino, 1998.
61. See Paul De Grauwe, *The Economics of Monetary Integration*, Oxford, Oxford University Press, 1992, Ch. 8.
62. For a discussion of this alternative interpretation, see David M. Andrews, C. Randall Henning and Louis W. Pauly, 'Monetary institutions, financial integration, and political authority', in David M. Andrews, C. Randall Henning and Louis W. Pauly (eds), *Governing the World's Money*, Ithaca, NY, Cornell University Press, 2002.
63. See Barry Eichengreen, *Globalizing Capital: A History of the International Monetary System*, Princeton, NJ, Princeton University Press, 1996, pp. 106–107.
64. See Peter B. Kenen, 'Currency unions and policy domains', in Andrews, Henning and Pauly (eds), *Governing the World's Money*.
65. Italy initially benefited from a broader band that took account of its higher inflation.
66. The convergence criteria concerned, respectively, the rate of inflation, the long-term interest rate, the exchange rate and public finances. In particular: (i) the inflation rate in the year before entry could not exceed by more than one and a half percentage points that of the three best-performing member states; (ii) the long-term nominal interest rate, again in the previous year, could not exceed by more than two percentage points that of the three best-performing member states; (iii) the exchange rate must have remained within the narrow fluctuation band of the EMS in the two years before entry; (iv) the ratio of government debt to GDP at the time of selection of candidate countries could not exceed 60 per cent (or if it did, had to show a clear downwards trend) and the ratio of the government deficit to gross domestic product could not exceed 3 per cent.
67. For these and other aspects of the autonomy of the European Central Bank, see Papadia and Santini. *La Banca centrale europea*, pp. 31–37.
68. See Eichengreen, *Globalizing Capital*, pp. 175–181.
69. Francesco Giavazzi and Marco Pagano, 'On the advantage of tying one's hands: EMS discipline and central bank credibility', *European Economic Review*, June 1998. Giavazzi and Pagano focused on the benefits of the ties in terms of the credibility of monetary policy, but equally – if not more – important were the effects on the public finances generated by the lowering of long-term rates. For example, the differential between the long-term rates in Italy and Germany, which easily exceeded six percentage points in 1992, had dropped to around two points at the end of 1996 and to less than 50 basis points one year later, and fluctuated around 20–30 cents in recent years. The decline led to massive savings in terms of interest payments, largely contributing to their reduction in relation to GDP, from 13 per cent in 1993 to 6.5 per cent in 2000 and 5.7 in 2002.
70. See, for example, Lorenzo Bini Smaghi and Daniel Gros, *Open Issues in European Central Banking*, London, Macmillan, 2000.
71. Susan Strange, *Casino Capitalism*, New York, Basil Blackwell, 1986, and *Mad Money*, Manchester, Manchester University Press, 1998; Eric Helleiner, *States and the Reemergence of Global Finance: From Bretton Woods to the 1990s*.

72. Barry Eichengreen, *Globalizing Capital*, Ch. 4.
73. Tommaso Padoa-Schioppa and Fabrizio Saccomanni, 'Managing a market-led global financial system', in Peter B. Kenen (ed.), *Managing the World Economy: Fifty Years after Bretton Woods*, Washington, DC, Institute for International Economics, 1994.
74. See Pier Carlo Padoan, 'EMU as an evolutionary process', in Andrews, Henning and Pauly (eds), *Governing the World's Money*.

CHAPTER 7

1. W. Stanley Jevons, *Money and the Mechanism of Exchange*, New York, Appleton, 1875; Knut Wicksell, *Interest and Prices*, London, Macmillan, 1936 (orig. *Geldzins und Güterpreise*, Jena, Fischer, 1898); John Maynard Keynes, *A Treatise on Money*, London, Macmillan, 1930; Ludwig von Mises, *Theory of Money and Credit*, London, Jonathan Cape, 1934 (orig. *Theorie des Geldes und der Unlaufsmittel*, Munich and Leipzig, Duncker & Humboldt, 1924).
2. Hicks, 'A suggestion for simplifying the theory of money', op. cit.
3. Typical is the literature on the optimal quantity of money, which is founded upon the opportunity cost of a stock of money, that is, a typical holding cost.
4. For a review of themes and results see Giannini, 'Determinazione del livello dei prezzi e politica "monetaria" in un'economia senza moneta', op. cit.
5. Bank for International Settlements, *Payment systems in the Group of Ten countries*, Basel, various years.
6. See, for example, Michael Woodford, 'Monetary policy in a world without money', *International Finance*, July 2000.
7. More properly, one should speak of payment definitiveness or finality, which is immediate in the former and deferred in the latter case. See Chapter 2, section 2.2.
8. As we shall see further on, in the past 30 years some hybrid systems have been created that combine features of net and of gross settlement.
9. Clearing is 'bilateral' when the balances are calculated for each participant vis-à-vis each other participant; it is 'multilateral' when at the end of the day the balance vis-à-vis the system is calculated for each participant.
10. As we shall see further on, today this is not always actually true, thanks to revisions of clearing and settlement systems for purposes of risk control.
11. For a formal treatment of the determination of the optimal payment interval and of the forces that tend to shorten it, see Paolo Angelini and Curzio Giannini, 'On the economics of interbank payment systems', *Economic Notes*, May–August 1994.
12. David B. Humphrey, 'Central banks and the payment system', in Anthony M. Santomero, Staffan Viotti and Anders Vredin (eds), *Challenges for Central Banking*, Boston, MA, Kluwer, 2001, pp. 150–151.
13. This schematic account does not do justice to the complexity of actual payment systems. For a more detailed treatment, see Bruce Summers (ed.), *The Payment System. Design, Management, and Supervision*, Washington, DC, International Monetary Fund, 1994.
14. McKinnon, *Money and Capital in Economic Development*, op. cit.; Shaw, *Financial Deepening in Economic Development*, op. cit.
15. Williamson and Mahar, 'A survey of financial liberalization', op. cit.
16. For an excellent review see Alfred Steinherr, *Derivatives: The Wild Beast of Finance*, Chichester, Wiley, 1998.
17. The phrase comes from David Folkerts-Landau, 'Derivatives: the new frontier in finance', in Tomas Balino and Carlo Cottarelli (eds), *Frameworks for Monetary Stability: Policy Issues and Country Experiences*, Washington, DC, International Monetary Fund, 1994.

18. Derivatives have a multiplicity of possible uses. For one thing, they may be used for active portfolio management to exploit opportunities for arbitrage. For instance, banks typically use a technique – 'dynamic hedging' – to cover the risks connected with balance sheet and off-balance sheet positions that consists in re-creating, for every option actually subscribed, a 'synthetic' option obtained by an appropriate combination of spot positions and positions in the option's reference financial instruments, so as to offset the risks perfectly. For this mechanism to work, however, the characteristics of the synthetic option must be continually adjusted to track the actual evolution of market prices. At the other end of the spectrum, derivatives can be used to take speculative positions worth many times the funds invested. This is the purpose of hedge funds, a new kind of intermediary that grew rapidly in the second half of the 1990s.
19. Raymond Goldsmith, *Financial Structure and Development*, New Haven, CT, Yale University Press, 1969, pp. 26–27.
20. John R. Hicks, 'A suggestion for simplifying the theory of money'.
21. Hans J. Blommestein and Bruce J. Summers, 'Banking and the payment system', in Summers (ed.), *The Payment System*, p. 26.
22. Board of Governors of the Federal Reserve System, *Controlling Risk in the Payment System*, Washington, DC, August 1988, p. 1.
23. Banca d'Italia, *Libro bianco sul sistema dei pagamenti in Italia*, Rome, April 1987, p. 111.
24. David B. Humphrey, 'Payments finality and risk of settlement failure', in Anthony Saunders and Lawrence J. White (eds), *Technology and the Regulation of Financial Markets*, Lexington, MA, Lexington Books, 1986. Not all comparable exercises for other countries produced such alarming results. For example, in the early 1990s the Italian clearing system was found to be practically free of systemic risk (Paolo Angelini, Giuseppe Maresca and Daniela Russo, 'Systemic risk in the netting system', *Journal of Banking and Finance*, June 1996).
25. See Chapter 6, section 6.4.
26. Peter M. Garber and Steven R. Weisbrod, *The Economics of Banking, Liquidity and Money*, Lexington, MA, Heath & Co., 1992, p. 288.
27. Angelini and Giannini, *On the Economics of Interbank Payment Systems*, p. 210.
28. Further, as Angelini and Giannini argue, pure gross settlement actually does entail a particular form of systemic risk, owing to the incentive for every participant to minimize its own money stock and to rely on others to inject the liquidity necessary with their own payment messages. This risk is known in the literature as 'gridlock'. In the figure, however, it is implicitly assumed that the stocks of monetary assets are sufficient to avert this danger.
29. The Settlement Finality Directive (Directive 98/26/EC) seeks to reduce systemic risks and to provide safeguards against the effects of bankruptcy and certainty over the applicable law. The Directive on Financial Collateral Arrangements (Directive 2002/47/EC) supplements the Settlement Finality Directive and governs some aspects of the law on collateral (for example the possibility of using collateral outside the country of issue) and rules on conflicts of law. The Directive on the Reorganisation and Winding-Up of Credit Institutions (Directive 2001/24/EC) introduces the principle of home-country control in cases of insolvency of a credit institution with branches in other member states, in order to guarantee that there be a single bankruptcy proceeding under a single bankruptcy law.
30. In April 1996 the Fed instituted a charge for intraday overdrafts above a set limit of 15 per cent on an annual basis. Rita Brizi, Ferdinando Sasso and Carlo Tresoldi, *Le banche e il sistema dei pagamenti*, Bologna, Il Mulino, 1998, p. 90.
31. On this see Angelini and Giannini, 'On the economics of interbank payment systems'.
32. For a summary of the issues and suggested solutions, see Curzio Giannini and Carlo Monticelli, 'Which target for monetary policy in Stage Three? Issues in the shaping of the European Payment System', *Weltwirtschaftliches Archiv*, October–December 1997.

33. Group of Thirty, *Clearance and Settlement Systems in the World's Securities Markets*, New York, March 1989.
34. For a more detailed treatment, see David Folkerts-Landau, Peter Garber and Dirk Schoenmaker, 'The reform of wholesale payment systems and its impact on financial markets', IMF Working Paper WP/96/37, April 1996.
35. The leaders, in a process that is still ongoing, were the Bank of Italy, with its 1997 White Paper 'Libro bianco sulla sorveglianza sul sistema dei pagamenti', and the Bank of England, whose report 'Oversight of payment systems' was released in 2000.
36. On the substance of this oversight, see Biagio Bossone and Massimo Cirasino, 'The oversight of the payment systems: a framework for the development and governance of payment systems in emerging economies', Cemla/World Bank Research Series, No. 1, July 2001.
37. The third alternative of assigning the function to a private institution, now being implemented via the Continuous Linked Settlement (CLS), was not even considered at the time.
38. Marco Rossi, *Payment Systems in the Financial Markets*, London, Macmillan, 1998, p. 58.
39. Ibid., p. 88.
40. Group of Ten, 'Report on consolidation in the financial sector', January 2001. The report is available on the BIS website (www.bis.org) and on those of the International Monetary Fund (IMF) and the OECD. An Italian version was produced by the Bank of Italy (Banca d'Italia, 'Il processo di consolidamento nel settore finanziario', Rome, 2001).
41. James F. Dingle, 'The elements of the global network for large-value funds transfers', Bank of Canada Working Papers, 2001-1, 2001.
42. For a full treatment, see Dingle, op. cit., and Charles M. Kahn and William Roberds, 'The CLS Bank: a solution to the risks of international payments settlement?' *Carnegie-Rochester Conference Series on Public Policy*, June 2001.
43. On this point, Jeffrey Lacker has remarked that: 'the ironic feature of CLS . . . is that the operations may actually encourage the use of central bank daylight credit. CLS itself will not have an explicit borrowing arrangement with any central bank, but members can use daylight overdrafts to transfer funds into CLS at the beginning of the settlement process. In other words, members' pay-ins are not limited by their initial balance at the central bank. A member bank could hypothetically meet all of its FX settlement obligations but end the day overdrawn at some central bank.' Jeffrey M. Lacker, 'A comment to Kahn and Roberds', in *Carnegie-Rochester Conference Series on Public Policy*, June 2001, p. 230.

EPILOGUE

1. Émile Durkheim, *De la division du travail social*, Paris, Alcan, 1893.
2. James, *The End of Globalization*, p. 216.
3. These works include: Claudio E.V. Borio, Neale Kennedy and Stephen D. Prowse, 'Exploring aggregate price fluctuations across countries: measurement, determinants and monetary policy implications', BIS Economic Papers, no. 40, April 1994; Claudio E.V. Borio and Philip Lowe, 'Asset prices, financial and monetary stability: exploring the nexus', BIS Economic Papers, no. 114, July 2002; Andrew D. Crockett, 'In search of anchors for financial and monetary stability', *Suerf Colloquium*, Vienna, April 2000 (also at www.bis.org, 'BIS speeches').
4. See the report of the G-10 working group on financial asset prices: Contact Group on Asset Prices, 'Turbulence in asset markets: the role of micro policies', Basel, January 2003 (also at www.bis.org).

5. The first reflections on this matter were conducted, at the initiative of the Bank of Italy, by a group of G-10 central banks. See Contact Group on the legal and institutional underpinnings of the international financial system, 'Insolvency arrangements and contract enforceability', Basel, September 2002 (also at www.bis.org and www.banca ditalia.it).
6. Charles Bean, 'Asset prices, financial imbalances and monetary policy: are inflation targets enough?' BIS Working Papers, no. 140, September 2003; see also Ignazio Visco's discussion in the same paper.
7. Hirsch, 'The Bagehot problem', op. cit.
8. Kenneth E. Boulding, 'The legitimacy of central banking', in Federal Reserve System Board of Governors, *Reappraisal of the Federal Reserve Discount Mechanism*, Vol. 2, Washington, DC, Federal Reserve System, 1979.

Index

representative democracy 251
repression, financial 227–228
'repudiated pyramid' hypothesis 248
reserve cities 97
reserve equalization mechanism 97
reserve requirements 141–142
reserves 15, 84
    Bank of England as depository of
        93–94
    Genoa accords 122, 123
    global 173
resumption rule 117–118
retail payment system 220, 226
revolutions 26
Rey Report 193, 194
Ricardo, D. xxvii, 58, 61, 64, 130–131
Ricardo, S. 58, 64
Richter, R. 9
risk
    commodification of risks 228
    payment system risk *see* payment
        system risks
Roberds, W. 38
Robinson, J. 180
Rogoff, K. 152–153
Rome Treaty 205
Roover, R. de 53
rules
    finality 36–39, 238–239
    resumption rule 117–118
runs on banks 81
    see also banking crises

safety net 196
saleability 17–18
Sannucci, V. 78
Schnadt, N. 81
Schumpeter, J. 27, 261
Schwartz, A. 23
Scotland 111
Second Bank of the US 66, 68–71, 79
Second World War 135, 143
securities payments 237, 240–241
settlement interval 224–225
Shafroth, J. 99, 270
shares 230
Shaw, E. 157, 227–228
SIC 240
signatures 53
silver standard 116–117

Simiand, F. 26–27
Simon, H. 6
Single European Act 1986 204
single market, EU 203
Smith, A. 58, 60–61, 258
Smith, V. 49, 56, 65, 89, 99
Snake, Monetary 206, 207
social conventions 8
social pact 145
social transfer payments 145, 146
Società Bancaria Italiana 104
Société Générale 101
soft law 195–204, 258
sovereignty 252
    international money 169–170,
        175–176, 192
    pooled sovereignty 175–179,
        204–214, 216–218
    renouncing monetary sovereignty
        160
    uncertain benefits of monetary
        sovereignty 160–161
Special Drawing Rights (SDRs)
    186–187
Stability and Growth Pact 209–210,
    211–214
stagflation 115, 148–150
    recovery from 253
Standing Committee on Banking
    Regulations and Supervisory
    Practices *see* Basel Committee
statalism 5–6
state 22, 252
    intervention in crises 24
    liberal and democratic xxxi, 251
    and market 22–23, 28
    nation-state *see* nation-state
    role in creating confidence 23, 25
    supervision and banknote issue 56,
        59
state banks (US) 68–9, 70, 71–72, 80,
    96–97
stock markets 256–257
store of value 219
Strange, S. 215
'strengthened pyramid' hypothesis 248
Stringher, B. 103–104
Strong, B. 120–121, 123–124, 132–133,
    141
structural controls 107–108, 109